ISBN 978-1-330-08456-4
PIBN 10021839

1 MONTH OF
FREE
READING

at

www.ForgottenBooks.com

By purchasing this book you are eligible for one month membership to ForgottenBooks.com, giving you unlimited access to our entire collection of over 700,000 titles via our web site and mobile apps.

To claim your free month visit: www.forgottenbooks.com/free21839

English
Français
Deutsche
Italiano
Español
Português

www.forgottenbooks.com

Mythology Photography **Fiction**
Fishing Christianity **Art** Cooking
Essays Buddhism Freemasonry
Medicine **Biology** Music **Ancient**
Egypt Evolution Carpentry Physics
Dance Geology **Mathematics** Fitness
Shakespeare **Folklore** Yoga Marketing
Confidence Immortality Biographies
Poetry **Psychology** Witchcraft
Electronics Chemistry History **Law**
Accounting **Philosophy** Anthropology
Alchemy Drama Quantum Mechanics
Atheism Sexual Health **Ancient History**
Entrepreneurship Languages Sport
Paleontology Needlework Islam
Metaphysics Investment Archaeology
Parenting Statistics Criminology
Motivational

BOOK

OF

COMMON PRAYER

ACCORDING TO THE USE OF

KING'S CHAPEL,

BOSTON.

BOSTON
LITTLE, BROWN, AND COMPANY.
1865.

UnIversity Press : Welch, Bigelow, & Co.,
CAMBRIDGE.

PREFACE

TO THE FIRST EDITION. MDCCLXXXV.

ANY truly great and learned men, of the Church of England, as well divines as laymen, have earnestly wished to see their Liturgy reformed; but hitherto all attempts to reform it have proved ineffectual. The late happy revolution here hath forever separated all the Episcopal Societies in the United States of America from the Church of England, of which the King of that country is the supreme head, to whom all Archbishops, Bishops, Priests, and Deacons of that Church are obliged to take an oath of allegiance and supremacy, at the time of their consecration or ordination. Being torn from that King and Church, the Society for whose use this Liturgy is published, think themselves at liberty, and well justified even by the declarations of the Church of England, in making such alterations as "the exigency of the times and occasions hath rendered expedient," and in expunging everything which gave, or might be suspected to give, offence to tender consciences; guiding themselves, however, by "the holy Scriptures, which," they heartily agree with the Church of England, "contain all things necessary to salvation," and that "whatsoever is not read therein, nor can be proved thereby, is not to be required of any man, that it should be believed as an article of faith, or be thought requisite or necessary to salvation."

In the thirty-fourth of the Articles of the Church of England, it is declared, that "it is not necessary that traditions and ceremonies be in all places one, or utterly like; for at all times they have been diverse, and may be changed according to the diversity of countries, times, and men's manners, so that nothing be ordained against God's word." And by the twentieth of those Articles it is declared, that "the Church hath power to decree rites and ceremonies, and authority in controversies of faith." What is there meant by the word Church, will appear from the nineteenth of those Articles, which declares, "The visible Church of Christ is a Congregation of faithful men, in which the pure word of God is preached, and the sacraments be duly ministered, according to CHRIST's ordinance, in all those things that of necessity are requisite to the same. As the Church of Hierusalem, Alexandria, and Antioch have erred, so also the Church of Rome hath erred, not only in living, and manner of ceremonies, but also in matters of faith." At the Reformation, when the Book of Common Prayer of the Church of England was compiled, the Committee appointed to execute that business were obliged to proceed very tenderly and with great delicacy, for fear of offending the whole body of the people, just torn from the idolatrous Church of Rome ; and many things were then retained, which have, in later times, given great offence to many truly pious Christians.

The Liturgy, contained in this volume, is such as no Christian, it is supposed, can take offence at, or find his conscience wounded in repeating. The Trinitarian, the Unitarian, the Calvinist, the Arminian will read nothing in it which can give him any reasonable umbrage. GOD is the sole object of worship in these prayers ; and as no man can come to GOD but by the one Mediator, JESUS CHRIST every petition is here offered in his name, in obedience to his positive command.* The Gloria Patri, made and introduced into the Liturgy of the Church of Rome by the decree of Pope Damasus, towards the latter part of the fourth century, and adopted into the Book of Common Prayer, is not in this Liturgy. Instead of that doxology, doxologies from the pure word of GOD are introduced. It is not our wish to make proselytes to any particular system of opinions of any particular sect of Christians. Our earnest desire is to live in brotherly love and peace with all men, and especially with those who call themselves the disciples of JESUS CHRIST.

In compiling this Liturgy great assistance hath been derived from the judicious corrections of the Reverend Mr. Lindsey, who hath reformed the Book of Common Prayer according to the Plan of the

* In the original Preface a large number of texts were quoted in support of this position, which it was not thought necessary to insert at present. This first edition was published in the year 1785.

truly pious and justly celebrated Doctor Samuel Clarke. Several of Mr. Lindsey's amendments are adopted entire. The alterations which are taken from him, and the others which are made, excepting the prayers for Congress and the General Court, are none of them novelties ; for they have been proposed and justified by some of the first divines of the Church of England.

A few passages in the Psalter, which are liable to be misconstrued or misapplied, are printed in Italics, and are designed to be omitted in repeating the Psalms.

PREFACE

TO THE EDITION OF MDCCCL.

'HE change introduced in the edition of 1785, and described in the foregoing Preface by Dr. Freeman, was of a kind which can never be looked back upon, by those who use this Liturgy, otherwise than with feelings of grateful satisfaction. In the then existing state of the Theological world, it required, on the part of Dr. Freeman and his associates, a fidelity to their convictions, a sincere and simple reverence for what they believed to be the truth of God, a disregard for all secondary and personal considerations, which will cause their names to be held in honor so long as the Church shall stand. It was an auspicious revolution which emancipated the forms of worship from the unwarranted restrictions of creeds framed by men, and restored the worshipper to the freedom of the Gospel.

In the successive editions published since 1785, the changes which appear consist principally of additions. They were made for the most part under the direction of Dr. Greenwood, whose pure taste and fervent piety eminently qualified him for the task. Since the first edition the Psalter has been abridged; and, wherever the sense or the diction appeared to require it, instead of the old translation, the version of the common English Bible, or some other approved translation, has been adopted. Several Occasional Services, a second Evening Service, Services for the annual Fast and Thanksgiving, Prayers for Families, Services for Sunday Schools, and Collects for particular occasions, have been added. Except in these particulars, the book remains in every important respect as it was. ·

All change, not obviously necessary, has been avoided. Experience has abundantly shown that it is difficult to improve these simple and venerable forms of worship, through which originally the most profound sentiments of devotion found utterance, and which still, better than any other human compositions, give expression to the religious wants and aspirations of the human heart. The substance of the Morning and of the Evening Service is derived from those early formularies of the primitive Church, from which the Lutheran and the English, the Greek and the Roman Churches, drew their respective modes of worship. The words which guide our devotional meditations have, in large part, been used for centuries, and are still used for the same purpose, by the great body of believers throughout Christendom. Many of the sentences are found in the earliest records of Christian devotion. The very phrases of invitation and benediction which we repeat, were repeated in secret chambers and torch-lighted catacombs, by those who commemorated Christ by night, at the peril of martyrdom on the morrow. The same words of blessing, "Peace be with you," "The Lord be with you," reminded men then, as now, of their common dependence on God. While theological speculations tend to separate Christians, our devotional forms have an opposite tendency to counteract this influence, by putting each worshipper into conscious relations with the whole Christian Church. Besides this, the associations which gradually collect around a Book of Common Prayer not only add to its interest and value, but in time constitute an essential part of the work itself. The child reads the same page which his parents read, and his devotions are warmed and hallowed by his remembrance of the affection and the faith of those, who may have been called from the worship of an earthly temple to a holier worship in Heaven. For such reasons as these, while additions have been made as circumstances required, it has been thought important to abstain carefully from all needless alterations.

NOTE

IN the present edition a few Collects from ancient liturgies, and Prayers for special occasions, have been added. The Confirmation Service, at page 249, is taken from the "Common Prayer for Christian Worship" of Dr. Sadler and Rev. James Martineau. It is not inserted as an obligatory service, but as enriching the devotional treasures of this Liturgy, and to meet the desire, sometimes felt in the early freshness of religious experience, for an open form of Christian profession.

The only other changes from the previous edition have been conformed to the principles laid down in the foregoing Preface, and are confined to some verbal alterations in the Psalter, and in the Occasioual Services.

CONTENTS

Contents.

Contents.

PRAYERS AND SERVICES FOR FAMILIES.

SERVICES FOR SUNDAY SCHOOLS.

TABLE OF HOLY DAYS

OBSERVED IN THIS CHURCH.

THE Christian year begins with ADVENT — the Coming of Christ. The four Sundays in Advent precede the Great Festival of our Saviour's Nativity. The First Sunday in Advent is always the nearest Sunday, before or after, to the Feast of St. Andrew (the first-called Apostle), which is on the 30th day of November. It is therefore on one of the seven days from November 27 to December 3.

CHRISTMAS — the Nativity of our Lord. This occurs on the 25th day of December. The Festival includes twelve days to the Epiphany. Twelfth Night is the twelfth from Christmas.

ST. STEPHEN'S DAY is the 26th of December.

EPIPHANY — the Manifestation of Christ to the Gentiles, is on the 6th of January. This applies particularly to the manifestation to the Wise Men of the East; and indirectly, to the manifestation at his Baptism, and to the manifestation of his miraculous powers at the Marriage Feast. The Sundays after Epiphany are numbered to Septuagesima Sunday, from one to six, according as Easter comes earlier or later.

THE CONVERSION OF ST. PAUL is commemorated on the 25th of January.

SEPTUAGESIMA SUNDAY is the third before Lent, and nearly the 70th day before Easter.

SEXAGESIMA SUNDAY is the second before Lent.

QUINQUAGESIMA SUNDAY is the next before Lent.

ASH-WEDNESDAY is the first day of Lent. The name is derived from Ashes, symbolic of fasting and self-mortification.

LENT — the Fast of Forty Days before Easter. From Ash-Wednesday to Easter are forty-six days; but the six Sundays are not counted, because it is not the custom of the Church to fast on Sundays, when we commemorate so great a blessing as our Saviour's resurrection.

PASSION WEEK — the week before Easter. The name is derived from the Latin word Passio, signifying suffering.

PALM SUNDAY — Day of Christ's Entrance into Jerusalem, is the next before Easter.

GOOD FRIDAY — Day of the Crucifixion, is the third day before Easter.

EASTER — Day of the Resurrection. Easter Day, on which the other Movable Feasts and Fasts depend, is the first Sunday after the full moon, which happens upon, or next after, the 21st day of March, the Vernal Equinox. If the full moon is on a Sunday, Easter Day is the Sunday after. Easter Day, from being nearly coincident with the Jewish Passover, and also because of the analogy between the sacrifice of Christ and that of the Lamb of the Paschal feast, is often alluded to in the same terms; and most nations give it a name derived from the Greek name of the Passover, Pascha.

ASCENSION DAY, called also Holy Thursday, is the fortieth day after Easter.

WHITSUNDAY — Giving of the Holy Spirit, is the fiftieth day after Easter. Whitsunday is so called, because, this day being one of the stated times for Baptism in the ancient Church, those who were baptized were clothed in white garments, as a type of spiritual purity.

The coincidence of this feast with the Jewish Festival of Pentecost, held in commemoration of the giving of the Law from Sinai, on the fiftieth day of the departure of the Israelites from Egypt, has caused this feast to be recognized as analogous to that, and often to be called by that name.

After Whitsunday, twenty-eight Sundays, or fewer, from about the middle of May to Advent, complete the year.

	1883	1869 1875 *1880	*1872	1866 1877	1874 1885	1871 1882	*1868	1873 1879 *1884	1865 *1876	1870 1881	1867 1878
	Jan.	Jan.	Jan.	Jan.	Jan.	Jan.	Jan.	Jan.	Jan.	Jan.	Jan.
1st S. of year.		3			4	1	4	5	1	2	
EPIPHANY.	6	6	6	6	6	6	6	6	6	6	6
1st S. after.	7	10	13	7	11	8	11	12	8	9	13
II.	14	17	20	14	18	15	18	19	15	16	20
III.				21	25	22	25 Feb.	26 Feb.	22	23	27 Feb.
IV.						29	1	2	29 Feb.	30 Feb.	3
V.					Feb.	Feb.			5	6	10
Septuages.	21	24	27 Feb.	28 Feb.	1	5	8	9	12	13	17
Sexages.	28 Feb.	31 Feb.	3	4	8	12	15	16	19	20	24 Mar.
Quinqua.	4	7	10	11	15	19	22	23	26 Mar.	27 Mar.	3
ASH-WED.	7	10	13	14	18	22	25 Mar.	26 Mar.	1	2	6
1st S. in Lent.	11	14	17	18	22 Mar.	26 Mar.	1	2	5	6	10
II.	18	21	24 Mar.	25 Mar.	1	5	8	9	12	13	17
III.	25 Mar.	28 Mar.	3	4	8	12	15	16	19	20	24
IV.	4	7	10	11	15	19	22	23	26 Apr.	27 Apr.	31 Apr.
V.	11	14	17	18	22	26 Apr.	29 Apr.	30 Apr.	2	3	7
VI.	18	21	24	25	29 Apr.	2	5	6	9	10	14
Good Friday.	23	26	29	30 Apr.	3	7	10	11	14	15	19
EASTER.	25 Apr.	28 Apr.	31 Apr.	1	5	9	12	13	16	17	21
1st S. after.	1	4	7	8	12	16	19	20	23	24 May	28 May
II.	8	11	14	15	19	23	26 May	27 May	30 May	1	5
III.	15	18	21	22	26 May	30 May	3	4	7	8	12
IV.	22	25 May	28 May	29 May	3	7	10	11	14	15	19
v. Ascension.	29 May	2	5	6	10	14	17	18	21	22	26 June
S. after Asc.	6	9	12	13	17	21	24	25 June	28 June	29 June	2
Whitsunday.	13	16	19	20	24	28 June	31 June	1	4	5	9
1st S. after.	20	23	26 June	27 June	31 June	4	7	8	11	12	16
II.	27	30	2	3	7	11	14	15	18	19	23

— Find the *year* at the head of the Table. In the column under the year, find the date of the Day. In the column at the left-hand margin is the name of the Day.

Sundays after Whitsunday.	1883	1869 1875 *1880	*1872	1866 1877	1874 1885	1871 1882	*1868	1873 1879 *1884	1865 *1876	1870 1881	1867 1878
	June	June	June	June	June	June	June	June	June	June	June
III.	3	6	9	10	14	18	21	22	25 July	26 July	30 July
IV.	10	13	16	17	21	25 July	28 July	29 July	2	3	7
V.	17	20	23	24 July	28 July	2	5	6	9	10	14
VI.	24 July	27 July	30 July	1	5	9	12	13	16	17	21
VII.	1	4	7	8	12	16	19	20	23	24	28 Aug.
VIII.	8	11	14	15	19	23	26 Aug.	27 Aug.	30 Aug.	31 Aug.	4
IX.	15	18	21	22	26 Aug.	30 Aug.	2	3	6	7	11
X.	22	25 Aug.	28 Aug.	29 Aug.	2	6	9	10	13	14	18
XI.	29 Aug.	1	4	5	9	13	16	17	20	21	25 Sep.
XII.	5	8	11	12	16	20	23	24	27 Sep.	28 Sep.	1
XIII.	12	15	18	19	23	27 Sep.	30 Sep.	31 Sep.	3	4	8
XIV.	19	22	25 Sep.	26 Sep.	30 Sep.	3	6	7	10	11	15
XV.	26 Sep.	29 Sep.	1	2	6	10	13	14	17	18	22
XVI.	2	5	8	9	13	17	20	21	24 Oct.	25 Oct.	29 Oct.
XVII.	9	12	15	16	20	24 Oct.	27 Oct.	28 Oct.	1	2	6
XVIII.	16	19	22	23	27 Oct.	1	4	5	8	9	13
XIX.	23	26 Oct.	29 Oct.	30 Oct.	4	8	11	12	15	16	20
XX.	30 Oct.	3	6	7	11	15	18	19	22	23	27 Nov.
XXI.	7	10	13	14	18	22	25 Nov.	26 Nov.	29 Nov.	30 Nov.	3
XXII.	14	17	20	21	25 Nov.	29 Nov.	1	2	5	6	10
XXIII.	21	24	27 Nov.	28 Nov.	1	5	8	9	12	13	17
XXIV.	28 Nov.	31 Nov.	3	4	8	12	15	16	19	20	24
XXV.	4	7	10	11	15	19	22	23	26		
XXVI.	11 Dec.	14	17 Dec.	18 Dec.	22	26 Dec.			Dec.		Dec.
Advent.	2	28 Dec.	1	2	29 Dec.	3	29 Dec.	30 Dec.	3	27 Dec.	1
2d S. in Adv.	9	5	8	9	6	10	6	7	10	4	8
III.	16	12	15	16	13	17	13	14	17	11	15
IV. Christmas.	23	19	22	23	20	24	20	21	24	18	22
1st S. after C.	30	26	29	30	27	31	27	28	31		29

— In Leap Years (marked thus *) one day must be added to the dates in the Table, in January and February, except for Epiphany ; and the Sundays after Epiphany will be as many as if Easter fell one day later.

PROPER

To be read from the Old Testament, at Morning and other Holy-Days

	MORNING.		EVENING.	
Sundays of Advent.				
1	Isaiah	1	Isaiah	2
2		5		24
3		25	26 or	28
4		30		32
CHRISTMAS DAY.		9 to v. 8		7 v. 10 to v. 17
Sundays after Christmas.				
1		35		40
2		41	42 or	43
Sundays after the Epiphany.				
1		44		45
2		51		52
3		55		56
4		57		59
5		61		62
6		65		66
Septuagesima.	Jerem.	7	Jerem.	10
Sexagesima.		22		35
Quinquagesima.	Lam.	1	Lam. v. 22 to v. 37	
LENT. ASH-WEDNES-DAY.	Isaiah	58	Jerem.	36 to v. 11
First Sunday.	Jerem.	9		17
2	Ezek.	14	Ezek.	18
3		20		33
4	Dan.	9	Mic.	6
5	Hab.	2 or 3	Hag.	1 or 2
6	Mal.	3	Mal.	4
GOOD FRIDAY.	Gen. 22 to v. 20		Isaiah	53
EASTER DAY.	Exod.	12	Dan.	12
Sundays after Easter.				
1	Hosea	6	Hosea	11

IT is not intended that the minister should be confined to the chapters selected in the above table, nor that every chapter should be read through. The minister is at liberty to change the Lesson whenever he thinks proper so to do; and also to read a portion only of the appointed chapter, if it is not convenient to read the whole.

LESSONS

...ng and Evening Prayer, on the Sundays throughout the Year.

	MORNING.	EVENING.
Sundays after Easter.		
2	Hosea 13	Hosea 14
3	Joel 3 v. 9	Amos 5
4	Mic. 4 or 5	Nahum 1
5	Zeph. 3	Zech. 1 or 2
Sunday after Ascension.	Zech. 8	10
WHITSUNDAY.	Deut. 16 to v. 18	Isaiah 11
Sundays after Whitsunday.		
1	Gen. 1	Gen. 2
2	3	6
3	37	40
4	41	42
5	43	44
6	45	47 to v. 12
7	48	50
8	Exod. 3	Exod. 5
9	6	15
10	20 to v. 18	Lev. 26
11	Numb. 20	Numb. 24
12	Deut. 4	Deut. 6
13	7 or 8	28 to v. 26
14	30 or 33	34
15	Josh. 1	Josh. 4
16	23 or 24	1 Sam. 3
17	1 Sam. 12	26
18	2 Sam. 1	2 Sam. 12
19	18	1 Kings 3
20	1 Kings 8	19
	v. 22	
21	21	2 Kings 5
22	2 Kings 17	25
23	Job 28	29
24	34	Prov. 1 or 2
25	Prov. 3 or 4	8
26	11	15
27	28	Ecc 12

The appointed Lessons from the New Testament are to be found under the daily Collects. The Gospel is to be read in the morning, and the Epistle in the evening.

Proper Psalms for particular days are to be found by referring to the Table of Contents.

MORNING PRAYER.

¶ *At the beginning of Morning Prayer, the Minister shall read one or more of the following Sentences of Scripture: and then shall read the Exhortation.*

⁘HEN the wicked man turneth away from his wickedness which he hath committed, and doeth that which is lawful and right, he shall save his soul alive. *Ezek.* xviii. 27.

I acknowledge my transgressions ; and my sin is ever before me. *Psal.* li. 3.

Hide thy face from my sins ; and blot out all mine iniquities. *Psal.* li. 9.

The sacrifices of God are a broken spirit ; a broken and a contrite heart, O God, thou wilt not despise. *Psal.* li. 17.

Rend your heart, and not your garments, and turn unto the Lord your God ; for he is gracious and merciful, slow to anger, and of great kindness, and repenteth him of the evil. *Joel* ii. 13.

To the Lord our God belong mercies and forgivenesses, though we have rebelled against him ; neither have we obeyed the voice of the Lord our God, to walk in his laws which he set before us. *Dan.* ix. 9, 10.

O Lord, correct me, but in measure; not in thine anger, lest thou bring me to nothing. *Jer.* x. 24.

Repent ye; for the kingdom of heaven is at hand. *St. Matt.* iii. 2.

I will arise, and go to my Father, and will say unto him, Father, I have sinned against heaven, and before thee, and am no more worthy to be called thy son. *St. Luke* xv. 18, 19.

Enter not into judgment with thy servant, O Lord; for in thy sight shall no man living be justified. *Psal.* cxliii. 2.

If we say that we have no sin, we deceive ourselves, and the truth is not in us; but if we confess our sins, God is faithful and just to forgive us our sins, and to cleanse us from all unrighteousness. 1 *John* i. 8, 9.

The hour cometh, and now is, when the true worshippers shall worship the Father in spirit and in truth; for the Father seeketh such to worship him. God is a spirit, and they who worship him must worship him in spirit and in truth. *St. John* iv. 23, 24.

EXHORTATION.

DEARLY beloved brethren, the Scripture moveth us in sundry places to acknowledge and confess our manifold sins and wickedness, and that we should not dissemble nor cloak them before the face of Almighty God our Heavenly Father; but confess them with an humble, lowly, penitent, and obedient heart; to the end that we may obtain forgiveness of the same, by his infinite goodness and mercy. And although we ought, at all times, humbly to acknowledge our sins before God; yet ought we chiefly so to do, when we assemble and meet together, to render thanks for the great benefits that we have received at his hands, to set forth his most worthy praise, to hear his most holy word, and to ask those things which are requisite and necessary, as well for the body as the soul. Wherefore I pray and beseech you, as many as are here present, to accompany me, with a pure heart and humble voice, unto the throne of the heavenly grace, saying with me —

¶ *A General Confession to be said by the Minister and People.*

ALMIGHTY and most merciful Father, We have erred and strayed from thy ways like lost sheep. We have followed too much the devices and desires of our own hearts. We have offended against thy holy laws. We have left undone those things which we ought to have done; And we have done those things which we ought not to have done. But thou, O Lord, have mercy upon us miserable offenders. Spare thou those, O God, who confess their faults. Restore thou those who are penitent, according to thy promises declared unto mankind in Christ Jesus our Lord. And grant, O most merciful Father, That we may hereafter live a godly, righteous, and sober life; To the glory of thy holy name. *Amen.*

¶ *The People shall answer here, and at the end of*
ı *P* , Amen.

¶ Th n s tall t e Minister sa this Pra er.

O LORD, we beseech thee, mercifully hear our prayers, and spare all those who confess their sins unto thee ; that they whose consciences by sin are accused, by thy merciful pardon may be absolved, through Christ our Lord. *Amen.*

¶ Then the Minister shall say the Lord's Prayer ; the People repeating it with him both here and wheresoever else it is used in Divine Service.

O UR Father, who art in heaven, Hallowed be thy name. Thy kingdom come ; Thy will be done on earth, as it is in heaven. Give us this day our daily bread. And forgive us our trespasses, As we forgive those who trespass against us. And lead us not into temptation, But deliver us from evil. For thine is the kingdom, and the power, and the glory, For ever and ever. *Amen.*

¶ Then likewise he shall say,

O LORD, open thou our lips ;
Answ. And our mouth shall show forth thy praise.

¶ Here, all standing up, the Minister shall say,

Min. Now unto the King eternal, immortal, invisible, the only wise God ;
Answ. Be honor and glory, through Jesus Christ, for ever and ever. 1 *Tim.* i. 17 ; *Rom.* xvi. 27. *Amen.*
Min. Praise ye the Lord.
Answ. The Lord's name be praised.

Venite, exultemus Domino.

O COME, let us sing unto the Lord ; let us heartily rejoice in the strength of our salvation.

Let us come before his presence with thanksgiving ; and show ourselves glad in him with psalms.

For the Lord is a great God ; and a great king above all gods.

In his hand are all the corners of the earth · and the strength of the hills is his also.

The sea is his, and he made it ; and his hands prepared the dry land.

O come, let us worship, and fall down, and kneel before the Lord our Maker.

For he is the Lord our God ; and we are the people of his pasture, and the sheep of his hand.

O worship the Lord in the beauty of holiness ; let the whole earth stand in awe of him.

For he cometh, for he cometh to judge the earth ; and with righteousness to judge the world, and the people with his truth.

¶ *The shall be said, by tl e Minister and People, alter- atelv, the Psal s f r the Da . And at tl e close of tl e Psa ns sl all be peated tl e follo ng Dox ol gy.*

NOW unto the King eternal, immortal, invisible, the only wise God ;

Be honor and glory, through Jesus Christ, for ever and ever. *Amen.*

¶ *Then may follow an Anthem, or a Voluntary on the Organ. After which the Minister shall read the*
FIRST LESSON, *taken out of the Old Testament ; and at the end of it he shall say,* Here endeth the First Lesson. ↲ *is l le s ~ or else sa d ly the Minister and People, alter nately, the following Hymn.*

Te Deum laudamus.

WE praise thee, O God ; we acknowledge thee to be the Lord.

All the earth doth worship thee, the Father everlasting.

To thee all angels cry aloud, the heavens and all the powers therein.

To thee cherubim and seraphim continually do cry,

Holy, holy, holy, Lord God of Sabaoth.

Heaven and earth are full of the majesty of thy glory.

The glorious company of the apostles, praise thee.

The goodly fellowship of the prophets, praise thee.

The noble army of martyrs, praise thee.

The holy Church, throughout all the world, doth acknowledge thee,

The Father of an infinite majesty ;

Thine honorable, true, and only Son ;

Also the Holy Ghost, the Comforter.

Thou art the King of glory, O Lord ;

And Jesus Christ is thy well beloved Son.

When thou gavest him to deliver man, it pleased thee that he should be born of a virgin.

When he had overcome the sharpness of death, he did open the kingdom of heaven to all believers.

He sitteth at the right hand of God, in the glory of the Father.

We believe, that he shall come to be our judge.

We therefore pray thee, help thy servants, whom thou hast redeemed through his most precious blood.

Make them to be numbered with thy saints, in glory everlasting.

O Lord, save thy people, and bless thine heritage.

Govern them, and lift them up for ever.

Day by day we magnify thee ;

And we worship thy name, ever, world without end.

Vouchsafe, O Lord, to keep us this day without sin.

O Lord, have mercy upon us ; have mercy upon us.

O Lord, let thy mercy lighten upon us, as our trust is in thee.

O Lord, in thee have we trusted ; let us never be confounded.

¶ *Or this Psalm*

Exaltabo te, Deus.   PSALM CXLV.

I WILL magnify thee, O God, my King ; and I will praise thy name for ever and ever.

Every day will I give thanks unto thee, and praise thy name for ever and ever.

Great is the Lord and marvellous, worthy to be praised ; there is no end of his greatness.

One generation shall praise thy works unto another, and declare thy power.

The memorial of thine abundant kindness shall be shown ; and men shall sing of thy righteousness.

The Lord is gracious and merciful, long suffering, and of great goodness.

The Lord is loving unto every man, and his mercy is over all his works.

All thy works praise thee, O Lord, and thy saints give thanks unto thee.

They show the glory of thy kingdom, and talk of thy power ;

That thy power, thy glory, and mightiness of thy kingdom might be known unto men.

Thy kingdom is an everlasting kingdom, and thy dominion endureth throughout all ages.

The Lord upholdeth all such as fall, and lifteth up all those who are down.

The eyes of all wait upon thee, O Lord, and thou givest them their meat in due season.

Thou openest thine hand, and fillest all things living with plenteousness.

The Lord is righteous in all his ways, and holy in all his works.

The Lord is nigh unto all those who call upon him ; yea, all such as call upon him faithfully.

He will fulfil the desire of those who fear him ; he also will hear their cry, and will help them.

The Lord preserveth all those who love him ; but scattereth abroad all the ungodly.

My mouth shall speak the praise of the Lord, and let all flesh give thanks unto his holy name for ever and ever. *Amen.*

¶ *Then shall the Minister read the* SECOND LESSON, *taken out of the New Testament : and at the end of it he shall say,* Here endeth the Second Lesson. *Then shall be sung, or else repeated by the Minister and People, alternately, the following Hymn.*

Benedictus. ST. LUKE I. 68.

BLESSED be the Lord God of Israel ; for he hath visited and redeemed his people ;

And hath raised up a mighty salvation for us, in the house of his servant David ;

As he spake by the mouth of his holy prophets, who have been since the world began ;

That we should be saved from our enemies, and from the hand of all who hate us.

¶ *Or this Psalm.*

Jubilate Deo. PSALM C.

O BE joyful in the Lord, all ye lands ; serve the Lord with gladness, and come before his presence with a song.

Be ye sure that the Lord he is God ; it is he who hath made us, and not we ourselves ; we are his people, and the sheep of his pasture.

O go your way into his gates with thanksgiving, and into his courts with praise ; be thankful unto him, and speak good of his name.

For the Lord is gracious, his mercy is **everlast-**ing, and his truth endureth from generation to generation.

Then shall be said these Prayers following, the Min-ister first saying,

Min. The Lord be with you.

Answ. And with thy spirit.

Min. Let us pray.

O Lord, show thy mercy upon us ;

Answ. And grant us thy salvation.

Min. O God, make clean our hearts within us ;

Answ. And take not thy Holy Spirit from us.

Then shall be said the COLLECT FOR THE DAY ; *and then the service shall proceed as followeth.*

THE COLLECT FOR PEACE.

O GOD, who art the author of peace, and lover of concord, in knowledge of whom standeth our eternal life, whose service is perfect freedom ; defend us thy humble servants in all assaults of our enemies, that we, surely trusting in thy defence, may not fear the power of any adversaries, through Jesus Christ our Lord. *Amen.*

THE COLLECT FOR GRACE.

O LORD, our Heavenly Father, almighty and everlasting God, who hast safely brought us to the beginning of this day; defend us in the same with thy mighty power ; and grant that this day we fall into no sin, neither run into any kind of danger ; but that all our doings may be ordered

by thy governance, to do always that which is
righteous in thy sight, through Jesus Christ our
Lord. *Amen.*

THE LITANY

OR GENERAL SUPPLICATION.

O GOD, our Heavenly Father, have mercy upon
us miserable sinners.

*O God, our Heavenly Father, have mercy upon us
miserable sinners.*

O God, who by thy Son hast redeemed the
world, have mercy upon us miserable sinners.

*O God, who by thy Son hast redeemed the world,
have mercy upon us miserable sinners.*

O God, who by thy Holy Spirit dost govern,
direct, and sanctify the hearts of thy faithful servants, have mercy upon us miserable sinners.

*O God, who by thy Holy Spirit dost govern, di-
rect, and sanctify the hearts of thy faithful servants,
have mercy upon us miserable sinners.*

Remember not, Lord, our offences, neither take
thou vengeance of our sins ; spare us, good Lord,
spare thy people whom thou hast redeemed by the
most precious blood of thy Son, and be not angry
with us for ever.

Spare us, good Lord.

From all evil and mischief ; from sin ; from the
assaults of temptation ; from thy wrath, and from
everlasting destruction,

Good Lord, deliver us.

From all blindness of heart ; from pride, vain-glory, and hypocrisy ; from envy, hatred, and mal-ice, and all uncharitableness ; from all inordinate and sinful affections, and from all the deceitful allurements of this transitory world,

Good Lord, deliver us.

From lightning, and tempest; from plague, pesti-lence, and famine ; from battle, and murder, and from death unprepared for,

Good Lord, deliver us.

From all sedition, privy conspiracy, and rebel-lion ; from all false doctrine, heresy, and schism ; from hardness of heart, and contempt of thy word and commandment,

Good Lord, deliver us.

In all time of our tribulation ; in all time of our prosperity ; in the hour of death, and in the day of judgment,

Good Lord, deliver us.

We sinners do beseech thee to hear us, O Lord God, and that it may please thee to rule and gov-ern thy holy Church universal in the right way ; and to illuminate all ministers of the Gospel with true knowledge, and understanding of thy word ; and that both by their preaching and living they may set it forth, and show it accordingly ;

We beseech thee to hear us, good Lord.

That it may please thee to endue the President of these United States, the Governor of this Com-monwealth, the Judges and Magistrates, and all others in authority, with wisdom and understand-ing ; giving them grace to execute justice and to maintain truth ·

We beseech thee to hear us, good Lord.

That it may please thee to bless all colleges and seminaries of learning; all instructors of youth, and all means of true knowledge, virtue, and Piety;

We beseech thee to hear us, good Lord.

That it may please thee to bless and keep all thy people; to give to all nations, unity, peace, and concord; and to give us a heart to love and fear thee, and diligently to live after thy commandments;

We beseech thee to hear us, good Lord.

That it may please thee to give to all thy people increase of grace, to hear meekly thy word, and to receive it with pure affection, and to bring forth the fruits of the Spirit;

We beseech thee to hear us, good Lord.

That it may please thee to bring into the way of truth all such as have erred, and are deceived; to strengthen such as do stand; to comfort and help the weak-hearted; to raise up those who fall; and finally to give us victory over all temptations;

We beseech thee to hear us, good Lord.

That it may please thee to succor, help, and comfort all who are in danger, necessity, and tribulation; to preserve all who travel by land or by water, all sick persons and young children; to show thy pity upon all prisoners and captives; to defend, and provide for, the fatherless children and widows, and all who are desolate and oppressed;

We beseech thee to hear us, good Lord.

That it may please thee to have mercy upon all men ;

We beseech thee to hear us, good Lord.

That it may please thee to forgive our enemies, persecutors, and slanderers, and to turn their hearts ;

We beseech thee to hear us, good Lord.

That it may please thee to give and preserve to our use the kindly fruits of the earth, so that in due time we may enjoy them ;

We beseech thee to hear us, good Lord.

That it may please thee to give us true repentance, to forgive us all our sins, negligences, and ignorances, and to endue us with the grace of thy holy Spirit, to amend our lives according to thy holy word ;

We beseech thee to hear us, good Lord.

O Lord, grant us thy peace.

Lord, have mercy upon us.

O Lord, deal not with us according to our sins ;

Neither reward us according to our iniquities.

WE humbly beseech thee, O Father, mercifully to look upon our infirmities ; and for the glory of thy name, turn from us all those evils which we most justly have deserved ; and grant that in all our troubles we may put our whole trust and confidence in thy mercy, and evermore serve thee in holiness and pureness of living, to thy honor and glory, through our only Mediator and Advocate, Jesus Christ our Lord. *Amen.*

☞ *The three Prayers following are to be said in the Morning at those times when the Litany is not said.*

A PRAYER FOR RULERS.

O LORD, our Heavenly Father, high and mighty, King of kings, Lord of lords, who dost from thy throne behold all the dwellers upon the earth; most heartily we beseech thee with thy favor to behold the President, Vice-President, and Congress of the United States, and so replenish them with the grace of thy holy Spirit, that they may always incline to thy will, and walk in thy way. Endue them plenteously with heavenly gifts, that in all their deliberations they may be enabled to promote the national prosperity, and to secure the peace, liberty, and safety of the United States throughout all generations. This we humbly ask in the name of Jesus Christ our Lord. *Amen.*

A PRAYER FOR THE CLERGY AND PEOPLE.

A LMIGHTY and everlasting God, who art the author of every good and perfect gift; send down upon all ministers of the Gospel, and upon all congregations committed to their charge, the needful spirit of thy grace; and, that they may truly please thee, pour upon them the continual dew of thy blessing. Grant this, O Heavenly Father, for thine infinite mercy's sake in Jesus Christ our Lord. *Amen.*

A PRAYER FOR ALL CONDITIONS OF MEN.

O GOD, the Creator and Preserver of all mankind, we humbly beseech thee for all sorts and conditions of men, that thou wouldest be pleased to make thy ways known unto them, thy saving health unto all nations. More especially we pray for the good estate of thy holy Church; that it may be so guided and governed by thy good Spirit, that all who profess and call themselves Christians may be led into the way of truth, and hold the faith in unity of spirit, in the bond of peace, and in righteousness of life. Finally, we commend to thy fatherly goodness all those who are any ways afflicted or distressed in mind, body, or estate; that it may please thee to comfort and relieve them according to their several necessities; giving them patience under their sufferings, and a happy issue out of all their afflictions; and this we humbly ask as disciples of Jesus Christ our Lord. *Amen.*

⁂ If any desire the Prayers of the Congregation, the Notes are to be read here by the Minister, and to be followed with the appropriate Prayers or Thanksgivings.

A GENERAL THANKSGIVING.

ALMIGHTY God, Father of all mercies, we thine unworthy servants do give thee most humble and hearty thanks for all thy goodness and loving kindness to us and to all men. We bless thee for our creation, preservation, and all the blessings of this life; but above all, for thine inestimable love in the redemption of the world by our Lord Jesus Christ; for the means of grace, and for the hope of glory. And we beseech thee, give us that due sense of all thy mercies, that our hearts may be unfeignedly thankful, and that we may show forth thy praise, not only with our lips, but in our lives, by giving up ourselves to thy service, and by walking before thee in holiness and righteousness all our days, through Jesus Christ our Lord; in whose name we ascribe unto thee all honor and glory, world without end. *Amen.*

A CONCLUDING PRAYER.

ALMIGHTY God, who hast given us grace, at this time, with one accord, to make our common supplications unto thee, and hast promised by thy beloved Son, that, where two or three are gathered together in his name, thou wilt grant their requests; fulfil now, O Lord, the desires and petitions of thy servants, as may be most expedient for them, granting us in this world knowledge of thy truth, and in the world to come life everlasting. *Amen.*

THE grace of our Lord Jesus Christ, and the love of God, and the fellowship of the Holy Ghost, be with us all evermore. *Amen.*

END OF MORNING PRAYER.

EVENING PRAYER.

HEN the wicked man turneth away from his wickedness which he hath committed, and doeth that which is lawful and right, he shall save his soul alive. *Ezek.* xviii. 27.

I acknowledge my transgressions; and my sin is ever before me. *Psal.* li. 3.

Hide thy face from my sins; and blot out all mine iniquities. *Psal.* li. 9.

The sacrifices of God are a broken spirit; a broken and a contrite heart, O God, thou wilt not despise. *Psal.* li. 17.

Rend your heart, and not your garments, and turn unto the Lord your God; for he is gracious and merciful, slow to anger, and of great kindness, and repenteth him of the evil. *Joel* ii. 13.

To the Lord our God belong mercies and for-givenesses, though we have rebelled against him; neither have we obeyed the voice of the Lord our God, to walk in his laws which he set before us. *Dan.* ix. 9, 10.

O Lord, correct me, but in measure; not in thine anger, lest thou bring me to nothing. *Jer.* x. 24.

Repent ye; for the kingdom of heaven is at hand. *St. Matt.* iii. 2.

I will arise, and go to my Father, and will say unto him, Father, I have sinned against heaven, and before thee, and am no more worthy to be called thy son. *St. Luke* xv. 18, 19.

Enter not into judgment with thy servant, O Lord; for in thy sight shall no man living be justified. *Psal.* cxliii. 2.

If **we** say that we have no sin, we deceive ourselves, and the truth is not in us; but if we confess our sins, God is faithful and just to forgive us our sins, and to cleanse us from all unrighteousness. 1 *John* i. 8, 9.

The hour cometh, and now is, when the true worshippers shall worship the Father in spirit and in truth; for the Father seeketh such to worship him. God is a spirit, and they who worship him must worship him in spirit and in truth. *St. John* iv. 23, 24.

EXHORTATION.

DEARLY beloved brethren, the Scripture moveth us in sundry places to acknowledge and confess our manifold sins and wickedness, and that we should not dissemble nor cloak them before the face of Almighty God our Heavenly Father; but confess them with an humble, lowly, penitent and obedient heart; to the end that we may obtain forgiveness of the same, by his infinite goodness and mercy. And although we ought, at all times, humbly to acknowledge our sins before God ; yet ought we chiefly so to do, when we assemble and meet together, to render thanks for the great benefits that we have received at his hands, to set forth his most worthy praise, to hear his most holy word, and to ask those things which are requisite and necessary, as well for the body as the soul. Wherefore I pray and beseech you, as many as are here present, to accompany me, with a pure heart and humble voice, unto the throne of the heavenly grace, saying with me —

LMIGHTY and most merciful Father, We have erred and strayed from thy ways like lost sheep. We have followed too much the devices and desires of our own hearts. We have offended against thy holy laws. We have left undone those things which we ought to have done ; And we have done those things which we ought not to have done. But thou, O Lord, have mercy upon us miserable offenders. Spare thou those, O God, who confess their faults. Restore thou those who are penitent, according to thy promises declared unto mankind in Christ Jesus our Lord. And grant, O most merciful Father, That we may hereafter live a godly, righteous, and sober life ; To the glory of thy holy name.

Amen.

ALMIGHTY God, the Father of our Lord Jesus Christ, who desirest not the death of a sinner, but rather that he should turn from his wickedness and live ; pardon and absolve all those who truly repent, and unfeignedly believe the holy Gospel. We beseech thee to grant us true repentance, and thy Holy Spirit ; that those things may please thee which we do at this present, and that the rest of our life hereafter may be pure and holy ; so that at the last we may come to thine eternal joy, through Jesus Christ our Lord. *Amen.*

O MOST mighty God and merciful Father, who hast compassion upon all men, and hatest nothing that thou hast made ; who wouldest not the death of a sinner, but that he should rather turn from his sin and be saved ; mercifully forgive us our trespasses ; receive and comfort us, who are grieved with the burden of our sins. Thy property is always to have mercy ; to thee only it appertaineth to forgive iniquity. Spare us, therefore, good Lord ; enter not into judgment with thy servants, who have sinned against thee : but so turn thine anger from us, who acknowledge our unworthiness, and repent us of our faults, and so make haste to help us in this world, that we may ever live with thee in the world to come, through Jesus Christ our Lord. *Amen.*

OUR Father, who art in heaven, Hallowed be thy name. Thy kingdom come; Thy will be done on earth, as it is in heaven. Give us this day our daily bread. And forgive us our trespasses, As we forgive those who trespass against us. And lead us not into temptation, But deliver us from evil. For thine is the kingdom, and the power, and the glory, For ever and ever. *Amen.*

LORD, open thou our lips;

Answ. And our mouth shall show forth thy praise.

Min. Now unto the King eternal, immortal, invisible, the only wise God;

Answ. Be honor and glory, through Jesus Christ, for ever and ever. *Amen.*

Min. Praise ye the Lord.

Answ. The Lord's name be praised.

NOW unto the King eternal, immortal, invisible, the only wise God;

Be honor and glory, through Jesus Christ, for ever and ever. *Amen.*

FIRST LESSON,

s   Here endeth the First Lesson.   7

Magnificat. ST. LUKE I. 46.

MY soul doth magnify the Lord, and my spirit hath rejoiced in God my Saviour.

For he hath regarded the lowliness of his hand-maiden.

For behold, from henceforth, all generations shall call me blessed.

For he who is mighty hath magnified me ; and holy is his name.

And his mercy is on them that fear him, through-out all generations.

He hath shown strength with his arm ; he hath scattered the proud in the imagination of their hearts.

He hath put down the mighty from their seat ; and hath exalted the humble and meek.

He hath filled the hungry with good things ; and the rich he hath sent empty away.

He, remembering his mercy, hath holpen his servant Israel, as he promised to òur forefathers, Abraham and his seed for ever.

¶ *Or* ei ι s *Ps* ›

Cantate Domino. PSALM XCVIII.

O SING unto the Lord a new song ; for he hath done marvellous things.

With his own right hand, and with his holy arm, hath he gotten himself the victory.

The Lord declared his salvation; his righteousness hath he openly shown in the sight of the heathen.

He hath remembered his mercy and truth toward the house of Israel; and all the ends of the world have seen the salvation of our God.

Show yourselves joyful unto the Lord, all ye lands; sing, rejoice, and give thanks.

Praise the Lord upon the harp; sing to the harp with a Psalm of thanksgiving;

With trumpets also and shawms, O show yourselves joyful before the Lord the king.

Let the sea make a noise, and all that therein is; the round world, and they that dwell therein.

Let the floods clap their hands; and let the hills be joyful together before the Lord; for he cometh to judge the earth.

With righteousness shall he judge the world, and the people with equity.

Here shall be read the SECOND LESSON.

Here endeth the Second Lesson.

Then shall be sung or said the following, except on Easter-day

Nunc dimittis. ST. LUKE II. 29.

LORD, now lettest thou thy servant depart in peace, according to thy word;

For mine eyes have seen thy salvation,

Which thou hast prepared before the face of all people;

To be a light to lighten the Gentiles ; and to be the glory of thy people Israel.

Deus misereatur. PSALM LXVII.

GOD be merciful unto us, and bless us ; and show us the light of his countenance, and be merciful unto us ;

That thy way may be known upon earth, thy saving health among all nations.

Let the people praise thee, O God ; yea, let all the people praise thee.

O let the nations rejoice and be glad ; for thou shalt judge the folk righteously, and govern the nations upon earth.

Let the people praise thee, O God ; yea, let all the people praise thee.

Then shall the earth bring forth her increase ; and God, even our own God, shall give us his blessing.

God shall bless us, and all the ends of the world shall fear him.

Then shall be said these words concerning the Min . . . . . first sung.

Min. The Lord be with you ;
Answ. And with thy spirit.
Min. Let us pray.
O Lord, show thy mercy upon us ;
Answ. And grant us thy salvation.
Min. O God, make clean our hearts within us ;
Answ. And take not thy Holy Spirit from us.

* *Here shall be said the Creed by the Ministers and the People the Minister . . . shall proceed as followeth.*

THE COLLECT FOR PEACE.

O GOD, from whom all holy desires, all good counsels, and all just works do proceed; give unto thy servants that peace which the world cannot give; that both our hearts may be set to obey thy commandments, and also that, being defended by thee from the fear of our enemies, we may pass our time in rest and quietness, through Jesus Christ our Saviour. *Amen.*

THE COLLECT FOR AID AGAINST ALL PERILS.

LIGHTEN our darkness, we beseech thee, O Lord, and by thy great mercy defend us from all perils and dangers of this night, for the honor of thy name, through Jesus Christ our Mediator and Advocate. *Amen.*

A PRAYER FOR RULERS.

O LORD, our Heavenly Father, high and mighty, King of kings, Lord of lords, who dost from thy throne behold all the dwellers upon the earth; most heartily we beseech thee with thy favor to behold the President, Vice-President, and Congress of the United States, and so replenish them with the grace of thy Holy Spirit, that they may always incline to thy will, and walk in thy way. Endue them plenteously with heavenly gifts, that in all their deliberations they may be enabled to promote the national prosperity, and to secure the peace, liberty, and safety of the United States throughout all generations. This we humbly ask in the name of Jesus Christ our Lord. *Amen.*

Evening Prayer.

A PRAYER FOR THE CLERGY AND PEOPLE.

ALMIGHTY and everlasting God, who art the author of every good and perfect gift; send down upon all ministers of the Gospel, and upon all congregations committed to their charge, the needful spirit of thy grace; and that they may truly please thee, pour upon them the continual dew of thy blessing. Grant this, O Heavenly Father, for thine infinite mercy's sake in Jesus Christ our Lord. *Amen.*

A PRAYER FOR ALL CONDITIONS OF MEN.

O GOD, the Creator and Preserver of all mankind, we humbly beseech thee for all sorts and conditions of men, that thou wouldest be pleased to make thy ways known unto them, thy saving health unto all nations. More especially we pray for the good estate of thy holy Church; that it may be so guided and governed by thy good Spirit, that all who profess and call themselves Christians may be led into the way of truth, and hold the faith in unity of spirit, in the bond of peace, and in righteousness of life. Finally, we commend to thy fatherly goodness all those who are any ways afflicted or distressed in mind, body, or estate; that it may please thee to comfort and relieve them according to their several necessities; giving them patience under their sufferings, and a happy issue out of all their afflictions; and this we humbly ask as disciples of Jesus Christ our Lord. *Amen.*

If there follow the Prayers of the Congregation, the ... ... by the Minister, followed

A GENERAL THANKSGIVING.

ALMIGHTY God, Father of all mercies, we thine unworthy servants do give thee most humble and hearty thanks for all thy goodness and loving kindness to us and to all men. We bless thee for our creation, preservation, and all the blessings of this life ; but above all, for thine inestimable love in the redemption of the world by our Lord Jesus Christ; for the means of grace, and for the hope of glory. And we beseech thee, give us that due sense of all thy mercies, that our hearts may be unfeignedly thankful, and that we may show forth thy praise, not only with our lips, but in our lives, by giving up ourselves to thy service, and by walking before thee in holiness and righteousness all our days, through Jesus Christ our Lord ; in whose name we ascribe unto thee all honor and glory, world without end. *Amen.*

A CONCLUDING PRAYER.

ALMIGHTY God, who hast given us grace, at this time, with one accord, to make our common supplications unto thee, and hast promised by thy beloved Son, that, where two or three are gathered together in his name, thou wilt grant their requests ; fulfil now, O Lord, the desires and petitions of thy servants, as may be most expedient for them, granting us in this world knowledge of thy truth, and in the world to come life everlasting. *Amen.*

THE grace of our Lord Jesus Christ, and the love of God, and the fellowship of the Holy Ghost, be with us all evermore. *Amen.*

END OF THE FIRST FORM OF EVENING PRAYER.

SECOND

FORM OF EVENING PRAYER.

FROM the rising of the sun, unto the going
down of the same, the Lord's name is to be
praised.

O magnify the Lord with me, and let us exalt
his name together; for with him is the fountain
of life, and in his light shall we see light.

Let our prayers be set forth in his sight as
incense; and the lifting up of our hands be an
evening sacrifice.

We will go into his tabernacle; we will worship
at his footstool; we will worship, and fall down,
and kneel before the Lord our Maker.

For he is kind to all, even unto the evil and
unthankful. He has nourished and brought us
up as children, though we have rebelled against
him.

Let us then go unto our Father, and say unto
him, Father, we have sinned against heaven and

in thy sight, and are no more worthy to be called thy children.

ALMIGHTY God and most merciful Father, Unto whom all hearts are open, and from whom no secrets are hid; With simplicity and godly sincerity would we seek thee, Confessing our unthankfulness, and our manifold offences. We deplore the sins which we have at any time committed, In thought or affection, in word or deed, Against each other and against thee. And we humbly beseech thee, Through thy mercy declared unto us by thy Son Jesus Christ, To look graciously upon us, and forgive us, And assist us to lay aside every weight, And the sins which so easily beset us; To mortify our evil and corrupt affections, And to subdue our thoughts and desires to the obedience of the Gospel. May we be convinced, O God, That till we know thee, we know nothing aright; That without thee, we have nothing of any worth; And in wandering from thee, we leave all that is truly good. Let us cast ourselves into the arms of thy mercy, And offer thee our whole being, our bodies and our souls, That they may be thy temple for ever. And wilt thou take us, O Lord, entirely into thy hands, with all that we have, And let nothing henceforward, either in life or death, ever separate us from thee any more. *Amen.*

THE LORD'S PRAYER.

OUR Father who art in heaven, Hallowed be thy name. Thy kingdom come; Thy will be done on earth, as it is in heaven. Give us this day our daily bread. And forgive us our trespasses, As we forgive those who trespass against us. And lead us not into temptation, But deliver us from evil. For thine is the kingdom, and the power, and the glory, For ever and ever. *Amen.*

O LORD, open thou our lips;
  Answ. And our mouths will show forth thy praise.
  Min. O God, make speed to save us.
  Answ. O Lord, make haste to help us.
  Min. O Lord, let thy mercy be shown upon us;
  Answ. As we do put our trust in thee.
  Min. Praise ye the Lord.
  Answ. The Lord's name be praised.

NOW unto the King eternal, immortal, invisible, the only wise God;
  Be honor and glory, through Jesus Christ, for ever and ever. *Amen.*

FIRST LESSON, *Here endeth the First Lesson.*

Cantate Domino. PSALM XCVIII.

O SING unto the Lord a new song; for he hath done marvellous things.

With his own right hand, and with his holy arm, hath he gotten himself the victory.

The Lord declared his salvation; his righteousness hath he openly shown in the sight of the heathen.

He hath remembered his mercy and truth toward the house of Israel; and all the ends of the world have seen the salvation of our God.

Show yourselves joyful unto the Lord, all ye lands; sing, rejoice, and give thanks.

Praise the Lord upon the harp; sing to the harp with a Psalm of thanksgiving;

With trumpets also and shawms, O show yourselves joyful before the Lord the king.

Let the sea make a noise, and all that therein is; the round world, and they that dwell therein.

Let the floods clap their hands; and let the hills be joyful together before the Lord; for he cometh to judge the earth.

With righteousness shall he judge the world, and the people with equity.

☛ *Or this.*

Quam dilecta ! PSALM LXXXIV.

O HOW amiable are thy dwellings, thou Lord of hosts !

My soul longeth, yea, even fainteth for the courts of the Lord; my heart and my flesh cry out for the living God.

As the sparrow findeth a house, and the swallow a nest where she may lay her young, so let me dwell at thine altars, O Lord of hosts, my king and my God.

Blessed are they who dwell in thy house; they will be always praising thee.

Blessed are the men whose strength is in thee; in whose heart are thy ways.

They will go from strength to strength, till every one of them appeareth before God in Sion.

For a day in thy courts is better than a thousand elsewhere. I had rather be a doorkeeper in the house of my God, than to dwell in the tents of ungodliness.

For the Lord God is a sun and shield; the Lord will give grace and glory; no good thing will he withhold from those who walk uprightly.

O Lord, God of hosts, blessed is the man who trusteth in thee.

☛ *T' , ͜ , ͜ ' , ͜]ʄ ͜ , ʒd ⁴' ·* SECOND LESSON

Here endeth the Second Lesson. *⧸ ͥ ͥ 'l ͥ ͨ*

Deus misereatur. PSALM LXVII.

GOD be merciful unto us, and bless us; and show us the light of his countenance, and be merciful unto us;

That thy way may be known upon earth, thy saving health among all nations.

Let the people praise thee, O God; yea, let all the people praise thee.

O let the nations rejoice and be glad; for thou shalt judge the folk righteously, and govern the nations upon earth.

Let the people praise thee, O God; yea, let all the people praise thee.

Then shall the earth bring forth her increase; and God, even our own God, shall give us his blessing.

God shall bless us, and all the ends of the world shall fear him.

Levavi oculos meos. PSALM CXXI.

WILL lift up mine eyes unto the hills, from whence cometh my help.

My help cometh from the Lord, who hath made heaven and earth.

He will not suffer thy foot to be moved; he who keepeth thee will not sleep.

Behold, he who keepeth his people shall neither slumber nor sleep.

The Lord himself is thy keeper; the Lord is thy shade upon thy right hand.

The sun shall not smite thee by day, neither the moon by night.

The Lord shall preserve thee from all evil ; it is even he who shall keep thy soul.

The Lord shall preserve thy going out and thy coming in, from this time forth for evermore.

Min.   The Lord be with you ;
Answ.   And with thy spirit.
Min.   Let us pray.
O Lord, show thy mercy upon us ;
Answ.   And grant us thy salvation.
Min.   O God, make clean our hearts within us ;
Answ.   And take not thy Holy Spirit from us.

Then shall the Minister say the following Prayers.

A PRAYER FOR AID AGAINST PERILS.

O THOU great Author of our being, who knowest all our wants, and who alone art able to supply them ; who perceivest all the dangers and evils to which we are exposed, and who alone canst defend us ; whither shall we go but unto thee ! We pray thee to compassionate our weakness, to guard us in peril, to direct us in doubt, and to save us from falling into sin.

In every exposure may thy shield be over us. From the evil that is around and within us, graciously deliver us. Make the path of duty plain before us, and keep us in it even unto the end.

Heavenly Father, we beseech thee to watch over us this night, and preserve us from all harm. In the night of affliction and trouble may we look up unto thee, and be comforted with the assurance that thou wilt hereafter wipe away all tears from our eyes. And when we come to the dark valley of the shadow of death, be thou our guide and comforter, and bring us to the regions of endless day.

O God, we commit ourselves entirely to thy disposal ; and whether we enjoy, or suffer, or live, or die, may we be mercifully accepted as thy children, and disciples of thy Son Jesus Christ. *Amen.*

INTERCESSIONS.

O THOU who art our Creator, Preserver, Governor, and Judge, we beseech thee to regard with thy favor all thy creatures, and to show thy mercy on all orders and conditions of men. Bless, we pray thee, all our rulers ; all those whose duty it is to administer justice ; and all who are in places of authority and trust. May our land be ever favored of the Most High God ; the abode of freedom, religion, virtue, truth, and peace. Let thy mercy descend upon thy whole Church ; purify it by thy spirit, and preserve it against all temptations and enemies ; that, offering to thee the never ceasing sacrifice of prayer and thanksgiving, it may advance thy honor, and be filled with thy grace, and partake of thy glory. Bless all its ministers, and clothe them with righteousness. Bless the means of education, and the instructors of youth. Enlighten the ignorant ; convert the unbelieving ; relieve and comfort all the persecuted and afflicted ; speak peace to troubled consciences ; strengthen the weak ; confirm the strong ; deliver the oppressed from him who spoileth him, and succor the needy who hath no helper. Redeem man, O God, from slavery, superstition, and crime ; send light, liberty, and peace over the whole earth ; and let the sun of righteousness arise upon all nations, with healing in his beams.

Hear our supplications, which we humbly address to thee in the name of Jesus Christ our Saviour, who ever liveth to make intercession for us, and through whom we render unto thee all honor and glory for ever. *Amen.*

GENERAL THANKSGIVING.

LORD, merciful and gracious, we, thy dependent offspring, would now humbly and sincerely thank thee, because thou hast given us life, and by thy bountiful providence hast always nourished, directed, and governed us. For our reason, education, and religion ; for all the gifts of nature, and of grace ; for our Saviour, Christ ; for our redemption, and instruction in the truth ; for thy repeated calls to us ; for all the patience which has waited for us, and all the mercy which has spared us ; for all the enjoyments of this present life, and for all thy promises, and all our hopes of a better life to come, we bless and magnify thy holy name. And grant, O Lord, that thy mercies may be followed by our obedience ; and that we may so walk in the light of thy favor, and in the paths of thy commandments, that living here to thy praise, we may at last be received to thyself, to rejoice for ever in thy presence ; which we ask in the name, and as disciples, of him who died that we might live, through whom to thee be ascribed all thanksgiving and praise, both now and for ever. *Amen.*

CONCLUDING PRAYER.

ETERNAL and all-seeing God, we thy creatures sink into nothing before thy supreme majesty ; we feel our weakness ; we acknowledge our folly ; we repeatedly bewail our sins ; thee only we adore with awful veneration ; thee we would thank with fervent zeal ; to thy power we humbly submit; of thy goodness we devoutly implore protection ; on thy wisdom we firmly and cheerfully rely. Whenever we address thee, O Father, if our prayers are unwise, wilt thou pity us ; if they are presumptuous, wilt thou pardon us ; if acceptable to thee, grant them, all-powerful God ; and as we now express our submission to thy decrees, adore thy providence, and bless thy dispensations, so, in that future state, to which we reverently hope thy goodness will raise us, may we continue praising, venerating, worshipping thee, more and more, through worlds without number, and ages without end. *Amen.*

THE grace of our Lord Jesus Christ, and the love of God, and the fellowship of the Holy Spirit, be with us all evermore. *Amen.*

END OF THE SECOND FORM OF EVENING PRAYER.

OCCASIONAL

PRAYERS AND THANKSGIVINGS.

PRAYERS.

FOR A SICK PERSON.

O GOD, who hast taught us at all times and in every condition to make our requests known unto thee; we offer up our humble supplications in behalf of thy servant, who is laboring under pain and sickness. Look down upon *him* with mercy, and let the consideration of thy goodness strengthen and comfort *his* soul in the time of affliction. We pray, with submission to thy wise providence, that thou wouldest be pleased to remove *his* disorder and restore *him* to health. Graciously prolong *his* days upon earth; and grant that *his* affliction may produce the fruit of righteousness to the honor of thy name. By the sadness of *his* countenance may *his* heart be made better ; and may *he* live to manifest *his* thankfulness to thee *his* great preserver.

[* But if this affliction should be unto death, may thy servant be prepared to give *himself* up into thy hands with Christian patience and fortitude, in joyful expectation of thy mercy unto eternal life. Give *him* unfeigned repentance for all *his* sins and a firm reliance on thy great mercies declared unto mankind by Jesus Christ our Lord. May the hope of thy favor support *him* in the hour of death ; may *he* leave the world in peace ; may *he* be received into thy heavenly kingdom, and made a partaker of that happiness which eye hath not seen, nor ear heard, nor hath it entered into the heart of man to conceive.]

O God, command thy blessing upon thy servant, even life evermore, through Jesus Christ our Lord and Saviour. *Amen.*

FOR A SICK CHILD.

O GOD, the fountain of all mercy, we offer up our humble prayers unto thee in behalf of the child, on whom thou hast seen fit to lay thine afflicting hand. We beseech thee, if it be thy will, to remove the disorder under which *he* labors, and restore *him* to health and strength. Suffer not the wishes of *his* parents to be disappointed, but in thy great mercy spare *him* to be the comfort and support of their advancing years, and to be useful in the world. But whatever thou

* *This is to be said when there is small hope of recovery.*

hast determined concerning *him*, thy will, O God, be done. Into thy hands we commit ourselves and all our enjoyments, and we humbly pray that, by all the dispensations of thy providence, we may be trained up for that world where pain, and sorrow, and death shall be known no more. *Amen.*

FOR A PERSON IN AFFLICTION.

O MERCIFUL God and Heavenly Father, who hast taught us in thy holy word that thou dost not willingly afflict or grieve the children of men ; look with pity, we beseech thee, upon the sorrows of thy servant for whom our prayers are desired. Remember *him*, O Lord, in mercy ; sanctify to *him* thy fatherly correction ; endue *his* soul with patience under *his* affliction, and with resignation to thy holy will. Comfort *him* with a sense of thy goodness ; lift up the light of thy countenance upon *him*, and give *him* peace through Jesus Christ our Lord. *Amen.*

Or this.

O GOD, gracious and merciful, who bindest up the broken heart, and pitiest the sorrows of those who fear thee, fulfil to thy *servant*, for whom our prayers are now desired, the promises of thy word. Sanctify to *him*, we beseech thee, thy correcting hand. Suffer *him* not to faint under thy rebuke. Let not *his* faith fail, nor *his* fortitude be overcome, nor *his* patience nor *his* hope depart from *him*. Enlighten the darkness which covers *him*, by the cheering truths of religion. Let the remembrance of thy goodness comfort *his* heart. Let the conviction of thy wisdom fortify *his* soul. Enable *him* to resign unto thee the object of *his* affections, in the assurance that, as thou hast appointed unto all men once to die, so after death will be a joyful resurrection, when they who sleep in Jesus shall awake to everlasting life, and friends shall meet again, to separate no more. *Amen.*

AFTER THE DEATH OF THE AGED.

O THOU who art the God of the fathers and of the children, grant, we beseech thee, unto thy servants for whom our prayers are desired, the sure comforts of thy Spirit.

Make them grateful for the length of years in which thou hast blessed them with a faithful companionship, and with wise and loving counsels. Cause them to recognize the mercy which has permitted them in their turn to care for *him* who watched over their childhood and youth.

Teach them to perceive thy hand in everything which smoothed the path of declining years, and fulfilled thy promise that the gray hairs of the righteous should be a crown of glory. And grant that they also may so serve thee in their generation that they may be prepared for the home where thou wilt at length gather together thy family in Jesus Christ our Lord. *Amen.*

FOR A PERSON AT SEA, OR GOING TO SEA.

O ETERNAL Lord God, who alone spreadest out the heavens, and rulest the raging of the sea; be pleased to receive into thine almighty and most gracious protection the person of thy servant, for whom our prayers are desired. Preserve *him* from the dangers of the sea, from sickness, from the violence of enemies, and from every evil to which *he* may be exposed. Conduct *him* in safety to the desired haven, with a grateful sense of thy mercies, through Jesus Christ our Lord. *Amen.*

FOR MALEFACTORS AFTER CONDEMNATION.

O MOST gracious and merciful God, we earnestly beseech thee to look down upon *those* *persons* recommended to our prayers, who now lie under the sentence of the law, and are appointed to die Visit *them*, O Lord, with thy compassion; make *them* sensible of the miserable condition to which *their* wickedness has reduced them, and give *them* true and unfeigned repentance. O God, in judgment remember mercy, and whatever sufferings *they* are to endure in this world, deliver *them* from the bitter pains of eternal death. Pardon *their* sins, and save *their* souls, for the sake of thine infinite goodness, in Jesus Christ our Lord. *Amen.*

FOR THE GENERAL COURT,

TO BE READ DURING THEIR SESSION.

MOST gracious God, we humbly beseech thee, for the Legislature of this Commonwealth, at this time assembled, that thou wouldest be pleased to direct and prosper all their consultations, to the advancement of thy glory, and the safety, honor, and welfare of thy people; that all things may be so ordered and settled, by their endeavors, upon the best and surest foundations, that peace and happiness, truth and justice, religion and piety, may be established among us for all generations. These and all other necessaries for them, and for us, we humbly beg, in the name of Jesus Christ, our most blessed Lord and Saviour. *Amen.*

A COLLECT FOR SPRING.

O LORD, the Creator and Preserver of all things, who with unerring wisdom maintainest the beauty and order of thy works; we look up with joy and confidence unto thy gracious power, which causes the returning seasons to know their place. Bless, we beseech thee, the springing of the year, and enrich the earth with the rain of heaven. May grass grow for the cattle, and herbs and fruits for the service of man. May our pastures be clothed with flocks, our valleys covered with corn, and the year crowned with thy goodness; and may we so improve the various blessings of thy providence in this world, as to be prepared for the unchangeable felicities of thine everlasting kingdom, through Jesus Christ our Lord. *Amen.*

FOR SEASONABLE WEATHER.

O GOD, our Heavenly Father, whose gift it is that the earth is fruitful and bringeth forth its increase for our sustenance and comfort; we humbly beseech thee to send us in this our necessity such seasonable weather, that we may receive the fruits thereof in due time ; and grant that we may show forth our thankfulness to thee for all thy mercies, by a sincere obedience to thy holy laws, which thou hast taught us by Jesus Christ our Lord. *Amen.*

IN TIME OF GREAT SCARCITY.

O GOD, our Heavenly Father, who hast mercifully given us life, and on whom we depend for its support and preservation ; mercifully behold, we beseech thee, the present afflictions of thy people ; alleviate the distresses of the miserable, and may the cries of the poor come unto thee ; increase the fruits of the earth by thy heavenly benediction ; may our scarcity be turned into plenty, and grant that we may improve the bounties of thy providence to thy praise, by relieving the distresses of others, and by thankfully acknowledging thee the giver of every good and perfect gift, through Jesus Christ our Lord. *Amen.*

IN TIME OF SICKNESS.

ALMIGHTY and most wise God, whose never-failing providence ordereth all things both in heaven and on earth ; we humbly direct our addresses unto thee, in this time of our calamity, beseeching thee in behalf of our fellow-creatures and friends, who are suffering under the grievous sickness with which thou art pleased to visit us. May the everlasting arm of thy mercy support them, in this time of their distress. Sanctify this general affliction to the reformation of our manners, and the improvement of our virtue ; and cause us to rejoice in the humble hope that everything shall work together for good. In the midst of life we are in death ; of whom may we seek for succor, but of thee, O God. Restrain the progress of this disorder, if it be agreeable to thy blessed will. May those lives which are yet spared be devoted to thy service, and may we, and all thy servants, be prepared for every event of thy providence, that whether we live, we may live unto the Lord, or whether we die, we may die unto the Lord, and whether living or dying, may have an interest in thy mercies unto eternal life, through Jesus Christ our Saviour. *Amen.*

IN TIME OF WAR.

ALMIGHTY God, who art a strong tower of defence unto all who do put their trust in thee, we humbly beseech thee in this time of our danger to be the defender of our country. Give us not up into the hands of our enemies, and preserve our land from the desolations of war. Have mercy upon us, O God ; have mercy upon thy people. Avert the evils we have deserved ; continue thy favor and protection to us ; and grant that these present sufferings may work within us a spirit of loyalty, and reformation, and obedience to thy will.

In all our battles, trials, and dangers, support us with heavenly help, and give unto us such victory as shall hasten the coming of honorable and abiding peace.

And this we humbly beg for thy mercy's sake, in Jesus Christ our Lord. *Amen.*

¶ *Or this.*

O GOD, whose loving mercies are over all thy children, we humbly commend to thy tender care and sure protection thy servants who have gone forth to defend us. Let thy fatherly hand be over them; let thy Holy Spirit be with them day by day ; with thy loving-kindness defend them as with a shield. Grant that in the perils that beset them they may gain a steadfast hope in thee, and if it be thy merciful will, we beseech thee, bring them out of their trial in safety, with hearts to love thee and to show forth thy praises forever.

Strengthen with the comforts of thy Spirit all who are sick, or wounded, or in prison for our sakes ; and sustain them with that glorious hope by which alone thy servants can have victory in suffering and death.

O Thou who art our refuge and our stay, comfort all whom thou hast stricken ; let their sighing come before thee ; uphold them with thy patience in anxiety and sorrow ; and cause them to look to thee with childlike trust ; which we ask in the name of thy dear Son the Prince of Peace. *Amen.*

THANKSGIVINGS.

FOR RECOVERY FROM SICKNESS.

( ) LORD, our Heavenly Father, who redeemest the lives of thy servants from destruction, and givest health, and life, and blessing ; accept the sincere and humble thanksgivings of thy servant, whom thou hast raised from a bed of sickness, and restorèd to some good measure of health and strength. We praise thee for this gracious instance of thy goodness ; may the remembrance of thy late mercy to *him* have a happy and lasting influence upon *his* mind, and establish the good resolutions *he* may have formed ; and may that life, which thy mercy prolongs, be devoted to thy service, in a constant obedience to thy holy commandments, through Jesus Christ our Lord. *Amen.*

A GENERAL THANKSGIVING.

LMIGHTY God our most gracious preserver, we offer up to thee our united thanksgivings for thy great goodness to thy *servants* in the mercies which thou hast vouchsafed to *them.* May *their* hearts be filled with unfeigned thankfulness to thee *their* benefactor ; and may *they* spend the remainder of *their* days in a course of obedience to thy commandments, that at last *they* may be partakers of eternal glory and happiness in the world to come, through Jesus Christ our Lord. *Amen.*

ON THE BIRTH OF A CHILD.

GRACIOUS God, we thank thee that thou hast given to thy *servants* a new object of affection and concern. Let *them* receive *their* child as from thee, and in gratitude dedicate it to thee. Will it please thee to watch over its life and health, to unfold its faculties, to make it a blessing to *them* and an instrument of good to society, wherever its lot may be cast. Help *them* to feel *their* obligations to it as Christian parents. Above all wilt thou early sanctify it in all its faculties and affections, and let it become a child of God. And whether earlier or later thou shalt take it from this scene of discipline, may it not have lived in vain; and this we humbly ask in the name of Jesus Christ our Lord. *Amen.*

FOR A SAFE RETURN FROM SEA.

ALMIGHTY God, the preserver of all thy creatures, and the confidence of the ends of the earth, and of those who are afar off upon the seas; we offer up unto thee our united thanksgivings for the signal mercies thou hast vouchsafed to thy servant whom thou hast preserved in *his* voyage; that thou hast protected *him* from every danger to which *he* was exposed; and hast restored *him* to *his* friends in safety. Write a law of thankfulness upon *his* heart, and hereby engage *him* to a diligent and grateful obedience to all thy commandments, through Jesus Christ our Lord. *Amen.*

FOR RAIN.

O GOD, our Heavenly Father, who by thy gracious providence dost cause the former and the latter rain to descend upon the earth, that it may bring forth fruit for the use of man ; we give thee humble thanks that it hath pleased thee in our great necessity to send a joyful rain upon the earth, and to enrich the furrows thereof with the plentiful dews of heaven. Thou hast filled our hearts with joy and gladness. We pray thee to continue to us the genial influences of the sun and rain, and to make us truly thankful for all thy mercies, through Jesus Christ our Lord. *Amen.*

FOR A PLENTIFUL SEASON.

A LMIGHTY and ever blessed God, who mercifully suppliest the wants of thy creatures, and art continually giving testimonies of thy gracious providence ; we rejoice at this time, with humble thankfulness, in the gifts of thine undeserved bounty, that thou hast caused the earth to yield its increase, and crowned the year with thy goodness. While thou art thus sending down thy blessings upon us, may we be disposed to live in a sober, temperate, and charitable enjoyment of them, and to bring forth the fruits of holiness and righteousness all the days of our life, through Jesus Christ our Lord. *Amen.*

FOR DELIVERANCE FROM A GENERAL SICKNESS.

O LORD God, who hast wounded us for our sins, and consumed us for our transgressions, by thy late heavy and dreadful visitation ; and now in the midst of judgment remembering mercy, hast redeemed our souls from death ; we offer unto thy fatherly goodness, ourselves, our souls, and bodies, which thou hast delivered, to be a living sacrifice unto thee ; always praising and magnifying thy mercies in the midst of thy Church, through Jesus Christ our Lord. *Amen.*

FOR PEACE AND DELIVERANCE FROM OUR ENEMIES.

ALMIGHTY God, who art a strong tower of defence unto thy servants against the face of their enemies ; we yield thee praise and thanksgiving for our deliverance from those great dangers wherewith we were compassed. We acknowledge it of thy goodness that we were not delivered over as a prey unto them ; beseeching thee still to continue such thy mercies towards us, that all the world may know that thou art our saviour and mighty deliverer, through Jesus Christ our Lord. *Amen.*

FOR RESTORING PUBLIC PEACE AT HOME.

O ETERNAL God, our Heavenly Father, who alone makest men to be of one mind in a house, and stillest the outrage of a violent and unruly people ; we bless thy holy name, that it hath pleased thee to appease the seditious tumults which have been lately raised up amongst us ; and we most humbly beseech thee, to grant to all of us grace, that we may henceforth obediently walk in thy holy commandments, and, leading a quiet and peaceable life in all godliness and honesty, may continually offer unto thee our sacrifice of praise and thanksgiving for these thy mercies toward us, through Jesus Christ our Lord. *Amen.*

FOR THE CLOSE OF THE YEAR.

OD of our lives, who art unchanged and unchangeable, without beginning and without end ; we render thee our humble thanks that thou hast brought us through the year, which is now closing, by thy mighty and outstretched arm. Thy candle hath shone upon our tabernacle, and thy smiles have gladdened our hearts. We thank thee for the care which thou hast extended to us, and the blessings which thou hast bestowed upon us. We have cause to be grateful, and we have cause also to be humble, in our review of the past. Much of our time has been wasted or misspent. O reward us not according to our iniquities, and let not thy compassions cease from us ; but graciously prolong to us the day of grace and the means of salvation. Sanctify to us the afflictions which thou hast appointed us to bear, and grant that they may contribute to our eternal welfare and peace. We commend ourselves to thy holy keeping. Prepare us for life ; prepare us for death, and for eternity. May we go on our way with new resolutions of obedience, new gratitude for thy mercies, and new vigor to perform thy will. And when our time shall be no more, receive us to thyself in glory ; through Jesus Christ our Lord. *Amen.*

END OF THE PRAYERS AND THANKSGIVINGS.

COLLECTS, GOSPELS, AND EPISTLES.

The Coming of our Lord.

THE COLLECT.

* LMIGHTY God, give us grace that we may cast away the works of darkness, and put upon us the armor of light, now in the time of this mortal life, in which thy Son Jesus Christ came to visit us in great humility ; that in the last day, when he shall come again in his glorious majesty, to judge both the living and dead, we may rise to the life immortal. And this we beg in the name of our Mediator ; through whom we ascribe unto thee all honor and glory, now and ever. *Amen.*

THE GOSPEL.

St. Matt. xxi. I.

HEN they drew nigh unto Jerusalem, and were come to Bethphage, unto the Mount of Olives, then sent Jesus two disciples, saying unto them, Go into the village over against you, and straightway ye shall find an ass tied, and a colt with her; loose them, and bring them unto me. And if any man say aught unto you, ye shall say, the Lord hath need of them; and straightway he will send them. All this was done, that it might be fulfilled which was spoken by the prophet, saying, Tell ye the daughter of Sion, behold thy King cometh unto thee, meek, and sitting upon an ass, and a colt the foal of an ass. And the disciples went and did as Jesus commanded them, and brought the ass and the colt, and put on them their clothes, and they set him thereon. And a very great multitude spread their garments in the way; others cut down branches from the trees, and strewed them in the way. And the multitudes that went before, and that followed, cried, saying, Hosanna to the Son of David; blessed is he that cometh in the name of the Lord, Hosanna in the highest. And when he was come into Jerusalem, all the city was moved, saying, Who is this? And the multitude said, This is Jesus the Prophet, of Nazareth of Galilee. And Jesus went into the temple of God, and cast out all them that sold and bought in the temple, and overthrew the tables of the money-changers, and the seats of them that sold doves, and said to them, It is written, my house shall be called the house of prayer, but ye have made it a den of thieves.

THE EPISTLE.

Rom. xiii. 8.

OWE no man anything but to love one another; for he that loveth another, hath fulfilled the law. For this, thou shalt not commit adultery, thou shalt not kill, thou shalt not steal, thou shalt not bear false witness, thou shalt not covet, and if there be any other commandment, it is briefly comprehended in this saying, namely, thou shalt love thy neighbor as thyself Love worketh no ill to his neighbor; therefore love is the fulfilling of the law. And that do, knowing the time, that now it is high time to awake out of sleep, for now is our salvation nearer than when we believed. The night is far spent, the day is at hand; let us therefore cast off the works of darkness, and let us put on the armor of light.

The Second Sunday in Advent.

THE COLLECT.

BLESSED Lord, who hast caused all holy Scriptures to be written for our learning; grant that we may in such wise hear them, read, mark, learn, and inwardly digest them, that, by patience and comfort of thy holy word, we may embrace and ever hold fast the blessed hope of everlasting life, which thou hast given us in our Saviour Jesus Christ. *Amen.*

THE GOSPEL.

St. Luke, xxi. 25.

AND there shall be signs in the sun, and in the moon, and in the stars ; and upon the earth distress of nations, with perplexity ; the sea and the waves roaring ; men's hearts failing them for fear, and for looking after those things which are coming on the earth ; for the powers of heaven shall be shaken. And then shall they see the Son of Man coming in a cloud, with power and great glory. And when these things begin to come to pass, then look up, and lift up your heads, for your redemption draweth nigh. And he spake to them a parable : Behold the fig-tree, and all the trees ; when they now shoot forth, ye see and know of your own selves, that summer is now nigh at hand. So likewise ye, when ye see these things come to pass, know ye that the kingdom of God is nigh at hand. Verily I say unto you, this gencration shall not pass away, till all be fulfilled ; heaven and earth shall pass away, but my word shall not pass away.

THE EPISTLE.

Rom. xv. 4.

HATSOEVER things were written aforetime, were written for our learning, that we, through patience and comfort of the Scriptures, might have hope. Now the God of patience and consolation grant you to be like-minded one toward another, according to Christ Jesus, that ye may with one mind and one mouth glorify God, even the Father of our Lord Jesus Christ. Wherefore receive ye one another, as Christ also received us, to the glory of God. Now, I say, that Jesus Christ was a minister of the circumcision, for the truth of God, to confirm the promises made unto the fathers, and that the Gentiles might glorify God for his mercy; as it is written, For this cause I will confess to thee among the Gentiles, and sing unto thy name. And again he saith, Rejoice, ye Gentiles, with his people. And again, Praise the Lord, all ye Gentiles, and laud him, all ye people. And again, Isaiah saith, There shall be a root of Jesse, and he who shall rise to reign over the Gentiles, in him shall the Gentiles trust. Now the God of hope fill you with all joy and peace in believing, that ye may abound in hope, through the power of the Holy Ghost.

The Third Sunday in Advent.

THE COLLECT.

GOD, the Father of Jesus Christ our Lord, who at his first coming didst send a messenger to prepare his way before him ; grant that the ministers of thy word may likewise so prepare and make ready his way, by turning the hearts of the disobedient to the wisdom of the just, that at his second coming to judge the world, we may be found an acceptable people in thy sight. And this we beg in the name of Jesus Christ, through whom we ascribe unto thee all honor and glory, now and ever. *Amen.*

THE GOSPEL.

St. Matt. xi. 2.

NOW when John had heard in the prison the works of Christ, he sent two of his disciples, and said unto him, Art thou he who should come, or do we look for another? Jesus answered and said unto them, Go and show John again those things which ye do hear and see; the blind receive their sight, and the lame walk, the lepers are cleansed, and the deaf hear, the dead are raised up, and the poor have the Gospel preached unto them; and blessed is he whosoever shall not be offended in me. And as they departed, Jesus began to say unto the multitudes, concerning John, What went ye out into the wilderness to see? A reed shaken with the wind? But what went ye out to see? A man clothed in soft raiment? Behold they who wear soft clothing are in kings' houses. But what went ye out to see? A prophet? yea, I say unto you, and more than a prophet. For this is he of whom it is written, Behold, I send my messenger before thy face, which shall prepare thy way before thee.

THE EPISTLE.

1 Cor. iv. 1.

LET a man so account of us, as of the ministers of Christ, and stewards of the mysteries of

God. Moreover, it is required in stewards, that a man be found faithful. But with me it is a very small thing, that I should be judged of you, or of man's judgment; because I do not condemn mine own self. For I know nothing against myself; yet am I not hereby justified; but he that judgeth me is the Lord. Therefore judge nothing before the time, until the Lord come, who both will bring to light the hidden things of darkness, and will make manifest the counsels of the hearts; and then shall every man have praise of God.

The Fourth Sunday in Advent.

THE COLLECT.

O LORD, raise up, we pray thee, thy power, and come among us, and with great might succor us; that whereas, through our sins and wickedness, we are hindered in running the race which is set before us, thy bountiful grace and mercy may speedily help and deliver us, through Jesus Christ our Lord. *Amen.*

THE GOSPEL.

St. John, i. 19.

THIS is the record of John when the Jews sent Priests and Levites from Jerusalem to ask him, Who art thou? And he confessed, and denied not; but confessed, I am not the Christ. And they asked him, What then? Art thou Elias? And he saith, I am not. Art thou that prophet?

And he answered, No. Then said they unto him, Who art thou? that we may give an answer to them that sent us; what sayest thou of thyself? He said, I am the voice of one crying in the wilderness, Make straight the way of the Lord, as said the prophet Isaiah. And they who were sent were of the Pharisees. And they asked him, and said unto him, Why baptizest thou then, if thou be not that Christ, nor Elias, neither that prophet? John answered them, saying, I baptize with water; but there standeth one among you, whom ye know not; he it is, who, coming after me, is preferred before me, whose shoe's latchet I am not worthy to unloose. These things were done in Bethabara, beyond Jordan, where John was baptizing.

THE EPISTLE.

Phil. iv. 4.

REJOICE in the Lord alway; and again I say, rejoice. Let your moderation be known unto all men. The Lord is at hand. Be careful for nothing; but in everything by prayer and supplication with thanksgiving, let your requests be made known unto God. And the peace of God, which passeth all understanding, shall keep your hearts and minds through Christ Jesus. Finally, brethren, whatsoever things are true, whatsoever things are honest, whatsoever things are just, whatsoever things are pure, whatsoever things are lovely, whatsoever things are of good report, if there be any virtue, and if there be any praise, think on these things. Those things which ye have both learned, and received, and heard, and seen in me do ; and the God of peace shall be with you.

Christmas Day.

The Nativity of our Lord.

THE COLLECT.

ALMIGHTY GOD, who hast given us thine only-begotten Son to take our nature upon him, and as at this time to be born of a virgin ; grant that we, being regenerate, and made thy children by adoption and grace, may daily be renewed by thy Holy Spirit. And this we beg in the name óf Jesus Christ, through whom we ascribe unto thee all honor and glory, now and ever. *Amen.*

THE GOSPEL.

St. John, i. 1.

IN the beginning was the Word, and the Word was with God, and the Word was God. The same was in the beginning with God. All things were made by him ; and without him was not anything made, that was made. In him was life, and the life was the light of men. And the light shineth in darkness ; and the darkness comprehended it not. There was a man sent from God, whose name was John. The same came for a witness, to bear witness of the light, that all men through him might believe. He was not that light, but was sent to bear witness of that light. That was the true light, which lighteth every man that cometh into the world. He was in the world, and the world was made by him ; and the world knew him not. He came unto his own, and his own received him not ; but as many as received him, to them gave he power to become the sons of God, even to those who believe on his name ; who were born not of blood, nor of the will of the flesh, nor of the will of man, but of God. And the Word was made flesh, and dwelt among us, and we beheld his glory, the glory of the only-begotten of the Father, full of grace and truth.

THE EPISTLE.

Heb. i. I.

GOD who at sundry times, and in divers manners, spake in times past unto the fathers by the prophets, hath in these last days spoken unto us by his Son, whom he hath appointed heir of all things, by whom also he made the worlds. Who being the brightness of his glory, and the express image of his person, and upholding all things by the word of his power, when he had by himself purged our sins, sat down on the right hand of the Majesty on high ; being made so much better than the angels, as he hath by inheritance obtained a more excellent name than they. For unto which of the angels said he at any time, Thou art my Son, this day have I begotten thee? and again, I will be to him a Father, and he shall be to me a Son? And again, when he bringeth in the first-begotten into the world, he saith, And let all the angels of God worship him. And of the angels he saith, Who maketh his angels spirits, and his ministers a flame of fire. But unto the Son he saith, Thy throne, O God, is for ever and ever; a sceptre of righteousness, is the sceptre of thy kingdom. Thou hast loved righteousness, and hated iniquity; therefore God, even thy God, hath anointed thee with the oil of gladness above thy fellows. And, Thou, Lord, in the beginning hast laid the foundation of the earth; and the heavens are the works of thine hands. They shall perish, but thou remainest; and they all shall wax old as doth a garment; and as a vesture shalt thou fold them up, and they shall be changed; but thou art the same, and thy years shall not fail.

The Sunday after Christmas Day.

THE COLLECT.

SOURCE of all light and truth, who didst send thy Son Jesus Christ into the world, that the world through him might be saved, grant, we beseech thee, that the light of his doctrine and life may shine into our hearts, and dispel our darkness, and direct our steps, and lead us at last to the unspeakable glories and felicities of thy heavenly kingdom; which we beg in the name of our Saviour, ascribing to thee everlasting praises. *Amen.*

THE GOSPEL.

St. Luke ii. 15.

AND it came to pass, as the angels were gone away from them into heaven, the shepherds said one to another, Let us now go even unto Bethlehem, and see this thing which is come to pass, which the Lord hath made known unto us. And they came with haste, and found Mary and Joseph, and the babe lying in a manger. And when they had seen it, they made known abroad the saying which was told them concerning this child. And all they that heard it wondered at those things which were told them by the shepherds. But Mary kept all these things and pondered them in her heart. And the shepherds returned, glorifying and praising God for all the things that they had heard and seen, as it was told unto them. And when eight days were aecomplished for the circumcising of the child, his name was called JESUS.

THE EPISTLE.

Gal. iv. 1.

NOW I say, that the heir, as long as he is a child, differeth nothing from a servant, though he be lord of all ; but is under tutors and governors, until the time appointed of the father. Even so we, when we were children, were in bondage under the elements of the world. But when the fulness of the time was come, God sent forth his Son, made of a woman, made under the law, to redeem those who were under the law, that we might receive the adoption of sons. And because ye are sons, God hath sent forth the spirit of his Son into your hearts, crying, Abba, Father. Wherefore thou art no more a servant, but a son ; and if a son, then an heir of God, through Christ.

The First Sunday in the Year

THE COLLECT.

O GOD, the unfailing source of light and mercy, who hast brought us to the beginning of this year, and art sparing us to love thee, and to keep thy commandments, give us, we beseech thee, a solemn sense of the importance of time, and of diligence in improving the talents thou hast placed in our hands ; and enable us so faithfully to discharge our duty in this life, that when we shall appear before thee at thy great tribunal, we may be found worthy of that eternal kingdom which thou hast promised by Jesus Christ our Lord. *Amen.*

THE GOSPEL.

St. Matt. xxv. 14.

FOR the kingdom of heaven is as a man travelling into a far country, who called his own servants, and delivered unto them his goods. And unto one he gave five talents, to another two, and to another one ; to every man according to his several ability ; and straightway took his journey.

Then he who had received the five talents went and traded with the same, and made them other five talents. And likewise he who had received two, he also gained other two. But he who had received one, went and digged in the earth, and hid his lord's money. After a long time, the lord of those servants cometh and reckoneth with them. And so he who had received five talents came and brought other five talents, saying, Lord, thou dcliveredst unto me five talents ; behold, I have gained beside them, five talents more. His lord said unto him, Well done, thou good and faithful servant; thou hast been faithful over a few things, I will make thee ruler over many things ; enter thou into the joy of thy lord. He also that had received two talents came and said, Lord, thou deliveredst unto me two talents ; behold, I have gained two other talents beside them. His lord said unto him, Well done, good and faithful servant ; thou hast been faithful over a few things, I will make thee ruler over many things ; enter thou into the joy of thy lord. Then he who had received the one talent came, and said, Lord, I knew thee, that thou art an hard man, reaping where thou hast not sown, and gathering where thou hast not strawed ; and I was afraid, and went and hid thy talent in the earth ; lo, there thou hast that is thine. His lord answered, and said unto him, Thou wicked and slothful servant, thou knewest that I reap where I sowed not, and gather where I have not strawed ; thou oughtest, therefore, to have put my money to the exchangers, and then at my coming I should have received mine own with usury. Take, therefore, the talent from him, and give it unto him who hath ten talents. For unto every one who hath shall be given, and he shall have abundance ; but from him who hath not, shall be taken away even that which he hath. And cast ye the unprofitable servant into outer darkness ; there shall be weeping and gnashing of teeth.

THE EPISTLE.

1 St. Pet. i. 13.

WHEREFORE gird up the loins of your mind, be sober, and hope to the end, for the grace that is to be brought unto you at the revelation of Jesus Christ. As obedient children, do not fashion yourselves according to the former lusts in your ignorance ; but as he who hath called you is holy, so be ye holy in all manner of conversation ; because it is written, Be ye holy, for I am holy. And if ye call on the Father, who, without respect of persons, judgeth according to every man's work, pass the time of your sojourning here in fear ; for as much as ye know that ye were not redeemed with corruptible things, such as silver and gold, from your vain conversation, received by tradition from your fathers, but with the precious blood of Christ, as of a lamb without blemish and without spot ; who verily was foreordained before the foundation of the world, but was manifest in these last times for you, who by him do believe in God who raised him up from the dead, and gave him glory, that your faith and hope might be in God. Seeing ye have purified your souls in obeying the truth through the Spirit, unto unfeigned love of the brethren, see that ye love one another, with a pure heart fervently; being born again, not of corruptible seed, but of incorruptible, by the word of God, which liveth and abideth forever. For all flesh is as grass, and all the glory of man as the flower of grass; the grass withereth, and the flower thereof falleth away; but the word of the Lord endureth forever. And this is the word, which by the Gospel is preached unto you.

The Epiphany, or the Manifestation of Christ to the Gentiles.

THE COLLECT.

O GOD, who by the leading of a star didst manifest thy only begotten Son to the Gentiles; mercifully grant, that we who know thee now by faith, may after this life have the fruition of thy glorious Godhead, through Jesus Christ our Lord. *Amen.*

THE GOSPEL.

St. Matf. ii. 1.

WHEN Jesus was born in Bethlehem of Judea, in the days of Herod the king, behold, there came wise men from the east to Jerusalem, saying, Where is he who is born King of the Jews? for we have seen his star in the east, and are come to worship him. When Herod the king had heard these things, he was troubled, and all Jerusalem with him. And when he had gathered all the chief priests and scribes of the people together, he demanded of them, where Christ should be born. And they said unto him, In Bethlehem of Judea ; for thus it is written by the prophet, And thou, Bethlehem, in the land of Juda, art not the least among the princes of Juda ; for out of thee shall come a Governor who shall rule my people Israel. Then Herod, when he had privily called the wise men, inquired of them diligently what time the star appeared. And he sent them to Bethlehem, and said, Go, and search diligently for the young child, and when ye have found him, bring me word again, that I may come and worship him also. When they had heard the king, they departed ; and lo, the star which they saw in the east went before them, till it came and stood over where the young child was. When they saw the star, they rejoiced with exceeding great joy. And when they were come into the house, they saw the young child with Mary his mother, and fell down and worshipped him ; and when they had opened their treasures, they presented unto him gifts ; gold, and frankincense, and myrrh. And being warned of God in a dream, that they should not return to Herod, they departed into their own country another way.

THE EPISTLE.

Ephes. iii. 1.

FOR this cause, I Paul, am the prisoner of Jesus Christ for you Gentiles ; for ye have heard of the dispensation of the grace of God, which is given me to you ward ; how that by revelation he made known unto me the mystery, (as I wrote afore in a few words, whereby, when ye read, ye may understand my knowledge in the mystery of Christ,) which in other ages was not made known unto the sons of men, as it is now revealed unto his holy apostles and prophets by the Spirit ; that the Gentiles should be fellow heirs, and of the same body, and partakers of his promise in Christ, by the Gospel ; whereof I was made a minister, according to the grace of God given unto me by the working of his power. Unto me, who am less than the least of all saints, is this grace given, that I should preach among the Gentiles the unsearchable riches of Christ ; and to make all men see what is the fellowship of the mystery, which from the beginning of the world hath been hid in God, who created all things ; to the intent that now unto the principalities and powers in heavenly places might be known, by the Church, the manifold wisdom of God, according to the eternal purpose which he purposed in Christ Jesus our Lord ; in whom we have boldness, and access with confidence by the faith of him.

The First Sunday after the Epiphany.

THE COLLECT.

O LORD, we beseech thee mercifully to receive the prayers of thy people who call upon thee ;

and grant that they may both perceive and know what things they ought to do, and also may have grace and power faithfully to fulfil the same, through Jesus Christ our Lord. *Amen.*

THE GOSPEL.

St. Luke ii. 41.

NOW his parents went to Jerusalem every year at the feast of the passover. And when he was twelve years old, they went up to Jerusalem, after the custom of the feast. And when they had fulfilled the days, as they returned, the child Jesus tarried behind in Jerusalem ; and Joseph and his mother knew not of it. But they, supposing him to have been in the company, went a day's journey ; and they sought him among their kinsfolk and acquaintance. And when they found him not, they turned back again to Jerusalem, seeking him. And it came to pass, that after three days they found him in the temple, sitting in the midst of the doctors, both hearing them, and asking them questions. And all who heard him were astonished at his understanding and answers. And when they saw him, they were amazed ; and his mother said unto him, Son, why hast thou thus dealt with us ? behold, thy father and I have sought thee sorrowing. And he said unto them, How is it that ye sought me ? wist ye not that I must be about my Father's business ? And they understood not the saying which he spake unto them. And he went down with them, and came to Nazareth, and was subject unto them ; but his mother kept all these sayings in her heart. And Jesus increased in wisdom and stature, and in favor with God and man.

THE EPISTLE.

Rom. xii. 1.

I BESEECH you therefore, brethren, by the mercies of God, that ye present your bodies a living sacrifice, holy, acceptable unto God, which is your reasonable service. And be not conformed to this world ; but be ye transformed by the renewing of your mind, that ye may prove what is that good, and acceptable, and perfect will of God. For I say, through the grace given unto me, to every man who is among you, not to think of himself more highly than he ought to think ; but to think soberly, according as God hath dealt to every man the measure of faith. For as we have many members in one body, and all members have not the same office, so we, being many, are one body in Christ, and every one members one of another.

The Second Sunday after the Epiphany

THE COLLECT.

ALMIGHTY and most merciful God, we beseech thee to grant us thy grace, that in all the relations of life we may do justly, and love mercy, and walk humbly before thee ; so that at last we may be received to the society of the just made perfect in thy heavenly kingdom, through Jesus Christ our Lord. *Amen.*

THE GOSPEL.

St. John ii. 1.

A ND the third day there was a marriage in Cana of Galilee ; and the mother of Jesus was there ; and both Jesus was called, and his disciples, to the marriage. And when they wanted wine, the mother of Jesus saith unto him, They have no wine. Jesus saith unto her, Woman, what have I to do with thee? Mine hour is not yet come. His mother saith unto the servants, Whatsoever he saith unto you, do it. And there were set there six water-pots of stone, after the manner of the purifying of the Jews, containing two or three firkins apiece. Jesus saith unto them, Fill the water-pots with water. And they filled them up to the brim. And he saith unto them, Draw out now, and bear unto the governor of the feast. And they bare it. When the ruler of the feast had tasted the water that was made wine, and knew not whence it was, (but the servants who drew the water knew,) the governor of the feast called the bridegroom, and said unto him, Every man at the beginning doth set forth good wine ; and when men have well drunk, then that which is worse ; but thou hast kept the good wine until now. This beginning of miracles did Jesus in Cana of Galilee, and manifested forth his glory ; and his disciples believed on him.

THE EPISTLE.

Rom. xii. 6.

H AVING then gifts, differing according to the grace that is given to us, whether prophecy, let us prophesy according to the proportion of faith ; or ministry, let us wait on our ministering ; or he who teacheth, on teaching ; or he who exhorteth, on exhortation ; he who giveth, let him do it with simplicity ; he who ruleth, with diligence ; he who showeth mercy, with cheerfulness. Let love be without dissimulation. Abhor that which is evil, cleave to that which is good. Be kindly affectioned one to another with brotherly love, in honor preferring one another ; not slothful in business ; fervent in spirit ; serving the Lord ; rejoicing in hope ; patient in tribulation ; continuing instant in prayer ; distributing to the necessity of saints ; given to hospitality. Bless those who persecute you ; bless, and curse not. Rejoice with those who do rejoice, and weep with those who weep. Be of the same mind one toward another. Mind not high things, but condescend to men of low estate.

The Third Sunday after the Epiphany.

THE COLLECT.

O THOU most holy and perfect God, teach us to love one another with pure hearts fervently ; to exercise forbearance and forgiveness toward our enemies ; to recompense to no man evil for evil ; and to be merciful, as thou, Father in heaven, art merciful. Grant this, we humbly beseech thee, in the name of Jesus Christ our Lord. *Amen.*

THE GOSPEL.

St. Matt. viii. 1.

WHEN he was come down from the mountain, great multitudes followed him. And behold, there came a leper and worshipped him, saying, Lord, if thou wilt thou canst make me clean. And Jesus put forth his hand, and touched him, saying, I will; be thou clean. And immediately his leprosy was cleansed. And Jesus saith unto him, See thou tell no man; but go thy way, show thyself to the priest, and offer the gift that Moses commanded, for a testimony unto them. And when Jesus was entered into Capernaum, there came unto him a centurion, beseeching him, and saying, Lord, my servant lieth at home sick of the palsy, grievously tormented. And Jesus saith unto him, I will come and heal him. The centurion answered and said, Lord, I am not worthy that thou shouldest come under my roof; but speak the word only, and my servant shall be healed. For I am a man under authority, having soldiers under me; and I say unto this man, Go, and he goeth; and to another, Come, and he cometh; and to my servant, Do this, and he doeth it. When Jesus heard it, he marvelled, and said to those who followed, Verily I say unto you, I have not found so great faith, no, not in Israel. And I say unto you, that many shall come from the east and west, and shall sit down with Abraham, and Isaac, and Jacob in the kingdom of heaven; but the children of the kingdom shall be cast out into outer darkness; there shall be weeping and gnashing of teeth. And Jesus said unto the centurion, Go thy way; and as thou hast believed, so be it done unto thee. And his servant was healed in the self same hour.

THE EPISTLE.

Rom. xii. 16.

BE not wise in your own conceits. Recompense to no man evil for evil. Provide things honest in the sight of all men. If it be possible, as much as lieth in you, live peaceably with all men. Dearly beloved, avenge not yourselves, but rather give place unto wrath; for it is written, Vengeance is mine; I will repay, saith the Lord. Therefore if thine enemy hunger, feed him; if he thirst, give him drink; for in so doing thou shalt heap coals of fire on his head. Be not overcome of evil, but overcome evil with good.

The Fourth Sunday after the Epiphany.

THE COLLECT.

O GOD, who knowest us to be set in the midst of so many and great dangers, that, by reason of the frailty of our nature, we cannot always stand upright; grant to us such strength and protection as may support us in all dangers, and carry us through all temptations, through Jesus Christ our Lord. *Amen.*

THE GOSPEL.

St. Matt. viii. 16.

WHEN the even was come, they brought unto him many that were possessed with devils · and he cast out the spirits with his word, and healed all that were sick : That it might be fulfilled which was spoken by Esaias the prophet, saying, Himself took our infirmities, and bare our sicknesses. Now when Jesus saw great multitudes about him, he gave commandment to depart unto the other side. And a certain scribe came, and said unto him, Master, I will follow thee whithersoever thou goest. And Jesus saith unto him, The foxes have holes, and the birds of the air have nests ; but the Son of man hath not where to lay his head. And another of his disciples said unto him, Lord, suffer me first to go and bury my father. But Jesus said unto him, Follow me ; and let the dead bury their dead. And when he was entered into a ship, his disciples followed him. And behold, there arose a great tempest in the sea, insomuch that the ship was covered with the waves ; but he was asleep. And his disciples came to him, and awoke him, saying, Lord, save us, we perish. And he saith unto them, Why are ye fearful, O ye of little faith? Then he arose, and rebuked the winds and the sea, and there was a great calm. But the men marvelled, saying, What manner of man is this, that even the winds and the sea obey him?

THE EPISTLE.

Rom. xiii. 1.

LET every soul be subject unto the higher powers ; for there is no power but of God ; the
powers that be are ordained of God. Whosoever
therefore resisteth the power, resisteth the ordinance of God ; and they who resist, shall receive
to themselves punishment. For rulers are not a
terror to good works, but to the evil. Wilt thou
then not be afraid of the power? Do that which
is good, and thou shalt have praise of the same ;
for he is the minister of God to thee for good. But
if thou do that which is evil, be afraid ; for he
beareth not the sword in vain ; for he is the minister of God, a revenger to execute wrath upon
him who doeth evil. Wherefore ye must needs be
subject, not only for wrath, but also for conscience'
sake. For, for this cause pay ye tribute also ; for
they are God's ministers, attending continually upon
this very thing. Render therefore to all their dues ;
tribute to whom tribute is due, custom to whom
custom, fear to whom fear, honor to whom honor.

The Fifth Sunday after the Epiphany.

THE COLLECT.

O LORD, we beseech thee to keep thy Church
and household continually in thy true religion ; that they, who do lean only upon the hope
of thy heavenly grace, may evermore be defended

by thy mighty power, through Jesus Christ our Lord. *Amen.*

THE GOSPEL.

St. Matt. xiii. 24.

THE kingdom of heaven is likened unto a man who sowed good seed in his field. But while men slept, his enemy came and sowed tares among the wheat, and went his way. But when the blade was sprung up, and brought forth fruit, then appeared the tares also. So the servants of the householder came and said unto him, Sir, didst not thou sow good seed in thy field? From whence then hath it tares? He said unto them, An enemy hath done this. The servants said unto him, Wilt thou then that we go and gather them up? But he said, Nay; lest while ye gather up the tares, ye root up the wheat with them. Let both grow together until the harvest; and in the time of harvest I will say to the reapers, Gather ye together first the tares, and bind them in bundles to burn them; but gather the wheat into my barn.

THE EPISTLE.

Col. iii. 12.

PUT on therefore, as the elect of God, holy and beloved, affections of pity, kindness, humbleness of mind, meekness, long-suffering; forbearing one another, and forgiving one another, if any man have a quarrel against any; even as Christ forgave you, so also do ye. And above all these things, put on charity, which is the bond of perfectness. And let the peace of God rule in your hearts, to the which also ye are called in one body ; and be ye thankful. Let the word of Christ dwell in you richly in all wisdom ; teaching and admonishing one another in psalms, and hymns, and spiritual songs, singing with grace in your hearts to the Lord. And whatsoever ye do, in word or deed, do all in the name of the Lord Jesus, giving thanks to God and the Father through him.

The Sixth Sunday after the Epiphany.

THE COLLECT.

O GOD, whose blessed Son was manifested, that he might make us the sons of God, and heirs of eternal life ; grant us, we beseech thee, that having this hope, we may purify ourselves even as he is pure ; that when he shall appear again with power and great glory, we may be made like unto him in his glorious kingdom ; where we may ascribe blessing, and honor, and glory, and power, to Him who sitteth upon the throne, and to the Lamb for ever and ever. *Amen.*

THE GOSPEL.

St. Matt. xxiv. 23.

THEN if any man shall say unto you, Lo, here is Christ, or there, believe it not. For there shall arise false Christs, and false prophets, and shall show great signs and wonders ; insomuch that, if it were possible, they shall deceive the very elect. Behold, I have told you before. Wherefore, if they shall say unto you, Behold, he is in the desert, go not forth ; Behold, he is in the secret chambers, believe it not. For as the lightning cometh out of the east, and shineth even unto the west, so shall also the coming of the Son of Man be. For wheresoever the carcass is, there will the eagles be gathered together. Immediately after the tribulation of those days, shall the sun be darkened, and the moon shall not give her light, and the stars shall fall from heaven ; and the powers of the heavens shall be shaken. And then shall appear the sign of the Son of Man in heaven ; and then shall all the tribes of the earth mourn, and they shall see the Son of Man coming in the clouds of heaven, with power and great glory. And he shall send his angels with a great sound of a trumpet, and they shall gather together his elect from the four winds, from one end of heaven to the other.

THE EPISTLE.

1 St. John iii. 1.

BEHOLD, what manner of love the Father hath bestowed upon us, that we should be called the sons of God. Therefore the world knoweth us not, because it knew him not. Beloved, now are we the sons of God, and it doth not yet appear what we shall be ; but we know, that when he shal appear, we shall be like him ; for we shall see him as he is. And every man who hath this hope in him purifieth himself, even as he is pure. Whosoever committeth sin, transgresseth also the law ; for sin is the transgression of the law. And ye know that he was manifested to take away our sins ; and in him is no sin. Whosoever abideth in him, sinneth not ; whosoever sinneth, hath not seen him, neither known him. Little children, let no man deceive you ; he who doeth righteousness is righteous, even as he is righteous. He who committeth sin is of the devil ; for the devil sinneth from the beginning. For this purpose the Son of God was manifested, that he might destroy the works of the devil.

The Sunday called Sexagesima, or the Third Sunday before Lent.

THE COLLECT.

G RANT unto us, O merciful Father, resolution and constancy to persevere in the path of our duty to the end of our lives. Let no prospect of danger deter us from doing that which is right, nor any enticement of evil example tempt us to forfeit our hope of immortality. Preserve us, we humbly beseech thee, from every evil way, and conduct us in the paths of innocence and virtue to eternal life ; which we ask in the name and as disciples of Jesus Christ our Lord. *Amen.*

THE GOSPEL.

St. Matt. xx. 1.

THE kingdom of heaven is like unto a man who is an householder, who went out early in the morning to hire laborers into his vineyard. And when he had agreed with the laborers for a penny a day, he sent them into his vineyard. And he went out about the third hour, and saw others standing idle in the market-place, and said unto them, Go ye also into the vineyard, and whatsoever is right I will give you. And they went their way. Again he went out about the sixth and ninth hour, and did likewise. And about the eleventh hour he went out, and found others standing idle, and said unto them, Why stand ye here all the day idle? They said unto him, Because no man hath hired us. He saith unto them, Go ye also into the vineyard, and whatsoever is right, that shall ye receive. So when even was come, the lord of the vineyard saith unto his steward, Call the laborers, and give them their hire, beginning from the last unto the first. And when they came who were hired about the eleventh hour, they received every man a penny. But when the first came, they supposed they should have received more; and they likewise received every man a penny. And when they had received it, they murmured against the good man of the house, saying, These last have wrought but one hour, and thou hast made them equal unto us, who have borne the burden and heat of the day. But he answered one of them, and said, Friend, I do thee no wrong. Didst thou not agree with me for a penny? Take that thine is, and go thy way. I will give unto this last even as unto thee. Is it not lawful for me to do what I will with my own? Is thine eye evil, because I am good? So the last shall be first, and the first last; for many be called, but few chosen.

THE EPISTLE.

1 Cor. ix. 24.

K NOW ye not, that they who run in a race, run all, but one receiveth the prize? So run, that ye may obtain. And every man who striveth for the mastery is temperate in all things. Now they do it to obtain a corruptible crown, but we an incorruptible. I therefore so run, not as uncertainly; so fight I, not as one that beateth the air; but I keep under my body, and bring it into subjection, lest that, by any means, when I have preached to others, I myself should be a castaway.

The Sunday called Sexagesima, or the Second Sunday before Lent.

THE COLLECT.

O LORD God, who seest that we put not our trust in anything which we do; mercifully grant, that by thy power we may be defended against all adversity, through Jesus Christ our Lord. *Amen.*

THE GOSPEL.

St. Luke viii. 4.

WHEN much people were gathered together, and were come to him out of every city, he spake by a parable. A sower went out to sow his seed. And as he sowed, some fell by the wayside; and it was trodden down, and the fowls of the air devoured it. And some fell upon a rock; and as soon as it was sprung up, it withered away, because it lacked moisture. And some fell among thorns; and the thorns sprang up with it, and choked it. And other fell on good ground, and sprang up, and bare fruit an hundred-fold. And when he had said these things, he cried, He who hath ears to hear, let him hear. And his disciples asked him, saying, What might this parable be? And he said, Unto you it is given to know the mysteries of the kingdom of God; but to others in parables; that seeing they might not see, and hearing they might not understand. Now the parable is this. The seed is the word of God. Those by the wayside are they who hear; then cometh the devil, and taketh away the word out of their hearts, lest they should believe and be saved. They on the rock are they who, when they hear, receive the word with joy; and these have no root; who for a while believe, and in time of temptation fall away. And that which fell among thorns, are they who, when they have heard, go forth, and are choked with cares, and riches, and pleasures of this life, and bring no fruit to perfection. But that on the good ground, are they who, in an honest and good heart, having heard the word, keep it, and bring forth fruit with patience.

THE EPISTLE.

2 Cor. xi. 19.

YE suffer fools gladly, seeing ye yourselves are wise. For ye suffer, if a man bring you into bondage, if a man devour you, if a man take of you, if a man exalt himself, if a man smite you on the face. I speak as concerning reproach, as though we had been weak ; howbeit, wheresoever any is bold, (I speak foolishly,) I am bold also. Are they Hebrews? so am I. Are they the seed of Abraham? so am I. Are they ministers of Christ? (I speak as a fool,) I am more ; in labors more abundant, in stripes above measure, in prisons more frequent, in death oft. Of the Jews five times received I forty stripes, save one. Thrice was I beaten with rods, once was I stoned, thrice I suffered ship-wreck, a night and a day I have been in the deep; in journeyings often, in perils of waters, in perils of robbers, in perils of mine own country-men, in perils by the heathen, in perils in the city, in perils in the wilderness, in perils in the sea, in perils among false brethren ; in weariness and painfulness, in watchings often, in hunger and thirst, in fastings often, in cold and naked-ness ; besides those things which are without, that which cometh upon me daily, the care of all the churches. Who is weak, and I am not weak ? who is offended, and I burn not ? If I must needs glory, I will glory of the things which concern mine infirmities. The God and Father of our Lord Jesus Christ, who is blessed forevermore, knoweth that I lie not.

The Sunday call'd Quinquagesima, or the next Sunday before Lent.

THE COLLECT.

O LORD, who hast taught us that all our doings without charity are nothing worth ; send thy holy Spirit and pour into our hearts that most excellent gift of charity, the very bond of peace, and of all virtues ; without which whosoever liveth is counted dead before thee. Grant this, O Lord, for thy mercy's sake in Jesus Christ our Saviour. *Amen.*

THE GOSPEL.

St. Luke xviii. 31.

THEN he took unto him the twelve, and said unto them, Behold, we go up to Jerusalem, and all things that are written by the prophets, concerning the Son of Man, shall be accomplished. For he shall be delivered unto the Gentiles, and shall be mocked, and spitefully entreated, and spitted on. And they shall scourge him, and put him to death ; and the third day he shall rise again. And they understood none of these things ; and this saying was hid from them, neither knew they the things which were spoken. And it came to pass, that as he was come nigh unto Jericho, a certain blind man sat by the wayside, begging; and hearing the multitude pass by, he asked what it meant. And they told him, that Jesus of Nazareth passeth by. And he cried, saying, Jesus, thou son of David, have mercy on me. And they who went before rebuked him, that he should hold his peace; but he cried so much the more, Thou son of David, have mercy on me. And Jesus stood, and commanded him to be brought unto him. And when he was come near, he asked him, saying, What wilt thou that I should do unto thee? And he said, Lord, that I may receive my sight. And Jesus said unto him, Receive thy sight; thy faith hath saved thee. And immediately he received his sight, and followed him, glorifying God. And all the people, when they saw it, gave praise unto God.

THE EPISTLE.

1 Cor. xiii. 1.

THOUGH I speak with the tongues of men and of angels, and have not charity, I am become as sounding brass, or a tinkling cymbal. And though I have the gift of prophecy, and understand all mysteries, and all knowledge; and though I have all faith, so that I could remove mountains, and have not charity, I am nothing. And though I bestow all my goods to feed the poor, and though I give my body to be burned, and have not charity, it profiteth me nothing. Charity suffereth long, and is kind; charity envieth not; charity vaunteth not itself, is not puffed up, doth not behave itself unseemly, seeketh not her own, is not easily provoked, thinketh no evil ; rejoiceth not in iniquity, but rejoiceth in the truth ; beareth all things, believeth all things, hopeth all things, endureth all things. Charity never faileth ; but whether there be prophecies, they shall fail ; whether there be tongues, they shall cease ; whether there be knowledge, it shall vanish away. For we know in part, and we prophesy in part. But when that which is perfect is come, then that which is in part shall be done away. When I was a child, I spake as a child, I understood as a child, I thought as a child ; but when I became a man, I put away childish things. For now we see through a glass, darkly ; but then face to face. Now I know in part ; but then shall I know, even as also I am known. And now abideth faith, hope, charity, these three ; but the greatest of these is charity.

Ash - Wednesday, or the First Day in Lent, the First of Lent Days of the Easter.

THE COLLECT.

ALMIGHTY and everlasting God, who hatest nothing which thou hast made, and dost forgive the sins of all those who are penitent ; create and make in us new and contrite hearts ; that we, worthily lamenting our sins, and acknowledging our wretchedness, may obtain of thee, the God of all mercy, perfect remission and forgiveness; through Jesus Christ our Lord. *Amen.*

THE GOSPEL.

St. Matt. vi. 16.

WHEN ye fast, be not, as the hypocrites, of a sad countenance; for they disfigure their faces, that they may appear unto men to fast. Verily I say unto you, they have their reward. But thou, when thou fastest, anoint thine head, and wash thy face; that thou appear not unto men to fast, but unto thy Father who is in secret; and thy Father, who seeth in secret, shall reward thee openly. Lay not up for yourselves treasures upon earth, where moth and rust do corrupt, and where thieves break through and steal; but lay up for yourselves treasures in heaven, where neither moth nor rust doth corrupt, and where thieves do not break through nor steal. For where your treasure is, there will your heart be also.

FOR THE EPISTLE.

Joel ii. 12.

TURN ye even to me, saith the Lord, with all your heart, and with fasting, and with weeping, and with mourning. And rend your heart, and not your garments, and turn unto the Lord your God; for he is gracious and merciful, slow to anger, and of great kindness, and repenteth him of the evil. Who knoweth if he will return, and repent, and leave a blessing behind him, even a meat-offering and a drink-offering unto the Lord your God? Blow the trumpet in Zion, sanctify a fast, call a solemn assembly ; gather the people, sanctify the congregation, assemble the elders, gather the children, and those who suck the breasts ; let the bridegroom go forth of his chamber, and the bride out of her closet ; let the priests, the ministers of the Lord, weep between the porch and the altar, and let them say, Spare thy people, O Lord, and give not thine heritage to reproach, that the heathen should rule over them. Wherefore should they say among the people, Where is their God?

The First Sunday in Lent.

THE COLLECT.

O GOD, whose Son, Jesus Christ our Lord, for our sake, did fast forty days and forty nights ; give us grace to use such abstinence, that our flesh being subdued to the spirit, we may ever obey thy godly motions in righteousness and true holiness, to thy honor and glory, who livest and reignest one God, world without end. *Amen.*

THE GOSPEL.

St. Matt. iv. 1.

THEN was Jesus led up of the spirit into the wilderness to be tempted of the devil. And when he had fasted forty days and forty nights, he was afterward an hungered. And when the tempter came to him, he said, If thou be the Son of God, command that these stones be made bread. But he answered and said, It is written, Man shall not live by bread alone, but by every word that proceedeth out of the mouth of God. Then the devil taketh him up into the holy city, and setteth him on a pinnacle of the temple, and saith unto him, If thou be the Son of God, cast thyself down ; for it is written, He shall give his angels charge concerning thee, and in their hands they shall bear thee up, lest at any time thou dash thy foot against a stone. Jesus said unto him, It is written again, Thou shalt not tempt the Lord thy God. Again, the devil taketh him up into an exceeding high mountain, and showeth him all the kingdoms of the world, and the glory of them ; and saith unto him, All these things will I give thee, if thou wilt fall down and worship me. Then saith Jesus unto him, Get thee hence, Satan ; for it is written, Thou shalt worship the Lord thy God, and him only shalt thou serve. Then the devil leaveth him ; and behold, angels came and ministered unto him.

THE EPISTLE.

2 Cor. vi. 1.

WE, then, as workers together with Christ, beseech you also, that ye receive not the grace of God in vain. For he saith, I have heard thee in a time accepted, and in the day of salvation have I succored thee. Behold, now is the accepted time ; behold, now is the day of salvation. We give no offence in anything, that the ministry be not blamed; but in all things approve ourselves as the ministers of God, in much patience, in afflictions, in necessities, in distresses, in stripes, in imprisonments, in tumults, in labors, in watchings, in fastings; by pureness, by knowledge, by long-suffering, by kindness, by the Holy Spirit, by love unfeigned, by the word of truth, by the power of God, by the armor of righteousness on the right hand and on the left, by honor and dishonor, by evil report and good report; as deceivers, and yet true; as unknown, and yet well known; as dying, and, behold, we live; as chastened, and not killed; as sorrowful, yet always rejoicing; as poor, yet making many rich; as having nothing, and yet possessing all things.

THE COLLECT.

ALMIGHTY God, who seest that we have no power of ourselves to help ourselves; keep us both outwardly in our bodies, and inwardly in our souls; that we may be defended from all adversities which may happen to the body, and from all evil thoughts which may assault and hurt the soul, through Jesus Christ our Lord. *Amen.*

THE GOSPEL.

St. Matt. xv. 21.

JESUS went thence, and departed into the coasts of Tyre and Sidon. And behold, a woman of

Canaan came out of the same coasts, and cried unto him, saying, Have mercy on me, O Lord, thou son of David ; my daughter is grievously vexed with a devil. But he answered her not a word. And his disciples came and besought him, saying, Send her away, for she crieth after us. Then he answered and said, I am not sent, but unto the lost sheep of the house of Israel. Then came she and worshipped him, saying, Lord, help me. But he answered and said, It is not meet to take the children's bread, and to cast it to dogs. And she said, Truth, Lord ; yet the dogs eat of the crumbs which fall from their master's table. Then Jesus answered and said unto her, O woman, great is thy faith ; be it unto thee even as thou wilt. And her daughter was made whole from that very hour.

THE EPISTLE.

St. James i. 2.

MY brethren, count it all joy when ye fall into divers temptations ; knowing this, that the trying of your faith worketh patience. But let patience have her perfect work, that ye may be perfect and entire, wanting nothing. If any of you lack wisdom, let him ask of God, who giveth to all men liberally, and upbraideth not ; and it shall be given him. But let him ask in faith, nothing wavering. For he that wavereth is like a wave of the sea, driven with the wind, and tossed. And let not that man think that he shall receive anything of the Lord. A double-minded man is unstable in all his ways. Let the brother of low degree rejoice in that he is exalted ; but the rich, in that he is made low ; because, as the flower of the grass, he shall pass away. For the sun is no sooner risen with a burning heat, but it withereth the grass, and the flower thereof falleth, and the grace of the fashion of it perisheth ; so also shall the rich man fade away in his ways. Blessed is the man that endureth temptation ; for, when he is tried, he shall receive the crown of life, which the Lord hath promised to them that love him. Let no man say, when he is tempted, I am tempted of God ; for God cannot be tempted with evil, neither tempteth he any man ; but every man is tempted, when he is drawn away of his own lust, and enticed. Then, when lust hath conceived, it bringeth forth sin ; and sin, when it is finished, bringeth forth death.

THE COLLECT.

WE pray, O merciful God, that all holy affections may be established in our hearts, and that our lives may be adorned with all good actions ; that while we live we may enjoy the testimony of a good conscience, and the hope of thy favor, and that after death we may receive an everlasting reward in the kingdom of heaven, through thine infinite mercy, manifested unto us by Jesus Christ our Saviour. *Amen.*

THE GOSPEL.

St. Luke xi. 14.

ESUS was casting out a devil, and it was dumb. And it came to pass, when the devil was gone out, the dumb spake. And the people wondered; but some of them said, He casteth out devils through Beelzebub, the chief of the devils. And others, tempting him, sought of him a sign from heaven. But he, knowing their thoughts, said unto them, Every kingdom divided against itself, is brought to desolation; and a house divided against a house, falleth. If Satan also be divided against himself, how shall his kingdom stand? because ye say that I cast out devils through Beelzebub. And if I by Beelzebub cast out devils, by whom do your sons cast them out? therefore shall they be your judges. But if I with the finger of God cast out devils, no doubt the kingdom of God is come upon you. When a strong man armed keepeth his palace, his goods are in peace; but when a stronger than he shall come upon him, and overcome him, he taketh from him all his armor wherein he trusted, and divideth his spoils. He who is not with me, is against me; and he who gathereth not with me, scattereth. When the unclean spirit is gone out of a man, he walketh through dry places, seeking rest; and, finding none, he saith, I will return unto my house, whence I came out. And when he cometh, he findeth it swept and garnished. Then goeth he, and taketh to himself seven other spirits more wicked than himself; and they enter in, and dwell there ; and the last state of that man is worse than the first.

THE EPISTLE.

Ephes. v. 1.

ᴦ E ye therefore followers of God, as dear children ; and walk in love, as Christ also hath loved us, and hath given himself for us, an offering and a sacrifice to God for a sweet-smelling savor. But fornication, and all uncleanness, or covetousness, let it not be once named amongst you, as becometh saints ; neither filthiness, nor foolish talking, nor jesting, which are not seemly ; but rather giving of thanks. For this ye know, that no fornicator, nor unclean person, nor covetous man, who is an idolater, hath any inheritance in the kingdom of Christ, and of God. Let no man deceive you with vain words ; for because of these things cometh the wrath of God upon the children of disobedience. Be not ye therefore partakers with them. For ye were once darkness, but now are ye light in the Lord ; walk as children of light, (for the fruit of the light is in all goodness, and righteousness, and truth,) proving what is acceptable unto the Lord. And have no fellowship with the unfruitful works of darkness, but rather reprove them ; for it is a shame even to speak of those things which are done of them in secret. But all things that are reproved, are made manifest by the light ; for whatsoever doth make manifest, is light. Wherefore he saith, Awake, thou who sleepest, and arise from the dead, and Christ shall give thee light.

The Fourth Sunday in Lent.

THE COLLECT.

GRANT, we beseech thee, Almighty God, that we, who for our evil deeds do worthily deserve to be punished, by the comfort of thy grace may mercifully be relieved, through our Lord and Saviour Jesus Christ. *Amen.*

THE GOSPEL.

St. John vi. 1.

JESUS went over the sea of Galilee, which is the sea of Tiberias. And a great multitude followed him, because they saw his miracles which he did on them who were diseased. And Jesus went up into a mountain, and there he sat with his disciples. And the Passover, a feast of the Jews, was nigh. When Jesus then lifted up his eyes, and saw a great company come unto him, he saith unto Philip, Whence shall we buy bread, that these may eat? (And this he said to prove him; for he himself knew what he would do.) Philip answered him, Two hundred pennyworth of bread is not sufficient for them, that every one of them may take a little. One of his disciples, Andrew, Simon Peter's brother, saith unto him, There is a lad here, who hath five barley loaves, and two small fishes; but what are they among so many? And Jesus said, Make the men sit down. Now there was much grass in the place. So the men sat down, in number about five thousand. And Jesus took the loaves; and when he had given thanks, he distributed to the disciples, and the disciples to them who were set down, and likewise of the fishes, as much as they would. When they were filled, he said unto his disciples, Gather up the fragments which remain, that nothing be lost. Therefore they gathered them together, and filled twelve baskets with the fragments of the five barley loaves, which remained over and above unto them that had eaten. Then those men, when they had seen the miracle that Jesus did, said, This is of a truth that Prophet, who should come into the world.

THE EPISTLE.

St. James iv. 8.

DRAW nigh to God, and he will draw nigh to you. Cleanse your hands, ye sinners; and purify your hearts, ye double-minded. Be afflicted, and mourn, and weep; let your laughter be turned to mourning, and your joy to heaviness. Humble yourselves in the sight of the Lord, and he shall lift you up. Speak not evil one of another, brethren. He that speaketh evil of his brother, and judgeth his brother, speaketh evil of the law, and judgeth the law; but if thou judge the law, thou art not a doer of the law, but a judge. There is one Lawgiver, who is able to save and to destroy. Who art thou that judgest another? Go to, now, ye that say, To-day or to-morrow we will go into such a city, and continue there a year, and buy and sell, and get gain; whereas ye know not what shall be on the morrow. For what is your life? It is even a vapor, that appeareth for a little time, and then vanisheth away.

THE COLLECT.

E beseech thee, O Father, who delightest in mercy, and art not willing that any should perish, to grant unto us the pardon of all our sins, and a joyful hope of thine approbation; and to assist us in forsaking all our evil ways, and returning to the path of thy commandments; that when our days on earth shall be finished, we may obtain everlasting life, through Jesus Christ our Lord. *Amen.*

THE GOSPEL.

St. John viii. 46.

ESUS said, Which of you convinceth me of sin? And if I say the truth, why do ye not believe me? He who is of God, heareth God's words; ye therefore hear them not, because ye are not of God. Then answered the Jews, and said unto him, Say we not well, that thou art a Samaritan, and hast a devil? Jesus answered, I have not a devil; but I honor my Father, and ye do dishonor me. And I seek not mine own glory; but there is one that seeketh and judgeth. Verily, verily, I say unto you, If a man keep my saying, he shall never see death. Then said the Jews unto him,

Now we know that thou hast a devil. Abraham is dead, and the prophets ; and thou sayest, If a man keep my saying, he shall never taste of death. Art thou greater than our father Abraham, who is dead ? and the prophets are dead ; whom makest thou thyself? Jesus answered, If I honor myself, my honor is nothing ; it is my Father who honoreth me, of whom ye say, that he is your God ; yet ye have not known him ; but I know him ; and if I say, I know him not, I shall be a liar like unto you ; but I know him, and keep his saying. Your father Abraham rejoiced to see my day ; and he saw it and was glad. Then said the Jews unto him, Thou art not yet fifty years old, and hast thou seen Abraham? Jesus said unto them, Verily, verily, I say unto you, Before Abraham was, I am. Then took they up stones to cast at him ; but Jesus hid himself, and went out of the temple.

THE EPISTLE.

Heb. ix. 11.

CHRIST, being come, a high-priest of good things to come, by a greater and more perfect tabernacle, not made with hands, that is to say, not of this building ; neither by the blood of goats and calves, but by his own blood, entered in once into the holy place, having obtained eternal redemption for us. For if the blood of bulls and of goats, and the ashes of a heifer sprinkling the unclean, sanctifieth to the purifying of the flesh, how much more shall the blood of Christ, who through the eternal

Spirit offered himself without spot to God, purge your conscience from dead works to serve the living God? And for this cause he is the Mediator of the new testament, that by means of death for the redemption of the transgressions that were under the first testament, they who are called might receive the promise of eternal inheritance.

The Sunday next before Easter, called Palm Sunday.

THE COLLECT.

LMIGHTY and everlasting God, who, of thy tender love toward mankind, hast sent thy Son, our Saviour Jesus Christ, to take upon him our flesh, and to suffer death upon the cross, that all mankind should follow the example of his great humility; mercifully grant, that we may both follow the example of his patience, and also be made partakers of his resurrection, through the same Jesus Christ our Lord. *Amen.*

THE GOSPEL.

St. Matt. xxvii. 1.

HEN the morning was come, all the chief priests and elders of the people took counsel against Jesus, to put him to death. And when they had bound him, they led him away, and delivered him to Pontius Pilate the governor. Then Judas, who had betrayed him, when he saw that he was condemned, repented himself, and brought again the thirty pieces of silver to the chief priests and elders, saying, I have sinned, in that I have betrayed innocent blood. And they said, What is that to us? see thou to that. And he cast down the pieces of silver in the temple, and departed, and went and hanged himself. And the chief priests took the silver pieces, and said, It is not lawful to put them into the treasury, because it is the price of blood. And they took counsel, and bought with them the Potter's Field, to bury strangers in. Wherefore that field was called The Field of Blood, unto this day. Then was fulfilled that which was spoken by Jeremiah the prophet, saying, And they took the thirty pieces of silver, the price of him who was valued, whom they of the children of Israel did value, and gave them for the Potter's Field, as the Lord appointed me. And Jesus stood before the governor ; and the governor asked him, saying, Art thou the King of the Jews? And Jesus said unto him, Thou sayest. And when he was accused by the chief priests and elders, he answered nothing. Then said Pilate unto him, Hearest thou not how many things they witness against thee? And he answered him to never a word ; insomuch that the governor marvelled greatly. Now, at that feast, the governor was wont to release unto the people a prisoner, whom they would. And they had then a notable prisoner, called Barabbas. Therefore, when they were gathered together, Pilate said unto them, Whom will ye that I release unto you? Barabbas, or Jesus, who is called Christ?

For he knew that for envy they had delivered him. When he was set down on the judgment-seat, his wife sent unto him, saying, Have thou nothing to do with that just man ; for I have suffered many things this day in a dream, because of him. But the chief priests and elders persuaded the multitude that they should ask Barabbas, and destroy Jesus. The governor answered and said unto them, Whether of the twain will ye that I release unto you ? They said, Barabbas. Pilate saith unto them, What shall I do then with Jesus, who is called Christ ? They all say unto him, Let him be crucified. And the governor said, Why, what evil hath he done ? But they cried out the more, saying, Let him be crucified. When Pilate saw that he could prevail nothing, but that rather a tumult was made, he took water, and washed his hands before the multitude, saying, I am innocent of the blood of this just person ; see ye to it. Then answered all the people, and said, His blood be on us, and on our children. Then released he Barabbas unto them ; and when he had scourged Jesus, he delivered him to be crucified. Then the soldiers of the governor took Jesus into the common hall, and gathered unto him the whole band of soldiers. And they stripped him, and put on him a scarlet robe. And when they had platted a crown of thorns, they put it upon his head, and a reed in his right hand ; and they bowed the knee before him, and mocked him, saying, Hail, King of the Jews. And they spit upon him, and took the reed, and smote him on the head. And after they had mocked him, they took the robe off from him, and put his own raiment on him, and led him away to crucify him. And as they came out, they found a man of Cyrene, Simon by name ; him they compelled to bear his cross. And when they were come unto a place called Golgotha, that is to say, a Place of a Skull, they gave him vinegar to drink, mingled with gall ; and when he had tasted thereof, he would not drink. And they crucified him, and parted his garments, casting lots. And sitting down, they watched him there. And they set up over his head, his accusation written, THIS IS JESUS THE KING OF THE JEWS. Then were there two thieves crucified with him ; one on the right hand, and another on the left. And they who passed by reviled him, wagging their heads, and saying, Thou who destroyest the temple, and buildest it in three days, save thyself. If thou be the Son of God, come down from the cross. Likewise also the chief priests, mocking him, with the scribes and elders, said, He saved others, himself he cannot save. If he be the King of Israel, let him now come down from the cross, and we will believe him. He trusted in God ; let Him deliver him now, if He will have him ; for he said, I am the Son of God. The thieves also, who were crucified with him, cast the same in his teeth. Now from the sixth hour, there was darkness over all the land, unto the ninth hour. And about the ninth hour Jesus cried with a loud voice, saying, *Eli, Eli, lama sabachthani ?* that is to say, My God, My God, why hast thou forsaken me ? Some of them that stood there, when they heard that, said, This man calleth for Elias. And straightway one of them ran, and took a sponge, and filled it with vinegar, and put it on a reed, and gave him to drink. The rest said, Let be, let us see whether Elias will come to save him. Jesus, when he had cried again with a loud voice, yielded up the ghost. And behold, the veil of the temple was rent in twain, from the top to the bottom ; and the earth did quake, and the rocks rent, and the graves were opened, and many bodies of the saints who slept, arose, and came out of the graves, after his resurrection, and went into the holy city, and appeared unto many. Now when the centurion, and they that were with him, watching Jesus, saw the earthquake, and those things that were done, they feared greatly, saying, Truly this was the Son of God.

Or this.

St. Luke xix. 29 – 44.

AND it came to pass, when he was come nigh to Bethphage and Bethany, at the mount called the Mount of Olives, he sent two of his disciples, saying, Go ye into the village over against you ; in the which at your entering ye shall find a colt tied, whereon yet never man sat : loose him, and bring him hither. And if any man ask you, Why do ye loose him ? thus shall ye say unto him, Because the Lord hath need of him. And they that were sent went their way, and found even as he had said unto them. And as they were loosing the colt, the owners thereof said unto them, Why loose ye the colt? And they said, The Lord hath need of him. And they brought him to Jesus; and they cast their garments upon the colt, and they set Jesus thereon. And as he went, they spread their clothes in the way. And when he was come nigh, even now at the descent of the Mount of Olives, the whole multitude of the disciples began to rejoice and praise God with a loud voice for all the mighty works that they had seen; saying, Blessed be the King that cometh in the name of the Lord; peace in heaven, and glory in the highest. And some of the Pharisees from among the multitude said unto him, Master, rebuke thy disciples. And he answered and said unto them, I tell you that, if these should hold their peace, the stones would immediately cry out. And when he was come near, he beheld the city, and wept over it, saying, If thou hadst known, even thou, at least in this thy day, the things which belong unto thy peace! but now they are hid from thine eyes. For the days shall come upon thee, that thine enemies shall cast a trench about thee, and compass thee round, and keep thee in on every side, and shall lay thee even with the ground, and thy children within thee; and they shall not leave in thee one stone upon another; because thou knewest not the time of thy visitation.

Good Friday.

Phil. ii. 4.

OOK not every man on his own things, but every man also on the things of others. Let this mind be in you, which was also in Christ Jesus; who, being in the form of God, did not think of eagerly retaining his likeness to God, but emptied himself of it, taking the form of a servant, being made in the likeness of men; and, being formed in fashion as a man, he humbled himself, and became obedient unto death, even the death of the cross. Wherefore God also hath highly exalted him, and given him a name, which is above every name; that at the name of Jesus, every knee should bow, of things in heaven, and things in earth, and things under the earth; and that every tongue should confess that Jesus Christ is Lord, to the glory of God, the Father.

THE COLLECTS.

LMIGHTY God, we beseech thee graciously to behold this thy family, for which our Lord Jesus Christ was contented to be betrayed, and given up into the hands of wicked men, and to suffer death upon the cross. And this we beg in the name of our Mediator; through whom we ascribe unto thee all honor and glory, now and ever. *Amen.*

LMIGHTY and everlasting God, by whose Spirit the whole body of the Church is governed and sanctified; receive our supplications and prayers, which we offer before thee for all estates of men in thy holy Church, that every member of the same, in his vocation and ministry, may truly and faithfully serve thee, through our Lord and Saviour Jesus Christ. *Amen.*

MERCIFUL God, who hast made all men, and hatest nothing that thou hast made, nor wouldest the death of a sinner, but rather that he should be converted, and live; have mercy upon all unbelievers and heathen, and take from them all ignorance, hardness of heart, and contempt of thy word; and so fetch them home, blessed Lord, to thy flock, that they may be saved among the remnant of the true Israelites, and be made one fold under one shepherd, Jesus Christ our Lord. *Amen.*

THE GOSPEL.

St. John xix. 1.

ILATE therefore took Jesus, and scourged him. And the soldiers platted a crown of thorns, and put it on his head, and they put on him a purple robe, and said, Hail, King of the Jews; and they smote him with their hands. Pilate therefore went forth again, and saith unto them, Behold, I bring him forth to you, that ye may know that I find no fault in him. Then came Jesus forth, wearing the crown of thorns, and the purple robe.

And Pilate saith unto them, Behold the man. When the chief priests, therefore, and officers saw him, they cried out, saying, Crucify him, crucify him. Pilate saith unto them, Take ye him, and crucify him ; for I find no fault in him. The Jews answered him, We have a law, and by our law he ought to die, because he made himself the Son of God. When Pilate therefore heard that saying, he was the more afraid ; and went again into the judgment-hall, and saith unto Jesus, Whence art thou? But Jesus gave him no answer. Then saith Pilate unto him, Speakest thou not unto me ? knowest thou not that I have power to crucify thee, and have power to release thee? Jesus answered, Thou couldest have no power at all against me, except it were given thee from above ; therefore he who delivered me unto thee hath the greater sin. And from thenceforth Pilate sought to release him ; but the Jews cried out, saying, If thou let this man go, thou art not Cæsar's friend ; whosoever maketh himself a king, speaketh against Cæsar. When Pilate therefore heard that saying, he brought Jesus forth, and sat down in the judgment-seat, in a place that is called the Pavement, but in the Hebrew, Gabbatha. And it was the preparation of the Passover, and about the sixth hour ; and he saith unto the Jews, Behold your King! But they cried out, Away with him, away with him, crucify him! Pilate saith unto them, Shall I crucify your King? The chief priests answered, We have no King but Cæsar. Then delivered he him therefore unto them to be crucified. And they took Jesus and led him away.

And he, bearing his cross, went forth into a place called the Place of a Skull, which is called in the Hebrew, Golgotha; where they crucified him, and two others with him, on either side one, and Jesus in the midst. And Pilate wrote a title, and put it on the cross; and the writing was, JESUS OF NAZARETH, THE KING OF THE JEWS. This title then read many of the Jews; for the place where Jesus was crucified was nigh to the city; and it was written in Hebrew, and Greek, and Latin. Then said the chief priests of the Jews to Pilate, Write not, The King of the Jews; but that he said, I am King of the Jews. Pilate answered, What I have written, I have written. Then the soldiers, when they had crucified Jesus, took his garments, and made four parts, to every soldier a part; and also his coat. Now the coat was without seam, woven from the top throughout. They said therefore among themselves, Let us not rend it, but cast lots for it, whose it shall be; that the Scripture might be fulfilled, which saith, They parted my raiment among them, and for my vesture they did cast lots. These things therefore the soldiers did. Now there stood by the cross of Jesus, his mother, and his mother's sister, Mary the wife of Cleophas, and Mary Magdalene. When Jesus therefore saw his mother and the disciple standing by, whom he loved, he saith unto his mother, Woman, behold thy son! Then saith he to the disciple, Behold thy mother! And from that hour that disciple took her unto his own home. After this, Jesus, knowing that all things were now accomplished, that the Scripture might be fulfilled, saith, I thirst. Now there was set a vessel full of vinegar ; and they filled a sponge with vinegar, and put it upon hyssop, and put it to his mouth. When Jesus therefore had received the vinegar, he said, It is finished ; and he bowed his head, and gave up the ghost. The Jews therefore, because it was the preparation, that the bodies should not remain upon the cross on the Sabbath day, (for that Sabbath day was a high day,) besought Pilate that their legs might be broken, and that they might be taken away. Then came the soldiers, and brake the legs of the first, and of the other who was crucified with him. But when they came to Jesus, and saw that he was dead already, they brake not his legs ; but one of the soldiers with a spear pierced his side ; and forthwith came thereout blood and water. And he that saw it, bare record, and his record is true ; and he knoweth that he saith true, that ye might believe. For these things were done, that the Scripture should be fulfilled, A bone of him shall not be broken. And again, another Scripture saith, They shall look on him whom they pierced.

THE EPISTLE.

Heb. x. I.

THE law, having a shadow of good things to come, and not the very image of the things, can never, with those sacrifices which they offered year by year continually, make the comers thereunto perfect. For then would they not have ceased to be offered, because that the worshippers, once purged, should have had no more conscience of sins? But in those sacrifices there is a remembrance again made of sins every year. For it is not possible that the blood of bulls and of goats should take away sins. Wherefore, when he cometh into the world, he saith, Sacrifice and offering thou wouldest not, but a body hast thou prepared me. In burnt-offerings and sacrifices for sin thou hast no pleasure. Then said I, Lo, I come, (in the volume of the book it is written of me,) to do thy will, O God. After saying first, Sacrifice and offering, and burnt-offerings, and offering for sin, thou wouldest not, neither hadst pleasure therein, which are offered by the law, then said he, Lo, I come to do thy will, O God. He taketh away the first, that he may establish the second. By the which will we are sanctified, through the offering of the body of Jesus Christ once for all. And every priest standeth daily ministering and offering oftentimes the same sacrifices, which can never take away sins ; but this man, after he had offered one sacrifice for sins, forever sat down on the right hand of God ; from henceforth expecting till his enemies be made his footstool. For by one offering he hath perfected forever those who are sanctified. Whereof the Holy Spirit also is a witness to us. For after that he had said before, This is the covenant that I will make with them after those days, the Lord saith, I will put my laws into their hearts, and in their minds will I write them ; and their sins and iniquities will I remember no more. Now

where remission of these is, there is no more offering for sin. Having therefore, brethren, boldness
to enter into the holiest by the blood of Jesus, by
a new and living way, which he hath consecrated
for us, through the veil, that is to say, his flesh ;
and having a high-priest over the house of God ;
let us draw near with a true heart, in full assurance
of faith, having our hearts sprinkled from an evil
conscience, and our bodies washed with pure water.
Let us hold fast the profession of our faith without
wavering ; for he is faithful who promised ; and let
us consider one another to provoke unto love and
to good works ; not forsaking the assembling of
ourselves together, as the manner of some is ; but
exhorting one another ; and so much the more, as
ye see the day approaching.

THE COLLECT.

MERCIFUL God, by whose power thy Son
Jesus Christ hath overcome death, and opened
unto us the gates of everlasting life ; grant that we,
thy servants, having this hope, may purify ourselves,
even as he is pure ; and by continually mortifying
our corrupt affections, may pass the grave and gate
of death, to our joyful resurrection ; which we ask
as disciples of him, who died, and was buried, and
rose again for us, thy Son Jesus Christ our Lord.
Amen.

THE GOSPEL.

St. John xx. I.

THE first day of the week cometh Mary Magdalene early, when it was yet dark, unto the sepulchre, and seeth the stone taken away from the sepulchre. Then she runneth, and cometh to Simon Peter, and to the other disciple, whom Jesus loved, and saith unto them, They have taken away the Lord out of the sepulchre, and we know not where they have laid him. Peter therefore went forth, and that other disciple, and came to the sepulchre. So they ran both together; and the other disciple did outrun Peter, and came first to the sepulchre; and he stooped down, and looking in, saw the linen clothes lying; yet went he not in. Then cometh Simon Peter, following him, and went into the sepulchre, and seeth the linen clothes lie, and the napkin that was about his head, not lying with the linen clothes, but wrapped together in a place by itself. Then went in also that other disciple, who came first to the sepulchre, and he saw, and believed. For as yet they knew not the Scripture, that he must rise again from the dead. Then the disciples went away again unto their own home.

THE EPISTLE.

Col. iii. I.

F ye then be risen with Christ, seek those things which are above, where Christ sitteth on the right hand of God. Set your affection on things above, not on things on the earth. For ye are dead, and your life is hid with Christ in God. When Christ, who is our life, shall appear, then shall ye also appear with him in glory. Mortify therefore your members which are upon the earth ; fornication, uncleanness, inordinate affection, evil concupiscence, and covetousness, which is idolatry ; for which things' sake the wrath of God cometh on the children of disobedience ; in the which, ye also walked sometime, when ye lived in them. But now ye also put away all these ; anger, wrath, malice, blasphemy, filthy communication out of your mouth. Lie not one to another, seeing that ye have put off the old man with his deeds, and have put on the new man, which is renewed in knowledge after the image of him who created him ; where there is neither Greek nor Jew, circumcision nor uncircumcision, Barbarian, Scythian, bond nor free ; but Christ is all and in all.

The First Sunday after Easter

THE COLLECT.

ALMIGHTY Father, who hast given thine only Son to die for our sins, and to rise again for our justification ; grant us so to put away the leaven of malice and wickedness, that we may always serve thee in pureness of living and truth, through Jesus Christ our Lord. *Amen.*

THE GOSPEL.

St. John xx. 19.

THE same day at evening, being the first day of the week, when the doors were shut, where the disciples were assembled, for fear of the Jews, came Jesus and stood in the midst, and saith unto them, Peace be unto you. And when he had so said, he showed unto them his hands and his side. Then were the disciples glad, when they saw the Lord. Then said Jesus to them again, Peace be unto you. As my Father hath sent me, even so send I you. And when he had said this, he breathed on them, and said unto them, Receive ye the Holy Spirit. Whosesoever sins ye remit, they are remitted unto them ; and whosesoever sins ye retain, they are retained.

THE EPISTLE.

I St. John v. 4.

WHATSOEVER is born of God overcometh the world ; and this is the victory that overcometh the world, even our faith. Who is he who overcometh the world, but he who believeth that Jesus is the Son of God? This is he who came by water and blood, even Jesus Christ ; not by water only, but by water and blood. And it is the Spirit that beareth witness, because the Spirit is truth. For there are three who bear record, the Spirit, and the water, and the blood ; and these three agree in one. If we receive the witness of men, the witness of God is greater ; for this is the

witness of God, which he hath testified of his Son.
He who believeth on the Son of God hath the
witness in himself ; he who believeth not God,
hath made him a liar, because he believeth not the
record that God gave of his Son. And this is the
record, that God hath given to us eternal life, and
this life is in his Son. He who hath the Son, hath
life ; and he who hath not the Son of God, hath not
life.

The Second Sunday after Easter

THE COLLECT.

A LMIGHTY God, who hast given thine only
Son to be unto us both a sacrifice for sin, and
also an example of godly life ; give us grace, that
we may always most thankfully receive this inestimable benefit, and daily endeavor ourselves to follow the blessed steps of his most holy life, through
the same Jesus Christ our Lord. *Amen.*

THE GOSPEL.

St. John x. 11.

JESUS said, I am the good shepherd. The good
shepherd giveth his life for the sheep. But he
who is a hireling, and not the shepherd, whose
own the sheep are not, seeth the wolf coming, and
leaveth the sheep, and fleeth ; and the wolf catch-
eth them, and scattereth the sheep. The hireling
fleeth, because he is a hireling, and careth not for
the sheep. I am the good shepherd, and know
my sheep, and am known of mine, as the Father

knoweth me, and I know the Father; and I lay down my life for the sheep. And other sheep I have, which are not of this fold; them also I must bring, and they shall hear my voice; and there shall be one fold, and one shepherd.

THE EPISTLE.

1 St. Pet. ii. 19.

THIS is thankworthy, if a man, for conscience toward God, endure grief, suffering wrongfully. For what glory is it, if, when ye be buffeted for your faults, ye shall take it patiently? But if, when ye do well, and suffer for it, ye take it patiently, this is acceptable with God. For even hereunto were ye called; because Christ also suffered for us, leaving us an example, that ye should follow his steps; who did no sin, neither was guile found in his mouth; who, when he was reviled, reviled not again; when he suffered, he threatened not, but committed himself to him who judgeth righteously; who his own self bare our sins in his own body on the tree, that we, being dead to sin, should live unto righteousness; by whose stripes ye were healed. For ye were as sheep going astray; but are now returned unto the shepherd and bishop of your souls.

THE COLLECT.

ALMIGHTY God, who showest to those who are in error, the light of thy truth, to the in-

tent that they may return into the way of righteousness ; grant unto all those who are admitted into
the fellowship of Christ's religion, that they may
avoid those things that are contrary to their profession, and follow all such things as are agreeable
to the same, through Jesus Christ our Lord. *Amen.*

THE GOSPEL.

St. John xvi. 16.

JESUS said to his disciples, A little while and ye
shall not see me ; and again a little while, and
ye shall see me ; because I go to the Father.   Then
said some of his disciples among themselves, What
is this that he saith unto us, A little while, and ye
shall not see me ; and again a little while, and ye
shall see me ; and, Because I go to the Father?
They said therefore, What is this that he saith, A
little while ?   We cannot tell what he saith.   Now
Jesus knew that they were desirous to ask him, and
said unto them, Do ye inquire among yourselves
of that I said, A little while, and ye shall not see
me ; and again, a little while, and ye shall see me ?
Verily, verily, I say unto you, that ye shall weep
and lament, but the world shall rejoice ; and ye
shall be sorrowful, but your sorrow shall be turned
into joy.

THE EPISTLE.

1 St. Pet. ii. 11.

DEARLY beloved, I beseech you as strangers
and pilgrims, abstain from fleshly lusts, which
war against the soul ; having your conversation

honest among the Gentiles ; that whereas they speak against you as evil doers, they may, by your good works which they shall behold, glorify God in the day of visitation. Submit yourselves to every ordinance of man, for the Lord's sake ; whether it be to the king, as supreme ; or unto governors, as unto them that are sent by him for the punishment of evil doers, and for the praise of them that do well. For so is the will of God, that with well doing ye may put to silence the ignorance of foolish men ; as free, and not using your liberty for a cloak of maliciousness, but as the servants of God. Honor all men ; love the brotherhood ; fear God ; honor the king.

The F… S… …ft… …ast…r

THE COLLECT.

O ALMIGHTY God, who alone canst order the unruly wills and affections of sinful men ; grant unto thy people, that they may love the thing which thou commandest, and desire that which thou dost promise ; that so, among the sundry and manifold changes of the world, our hearts may surely there be fixed, where true joys are to be found, through Jesus Christ our Lord. *Amen.*

THE GOSPEL.

St. John xvi. 5.

J ESUS said unto his disciples, Now I go my way to him who sent me ; and none of you asketh me, Whither goest thou ? but, because I have said these things unto you, sorrow hath filled your heart. Nevertheless, I tell you the truth ; it is expedient for you that I go away; for if I go not away, the Comforter will not come unto you ; but if I depart, I will send him unto you. And when he is come, he will reprove the world of sin, and of righteousness, and of judgment ; of sin, because they believe not on me ; of righteousness, because I go to my Father, and ye see me no more ; of judgment, because the prince of this world is judged. I have yet many things to say unto you, but ye cannot bear them now. Howbeit, when he, the Spirit of truth, is come, he will guide you into all truth ; for he shall not speak of himself, but whatsoever he shall hear, that shall he speak ; and he will show you things to come. He shall glorify me ; for he shall receive of mine, and shall show it unto you. All things that the Father hath are mine ; therefore said I, that he shall receive of mine, and show it unto you.

THE EPISTLE.

St. James i. 17.

E VERY good gift, and every perfect gift, is from above, and cometh down from the Father of lights, with whom is no variableness, neither shadow of turning. Of his own will begat he us with the word of truth, that we should be a kind of first fruits of his creatures. Wherefore, my beloved brethren, let every man be swift to hear, slow to speak, slow to wrath; for the wrath of man worketh not the righteousness of God. Wherefore lay apart all filthiness and superfluity of malice, and receive with meekness the ingrafted word, which is able to save your souls.

ι ι ι ι ˉ Ͻ ι ι ι αf ˉ L̉ ɔt ,

THE COLLECT.

O LORD, from whom all good things do come; grant to us thy humble servants, that by thy holy inspiration we may think those things that are good, and by thy merciful guiding may perform the same, through our Lord Jesus Christ. *Amen.*

THE GOSPEL.

St. John xvi. 23.

VERILY, verily, I say unto you, Whatsoever ye shall ask the Father in my name, he will give it you. Hitherto have ye asked nothing in my name; ask, and ye shall receive, that your joy may be full. These things have I spoken unto you in proverbs; the time cometh when I shall no more speak to you in proverbs; but I shall show you plainly of the Father. At that day ye shall ask in my name; and I say not unto you, that I will pray the Father for you; for the Father himself loveth you, because ye have loved me, and have believed that I came out from God. I came forth from the Father, and am come into the world; again I leave the world, and go to the Father. His disciples said unto him, Lo, now speakest thou plainly, and speakest no proverb. Now are we sure that thou knowest all things, and needest not that any man should ask thee ; by this we believe that thou camest forth from God. Jesus answered them, Do ye now believe? Behold, the hour cometh, yea, is now come, that ye shall be scattered every man to his own, and shall leave me alone ; and yet I am not alone, because the Father is with me. These things I have spoken unto you, that in me ye might have peace. In the world ye shall have tribulation ; but be of good cheer, I have over-come the world.

THE EPISTLE.

St. James i. 22.

BE ye doers of the word, and not hearers only deceiving your own selves. For if any be a hearer of the word, and not a doer, he is like unto a man beholding his natural face in a glass. For he beholdeth himself and goeth his way, and straight-way forgetteth what manner of man he was. But whoso looketh into the perfect law of liberty, and continueth therein, he being not a forgetful hearer, but a doer of the work, this man shall be blessed in his deed. If any man among you seem to be religious, and bridleth not his tongue, but deceiveth his own heart, this man's religion is vain. Pure religion, and undefiled, before God and the Father, is this, To visit the fatherless and widows in their affliction, and to keep himself unspotted from the world.

The Asersion Day.

THE COLLECT.

GRANT, we beseech thee, Almighty God, that like as we do believe thy only begotten Son, our Lord Jesus Christ, to have ascended into the heavens, so we may also in heart and mind thither ascend, and with him continually dwell, who liveth to make intercession for us, at the right hand of God, for ever and ever. *Amen.*

THE GOSPEL.

St. Mark xvi. 14.

JESUS appeared unto the eleven, as they sat at meat, and upbraided them with their unbelief and hardness of heart, because they believed not those who had seen him after he was risen. And he said unto them, Go ye into all the world, and preach the gospel to every creature. He who believeth and is baptized, shall be saved ; but he who believeth not shall be damned. And these signs shall follow them who believe. In my name shall they cast out devils ; they shall speak with new tongues ; they shall take up serpents ; and if they drink any deadly thing, it shall not hurt them ; they shall lay hands on the sick, and they shall recover. So then, after the Lord had spoken unto them, he was received up into heaven, and sat on the right hand of God. And they went forth and preached everywhere, the Lord working with them, and confirming the word with signs following.

The Ascension Day.

FOR THE EPISTLE.

Acts i. 1.

THE former treatise have I made, O Theophilus, of all that Jesus began both to do and teach, until the day in which he was taken up, after that he, through the Holy Spirit, had given commandments unto the Apostles whom he had chosen; to whom also he showed himself alive, after his passion, by many infallible proofs; being seen of them forty days, and speaking of the things pertaining to the kingdom of God. And being assembled together with them, he commanded them that they should not depart from Jerusalem, but wait for the promise of the Father, which, saith he, ye have heard of me. For John truly baptized with water; but ye shall be baptized with the Holy Spirit, not many days hence. When they therefore were come together, they asked of him, saying, Lord, wilt thou at this time restore again the kingdom to Israel? And he said unto them, It is not for you to know the times or the seasons, which the Father hath put in his own power. But ye shall receive power after that the Holy Spirit is come upon you; and ye shall be witnesses unto me, both in Jerusalem, and in all Judea, and in Samaria, and unto the uttermost part of the earth. And when he had spoken these things, while they beheld, he was taken up, and a cloud received him out of their sight. And while they looked steadfastly toward heaven, as he went up, behold, two men stood by them in white apparel; who also said, Ye men of

Galilee, why stand ye gazing up into heaven? This same Jesus who is taken up from you into heaven, shall so come in like manner as ye have seen him go into heaven.

The Sunday after Ascension Day.

THE COLLECT.

O GOD, the King of glory, who hast exalted thine only Son Jesus Christ with great triumph unto thy kingdom in heaven; we beseech thee leave us not comfortless; but send to us thine Holy Spirit to comfort us, and exalt us unto the same place whither our Saviour Christ is gone before, who liveth to make intercession for us at the right hand of God for ever and ever. *Amen.*

THE GOSPEL.

St. John xv. 26.

WHEN the Comforter is come, whom I will send unto you from the Father, even the Spirit of truth, which proceedeth from the Father, he shall testify of me; and ye also shall bear witness, because ye have been with me from the beginning. These things have I spoken unto you, that ye should not be offended. They shall put you out of the synagogues; yea, the time cometh, that whosoever killeth you, will think that he doeth God service. And these things will they do unto you, because they have not known the Father, nor me. But these things have I told you, that when the time shall come, ye may remember that I told you of them.

THE EPISTLE.

1 St. Pet. iv. 7.

THE end of all things is at hand. Be ye therefore sober, and watch unto prayer. And above all things have fervent charity among yourselves; for charity shall cover a multitude of sins. Use hospitality one to another, without grudging. As every man hath received the gift, even so minister the same one to another, as good stewards of the manifold grace of God. If any man speak, let him speak as the oracles of God. If any man minister, let him do it as of the ability which God giveth; that God in all things may be glorified through Jesus Christ, to whom be praise and dominion for ever and ever. *Amen.*

THE COLLECT.

GOD, who as at this time, didst teach the hearts of thy faithful people, by the sending to·them the light of thy Holy Spirit; grant us by the same Spirit to have a right judgment in all things, and evermore to rejoice in his holy comfort, through Christ Jesus our Saviour; in whose name we ascribe unto thee all honor and glory now and forever. *Amen.*

THE GOSPEL.

St. John xiv. 15.

JESUS said unto his disciples, If ye love me, keep my commandments. And I will pray the Father, and he shall give you another Comforter, that he may abide with you forever ; even the Spirit of truth ; whom the world cannot receive, because it seeth him not, neither knoweth him ; but ye know him ; for he dwelleth with you, and shall be in you. I will not leave you comfortless ; I will come to you. Yet a little while, and the world seeth me no more ; but ye see me ; because I live, ye shall live also. At that day ye shall know that I am in my Father, and ye in me, and I in you. He who hath my commandments, and keepeth them, he it is who loveth me ; and he who loveth me shall be loved of my Father, and I will love him, and will manifest myself to him. Judas saith unto him, (not Iscariot,) Lord, how is it that thou wilt manifest thyself unto us, and not unto the world ? Jesus answered and said unto him, If a man love me, he will keep my words ; and my Father will love him, and we will come unto him, and make our abode with him. He who loveth me not, keepeth not my sayings ; and the word which ye hear, is not mine, but the Father's, who sent me. These things have I spoken unto you, being yet present with you ; but the Comforter, who is the Holy Spirit, whom the Father will send in my name, he shall teach you all things, and bring all things to your remembrance, whatsoever I have said unto you.

Peace I leave with you, my peace I give unto you ; not as the world giveth, give I unto you. Let not your heart be troubled, neither let it be afraid. Ye have heard how I said unto you, I go away, and come again unto you. If ye loved me, ye would rejoice, because I said, I go unto the Father ; for the Father is greater than I. And now I have told you before it come to pass, that, when it is come to pass, ye might believe. Hereafter, I will not talk much with you ; for the prince of this world cometh, and hath nothing in me. But that the world may know that I love the Father, and as the Father gave me commandment, even so I do.

FOR THE EPISTLE.

Acts ii. 1.

❡ HEN the day of Pentecost was fully come, they were all with one accord in one place. And suddenly there came a sound from heaven, as of a rushing mighty wind, and it filled all the house where they were sitting. And there appeared unto them cloven tongues, like as of fire, which sat upon each of them. And they were all filled with the Holy Spirit, and began to speak with other tongues, as the Spirit gave them utterance. And there were dwelling at Jerusalem Jews, devout men, out of every nation under heaven. Now when this was noised abroad, the multitude came together, and were confounded, because that every man heard them speak in his own language. And they were all amazed, and marvelled, saying one to another,

Behold, are not all these, who speak, Galileans? And how hear we every man in our own tongue, wherein we were born? Parthians, and Medes, and Elamites, and the dwellers in Mesopotamia, and in Judea, and Cappadocia, in Pontus and Asia, Phrygia and Pamphylia, in Egypt, and in the parts of Lybia about Cyrene, and strangers of Rome, Jews and proselytes, Cretes and Arabians, we do hear them speak in our tongues the wonderful works of God.

The First Sunday aft.

THE COLLECT.

ALMIGHTY and everlasting God, who hast given us thy servants grace, by the confession of a true faith, to acknowledge the glory of thy eternal Godhead; we beseech thee that thou wouldest keep us steadfast in this faith, and evermore defend us from all adversities, who livest and reignest one God, world without end. *Amen.*

THE GOSPEL.

St. John iii. 1.

THERE was a man of the Pharisees, named Nicodemus, a ruler of the Jews; the same came to Jesus by night, and said unto him, Rabbi, we know that thou art a teacher come from God; for no man can do these miracles that thou doest, except God be with him. Jesus answered and said unto him, Verily, verily, I say unto thee, except a man be born again, he cannot see the kingdom of God. Nicodemus saith unto him, How can a man be born when he is old? can he enter the second time into his mother's womb, and be born? Jesus answered, Verily, verily, I say unto thee, except a man be born of water and of the Spirit, he cannot see the kingdom of God. That which is born of the flesh, is flesh; and that which is born of the Spirit, is spirit. Marvel not that I said unto thee, Ye must be born again. The wind bloweth where it listeth, and thou hearest the sound thereof, but canst not tell whence it cometh, and whither it goeth; so is every one who is born of the Spirit. Nicodemus answered and said unto him, How can these things be? Jesus answered and said unto him, Art thou a master of Israel, and knowest not these things? Verily, verily, I say unto thee, We speak that we do know, and testify that we have seen; and ye receive not our witness. If I have told you earthly things, and ye believe not, how shall ye believe, if I tell you of heavenly things? And no man hath ascended up to heaven, but he who came down from heaven, even the Son of Man, who is in heaven. And as Moses lifted up the serpent in the wilderness, even so must the Son of Man be lifted up; that whosoever believeth in him, should not perish, but have eternal life.

FOR THE EPISTLE.

Rev. iv. 1.

AFTER this I looked, and, behold, a door was opened in heaven; and the first voice which I heard was as it were of a trumpet talking with me; which said, Come up hither, and I will show thee things which must be hereafter. And immediately I was in the spirit; and behold, a throne was set in heaven, and one sat on the throne; and he who sat, was to look upon like a jasper and a sardine stone; and there was a rainbow round about the throne, in sight like unto an emerald. And round about the throne were four and twenty seats; and upon the seats I saw four and twenty elders sitting, clothed in white raiment; and they had on their heads crowns of gold. And out of the throne proceeded lightnings, and thunderings, and voices; and there were seven lamps of fire burning before the throne, which are the seven spirits of God. And before the throne there was a sea of glass, like unto crystal; and in the midst of the throne, and round about the throne, were four beasts, full of eyes before and behind. And the first beast was like a lion, and the second beast like a calf, and the third beast had a face as a man, and the fourth beast was like a flying eagle. And the four beasts had each of them six wings about him; and they were full of eyes within; and they rest not day and night, saying, Holy, holy, holy, Lord God Almighty, who was, and is, and is to come. And when those beasts give glory, and honor, and thanks to him who sat on the throne, who liveth for ever and ever, the four and twenty elders fall down before him who sat on the throne, and worship him who liveth for ever and ever, and cast their crowns before the throne, saying, Thou art worthy, O Lord, to receive glory, and honor, and power; for thou hast created all things, and for thy pleasure they are, and were created.

The Second Sunday after Whitsunday.

THE COLLECT.

O GOD, the strength of all those who put their trust in thee; mercifully accept our prayers; and because, through the weakness of our mortal nature, we can do no good thing without thee, grant us the help of thy grace, that in keeping thy commandments, we may please thee both in will and deed, through Jesus Christ our Lord. *Amen.*

THE GOSPEL.

St. Luke xvi. 19.

THERE was a certain rich man, who was clothed in purple and fine linen, and fared sumptuously every day. And there was a certain beggar, named Lazarus, who was laid at his gate, full of sores, and desiring to be fed with the crumbs which fell from the rich man's table; moreover, the dogs came and licked his sores. And it came to pass, that the beggar died, and was carried by the angels into

Abraham's bosom. The rich man also died, and was buried. And in hell he lifted up his eyes, being in torments, and seeth Abraham afar off, and Lazarus in his bosom. And he cried and said, Father Abraham, have mercy on me, and send Lazarus, that he may dip the tip of his finger in water, and cool my tongue; for I am tormented in this flame. But Abraham said, Son, remember that thou in thy lifetime receivedst thy good things, and likewise Lazarus evil things; but now he is comforted, and thou art tormented. And beside all this, between us and you there is a great gulf fixed; so that they who would pass from hence to you, cannot; neither can they pass to us, who would come from thence. Then he said, I pray thee therefore, father, that thou wouldest send him to my father's house; for I have five brethren; that he may testify unto them, lest they also come into this place of torment. Abraham saith unto him, They have Moses and the prophets, let them hear them. And he said, Nay, father Abraham; but if one went unto them from the dead, they will repent. And he said unto him, If they hear not Moses and the prophets, neither will they be persuaded, though one rose from the dead.

THE EPISTLE.

1 St. John iv. 7.

BELOVED, let us love one another; for love is of God; and every one who loveth, is born of God, and knoweth God. He who loveth not, knoweth not God ; for God is love. In this was manifested the love of God toward us, because that God sent his only begotten Son into the world, that we might live through him. Herein is love, not that we loved God, but that he loved us, and sent his Son to be the propitiation for our sins. Beloved, if God so loved us, we ought also to love one another. No man hath seen God at any time. If we love one another, God dwelleth in us, and his love is perfected in us. Hereby know we that we dwell in him, and he in us, because he hath given us of his Spirit. And we have seen and do testify, that the Father sent the Son to be the Saviour of the world. Whosoever shall confess that Jesus is the Son of God, God dwelleth in him, and he in God. And we have known and believed the love that God hath to us. God is love ; and he who dwelleth in love, dwelleth in God, and God in him. Herein is our love made perfect, that we may have boldness in the day of judgment; because as he is, so are we in this world. There is no fear in love ; but perfect love casteth out fear ; because fear hath torment ; he who feareth is not made perfect in love. We love him, because he first loved us. If a man say, I love God, and hateth his brother, he is a liar ; for he who loveth not his brother whom he hath seen, how can he love God whom he hath not seen? And this commandment have we from him, That he who loveth God, love his brother also.

The Third Sunday after Whitsunday.

THE COLLECT.

O LORD, who never failest to help and govern those whom thou dost bring up in thy steadfast fear and love ; keep us, we beseech thee, under the protection of thy good providence, and make us to have a perpetual fear and love of thy holy name, through Jesus Christ our Lord. *Amen.*

THE GOSPEL.

St. Luke xiv. 16.

¶ CERTAIN man made a great supper, and bade many ; and sent his servant, at supper time, to say to those who were bidden, Come, for all things are now ready. And they all with one consent began to make excuse. The first said unto him, I have bought a piece of ground, and I must needs go and see it ; I pray thee have me excused. And another said, I have bought five yoke of oxen, and I go to prove them ; I pray thee have me excused. And another said, I have married a wife, and therefore I cannot come. So that servant came, and showed his lord these things. Then the master of the house, being angry, said to his servant, Go out quickly into the streets and lanes of the city, and bring in hither the poor, and the maimed, and the halt, and the blind. And the servant said, Lord, it is done as thou hast commanded, and yet there is room. And the lord said unto the servant, Go out into the highways and hedges, and compel them to come in, that my house may be filled. For I say unto you, that none, of those men who were bidden, shall taste of my supper.

THE EPISTLE.

1 St. John iii. 13.

MARVEL not, my brethren, if the world hate you. We know that we have passed from death unto life, because we love the brethren. He who loveth not his brother, abideth in death. Whosoever hateth his brother, is a murderer; and ye know that no murderer hath eternal life abiding in him. Hereby perceive we love, because he laid down his life for us; and we ought to lay down our lives for the brethren. But whoso hath this world's good, and seeth his brother have need, and shutteth up his bowels of compassion from him; how dwelleth the love of God in him? My little children, let us not love in word, neither in tongue; but in deed, and in truth. And hereby we know that we are of the truth, and shall assure our hearts before him; for if our heart condemn us, God is greater than our heart, and knoweth all things. Beloved, if our heart condemn us not, then have we confidence toward God; and whatsoever we ask, we receive of him, because we keep his commandments, and do those things that are pleasing in his sight. And this is his commandment, That we should believe on the name of his Son Jesus Christ, and love one another, as he gave us commandment. And he, who keepeth his commandments, dwelleth in him, and he in him ; and hereby we know that he abideth in us, by the Spirit which he hath given us.

The Fourth Sunday after Whitsunday.

THE COLLECT.

LORD, we beseech thee mercifully to hear us, and grant that we, truly seeking thine aid, may by thy mighty power be defended, and by thy gracious mercy be comforted in all dangers and adversities, through Jesus Christ our Lord. *Amen.*

THE GOSPEL.

St. Luke xv. 1.

THEN drew near unto him all the publicans and sinners, to hear him. And the Pharisees and scribes murmured, saying, This man receiveth sinners, and eateth with them. And he spake this parable unto them, saying, What man of you, having a hundred sheep, if he lose one of them, doth not leave the ninety and nine in the wilderness, and go after that which is lost, until he find it ? And when he hath found it, he layeth it on his shoulders, rejoicing. And when he cometh home, he calleth together his friends and neighbors, saying unto them, Rejoice with me, for I have found my sheep which was lost. I say unto you, that likewise joy shall be in heaven over one sinner who repenteth, more than over ninety and nine just persons who need no repentance. Either what woman, having ten pieces of silver, if she lose one piece, doth not light a candle, and sweep the house, and seek diligently till she find it? And when she hath found it, she calleth her friends and her neighbors together, saying, Rejoice with me, for I have found the piece which I had lost. Likewise I say unto you, there is joy in the presence of the angels of God, over one sinner who repenteth.

THE EPISTLE.

1 St. Pet. v. 5.

ALL of you be subject one to another, and be clothed with humility; for God resisteth the proud, and giveth grace to the humble. Humble yourselves therefore under the mighty hand of God, that he may exalt you in due time; casting all your care upon him; for he careth for you. Be sober, be vigilant; because your adversary, the devil, as a roaring lion, walketh about, seeking whom he may devour; whom resist, steadfast in the faith, knowing that the same afflictions are accomplished in your brethren who are in the world. But the God of all grace, who hath called us unto his eternal glory by Christ Jesus, after that ye have suffered awhile, make you perfect, stablish, strengthen, settle you. To him be glory and dominion for ever and ever. *Amen.*

The Fifth Sunday after Whitsunday.

THE COLLECT.

C GOD, the protector of all who trust in thee, without whom nothing is strong, nothing is holy ; increase and multiply upon us thy mercy, that thou being our ruler and guide, we may so pass through things temporal, that we finally lose not the things eternal. Grant this, O heavenly Father, through Jesus Christ our Lord. *Amen.*

THE GOSPEL.

St. Luke vi. 36.

ʙ E ye therefore merciful, as your Father also is merciful. Judge not, and ye shall not be judged. Condemn not, and ye shall not be condemned. Forgive, and ye shall be forgiven. Give, and it shall be given unto you ; good measure, pressed down, and shaken together, and running over, shall men give into your bosom. For with the same measure that ye mete withal, it shall be measured to you again. And he spake a parable unto them ; Can the blind lead the blind? shall they not both fall into the ditch? The disciple is not above his master ; but every one who is perfect shall be as his master. And why beholdest thou the mote that is in thy brother's eye, but perceivest not the beam that is in thine own eye? Either how canst thou say to thy brother, Brother, let me pull out the mote that is in thine eye, when thou thyself beholdest not the beam that is in thine own eye? Thou hypocrite, cast out first the beam out of thine own eye, and then shalt thou see clearly to pull out the mote that is in thy brother's eye.

THE EPISTLE.

Rom. viii. 31.

WHAT shall we then say to these things? If God be for us, who can be against us? He that spared not his own Son, but delivered him up for us all, how shall he not with him also freely give us all things? Who shall lay anything to the charge of God's elect? It is God that justifieth; who is he that condemneth? It is Christ that died, yea, rather, that is risen again, who is even at the right hand of God, who also maketh intercession for us. Who shall separate us from the love of Christ? Shall tribulation, or distress, or persecution, or famine, or nakedness, or peril, or sword? as it is written, For thy sake we are killed all the day long; we are accounted as sheep for the slaughter. Nay, in all these things, we are more than conquerors, through him who loved us. For I am persuaded, that neither death, nor life, nor angels, nor principalities, nor powers, nor things present, nor things to come, nor height, nor depth, nor any other creature, shall be able to separate us from the love of God, which is in Christ Jesus our Lord.

The Sixth Sunday after Whitsunday.

THE COLLECT.

GRANT, O Lord, we beseech thee, that the course of this world may be so peaceably ordered by thy governance, that thy Church may joyfully serve thee in all godly quietness, through Jesus Christ our Lord. *Amen.*

THE GOSPEL.

St. Luke v. 1.

IT came to pass, that as the people pressed upon him to hear the word of God, he stood by the lake of Gennesaret, and saw two ships standing by the lake; but the fishermen were gone out of them, and were washing their nets. And he entered into one of the ships, which was Simon's, and prayed him that he would thrust out a little from the land. And he sat down, and taught the people out of the ship. Now when he had left speaking, he said unto Simon, Launch out into the deep, and let down your nets for a draught. And Simon answering, said unto him, Master, we have toiled all the night, and have taken nothing; nevertheless, at thy word I will let down the net. And when they had done this, they enclosed a great multitude of fishes, and their net brake. And they beckoned unto their partners who were in the other ship, that they should come and help them. And they came, and filled both the ships, so that they began to sink. When Simon Peter saw it, he fell down at Jesus' knees, saying, Depart from me, for I am a sinful man, O Lord. For he was astonished, and all who were with him, at the draught of the fishes which they had taken ; and so was also James and John the sons of Zebedee, who were partners with Simon. And Jesus said unto Simon, Fear not ; from henceforth thou shalt catch men. And when they had brought their ships to land, they forsook all, and followed him.

THE EPISTLE.

1 St. Pet. iii. 8.

BE ye all of one mind, having compassion one of another ; love as brethren, be pitiful, be courteous ; not rendering evil for evil, or railing for railing, but contrariwise, blessing; knowing that ye are thereunto called, that ye should inherit a blessing. For he who will love life, and see good days, let him refrain his tongue from evil, and his lips that they speak no guile ; let him eschew evil, and do good ; let him seek peace, and ensue it. For the eyes of the Lord are over the righteous, and his ears are open unto their prayers ; but the face of the Lord is against those who do evil. And who is he who will harm you, if ye be followers of that which is good ? But and if ye suffer for right-eousness' sake, happy are ye ; and be not afraid of their terror, neither be troubled ; but sanctify the Lord God in your hearts ; and be ready always to give an answer to every man that asketh you a reason of the hope that is in you.

The Seventh Sunday after Whitsunday.

THE COLLECT.

O GOD, who hast prepared for those who love thee, such good things as pass man's understanding; pour into our hearts such love toward thee, that we, loving thee above all things, may obtain thy promises, which exceed all that we can desire, through Jesus Christ our Lord. *Amen.*

THE GOSPEL.

St. Matt. v. 20.

JESUS said unto his disciples, Except your righteousness shall exceed the righteousness of the Scribes and Pharisees, ye shall in no case enter into the kingdom of heaven. Ye have heard that it was said by them of old time, Thou shalt not kill; and whosoever shall kill, shall be in danger of the judgment. But I say unto you, that whosoever is angry with his brother, without a cause, shall be in danger of the judgment; and whosoever shall say to his brother, Raca, shall be in danger of the council; but whosoever shall say, Thou fool, shall be in danger of hell fire. Therefore, if thou bring thy gift to the altar, and there rememberest that thy brother hath aught against thee, leave there thy gift before the altar and go thy way; first be reconciled to thy brother, and then come and offer thy gift. Agree with thine adversary quickly, whilst thou art in the way with him; lest at any time the adversary deliver thee to the judge, and the judge deliver thee to the officer, and thou be cast into prison. Verily I say unto thee, thou shalt by no means come out thence, till thou hast paid the uttermost farthing.

THE EPISTLE.

Rom. vi. 3.

KNOW ye not, that so many of us as were baptized into Jesus Christ, were baptized into his death? Therefore we are buried with him by baptism into death; that like as Christ was raised up from the dead by the glory of the Father, even so we also should walk in newness of life. For if we have been planted together in the likeness of his death, we shall be also in the likeness of his resurrection; knowing this, that our old man is crucified with him, that the body of sin might be destroyed, that henceforth we should not serve sin; for he who is dead is free from sin. Now if we be dead with Christ, we believe that we shall also live with him; knowing that Christ being raised from the dead, dieth no more; death hath no more dominion over him. For in that he died, he died unto sin once; but in that he liveth, he liveth unto God. Likewise reckon ye also yourselves to be dead unto sin, but alive unto God, through Jesus Christ our Lord.

The Eighth Sunday after Whitsunday.

THE COLLECT.

LORD of all power and might, who art the author and giver of all good things; graft in our hearts the love of thy name, increase in us true religion, nourish us with all goodness, and of thy great mercy keep us in the same, through Jesus Christ our Lord. *Amen.*

THE GOSPEL.

St. Mark viii. 1.

IN those days, the multitude being very great, and having nothing to eat, Jesus called his disciples unto him, and saith unto them, I have compassion on the multitude, because they have now been with me three days, and have nothing to eat; and if I send them away fasting to their own houses, they will faint by the way ; for divers of them came from far. And his disciples answered him, From whence can a man satisfy these men with bread here in the wilderness? And he asked them, How many loaves have ye? and they said, Seven. And he commanded the people to sit down on the ground ; and he took the seven loaves, and gave thanks, and brake, and gave to his disciples to set before them ; and they did set them before the people. And they had a few small fishes ; and he blessed, and commanded to set them also before them. So they did eat, and were filled ; and they took up of the broken meat that was left seven baskets. And they who had eaten were about four thousand ; and he sent them away.

THE EPISTLE.

Rom. vi. 16.

K NOW ye not that to whom ye yield yourselves servants to obey, his servants ye are to whom ye obey ; whether of sin unto death, or of obedience unto righteousness? But God be thanked, that ye were the servants of sin, but ye have obeyed from the heart that form of doctrine which was delivered you. Being then made free from sin, ye became the servants of righteousness. I speak after the manner of men, because of the infirmity of your flesh. For as ye have yielded your members servants to uncleanness and to iniquity, unto iniquity; even so now yield your members servants to righteousness, unto holiness. For when ye were the servants of sin, ye were free from righteousness. What fruit had ye then in those things whereof ye are now ashamed? for the end of those things is death. But now, being made free from sin, and become servants to God, ye have your fruit unto holiness, and the end everlasting life. For the wages of sin is death ; but the gift of God is eternal life, through Jesus Christ our Lord.

The Ninth Sunday after Whitsunday.

THE COLLECT.

O GOD, whose never failing providence ordereth all things both in heaven and earth ; we humbly beseech thee to put away from us all hurtful

things, and to give us those things which be profitable for us, through Jesus Christ our Lord. *Amen.*

THE GOSPEL.

St. Matt. vii. 15.

BEWARE of false prophets, who come to you
in sheeps' clothing, but inwardly they are
ravening wolves. Ye shall know them by their
fruits. Do men gather grapes of thorns, or figs
of thistles? Even so every good tree bringeth
forth good fruit; but a corrupt tree bringeth forth
evil fruit. A good tree cannot bring forth evil
fruit, neither can a corrupt tree bring forth good
fruit. Every tree that bringeth not forth good
fruit, is hewn down, and cast into the fire. Wherefore by their fruits ye shall know them. Not every
one that saith unto me, Lord, Lord, shall enter
into the kingdom of heaven; but he that doeth
the will of my Father who is in heaven. Many
will say to me in that day, Lord, Lord, have we
not prophesied in thy name? and in thy name have
cast out devils? and in thy name done many wonderful works? And then will I profess unto them,
I never knew you; depart from me, ye that work
iniquity. Therefore whosoever heareth these sayings of mine, and doeth them, I will liken him
unto a wise man, who built his house upon a rock;
and the rain descended, and the floods came, and
the winds blew, and beat upon that house, and it
fell not; for it was founded upon a rock. And
every one that heareth these sayings of mine, and

doeth them not, shall be likened unto a foolish man, who built his house upon the sand ; and the rain descended, and the floods came, and the winds blew, and beat upon that house, and it fell ; and great was the fall of it. And it came to pass, when Jesus had ended these sayings, the people were astonished at his doctrine ; for he taught them as one having authority, and not as the scribes.

THE EPISTLE.

Rom. viii. 12.

BRETHREN, we are not debtors to the flesh, to live after the flesh ; for if ye live after the flesh, ye shall die ; but if ye, through the Spirit, do mortify the deeds of the body, ye shall live. For as many as are led by the Spirit of God, they are the sons of God. For ye have not received the spirit of bondage again to fear ; but ye have received the spirit of adoption, whereby we cry, Abba, Father. The Spirit itself beareth witness with our spirit that we are the children of God. And if children, then heirs ; heirs of God, and joint heirs with Christ ; if so be that we suffer with him, that we may be also glorified together.

The Tenth Sunday after Whitsunday.

THE COLLECT.

GRANT to us, Lord, we beseech thee, the spirit to think and do always such things as be right-.

ful ; that we, who cannot do anything that is good without thee, may by thee be enabled to live according to thy will, through Jesus Christ our Lord. *Amen.*

THE GOSPEL.

St. Luke xvi. I.

JESUS said unto his disciples, There was a certain rich man, who had a steward ; and the same was accused unto him, that he had wasted his goods. And he called him, and said unto him, How is it that I hear this of thee ? give an account of thy stewardship ; for thou mayest be no longer steward. Then the steward said within himself, What shall I do ? for my lord taketh away from me the stewardship. I cannot dig ; to beg I am ashamed. I am resolved what to do, that, when I am put out of the stewardship, they may receive me into their houses. So he called every one of his lord's debtors unto him, and said unto the first, How much owest thou unto my lord ? And he said, An hundred measures of oil. And he said unto him, Take thy bill, and sit down quickly, and write fifty. Then said he to another, And how much owest thou ? And he said, An hundred measures of wheat. And he said unto him, Take thy bill, and write fourscore. And the lord commended the unjust steward, because he had done wisely ; for the children of this world are in their generation wiser than the children of light. And I say unto you, Make to yourselves friends of the mammon of unrighteousness; that when ye fail, they may receive you into everlasting habitations.

THE EPISTLE.

Gal. vi. 1.

BRETHREN, if a man be overtaken in a fault, ye who are spiritual, restore such an one in the spirit of meekness; considering thyself, lest thou also be tempted. Bear ye one another's burdens, and so fulfil the law of Christ. For if a man think himself to be something, when he is nothing, he deceiveth himself. But let every man prove his own work, and then shall he have rejoicing in himself alone, and not in another. For every man shall bear his own burden. Let him that is taught in the word, communicate unto him that teacheth in all good things. Be not deceived; God is not mocked; for whatsoever a man soweth, that shall he also reap. For he that soweth to his flesh, shall of the flesh reap corruption; but he that soweth to the Spirit, shall of the Spirit reap life everlasting. And let us not be weary in well-doing; for in due season we shall reap, if we faint not. As we have therefore opportunity, let us do good unto all men, especially unto them who are of the household of faith.

The Eleventh Sunday after Whitsunday.

THE COLLECT.

LET thy merciful ears, O Lord, be open to the prayers of thy humble servants; and, that they may obtain their petitions, make them to ask such things as shall please thee, through Jesus Christ our Lord. *Amen.*

THE GOSPEL.

St. Luke xix. 41.

AND when he was come near, he beheld the city, and wept over it ; saying, If thou hadst known, even thou, at least in this thy day, the things which belong unto thy peace ! but now they are hid from thine eyes. For the days shall come upon thee, that thine enemies shall cast a trench about thee, and compass thee round, and keep thee in on every side, and shall lay thee even with the ground, and thy children within thee ; and they shall not leave in thee one stone upon another ; because thou knewest not the time of thy visitation. And he went into the temple, and began to cast out those who sold therein, and those who bought, saying unto them, It is written, My house is the house of prayer ; but ye have made it a den of thieves. And he taught daily in the temple.

THE EPISTLE.

1 Cor. xii. 1.

CONCERNING spiritual gifts, brethren, I would not have you ignorant. Ye know that ye were Gentiles, carried away unto these dumb idols, even as ye were led. Wherefore I give you to understand that no man speaking by the Spirit of God calleth Jesus accursed ; and that no man can say that Jesus is the Lord, but by the Holy Spirit. Now there are diversities of gifts, but the same Spirit. And there are differences of administrations, but the same Lord. And there are diversities of operations, but it is the same God who worketh all in all. But the manifestation of the Spirit is given to every man to profit withal. For to one is given by the Spirit the word of wisdom ; to another, the word of knowledge, by the same Spirit ; to another, faith, by the same Spirit ; to another, the gifts of healing, by the same Spirit ; to another, the working of miracles ; to another, prophecy ; to another, discerning of spirits ; to another, divers kinds of tongues ; to another, the interpretation of tongues. But all these worketh that one and the self-same Spirit, dividing to every man severally as he will.

The Twelfth Sunday after Whitsunday.

THE COLLECT.

O GOD, who declarest thy almighty power chiefly in showing mercy and pity ; mercifully grant unto us such a measure of thy grace, that we, running the way of thy commandments, may obtain thy gracious promises, and be made partakers of thy heavenly treasure, through Jesus Christ our Lord. *Amen.*

THE GOSPEL.

St. Luke xviii. 9.

JESUS spake this parable unto certain who trusted in themselves that they were righteous, and despised others. Two men went up into the temple to pray; the one a Pharisee, and the other a publican. The Pharisee stood, and prayed thus with himself; God, I thank thee, that I am not as other men are, extortioners, unjust, adulterers, or even as this publican. I fast twice in the week; I give tithes of all that I possess. And the publican, standing afar off, would not lift up so much as his eyes unto heaven, but smote upon his breast, saying, God be merciful to me a sinner. I tell you, this man went down to his house justified rather than the other; for every one who exalteth himself shall be abased; and he who humbleth himself shall be exalted.

THE EPISTLE.

I Cor. xv. I.

BRETHREN, I declare unto you the gospel which I preached unto you, which also ye have received, and wherein ye stand; by which also ye are saved, if ye keep in memory what I preached unto you, unless ye have believed in vain. For I delivered unto you, first of all, that which I also received, how that Christ died for our sins, according to the Scriptures; and that he was buried; and that he rose again the third day according to the Scriptures; and that he was seen of Cephas; then of the twelve. After that, he was seen of above five hundred brethren at once; of whom the greater part remain unto this present, but some are fallen asleep. After that, he was seen of James; then of all the apostles. And last of all he was seen of me also, as of one born out of due time. For I am the least of the apostles, that am not meet to be called an apostle, because I persecuted the Church of God. But by the grace of God I am what I am ; and his grace which was bestowed upon me, was not in vain ; but I labored more abundantly than they all ; yet not I, but the grace of God which was with me. Therefore, whether it were I or they, so we preach, and so ye believed.

The Thirteenth Sunday after Whitsunday

THE COLLECT.

ALMIGHTY and everlasting God, who art always more ready to hear than we are to pray, and art wont to give more than either we desire or deserve ; pour down upon us the abundance of thy mercy, forgiving us those things whereof our conscience is afraid, and giving us those good things which we are not worthy to ask, but through the mediation of thy Son. Jesus Christ our Lord. *Amen.*

THE GOSPEL.

St. Mark vii. 31.

JESUS, departing from the coasts of Tyre and Sidon, came unto the sea of Galilee, through the midst of the coasts of Decapolis. And they bring unto him one that was deaf, and had an impediment in his speech ; and they beseech him to put his hand upon him. And he took him aside from the multitude, and put his fingers into his ears, and he spit, and touched his tongue; and looking up to heaven, he sighed, and saith unto him, *Ephphatha*, that is, Be opened. And straightway his ears were opened, and the string of his tongue was loosed, and he spake plain. And he charged them that they should tell no man; but the more he charged them, so much the more a great deal they published it; and were beyond measure astonished, saying, He hath done all things well; he maketh both the deaf to hear, and the dumb to speak.

THE EPISTLE.

2 Cor. iii. 4.

SUCH trust have we through Christ toward God. Not that we are sufficient of ourselves to think anything as of ourselves; but our sufficiency is of God; who also hath made us able ministers of the new testament; not of the letter, but of the spirit; for the letter killeth, but the spirit giveth life. But if the ministration of death, written and engraven in stones, was glorious, so that the children of Israel could not steadfastly behold the face of Moses, for the glory of his countenance; which glory was to be done away; how shall not the ministration of the spirit be rather glorious? For if the ministration of condemnation be glory, much more doth the ministration of righteousness exceed in glory.

The Fourteenth Sunday after Whitsunday.

THE COLLECT.

A LMIGHTY and merciful God, of whose only gift it cometh, that thy faithful people do unto thee true and laudable service ; grant, we beseech thee, that we may so faithfully serve thee in this life, that we fail not finally to attain thy heavenly promises, through Jesus Christ our Lord. *Amen.*

THE GOSPEL.

St. Luke x. 23.

B LESSED are the eyes which see the things that ye see. For I tell you that many prophets and kings have desired to see those things which ye see, and have not seen them ; and to hear those things which ye hear, and have not heard them. And behold, a certain lawyer stood up, and tempted him, saying, Master, what shall I do to inherit eternal life ? He said unto him, What is written in the law ? how readest thou ? And he answering, said, Thou shalt love the Lord thy God with all thy heart, and with all thy soul, and with all thy strength, and with all thy mind ; and thy neighbor as thyself. And he said unto him, Thou hast answered right ; this do, and thou shalt live. But he, willing to justify himself, said unto Jesus, And who is my neighbor ? And Jesus answering, said, A certain man went down from Jerusalem to Jericho, and fell among thieves, who stripped him of his raiment, and wounded him, and departed, leaving him half dead. And by chance there came down a certain priest that way ; and when he saw him, he passed by on the other side. And likewise a Levite, when he was at the place, came and looked on him, and passed by on the other side. But a certain Samaritan, as he journeyed, came where he was ; and when he saw him, he had compassion on him, and went to him, and bound up his wounds, pouring in oil and wine, and set him on his own beast, and brought him to an inn, and took care of him. And on the morrow, when he departed, he took out two pence, and gave them to the host, and said unto him, Take care of him, and whatsoever thou spendest more, when I come again, I will repay thee. Which now of these three, thinkest thou, was neighbor unto him who fell among the thieves ? And he said, He who showed mercy on him. Then said Jesus unto him, Go, and do thou likewise.

THE EPISTLE.

1 Thess. v. 14.

NOW we exhort you, brethren, warn them that are unruly ; comfort the feeble-minded ; support the weak ; be patient toward all men. See that none render evil for evil unto any man ; but ever follow that which is good, both among yourselves, and to all men. Rejoice evermore. Pray without ceasing. In everything give thanks ; for this is the will of God, in Christ Jesus, concerning you. Quench not the Spirit. Despise not prophesyings. Prove all things ; hold fast that which is good. Abstain from all appearance of evil. And the very God of peace sanctify you wholly ; and I pray God your whole spirit, and soul, and body, be preserved blameless unto the coming of our Lord Jesus Christ.

The Fifteenth Sunday after Whitsunday

THE COLLECT.

ALMIGHTY and everlasting God, give unto us the increase of faith, hope, and charity ; and that we may obtain that which thou dost promise, make us to love that which thou dost command, through Jesus Christ our Lord. *Amen.*

THE GOSPEL.

St. Luke xvii. 11.

AND it came to pass, as Jesus went to Jerusalem, that he passed through the midst of Samaria and Galilee. And as he entered into a certain village, there met him ten men who were lepers, who stood afar off. And they lifted up their voices and said, Jesus, Master, have mercy on us. And when he saw them, he said unto them, Go, show yourselves unto the priests. And it came to pass, that, as they went, they were cleansed. And one of them, when he saw that he was healed, turned back, and with a loud voice glorified God, and fell down on his face at his feet, giving him thanks ; and he was a Samaritan. And Jesus said, Were there not ten cleansed ? but where are the nine ? There are not found who returned to give glory to God, save this stranger. And he said unto him, Arise, go thy way ; thy faith hath made thee whole.

THE EPISTLE.

1 Cor. iii. 16.

K NOW ye not that ye are the temple of God, and that the Spirit of God dwelleth in you ? If any man defile the temple of God, him shall God destroy ; for the temple of God is holy, which temple ye are. Let no man deceive himself. If any man among you seemeth to be wise in this world, let him become a fool, that he may be wise. For the wisdom of this world is foolishness with God ; for it is written, He taketh the wise in their own craftiness. And again, The Lord knoweth the thoughts of the wise, that they are vain. Therefore let no man glory in men. For all things are yours ; whether Paul, or Apollos, or Cephas, or the world, or life, or death, or things present, or things to come ; all are yours ; and ye are Christ's ; and Christ is God's.

The Sixteenth Sunday after Whitsunday

THE COLLECT.

K EEP, we beseech thee, O Lord, thy Church with thy perpetual mercy ; and because the frailty of man without thee cannot but fall, keep us ever by thy help from all things hurtful, and lead us to all things profitable to our salvation, through Jesus Christ our Lord. *Amen.*

THE GOSPEL.

St. Matt. vi. 24.

NO man can serve two masters; for either he will hate the one, and love the other, or else he will hold to the one, and despise the other. Ye cannot serve God and mammon. Therefore I say unto you, Take no thought for your life, what ye shall eat, or what ye shall drink; nor yet for your body, what ye shall put on; is not the life more than meat, and the body than raiment? Behold the fowls of the air; for they sow not, neither do they reap, nor gather into barns; yet your Heavenly Father feedeth them. Are ye not much better than they? Which of you by taking thought can add one cubit unto his stature? And why take ye thought for raiment? Consider the lilies of the field, how they grow; they toil not, neither do they spin; and yet I say unto you, that even Solomon in all his glory was not arrayed like one of these. Wherefore, if God so clothe the grass of the field, which to-day is, and to-morrow is cast into the oven, shall he not much more clothe you, O ye of little faith? Therefore take no thought, saying, What shall we eat? or, what shall we drink? or, wherewithal shall we be clothed? (for after all these things do the Gentiles seek,) for your Heavenly Father knoweth that ye have need of all these things. But seek ye first the kingdom of God, and his righteousness, and all these things shall be added unto you. Take therefore no thought for the morrow; for the morrow shall take thought for the things of itself. Sufficient unto the day is the evil thereof.

FOR THE EPISTLE.

Rev. ii. 1.

UTNTO the angel of the church of Ephesus write; These things saith he that holdeth the seven stars in his right hand, who walketh in the midst of the seven golden candlesticks; I know thy works, and thy labor, and thy patience, and how thou canst not bear those who are evil; and thou hast tried those who say they are apostles, and are not, and hast found them liars; and hast borne, and hast patience, and for my name's sake hast labored, and hast not fainted. Nevertheless, I have somewhat against thee, because thou hast left thy first love. Remember, therefore, from whence thou art fallen, and repent, and do the first works; or else I will come unto thee quickly, and will remove thy candlestick out of his place, except thou repent. But this thou hast, that thou hatest the deeds of the Nicolaitans, which I also hate. He that hath an ear, let him hear what the Spirit saith unto the churches; To him that overcometh will I give to eat of the tree of life, which is in the midst of the paradise of God.

The Seventeenth Sunday after Whitsunday.

THE COLLECT.

O LORD, we beseech thee, let thy continual pity cleanse and defend thy Church ; and because it cannot continue in safety without thy succor, preserve it evermore by thy help and goodness, through Jesus Christ our Lord. *Amen.*

THE GOSPEL.

St. Luke vii. 11.

AND it came to pass the day after, that Jesus went into a city called Nain ; and many of his disciples went with him, and much people. Now when he came nigh to the gate of the city, behold there was a dead man carried out, the only son of his mother, and she was a widow ; and much people of the city was with her. And when the Lord saw her, he had compassion on her, and said unto her, Weep not. And he came and touched the bier, and those who bare him stood still. And he said, Young man, I say unto thee, Arise. And he who was dead sat up, and began to speak ; and he delivered him to his mother. And there came a fear on all ; and they glorified God, saying, that a great prophet is risen up among us ; and that God hath visited his people. And this rumor of him went forth throughout all Judea, and throughout all the region round about.

THE EPISTLE.

Ephes. iii. 13.

I DESIRE that ye faint not at my tribulations for you, which is your glory. For this cause I bow my knees unto the Father of our Lord Jesus Christ, of whom the whole family in heaven and earth is named, that he would grant you, according to the riches of his glory, to be strengthened with might by his Spirit in the inner man ; that Christ may dwell in your hearts by faith ; that ye, being rooted and grounded in love, may be able to comprehend with all saints, what is the breadth, and length, and depth, and height, and to know the love of Christ, which passeth knowledge, that ye might be filled with all the fulness of God. Now unto him who is able to do exceeding abundantly above all that we ask or think, according to the power that worketh in us, unto him be glory in the Church, by Christ Jesus, throughout all ages, world without end. Amen.

The Eighteenth Sunday after Whitsunday.

THE COLLECT.

LORD, we pray thee, that thy grace may be always with us, to enlighten and purify, to defend and preserve us ; and make us continually to be given to all good works, through Jesus Christ our Lord. *Amen.*

THE GOSPEL.

St. Luke xiv. 1.

IT came to pass, as Jesus went into the house of one of the chief Pharisees, to eat bread on the Sabbath day, that they watched him. And behold, there was a certain man before him, who had the dropsy. And Jesus spake unto the lawyers and Pharisees, saying, Is it lawful to heal on the Sabbath day? And they held their peace. And he took him, and healed him, and let him go ; and answered them, saying, Which of you shall have an ass, or an ox, fallen into a pit, and will not straightway pull him out on the Sabbath day? And they could not answer him again to these things. And he put forth a parable to those who were bidden, when he marked how they chose out the chief rooms ; saying unto them, When thou art bidden of any man to a wedding, sit not down in the highest room ; lest a more honorable man than thou be bidden of him, and he who bade thee and him, come and say to thee, Give this man place ; and thou begin with shame to take the lowest room. But when thou art bidden, go and sit down in the lowest room, that when he who bade thee cometh, he may say unto thee, Friend, go up higher ; then shalt thou have worship in the presence of those who sit at meat with thee. For whosoever exalteth himself shall be abased ; and he who humbleth himself shall be exalted.

THE EPISTLE.

Ephes. iv. 1.

I THEREFORE, the prisoner of the Lord, beseech you, that ye walk worthy of the vocation wherewith ye are called ; with all lowliness and meekness, with long-suffering, forbearing one another in love ; endeavoring to keep the unity of the spirit in the bond of peace. There is one body, and one spirit, even as ye are called in one hope of your calling ; one Lord, one faith, one baptism, one God and Father of all, who is above all and through all, and in you all. But unto every one of us is given grace according to the measure of the gift of Christ. Wherefore it saith, When he ascended up on high, he led captivity captive, and gave gifts unto men. (Now that he ascended, what is it but that he also descended first into the lower parts of the earth? He that descended is the same also that ascended up far above all heavens, that he might fill all things.) And he gave some, apostles ; and some, prophets ; and some, evangelists ; and some, pastors and teachers ; for the perfecting of the saints, for the work of the ministry, for the edifying of the body of Christ ; till we all come in the unity of the faith, and of the knowledge of the Son of God, unto a perfect man, unto the measure of the stature of the fulness of Christ.

The Nineteenth Sunday after Whitsunday.

THE COLLECT.

L ORD, we beseech thee, grant thy people grace to withstand the temptations of the world without, and of evil passions within ; to make daily advances in wisdom and goodness ; and with pure hearts and minds to follow thee, the only God, through Jesus Christ our Lord. *Amen.*

THE GOSPEL.

St. Matt. xxii. 34.

W HEN the Pharisees had heard that Jesus had put the Sadducees to silence, they were gathered together. Then one of them, who was a lawyer, asked him a question, tempting him, and saying, Master, which is the great commandment in the law? Jesus said unto him, Thou shalt love the Lord thy God with all thy heart, and with all thy soul, and with all thy mind. This is the first and great commandment. And the second is like unto it, Thou shalt love thy neighbor as thyself. On these two commandments hang all the law and the prophets. While the Pharisees were gathered together, Jesus asked them, saying, What think ye of Christ? whose son is he? They say unto him, The son of David. He saith unto them, How then doth David in spirit call him Lord, saying, The Lord said unto my Lord, Sit thou on my right hand, till I make thine enemies thy footstool? If David then call him Lord, how is he his son? And no man was able to answer him a word, neither durst any man, from that day forth, ask him any more questions.

THE EPISTLE.

2 Cor. iv. 13.

WE, having the same spirit of faith, according as it is written, I believed, and therefore have I spoken ; we also believe, and therefore speak ; knowing that he who raised up the Lord Jesus, shall raise up us also by Jesus, and shall present us with you. For all things are for your sakes, that the abundant grace might, through the thanksgiving of many, redound to the glory of God. For which cause we faint not ; but though our outward man perish, yet the inward man is renewed day by day. For our light affliction, which is but for a moment, worketh for us a far more exceeding and eternal weight of glory ; while we look not at the things which are seen, but at the things which are not seen ; for the things which are seen are temporal ; but the things which are not seen are eternal.

The Twentieth Sunday after Whitsunday

THE COLLECT.

O GOD, forasmuch as without thee we are not able to please thee, mercifully grant that thy Holy Spirit may in all things direct and rule our hearts ; that they may be cleansed from everything which defileth, and always inclined to keep thy law, through our Saviour Jesus Christ. *Amen.*

THE GOSPEL.

St. Matt. ix. 1.

JESUS entered into a ship, and passed over, and came into his own city. And behold, they brought to him a man sick of the palsy, lying on a bed. And Jesus, seeing their faith, said unto the sick of the palsy, Son, be of good cheer, thy sins be forgiven thee. And behold, certain of the Scribes said within themselves, This man blasphemeth. And Jesus, knowing their thoughts, said, Wherefore think ye evil in your hearts? For whether is easier, to say, Thy sins be forgiven thee; or to say, Arise and walk? But that ye may know that the Son of Man hath power on earth to forgive sins, (then saith he to the sick of the palsy,) Arise, take up thy bed, and go unto thine house. And he arose, and departed to his house. But when the multitudes saw it, they marvelled, and glorified God, who had given such power unto men.

THE EPISTLE.

Ephes. iv. 17.

THIS I say therefore, and testify in the Lord, that ye henceforth walk not as other Gentiles walk, in the vanity of their mind, having the understanding darkened, being alienated from the life of God through the ignorance that is in them, because of the blindness of their heart; who, being past feeling, have given themselves over unto lasciviousness, to work all uncleanness with greediness. But ye have not so learned Christ; if so be that ye have heard him, and have been taught by him, as the truth is in Jesus, that ye put off, concerning the former conversation, the old man, which is corrupt according to the deceitful lusts, and be renewed in the spirit of your mind; and that ye put on the new man, which after God is created in righteousness and true holiness. Wherefore, putting away lying, speak every man truth with his neighbor; for we are members one of another. Be ye angry, and sin not; let not the sun go down upon your wrath; neither give place to the devil. Let him who stole, steal no more; but rather let him labor, working with his hands the thing which is good, that he may have to give to him who needeth. Let no corrupt communication proceed out of your mouth, but that which is good to the use of edifying, that it may minister grace unto the hearers. And grieve not the holy Spirit of God, whereby ye are sealed unto the day of redemption. Let all bitterness, and wrath, and anger, and clamor, and evil speaking, be put away from you, with all malice. And be ye kind one to another, tenderhearted, forgiving one another, even as God, in Christ, hath forgiven you.

The Twenty-first Sunday after Whitsunday

THE COLLECT.

O ALMIGHTY and most merciful God, of thy bountiful goodness keep us, we beseech thee, from all things that may hurt us; that we, being ready both in body and soul, may cheerfully accomplish those things that thou wouldest have done, through Jesus Christ our Lord. *Amen.*

THE GOSPEL.

St. Matt. xxii. I.

JESUS said, The kingdom of heaven is like unto a certain king, who made a marriage for his son; and sent forth his servants to call those who were bidden to the wedding; and they would not come. Again, he sent forth other servants, saying, Tell those who are bidden, Behold, I have prepared my dinner: my oxen and my fatlings are killed, and all things are ready; come unto the marriage. But they made light of it, and went their ways, one to his farm, another to his merchandise; and the remnant took his servants, and entreated them spitefully, and slew them. But when the king heard thereof, he was wroth; and he sent forth his armies, and destroyed those murderers, and burnt up their city. Then saith he to his servants, The wedding is ready, but they who were bidden were not worthy. Go ye therefore into the highways, and as many as ye shall find, bid to the marriage. So those servants went out into the highways, and gathered together all as many as they found, both bad and good ; and the wedding was furnished with guests. And when the king came in to see the guests, he saw there a man who had not on a wedding garment. And he saith unto him, Friend, how camest thou in hither, not having a wedding garment? And he was speechless. Then said the king to the servants, Bind him hand and foot, and take him away, and cast him into outer darkness ; there shall be weeping and gnashing of teeth. For many are called, but few are chosen.

THE EPISTLE.

2 St. Pet. i. 2.

GRACE and peace be multiplied unto you, through the knowledge of God, and of Jesus our Lord ; according as his divine power hath given unto us all things that pertain unto life and godliness, through the knowledge of him that hath called us to glory and virtue ; whereby are given unto us exceeding great and precious promises ; that by these ye might be partakers of the divine nature, having escaped the corruption that is in the world through lust. And besides this, giving all diligence, add to your faith virtue ; and to virtue, knowledge ; and to knowledge, temperance ; and to temperance, patience ; and to patience, godliness ; and to godliness, brotherly kindness ; and to brotherly kindness, charity. For if these things be in you, and abound, they make you that ye shall neither be barren nor unfruitful in the knowl-

edge of our Lord Jesus Christ. But he that lack-
eth these things is blind, and cannot see afar off,
and hath forgotten that he was purged from his
old sins. Wherefore the rather, brethren, give
diligence to make your calling and election sure;
for if ye do these things, ye shall never fall; for so
an entrance shall be ministered unto you abundantly into the everlasting kingdom of our Lord
and Saviour Jesus Christ.

The Twenty-second Sunday after Whitsunday.

THE COLLECT.

GRANT, we beseech thee, merciful Lord, to thy
faithful people, pardon and peace; that they
may be cleansed from all their sins, and serve thee
with a pure heart and a quiet mind, through Jesus
Christ our Lord. *Amen.*

THE GOSPEL.

St. John iv. 46.

THERE was a certain nobleman, whose son was
sick at Capernaum. When he heard that Jesus
was come out of Judea into Galilee, he went unto
him, and besought him that he would come down,
and heal his son; for he was at the point of death.
Then said Jesus unto him, Except ye see signs and
wonders, ye will not believe. The nobleman saith
unto him, Sir, come down ere my child die. Jesus
saith unto him, Go thy way, thy son liveth. And

the man believed the word that Jesus had spoken unto him, and he went his way. And as he was now going down, his servants met him, and told him, saying, Thy son liveth. Then inquired he of them the hour when he began to amend. And they said unto him, Yesterday, at the seventh hour, the fever left him. So the father knew that it was at the same hour in the which Jesus said unto him, Thy son liveth. And himself believed, and his whole house. This is again the second miracle that Jesus did, when he was come out of Judea into Galilee.

THE EPISTLE.

Ephes. vi.· 10.

M Y brethren, be strong in the Lord, and in the power of his might. Put on the whole armor of God, that ye may be able to stand against the wiles of the devil. For we wrestle not against flesh and blood, but against principalities, against powers, against the rulers of the darkness of this world, against spiritual wickedness in high places. Wherefore take unto you the whole armor of God, that ye may be able to withstand in the evil day, and having done all, to stand. Stand therefore, having your loins girt about with truth, and having on the breastplate of righteousness, and your feet shod with the preparation of the gospel of peace; above all taking the shield of faith, wherewith ye shall be able to quench all the fiery darts of the wicked. And take the helmet of salvation, and the sword of the Spirit, which is the word of God; praying always with all prayer and supplication in the spirit, and watching thereunto with all perseverance and supplication for all saints ; and for me, that utterance may be given unto me that I may open my mouth boldly, to make known the mystery of the gospel ; for which I am an ambassador in bonds ; that therein I may speak boldly, as I ought to speak.

Twenty-third Sunday after Whitsunday.

THE COLLECT.

ᴛ ORD, we beseech thee to keep thy household
  ⁻ the Church in continual godliness ; that through thy protection it may be free from all adversities, and devoutly given to serve thee in good works, to the glory of thy name, through Jesus Christ our Lord. *Amen.*

THE GOSPEL.

St. Matt. xviii. 21.

ᴘETER said unto Jesus, Lord, how oft shall my
  brother sin against me, and I forgive him ? till seven times ?   Jesus saith unto him, I say not unto thee, Until seven times ; but, Until seventy times seven.   Therefore is the kingdom of heaven likened unto a certain king, who would take account of his servants.   And when he had begun to reckon, one was brought unto him, who owed him ten thousand talents.   But forasmuch as he had not to pay, his lord commanded him to be sold, and his wife and

children, and all that he had, and payment to be made. The servant therefore fell down and worshipped him, saying, Lord, have patience with me, and I will pay thee all. Then the lord of that servant was moved with compassion, and loosed him, and forgave him the debt. But the same servant went out, and found one of his fellow-servants, who owed him an hundred pence ; and he laid hands on him, and took him by the throat, saying, Pay me that thou owest. And his fellow-servant fell down at his feet, and besought him, saying, Have patience with me, and I will pay thee all. And he would not ; but went and cast him into prison, till he should pay the debt. So when his fellow-servants saw what was done, they were very sorry, and came and told unto their lord all that was done. Then his lord, after that he had called him, said unto him, O thou wicked servant, I forgave thee all that debt, because thou desiredst me ; shouldest not thou also have had compassion on thy fellow-servant, even as I had pity on thee? And his lord was wroth, and delivered him to the tormentors, till he should pay all that was due unto him. So likewise shall my heavenly Father do also unto you, if ye from your hearts forgive not every one his brother their trespasses.

THE EPISTLE.

Phil. i. 3.

I THANK my God upon every remembrance of you, always, in every prayer of mine for you all, making request with joy, for your fellowship in the gospel, from the first day until now ; being confident of this very thing, that he who hath begun a good work in you, will perform it until the day of Jesus Christ ; even as it is meet for me to think this of you all, because I have you in my heart, inasmuch as both in my bonds, and in the defence and confirmation of the gospel, ye all are partakers of my grace. For God is my record, how greatly I long after you all in the affections of Jesus Christ. And this I pray, that your love may abound yet more and more in knowledge, and in all judgment ; that ye may approve things that are excellent ; that ye may be sincere and without offence till the day of Christ ; being filled with the fruits of righteousness, which are by Jesus Christ, unto the glory and praise of God.

The Twenty-fourth Sunday after Whitsunday.

THE COLLECT.

O GOD, our refuge and strength, who art the author of all godliness ; be ready, we beseech thee, to hear the devout prayers of thy Church ; and grant that those things which we ask faithfully, we may obtain effectually, through Jesus Christ our Lord. *Amen.*

THE GOSPEL.

St. Matt. xxii. 15.

T HEN went the Pharisees, and took counsel how they might entangle him in his talk. And they sent out unto him their disciples with the Herodians, saying, Master, we know that thou art true, and teachest the way of God in truth, neither carest thou for any man; for thou regardest not the person of men. Tell us therefore, what thinkest thou? is it lawful to give tribute unto Cæsar, or not? But Jesus perceived their wickedness, and said, Why tempt ye me, ye hypocrites? show me the tribute money. And they brought unto him a penny. And he saith unto them, Whose is this image and superscription? They say unto him, Cæsar's. Then saith he unto them, Render therefore unto Cæsar, the things which are Cæsar's, and unto God, the things that are God's. When they had heard these words, they marvelled, and left him, and went their way.

THE EPISTLE.

St. Jude 17.

BELOVED, remember ye the words which were spoken before of the apostles of our Lord Jesus Christ; how that they told you there should be mockers in the last time, who should walk after their own ungodly lusts. These be they who separate themselves, sensual, having not the Spirit. But ye, beloved, building up yourselves on your most holy faith, praying in the Holy Ghost, keep yourselves in the love of God, looking for the mercy of our Lord Jesus Christ unto eternal life. And of some have compassion, making a difference;

and others save with fear, pulling them out of the fire ; hating even the garment spotted by the flesh. Now unto him that is able to keep you from falling, and to present you faultless before the presence of his glory with exceeding joy, to the only wise God our Saviour, be glory and majesty, dominion and power, both now and ever. Amen.

The Twenty-fifth Sunday after Whitsunday.

THE COLLECT.

( ) LORD, we beseech thee, absolve thy people from their offences ; that through thy bountiful goodness we may all be delivered from the bands of those sins which by our frailty we have committed, and be brought into the glorious liberty of the children of God. Grant this, O heavenly Father, for thine infinite mercy's sake in Jesus Christ our Saviour. *Amen.*

THE GOSPEL.

St. Matt. ix. 18.

\ \ 'HILE Jesus spake these things unto John's disciples, behold, there came a certain ruler, and worshipped him, saying, My daughter is even now dead ; but come and lay thy hand upon her, and she shall live. And Jesus arose and followed him, and so did his disciples. And behold, a woman who was diseased with an issue of blood twelve years, came behind him, and touched the hem of his garment; for she said within herself, If I may but touch his garment, I shall be whole. But Jesus turned him about, and when he saw her, he said, Daughter, be of good comfort, thy faith hath made thee whole. And the woman was made whole from that hour. And when Jesus came into the ruler's house, and saw the minstrels and the people making a noise, he said unto them, Give place; for the maid is not dead, but sleepeth. And they laughed him to scorn. But when the people were put forth, he went in, and took her by the hand, and the maid arose. And the fame hereof went abroad into all that land.

THE EPISTLE.

Coloss. i. 3.

WE give thanks to God and the Father of our Lord Jesus Christ, praying always for you; since we heard of your faith in Christ Jesus, and of the love which you have to all the saints; for the hope which is laid up for you in heaven, whereof ye heard before in the word of the truth of the gospel, which is come unto you, as it is in all the world, and bringeth forth fruit, as it doth also in you, since the day ye heard of it, and knew the grace of God in truth; as ye also learned of Epaphras our dear fellow servant, who is for you a faithful minister of Christ; who also declared unto us your love in the Spirit. For this cause we also, since the day we heard it, do not cease to pray for you, and to desire that ye might be filled with the knowledge of his will, in all wisdom and spiritual understanding ; that ye might walk worthy of the Lord unto all pleasing, being fruitful in every good work, and increasing in the knowledge of God ; strengthened with all might according to his glorious power, unto all patience and long-suffering, with joyfulness ; giving thanks unto the Father, who hath made us meet to be partakers of the inheritance of the saints in light ; who hath delivered us from the power of darkness, and hath translated us into the kingdom of his dear Son.

The Twenty-sixth Sunday after Whitsunday

THE COLLECT.

O LORD, we beseech thee to encourage the hearts of thy faithful people, that they, always relying on thy power, and trusting in thy grace, may bring forth plenteously the fruit of good works, and of thee be plenteously rewarded, both in the world which now is, and that which is to come, through Jesus Christ our Lord. *Amen.*

THE GOSPEL.

St. John x. 22.

A ND it was at Jerusalem the feast of the dedication, and it was winter. And Jesus walked in the temple in Solomon's porch. Then came the

Jews round about him, and said unto him, How long dost thou make us to doubt? If thou be the Christ, tell us plainly. Jesus answered them, I told you, and ye believed not. The works that I do in my Father's name, they bear witness of me. But ye believe not; because ye are not of my sheep, as I said unto you. My sheep hear my voice, and I know them, and they follow me; and I give unto them eternal life; and they shall never perish, neither shall any man pluck them out of my hand. My Father, who gave them me, is greater than all; and no man is able to pluck them out of my Father's hand.

FOR THE EPISTLE.

Jer. xxiii. 5.

BEHOLD, the days come, saith the Lord, that I will raise unto David a righteous branch, and a king shall reign and prosper, and shall execute judgment and justice on the earth. In his days Judah shall be saved, and Israel shall dwell safely; and this is his name whereby he shall be called, THE LORD OUR RIGHTEOUSNESS. Therefore behold, the days come, saith the Lord, that they shall no more say, The Lord liveth who brought up the children of Israel out of the land of Egypt; but, The Lord liveth who brought up, and who led the seed of the house of Israel out of the north country, and from all countries whither I had driven them; and they shall dwell in their own land.

If there be any more Sundays before Advent Sunday, the Service of some of those Sundays which were omitted after the Epiphany, shall be used. And if there be fewer, the overplus may be omitted; provided that this last Collect, Gospel, and Epistle, shall always be read upon the Sunday next before

SELECTIONS FROM SAINTS' DAYS.

DECEMBER 26.

THE COLLECT.

GRANT, O Lord, that in all our sufferings here upon earth, for the testimony of thy truth, we may steadfastly look up to heaven, and by faith behold the glory that shall be revealed; and being filled with the Holy Spirit, may learn to love and bless our persecutors, by the example of the first martyr, Saint Stephen, who cried for his murderers to thee, and commended his spirit into the hands of the blessed Jesus, who standeth at the right hand of God, to succor all those who suffer for him, our only Mediator and Advocate. *Amen.*

THE GOSPEL.

St. Matt. xxiii. 34.

BEHOLD I send unto you prophets, and wise men, and scribes; and some of them ye shall kill and crucify; and some of them shall ye scourge in your synagogues, and persecute them from city to city ; that upon you may come all the righteous blood shed upon the earth, from the blood of righteous Abel unto the blood of Zacharias, son of Barachias, whom ye slew between the temple and the altar. Verily I say unto you, All these things shall come upon this generation. O Jerusalem, Jerusalem, thou that killest the prophets, and stonest them who are sent unto thee, how often would I have gathered thy children together, even as a hen gathereth her chickens under her wings, and ye would not ! Behold, your house is left unto you desolate. For I say unto you, Ye shall not see me henceforth, till ye shall say, Blessed is he that cometh in the name of the Lord.

FOR THE EPISTLE.

Acts vii. 55.

STEPHEN, being full of the Holy Ghost, looked up steadfastly into heaven, and saw the glory of God, and Jesus standing on the right hand of God, and said, Behold, I see the heavens opened, and the Son of Man standing on the right hand of God. Then they cried out with a loud voice, and stopped their ears, and ran upon him with one accord, and cast him out of the city, and stoned him ; and the witnesses laid down their clothes at a young man's feet, whose name was Saul. And they stoned Stephen, calling out, and saying, Lord Jesus, receive my spirit. And he kneeled down, and cried with a loud voice, Lord, lay not this sin to their charge. And when he had said this, he fell asleep.

The Innocents' Day.

DECEMBER 28.

THE COLLECT.

O ALMIGHTY God, who out of the mouths of babes and sucklings hast ordained strength, and madest infants to glorify thee by their deaths; mortify and kill all vices in us, and so strengthen us by thy grace, that by the innocency of our lives and constancy of our faith even unto death, we may glorify thy holy name, through Jesus Christ our Lord. *Amen.*

THE GOSPEL.

St. Matt. ii. 13.

THE angel of the Lord appeareth to Joseph in a dream, saying, Arise, and take the young child and his mother, and flee into Egypt, and be thou there until I bring thee word; for Herod will seek the young child to destroy him. When he arose, he took the young child and his mother by night, and departed into Egypt; and was there until the death of Herod; that it might be fulfilled which was spoken of the Lord by the prophet, saying, Out of Egypt have I called my son. Then Herod, when he saw that he was mocked of the wise men, was exceeding wroth, and sent forth, and slew all the children that were in Bethlehem, and in all the coasts thereof, from two years old and under, according to the time which he had diligently inquired of the wise men. Then was fulfilled that which was spoken by Jeremy the prophet, saying, In Rama was there a voice heard, lamentation, and weeping, and great mourning, Rachel weeping for her children, and would not be comforted, because they are not.

FOR THE EPISTLE.

Rev. xiv. 1.

ᴵ LOOKED, and lo, a Lamb stood on the mount Sion, and with him a hundred forty and four thousand, having his Father's name written in their foreheads. And I heard a voice from heaven as the voice of many waters, and as the voice of a great thunder; and I heard the voice of harpers harping with their harps. And they sung as it were a new song before the throne, and before the four beasts and the elders; and no man could learn that song but the hundred and forty and four thousand, which were redeemed from the earth. These are they which were not defiled with women; for they are virgins. These are they which follow the Lamb whithersoever he goeth. These were redeemed from among men, being the first-fruits unto God and to the Lamb. And in their mouth was found no guile; for they are without fault before the throne of God.

The Conversion of Saint Paul.

JANUARY 25.

THE COLLECT.

Ο GOD, who, through the preaching of the blessed apostle Saint Paul, hast caused the light of the Gospel to shine throughout the world; grant, we beseech thee, that we, having his wonderful conversion in remembrance, may show forth our thankfulness unto thee for the same, by following the holy doctrine which he taught, through Jesus Christ our Lord. *Amen.*

THE GOSPEL.

St. Matt. xix. 27.

PETER answered, and said unto Jesus, Behold, we have forsaken all, and followed thee; what shall we have therefore? And Jesus said unto them, Verily I say unto you, That ye who have followed me, in the regeneration, when the Son of Man shall sit in the throne of his glory, ye also shall sit upon twelve thrones, judging the twelve tribes of Israel. And every one that hath forsaken houses, or brethren, or sisters, or father, or mother, or wife, or children, or lands, for my name's sake, shall receive a hundred-fold, and shall inherit everlasting life. But many that are first shall be last, and the last shall be first.

FOR THE EPISTLE.

Acts ix. 1.

AND Saul, yet breathing out threatenings and slaughter against the disciples of the Lord, went unto the high-priest, and desired of him letters to Damascus to the synagogues, that if he found any of this way, whether they were men or women, he might bring them bound unto Jerusalem. And as he journeyed, he came near Damascus; and suddenly there shined round about him a light from heaven; and he fell to the earth, and heard a voice saying unto him, Saul, Saul, why persecutest thou me? And he said, Who art thou, Lord? And the Lord said, I am Jesus whom thou persecutest. It is hard for thee to kick against the pricks. And he, trembling and astonished, said, Lord, what wilt thou have me to do? And the Lord said unto him, Arise, and go into the city, and it shall be told thee what thou must do. And the men who journeyed with him stood speechless, hearing a voice, but seeing no man. And Saul arose from the earth; and when his eyes were opened, he saw no man; but they led him by the hand, and brought him into Damascus. And he was three days without sight, and neither did eat nor drink. And there was a certain disciple at Damascus, named Ananias; and to him said the Lord in a vision, Ananias. And he said, Behold, I am here, Lord. And the Lord said unto him, Arise, and go into the street, which is called Straight, and inquire in the house of Judas for one called Saul of Tarsus; for, behold, he prayeth, and hath seen in a vision a man named Ananias coming in, and putting his hand on him, that he might receive his sight. Then Ananias answered, Lord, I have heard by many of this man, how much evil he hath done to thy saints at Jerusalem; and here he hath authority from the chief priests to bind all that call on thy name. But the Lord said unto him, Go thy way; for he is a chosen vessel unto me, to bear my name before the Gentiles, and kings, and the children of Israel : for I will show him how great things he must suffer for my name's sake. And Ananias went his way, and entered into the house ; and putting his hands on him, said, Brother Saul, the Lord, even Jesus, that appeared unto thee in the way as thou camest, hath sent me, that thou mightest receive thy sight, and be filled with the Holy Ghost. And immediately there fell from his eyes as it had been scales ; and he received sight forthwith, and arose, and was baptized. And when he had received meat, he was strengthened. Then was Saul certain days with the disciples, who were at Damascus. And straightway he preached Christ in the synagogues, that he is the Son of God. But all who heard him were amazed, and said, Is not this he who destroyed them who called on this name in Jerusalem, and came hither for that intent, that he might bring them bound unto the chief priests? But Saul increased the more in strength, and confounded the Jews who dwelt at Damascus, proving that this is very Christ.

JUNE 24.

THE COLLECT. ·

A LMIGHTY God, by whose providence thy servant John Baptist was wonderfully born, and sent to prepare the way of thy Son, our Saviour, by preaching repentance ; make us so to follow his doctrine and holy life, that we may truly repent according to his preaching ; and, after his example, constantly speak the truth, boldly rebuke vice, and patiently suffer for the truth's sake ; through Jesus Christ our Lord. *Amen.*

THE GOSPEL.

St. Luke i. 57.

NOW Elisabeth's full time came, that she should be delivered ; and she brought forth a son. And her neighbors and her cousins heard how the Lord had showed great mercy upon her ; and they rejoiced with her. And it came to pass, that on the eighth day they came to circumcise the child ; and they called him Zacharias, after the name of his father. And his mother answered and said, Not so, but he shall be called John. And they said unto her, There is none of thy kindred that is called by this name. And they made signs to his father, how he would have him called. And he asked for a writing-table, and wrote, saying, His name is John. And they marvelled all. And his mouth was opened immediately, and his tongue loosed, and he spake, and praised God. And fear came on all who dwelt round about them ; and all these sayings were noised abroad throughout all the hill-country of Judea. And all they who heard them laid them up in their hearts, saying, What manner of child shall this be ! And the hand of the Lord was with him. And his father Zacharias was filled with the Holy Ghost, and prophesied, saying, Blessed be the Lord God of

Israel; for he hath visited and redeemed his people, and hath raised up a horn of salvation for us in the house of his servant David; as he spake by the mouth of his holy prophets, who have been since the world began; that we should be saved from our enemies, and from the hand of all that hate us; to perform the mercy promised to our fathers, and to remember his holy covenant, the oath which he sware to our father Abraham, that he would grant unto us, that we, being delivered out of the hand of our enemies, might serve him without fear, in holiness and righteousness before him, all the days of our life. And thou, child, shalt be called the Prophet of the Highest; for thou shalt go before the face of the Lord to prepare his ways; to give knowledge of salvation unto his people, by the remission of their sins, through the tender mercy of our God, whereby the day-spring from on high hath visited us, to give light to them that sit in darkness and in the shadow of death, to guide our feet into the way of peace. And the child grew, and waxed strong in spirit, and was in the deserts, till the day of his showing unto Israel.

FOR THE EPISTLE.

Isaiah xl. I.

COMFORT ye, comfort ye my people, saith your God. Speak ye comfortably to Jerusalem, and cry unto her, that her warfare is accomplished, that her iniquity is pardoned; for she hath received of the Lord's hand double for all her sins. The voice of him that crieth in the wilderness, Prepare ye the way of the Lord, make straight in the desert a highway for our God. Every valley shall be exalted, and every mountain and hill shall be made low ; and the crooked shall be made straight, and the rough places plain. And the glory of the Lord shall be revealed, and all flesh shall see it together: for the mouth of the Lord hath spoken it. The voice said, Cry. And he said, What shall I cry? All flesh is grass, and all the goodliness thereof is as the flower of the field ; the grass withereth, the flower fadeth ; because the spirit of the Lord bloweth upon it ; surely the people is grass. The grass withereth, the flower fadeth ; but the word of our God shall stand forever. O Zion, that bringest good tidings, get thee up into the high mountain ; O Jerusalem, that bringest good tidings, lift up thy voice with strength ; lift it up, be not afraid ; say unto the cities of Judah, Behold your God ! Behold, the Lord God will come with strong hand, and his arm shall rule for him ; behold, his reward is with him, and his work before him. He shall feed his flock like a shepherd ; he shall gather the lambs with his arm, and carry them in his bosom, and shall gently lead those that are with young.

All Saints' Day.

NOVEMBER 1.

THE COLLECT.

O ALMIGHTY God, who hast knit together thine elect, in one communion and fellowship, in the mystical body of thy Son Christ our Lord; grant us grace so to follow thy blessed Saints in all virtuous and godly living, that we may come to those unspeakable joys, which thou hast prepared for those who unfeignedly love thee, through Jesus Christ our Lord. *Amen.*

THE GOSPEL.

St. Matt. v. 1.

JESUS, seeing the multitudes, went up into a mountain; and when he was set, his disciples came unto him. And he opened his mouth, and taught them, saying, Blessed are the poor in spirit; for theirs is the kingdom of heaven. Blessed are they that mourn; for they shall be comforted. Blessed are the meek; for they shall inherit the earth. Blessed are they who do hunger and thirst after righteousness; for they shall be filled. Blessed are the merciful; for they shall obtain mercy. Blessed are the pure in heart; for they shall see God. Blessed are the peacemakers; for they shall be called the children of God. Blessed are they who are persecuted for righteousness' sake; for theirs is the kingdom of heaven. Blessed are ye, when men shall revile you, and persecute you, and shall say all manner of evil against you falsely, for my sake. Rejoice, and be exceeding glad; for great is your reward in heaven; for so persecuted they the prophets which were before you.

Rev. vii. 2.

AND I saw another angel ascending from the east, having the seal of the living God ; and he cried with a loud voice to the four angels, to whom it was given to hurt the earth and the sea, saying, Hurt not the earth, neither the sea, nor the trees, till we have sealed the servants of our God in their foreheads. And I heard the number of them who were sealed ; and there were sealed a hundred and forty and four thousand of all the tribes of the children of Israel. After this I beheld, and, lo, a great multitude, which no man could number, of all nations, and kindreds, and people, and tongues, stood before the throne, and before the Lamb, clothed with white robes, and palms in their hands ; and cried with a loud voice, saying, Salvation to our God who sitteth upon the throne, and unto the Lamb ! And all the angels stood round about the throne, and about the elders and the four beasts, and fell before the throne on their faces, and worshipped God, saying, Amen ; blessing, and glory, and wisdom, and thanksgiving, and honor, and power, and might, be unto our God for ever and ever. Amen. And one of the elders answered, saying unto me, What are these who are arrayed in white robes? and whence came they ? And I said unto him, Sir, thou knowest. And he said to me, These are they who came out of great tribulation, and have washed their robes, and made them white in the blood of the Lamb. Therefore are they before the throne of God, and serve him day and night in his temple; and he that sitteth on the throne shall dwell among them. They shall hunger no more, neither thirst any more; neither shall the sun light on them, nor any heat. For the Lamb who is in the midst of the throne shall feed them, and shall lead them unto living fountains of waters; and God shall wipe away all tears from their eyes.

END OF **THE** COLLECTS, GOSPELS, AND EPISTLES.

COLLECTS AND PRAYERS,

TO BE USED BEFORE OR AFTER SERMON.

The following Collects and Prayers are adapted to various subjects of discourse, and are arranged for the sake of convenience under several heads. The Minister is at liberty to use, instead of these Forms, that which is most fitted.

GENERAL COLLECTS.

O GOD, the eternal source of wisdom and purity, from whom all good counsels, all holy desires, and all just works do proceed ; we offer up our humble prayers unto thee, beseeching thee to enlighten our minds, and sanctify our hearts by thy heavenly truth. What we know not, teach thou us ; whatever is amiss in us, dispose us to reform ; whatever in us is good, assist us to carry forwards to perfection ; which we ask in the name and as disciples of Jesus Christ our Lord. *Amen.*

ALMIGHTY God, unto whom all hearts are open, all desires known, and from whom no secrets are hid ; cleanse the thoughts of our hearts by the inspiration of thy Holy Spirit, that we may perfectly love thee, and worthily magnify thy holy name, through Christ our Lord. *Amen.*

O ALMIGHTY Lord, and everlasting God, vouchsafe, we beseech thee, to direct, sanctify, and govern both our hearts and bodies, in the ways of thy laws, and in the works of thy commandments ; that through thy most mighty protection, both here and ever, we may be preserved in body and soul, through our Lord and Saviour Jesus. Christ. *Amen.*

ASSIST us, O Lord, in all our doings with thy most gracious favor, and further us with thy continual help, that in all our works begun, continued, and ended in thee, we may glorify thy holy name, and finally by thy mercy obtain everlasting life, through Jesus Christ our Lord. *Amen.*

ALMIGHTY God, the fountain of all wisdom, who knowest our necessities before we ask, and our ignorance in asking ; we beseech thee to have compassion upon our infirmities ; and those things which for our unworthiness we dare not, and for our blindness we cannot ask, vouchsafe to give us, for the sake of thine infinite mercy in Jesus Christ our Lord. *Amen.*

ASSIST us mercifully, O Lord, in these our supplications and prayers, and dispose the way of thy servants toward the attainment of everlasting salvation ; that among all the changes and chances of this mortal life, they may ever be defended by thy most gracious and ready help, through Jesus Christ our Lord. *Amen.*

GRANT, we beseech thee, Almighty God, that the words which we have heard this day with our outward ears, may, through thy grace, be so grafted inwardly in our hearts, that they may bring forth in us the fruit of good living, to the honor and praise of thy name, through Jesus Christ our Lord. *Amen.*

WE offer these our prayers unto thee, O God of mercy, with a humble confidence in thine unerring wisdom and perfect goodness. We beseech thee to overlook the imperfection, and to accept the sincerity of our devotions. Of thy great mercy, grant unto us such things as shall be good for us, though we may neglect to pray for them ; and deny us such things as would be hurtful to us, though we should earnestly desire them. Order all things for us, as seemeth right in thy sight ; and do us good, both now and forevermore, according to thy promises declared unto us by Jesus Christ our Lord. *Amen.*

ALMIGHTY God, who hast promised to hear the petitions of those who ask in thy Son's name ; we beseech thee mercifully to incline thine ears to us who have made now our prayers and supplications unto thee ; and grant that those things which we have faithfully asked according to thy will, may effectually be obtained, to the relief of our necessity, and to the setting forth of thy glory, through Jesus Christ our Lord. *Amen.*

ALMIGHTY God, giver of all temporal and spiritual good, grant unto us thy grace, we beseech thee, so to speak, so to hear, and so to learn, that the word of Christ may dwell in us richly in all wisdom, that our minds may be enlightened, our fears banished, our faith confirmed, and our way directed unto eternal life, through Jesus Christ our Lord. *Amen.*

O LIFE–GIVING Lord, and Bestower of all good things, who hast given unto men the blessed hope of everlasting life in our Lord Jesus Christ ; grant us to perform this service unto thee in holiness, that we may enjoy the blessedness to come ; and being evermore guarded by thy power, and guided into the light of truth, may continually render unto thee all glory and thanksgiving, through our Saviour Jesus Christ. *Amen.*

STRETCH forth, O Lord, thy mercy over thy servants, even the right hand of heavenly help ; that they may seek thee with their whole heart, and obtain what they rightly ask for ; through Christ our Lord. *Amen.*

WE beseech thee, O Lord, make thy servants alway to join together in seeking thee with their whole heart, to serve thee with submissive mind, humbly to implore thy mercy, and perpetually to rejoice in thy blessings; through Jesus Christ our Lord. *Amen.*

O GOD, the life of the faithful, the joy of the righteous, mercifully receive the prayers of thy suppliants, that the souls which thirst for thy promises may evermore be filled from thine abundance; through Jesus Christ our Lord. *Amen.*

TRUST AND SUBMISSION.

O GOD, the high and holy One who inhabitest eternity, we pray thee so to enlighten and strengthen us, that we may make thee our refuge and trust, our confidence and joy; let us rest our hearts and our hopes upon thee, through all the scenes and trials of this our short and uncertain life; that, when heaven and earth shall pass away, we may be found in thine eternal dwelling-place, rendering to thee all power, and glory, and praise, through Jesus Christ, for ever and ever. *Amen.*

O THOU, who alone art infinite in knowledge and wisdom, though thy ways are past our finding out, we are assured that they are just and right; and we would therefore submit all our desires to thy will, all our actions to thy government, and all our concerns to thy disposal; and in humility and self-abasement we would now and at all times offer up our prayers to thee, the only wise

God, through our Lord and Saviour Jesus Christ. *Amen.*

O THOU, who art the only living and true God unchangeable in thy nature, universal in thy presence, and uncontrollable in thy dominion, we pray that we may have worthy conceptions of thy greatness; that we may entertain a deep and lasting sense of thy goodness ; that we may fear thee as our Master, and honor thee as our Father ; and that, when we meet thee as our Judge, we may be accepted and pardoned, through Jesus Christ our Lord. *Amen.*

PEACE.

O GOD, who art Peace everlasting, whose chosen reward is the gift of peace, and who hast taught us that the peacemakers are thy children, pour thy sweet peace into our souls, that everything discordant may utterly vanish, and all that makes for peace be sweet to us forever. *Amen.*

THANKFULNESS.

O GOD, who chastisest us in thy love, and refreshest us amid thy chastening ; grant that for both we may ever be able to give thee thanks ; through Jesus Christ our Lord. *Amen.*

RELIGIOUS KNOWLEDGE.

GOD of wisdom and truth, from whom proceed all the treasures of knowledge, and who by thy Spirit hast given us understanding ; we thank thee that thou hast enabled us to know thee in thy works, to study thy word, and to hold communion with thee, the Father of our spirits. May we at all times be sensible of our connection with thee, and above all things fear to degrade the nature which thou hast given us. Mercifully assist our weakness; reclaim us from our errors; enlighten our minds; purify our hearts, and give us true repentance for our sins, through Jesus Christ our Lord. *Amen.*

O GOD, the Author of nature, whose energy sustains, whose presence animates, and whose gracious influence blesses the universe; assist us, we beseech thee, to form worthy apprehensions of thy nature and character, and, as far as our faculties will permit, to become acquainted with thy perfections and providence. And let our conceptions of thee produce in us the sentiments of veneration, gratitude, and submission, and lead us to a diligent imitation of thy moral perfections, and a constant obedience to thy laws, through Jesus Christ our Lord. *Amen.*

GRANT unto us, O most merciful Father, the spirit of wisdom and knowledge. Teach us to judge aright concerning thee, our Maker, and the duties which thou requirest of us; and let all religious truths deeply impress our hearts, and have a lasting influence on our behavior. Assist us to subdue every vicious affection, and to withstand every temptation; that we may manifest the sincerity of our repentance by the steadfastness of our obedience ; and that, not being weary of well-doing, we may finally obtain everlasting life, through Jesus Christ our Lord. *Amen.*

O GOD, who givest understanding to man, and instructest him out of thy law, grant unto us thy servants such knowledge as may best enable us to do good, and a sincere disposition rightly to improve the knowledge we possess. Preserve in us a constant remembrance of thine all-seeing eye. Deliver us from irregular desires, vain hopes, and weak fears ; and prepare us, by innocence and purity of manners, and a steadfast faith in thee, for all the events of this mortal life, and for our departure out of this world. By the constant exercise of piety, righteousness, and mercy ; by an humble, resigned, and contented spirit, may we become fitted for the society of the just made perfect in thine heavenly kingdom ; which we ask in the name, and as disciples, of Jesus Christ our Lord. *Amen.*

DIVINE ASSISTANCE.

O GOD, who art ever more ready to hear than we are to pray, and who hast promised the assistance of thy Holy Spirit to those who truly seek it, we humbly beseech thee to fulfil thy gracious promise to us thy servants, and grant us that light and help, without which we know nothing, and can do nothing ; O guide us by thy counsel, defend us by thy might, purify us by thy Spirit, and keep us in thy fear and love continually; and thine shall be the honor, and the glory, and the praise, through Jesus Christ our Lord. *Amen.*

WE humbly beseech thee, O Father, to assist and direct us in the attainment of the happiness for which thou hast designed us. Lift up the light of thy countenance upon us, to illuminate our minds with thy heavenly truth, that, being purged from error, prejudice, and vice, our desires and passions may be under the continual guidance of reason, and our actions may be conformed to thy most holy laws, through Jesus Christ our Lord. *Amen.*

O GOD, who bestowest thy mercy at all times on them that love thee, and in no place art distant from those that serve thee; direct the way of thy servants in thy will, that having thee for their Protector and Guide, they may walk without stumbling in the paths of righteousness; through Jesus Christ our Lord. *Amen.*

WE beseech thee, O Lord, mercifully to correct our wanderings, and by the guiding radiance of thy compassion to bring us to the salutary vision of thy truth, through Jesus Christ our Lord. *Amen.*

GUIDANCE.

BE thou, O Lord, our protection, who art our redemption; direct our minds by thy gracious presence, and watch over our paths with guiding love ; that among the snares which lie hidden in the path wherein we walk, we may so pass onward with hearts fixed on thee, that by the track of faith we may come to be where thou wouldest have us, through Christ our Lord. *Amen.*

PERSEVERANCE.

( ) GOD, who hast willed that the gate of mercy should stand open to the faithful ; look on us, and have mercy on us ; that we who by thy grace are following the path of thy will, may never turn aside from the ways of life ; through Jesus Christ our Lord. *Amen.*

O GOD, who bestowest this upon us by thy grace, that we should be made righteous instead of ungodly, blessed instead of miserable ; be present to thine own works, be present to thine own gifts ; that they in whom dwells a justifying faith may not lack a strong perseverance ; through Jesus Christ our Lord. *Amen.*

THE BIBLE.

( ) GOD, who in times past didst speak to the fathers by the prophets, and in these last days to us by thy Son ; we thank thee for the volume of thy holy word ; for the plain and ample directions it contains ; for the sublime instructions it affords ; for the consolations and hopes it presents to the penitent, the afflicted, and the dying ; for the immortal life it reveals to man ; for the eternal glory and happiness it promises to those who love, and strive to obey thee. May we be enabled, by the light and assistance which it gives to our ignorance and frailty, to order our steps aright; to keep thy laws and ordinances blameless ; and steadily to pursue that path of virtue and true holiness which leads to everlasting life. And this we humbly beg in the name of our Saviour Jesus Christ. *Amen.*

UNITY.

O GOD, the Father of our Lord Jesus Christ, our only Saviour, the Prince of Peace ; take away from us, we beseech thee, all bitter prejudice and uncharitableness, and whatsoever else may hinder us from godly union and concord ; that as there is but one body, and one spirit, and one hope of our calling, one Lord, one faith, one baptism, one God and Father of us all, so we may henceforth be all of one heart, and of one soul, united in one holy bond of truth and peace, of faith and charity, and may with one mind and one mouth glorify thee, through Jesus Christ our Lord. *Amen.*

CHRIST AND CHRISTIANITY.

WE thank thee, O Father in heaven, for the blessed Gospel of thy Son Jesus Christ ; for the light it sheds on thy nature, character, and providence, on the path of our duty, and on the future world. May this glorious light shine into our hearts, and cheer and sustain us, and lead us through the scenes and trials of this life, to the endless felicities of thy kingdom above. Which we ask in the name of our Saviour Jesus Christ. *Amen.*

A LMIGHTY and most merciful God, who wouldest have all men to be saved, and come to the knowledge of thy truth ; regard in mercy, we beseech thee, those parts of the earth where the Gospel is not known, and bring them to the knowledge, obedience, and love of the religion of thy dear Son. We also pray for the whole Christian world, that all who profess the faith of the Gospel may hold it in unity of spirit, in the bond of peace, and in holiness of life. We entreat thee, more particularly, to assist us to govern our hearts by the blessed law of charity, that, together with all our fellow-Christians, we may continually become here on earth more worthy of the glorious society in heaven, where charity never faileth ; which we beg in the name of Jesus Christ, the head of all things to the Church, through whom we ascribe to thee blessing and praise, for ever and ever. *Amen.*

O THOU God and Father of our Lord Jesus Christ, give us grace, we humbly beseech thee, to act in every relation and condition of life as thy children, disciples of thy Son, and members of the general family of mankind. May we love one another with pure hearts fervently ; and heartily unite our endeavors to promote each other's happiness ; that, in this life, we may experience how good and how pleasant it is for brethren to dwell together in unity ; and that we may be prepared for an eternal abode in the regions of endless peace and joy, through thine infinite mercy, declared unto us by Jesus Christ our Lord. *Amen.*

ALMIGHTY God, who hast given unto us thy Son Jesus Christ from heaven, give unto us also thy quickening grace, that we may be disposed to hear, and enabled to obey him ; that we may become his disciples, not in name only, but in deed ; that we may surrender to his guidance the minds which he came to enlighten, and the souls which he came to save ; and so follow him in this world, that we may reign with him in the world to come ; and thine shall be the honor and the praise, through the same Jesus Christ our Lord. *Amen.*

RESIGNATION.

O MOST gracious and merciful Father, we desire to resign ourselves and all our interests to thy disposal, in the humble hope that thy mercy will never forsake us, and that thou wilt cause all things to work together for our good. We would submit patiently to thy will under all our afflictions; and we humbly pray that we may so pass through the changes of this world, as finally to be prepared for the enjoyment of perfect and eternal happiness in the world to come, through Jesus Christ our Lord. *Amen.*

FOR THE AFFLICTED.

ALMIGHTY and everlasting God, the Comfort of the sad, the Strength of the suffering, let the prayers of those that cry out of any tribulation come unto thee; that all may rejoice to find that thy mercy is present with them in their afflictions; through Christ our Lord. *Amen.*

TEMPTATION.

LMIGHTY and most merciful God, it is our earnest desire and humble prayer that thou wouldest enable us to resist and overcome temptation. May neither the allurements of vicious pleasure, nor the difficulties of a virtuous course, deter us from the practice of our duty. To whatever trials our integrity may be exposed, may we have strength to preserve it uncorrupted; that, having endured temptation, we may receive the crown of eternal life, which thou hast promised to the righteous by Jesus Christ our Lord. *Amen.*

ROTECT, O Lord, thy suppliants, support their weakness, and wash away their earthly stains; and while they walk amid the darkness of this mortal life, do thou ever quicken them by thy light; deliver them in thy mercy from all evils, and grant unto them to attain the height of good; through Jesus Christ our Lord. *Amen.*

O GOD, the comforter of the humble, and the strength of the faithful, be merciful to thy suppliants; that human weakness, which by itself is prone to fall, may be evermore supported by thee to stand upright; through Jesus Christ our Lord. *Amen.*

PIETY AND MORALITY.

ALMIGHTY God, give us grace, we beseech thee, to keep thee and thy commandments continually before us; to live as in thy sight; to walk in thy fear; to make ourselves the objects of thy love. May our principles of duty be firm; our regard to thy laws constant; our desire of obeying and pleasing thee, the first desire of our souls. May all that we do be done to thy glory; that when this transitory life is over, we may enter into thy joy, and continue to worship and serve thee for ever and ever in thy heavenly kingdom; which we humbly ask in the name and as disciples of Jesus Christ our Lord. *Amen.*

REPENTANCE.

ALMIGHTY and most merciful Father, who knowest our weakness, and art acquainted with every action of our lives, and every secret of our hearts; we acknowledge in thy presence our imperfections and sins, and fervently pray that thou wouldest be gracious unto us, and forgive us; and help us to forsake all that is evil, and cleave to all that is good, and to make thee and thy approbation the objects of our supreme regard; so that we fail not at last to attain that eternal happiness which thou hast promised to thy faithful servants, through thine infinite mercy in Jesus Christ our Lord. *Amen.*

FORGIVENESS.

WE beseech thee, O Lord, in thy forgiving love, turn away what we deserve for our sins, nor let our offences prevail before thee, but let thy mercy always rise up to overcome them; through Jesus Christ our Lord. *Amen.*

TIME, DEATH, AND ETERNITY.

GRANT, O Lord and Heavenly Father, that, as our days on earth are multiplied, our good resolutions may be strengthened, and our powers of resisting temptations increased. Relieve the infirmities of our minds and bodies; grant us such strength as our duties may require, and such diligence as may improve those opportunities of good that shall be afforded us. Deliver us from evil thoughts; give us true repentance for the sins of our past lives; and as we draw nearer and nearer to the grave, increase our faith, enliven our hope, extend our charity, and purify our desires; and so help us, by thy Holy Spirit, that, when it shall be thy pleasure to call us hence, we may be received to everlasting happiness, through Jesus Christ our Lord. *Amen.*

WE humbly pray thee, O Father in heaven, to guide us through the darkness of this world, to guard us from its perils, to hold us up and strengthen us when we grow weary in our mortal way, and to lead us by thy chosen paths, through time and through death, to our eternal home in thy heavenly kingdom ; which we ask in the name of Jesus Christ our Lord. *Amen.*

LORD of life and death, of all ages and all worlds, give us to know the value of our fleeting years. While we have time, let us improve it as we ought ; let us not forsake thee in life, nor fall from thee in death ; and O keep us, we entreat thee, from that second death, which must come upon the heedless and impenitent. Save us, and bring us to dwell with thee, where weakness, danger, and death shall find no room. Grant this, O Lord, for thine infinite mercy's sake, through Jesus Christ our Lord. *Amen.*

CLOSE OF PUBLIC WORSHIP.

ALMIGHTY God, we humbly thank thee for the privileges of religious worship and instruction which we have at this time enjoyed. Forgive whatever thou hast seen amiss in us, and whatever may have been said contrary to the truth and to thy holy word. Accept the sincerity of our devotions, and cause the good seed of thy word to spring up, and bear a hundred-fold in our hearts and lives. Teach us to love thee more and serve thee better, day by day ; that when our days on earth are ended, we may be received to thine eternal joy, through Jesus Christ our Lord. *Amen.*

END OF THE COLLECTS AND PRAYERS.

ANTE-COMMUNION

OR

OFFICE OF THE COMMANDMENTS.

on which the Lord's Supper is to be administered.

COLLECT FOR PURITY.

ALMIGHTY God, unto whom all hearts are open, all desires known, and from whom no secrets are hid ; cleanse the thoughts of our hearts by the inspiration of thy Holy Spirit, that we may perfectly love thee, and worthily magnify thy holy name, through Christ our Lord. *Amen.*

Minister.

GOD spake these words and said, I am the Lord thy God ; thou shalt have no other gods but me.

People. Lord, have mercy upon us, and incline our hearts to keep this law.

Min. Thou shalt not make to thyself any graven image, nor the likeness of anything that is in heaven above, or in the earth beneath, or in the water under the earth. Thou shalt not bow down to them nor worship them; for I the Lord thy God am a jealous God, and visit the sins of the fathers upon the children, unto the third and fourth generation of those who hate me, and show mercy unto thousands of those who love me and keep my commandments.

Peo. Lord, have mercy upon us, and incline our hearts to keep this law.

Min. Thou shalt not take the name of the Lord thy God in vain; for the Lord will not hold him guiltless who taketh his name in vain.

Peo. Lord, have mercy upon us, and incline our hearts to keep this law.

Min. Remember that thou keep holy the Sabbath day. Six days shalt thou labor, and do all that thou hast to do; but the seventh is the Sabbath of the Lord thy God. In it thou shalt do no manner of work, thou, and thy son, and thy daughter, thy man-servant, and thy maid-servant, thy cattle, and the stranger that is within thy gates. For in six days the Lord made heaven and earth, the sea, and all that in them is, and rested the seventh day; wherefore the Lord blessed the seventh day, and hallowed it.

Peo. Lord, have mercy upon us, and incline our hearts to keep this law.

Min. Honor thy father and thy mother; that thy days may be long in the land which the Lord thy God giveth thee.

Peo. Lord, have mercy upon us, and incline our hearts to keep this law.

Min. Thou shalt do no murder.

Peo. Lord, have mercy upon us, and incline our hearts to keep this law.

Min. Thou shalt not commit adultery.

Peo. Lord, have mercy upon us, and incline our hearts to keep this law.

Min. Thou shalt not steal.

Peo. Lord, have mercy upon us, and incline our hearts to keep this law.

Min. Thou shalt not bear false witness against thy neighbor.

Peo. Lord, have mercy upon us, and incline our hearts to keep this law.

Min. Thou shalt not covet thy neighbor's house, thou shalt not covet thy neighbor's wife, nor his servant, nor his maid, nor his ox, nor his ass, nor anything that is his.

Peo. Lord, have mercy upon us, and write all these thy laws in our hearts, we beseech thee.

HEAR also what our Saviour Christ saith : The first of all the commandments is, Hear, O Israel ; The Lord our God is one Lord : and thou shalt love the Lord thy God with all thy heart, and with all thy soul, and with all thy mind, and with all thy strength.

This is the first commandment. And the second is like, namely, this :

Thou shalt love thy neighbor as thyself.

There is none other commandment greater than these.

Ante-Communion.

The Minister shall then announce the Communion in the following words :

On Sunday next will be administered unto all who are religiously and devoutly disposed, and who love the Lord Jesus Christ in sincerity, the holy ordinance of the Lord's Supper.

Other notices may also be given at this time, and then the Hymn and Sermon shall follow as usual.

The foregoing Office may be used after the Morning or Evening Prayer, or introduced in the course of either at such place as shall seem most proper and convenient.

END OF THE OFFICE OF THE COMMANDMENTS.

ADMINISTRATION OF THE LORD'S SUPPER,

OR

HOLY COMMUNION.

Begin the Service by reading the following Sentences, or such a portion of them as may be convenient, the

LET your light so shine before men, that they may see your good works, and glorify your Father who is in heaven. *St. Matt.* v. 16.

Lay not up for yourselves treasures upon earth, where moth and rust do corrupt, and where thieves break through and steal ; but lay up for yourselves treasures in heaven, where neither moth nor rust doth corrupt, and where thieves do not break through nor steal. *St. Matt.* vi. 19, 20.

Whatsoever ye would that men should do unto you, even so do unto them ; for this is the law and the prophets. *St. Matt.* vii. 12.

Not every one who saith unto me, Lord, Lord, shall enter into the kingdom of heaven ; but he who doeth the will of my Father who is in heaven. *St. Matt.* vii. 21.

He who soweth little shall reap little; and he who soweth plenteously shall reap plenteously. Let every man do according as he is disposed in his heart; not grudgingly, or of necessity; for God loveth a cheerful giver. 2 *Cor.* ix. 6, 7.

While we have time let us do good unto all men, and especially unto those who are of the household of faith. *Gal.* vi. 10.

Godliness is great riches, if a man be content with that he hath; for we brought nothing into the world, neither mav we carry anything out. 1 *Tim.* vi. 6, 7.

Charge those who are rich in this world, that they be ready to give, and glad to distribute; laying up in store for themselves a good foundation against the time to come, that they may attain eternal life. 1 *Tim.* vi. 17, 18, 19.

God is not unrighteous, that he will forget your works and labor that proceedeth of love, which ye have showed for his name's sake, who have ministered unto the saints, and yet do minister. *Heb.* vi. 10.

To do good, and to distribute, forget not; for with such sacrifices God is well pleased. *Heb.* xiii. 16.

Whoso hath this world's good, and seeth his brother have need, and shutteth up his compassion from him, how dwelleth the love of God in him? 1 *St. John* iii. 17.

Give alms of thy goods, and never turn thy face

from any poor man ; and then the face of the Lord shall not be turned away from thee. *Tob.* iv. 7.

Be merciful after thy power. If thou hast much, give plenteously ; if thou hast little, do thy diligence gladly to give of that little ; for so gatherest thou thyself a good reward in the day of necessity. *Tob.* iv. 8, 9.

He who hath pity upon the poor lendeth unto the Lord ; and look, what he layeth out, it shall be paid him again. *Prov.* xix. 17.

Blessed is the man who provideth for the sick and needy ; the Lord shall deliver him in the time of trouble. *Psal.* xli. 1.

I have shown you how that ye ought to support the weak, and to remember the words of the Lord Jesus, how he said, It is more blessed to give than to receive. *Acts* xx. 35.

Let us pray for the whole Church of Christ.

And the Minister shall say this, and all other Prayers and Confessions in the Communion Service, kneeling at the end of the table, so that the Congregation shall be on his right hand.

ALMIGHTY and ever-living God, who by thy holy apostle hast taught us to make prayers and supplications, and to give thanks for all men ; we humbly beseech thee most mercifully [*to accept our alms and oblations, and*] to receive these our prayers, which we offer unto thy Divine Majesty ; beseeching thee to inspire continually the universal

Church, with the spirit of truth, unity, and concord ; and grant that all they who do confess the name of Christ may agree in the truth of thy holy word, and live in unity and godly love. We beseech thee also to bless all Christian rulers and governors, and grant that all who are placed in authority over us may truly and impartially minister justice, to the punishment of wickedness and vice, and to the maintenance of true religion and virtue. Give grace, O Heavenly Father, to all Ministers of thy holy Gospel, that they may, both by their life and doctrine, set forth thy true and lively word, and rightly and duly administer thy holy ordinances. And to all thy people give thy heavenly grace ; and especially to this congregation here present; that, with meek heart and due reverence, they may hear and receive thy holy word, truly serving thee in holiness and righteousness all the days of their life. And we most humbly beseech thee of thy goodness, O Lord, to comfort and succor all those who in this transitory life are in trouble, sorrow, need, sickness, or any other adversity. And we also bless thy holy name, for all thy servants departed this life in thy faith and fear ; beseeching thee to give us grace, so to follow their good examples, that with them we may be partakers of thy beavenly kingdom. Grant this, O Father, for thine infinite mercy's sake, in Jesus Christ our Mediator and Advocate. *Amen.*

The Communion.

Then the Minister, standing before the Table, shall say to those who come to receive the holy Communion,

YᴱE who do truly and earnestly repent you of your sins, and are in love and charity with your neighbors, and intend to follow the commandments of God, and walk from henceforth in his holy ways, draw near with faith, and take this holy ordinance to your comfort; and make your humble confession to Almighty God, saying with me : —

Then shall this General Confession be made by the Minister and People.

ALMIGHTY God, Father of our Lord Jesus Christ, Maker of all things, Judge of all men; We acknowledge and bewail our manifold sins, Which we from time to time most grievously have committed, by thought, word, and deed, against thy Divine Majesty, Provoking most justly thy wrath and indignation against us. We do earnestly repent, and are heartily sorry for these our misdoings; The remembrance of which is grievous unto us. Have mercy upon us, Have mercy upon us, most merciful Father. In the name of thy Son our Lord Jesus Christ, we beseech thee to forgive us all that is past; And grant that we may ever hereafter serve and please thee in newness of life, To thy honor and glory, through Jesus Christ our Lord. *Amen.*

ALMIGHTY God, our Heavenly Father, who of thy great mercy hast promised forgiveness of sins to all those who, with hearty repentance, and true faith, turn unto thee ; have mercy upon us, pardon and deliver us from all our sins, confirm and strengthen us in all goodness, and bring us to everlasting life, through Jesus Christ our Lord. *Amen.*

Then the Minister, standing before the Table, shall say

HEAR what comfortable words our Saviour Christ saith unto all who truly turn to him :

Come unto me, all ye who labor, and are heavy laden, and I will give you rest :

God so loved the world, that he gave his only begotten Son, to the end that all who believe in him should not perish, but have everlasting life.

Hear also what St. Paul saith :

This is a true saying, and worthy of all men to be received, that Christ Jesus came into the world to save sinners.

Hear also what St. John saith :

If any man sin, we have an advocate with the Father, Jesus Christ the righteous, and he is the propitiation for our sins.

Lift up your hearts.
Answ. We lift them up unto the Lord.
Min. Let us give thanks unto our Lord God.
Answ. It is meet and right so to do.

Min. It is very meet, right, and our bounden duty, that we should at all times, and in all places, give thanks unto thee, O Lord, Holy Father, Almighty, Everlasting God;

Here shall follow the proper Preface, if there be any specially appointed; or else immediately shall follow.

THEREFORE, with Angels, and Archangels, and with all the company of heaven, we laud and magnify thy glorious name; evermore praising thee, and saying, Holy, holy, holy, Lord God of hosts; heaven and earth are full of thy glory. Glory be to thee, O Lord, most high. *Amen.*

PROPER PREFACES.

Upon Christmas Day.

BECAUSE thou didst send thy Son into the world, that the world through him might be saved. Therefore, with Angels, &c.

Upon Easter Day.

BUT chiefly are we bound to praise thee for the glorious resurrection of thy Son Jesus Christ our Lord; for he was offered for us, and is the Lamb of God that taketh away the sins of the world; who, by his death, hath destroyed death, and, by his rising to life again, hath restored to us everlasting life. Therefore, with Angels, &c.

Upon Ascension Day.

THROUGH thy most dearly beloved Son Jesus Christ our Lord; who, after his most glorious resurrection, manifestly appeared to all his Apostles, and in their sight ascended up into heaven to prepare a place for us; that where he is, thither we might also ascend, and reign with him in glory. Therefore, with Angels, &c.

Upon Whitsunday.

THROUGH Jesus Christ our Lord; according to whose most true promise, thy Holy Spirit was poured forth upon the Apostles, to teach them, and to lead them to all truth; giving them both the gift of divers languages, and also boldness, with fervent zeal, constantly to preach the Gospel unto all nations, whereby we have been brought out of darkness and error into the clear light and true knowledge of thee, and of thy Son Jesus Christ. Therefore, with Angels, &c.

Then shall the Minister say, in the name of all them who shall receive the Communion, this Prayer following.

WE do not presume to come to this thy table, O merciful Lord, trusting in our own righteousness, but in thy manifold and great mercies. We are not worthy so much as to gather up the crumbs under thy table: but thou art the same Lord, whose property is always to have mercy; grant us therefore, gracious Lord, so to partake of this holy ordinance, that our minds may be impressed with gratitude to thy dear Son Jesus Christ, and that we may evermore dwell in him, and he in us. *Amen.*

Then the Minister, standing before the Table, shall read the following account of the Institution, from 1 Cor. xi. 23, 25.

THE Lord Jesus, the same night that he was betrayed, took bread ; and when he had given thanks, he brake it, and said, Take, eat ; this is my body, which is broken for you ; this do in remembrance of me. After the same manner, also, he took the cup, when he had supped, saying, This cup is the new testament in my blood ; this do ye, as oft as ye drink it, in remembrance of me.

Then the Minister's shall break the Bread, and pour out the Wine; after which he shall say the Prayer fol-

ALMIGHTY God, our Heavenly Father, who, of thy tender mercy, didst give thine only Son Jesus Christ to suffer death upon the cross for our redemption ; who did institute, and in his holy Gospel command his disciples to continue a memorial of that his precious death ; hear us, O merciful Father, we most humbly beseech thee, and grant that we may receive this bread and wine, according to the holy institution, and in remembrance of the death and passion, of thy Son our Saviour Jesus Christ. *Amen.*

Then shall the Minister first receive the Communion in both kinds himself, saying when he taketh the Bread,

I take, and eat this in remembrance of Christ ;

Likewise, when he takes the Cup,

I drink this in remembrance of Christ;

4rd th n tprocced to deliver the same to the People. And when he delivereth the Bread to the People, he shall say,

Take, and eat this in remembrance of Christ.

And when the Minister delivereth the Cup to the People, he shall say,

Drink this in remembrance of Christ.

When all have received the Communion, a Psal or Hymn may be sung; and this ended, the following Prayer shall be said

OUR Father, who art in heaven, Hallowed be thy name. Thy kingdom come. Thy will be done on earth as it is in heaven. Give us this day our daily bread. And forgive us our trespasses, as we forgive those who trespass against us. And lead us not into temptation, but deliver us from evil. For thine is the kingdom, and the power, and the glory, for ever and ever. *Amen.*

O LORD and Heavenly Father, we thy humble servants earnestly desire thy fatherly goodness, mercifully to accept this our sacrifice of praise and thanksgiving ; beseeching thee to grant that, by the mediation of thy Son Jesus Christ, and through faith in him, we and thy whole Church may obtain remission of our sins, and all other benefits of his passion. And here we offer and present unto thee, O Lord, ourselves, our souls and bodies, to be a reasonable, holy, and lively sacrifice unto thee; humbly beseeching thee, that all we, who are partakers of this holy communion, may be filled with thy grace and heavenly benediction. And although we be unworthy, through our manifold sins, to offer unto thee any sacrifice, yet we beseech thee to accept this our bounden duty and service; not weighing our merits, but pardoning our offences, according to thine abundant mercies in Christ Jesus our Lord; through whom all honor and glory be unto thee, O Father Almighty, world without end. *Amen.*

Then shall the following Anthem be said by the Minister and People.

Gloria in excelsis.

GLORY be to God on high, and on earth peace, good will among men. We praise thee, we bless thee, we worship thee, we glorify thee, we give thanks to thee for the various manifestations of thy great glory, O Lord God, heavenly King, God the Father Almighty.

We bless thee for sending thy beloved Son into the world to save sinners; for exalting him unto thy right hand in heaven; for all the gifts and graces of thy Holy Spirit; and for the hope of eternal life.

For thou only art wise, and holy, and good; thou only art the Lord; thou only dost govern all things, both in heaven and earth. Therefore, blessing, and honor, and glory, and power, be unto thee who sittest upon the throne, and unto ·the Lamb for ever and ever. *Amen.*

T HE grace of our Lord Jesus Christ, and the love of God, and the fellowship of the Holy Ghost, be with us all evermore. *Amen.*

Or this

T HE peace of God, which passeth all under-standing, keep your hearts and minds in the knowledge and love of God and of his Son Jesus Christ our Lord ; and the blessing of God Almighty be among you, and remain with you always. *Amen.*

MEDITATIONS AND PRAYERS.

The following brief Meditations and Prayers may be used as Guides to Private Devotion before and after Communion.

MEDITATION BEFORE COMMUNING.

ACCORDING to the exhortation of St. Paul, let me examine myself, and so let me eat of that bread, and drink of that cup.

Do I approach the table of my Lord as his humble disciple; seeking his spirit and grace; relying on his word; remembering his great sufferings, and his shameful death, and his surpassing love for me and for all men, for whose salvation he suffered and died? Do I hate and renounce my sins? Am I in charity with all my neighbors? Am I anxious to follow my Saviour in loving and serving God? — I will wash my hands in innocency, O Lord, and so will I compass thine altar.

PRAYER.

BEHOLD, gracious Lord, I come to thy table, as one who is sick, to the great Physician. Let me worthily receive these elements of bread and wine, and fill me, O Lord, with that spiritual food, the body and blood of Christ, of which these are the outward signs ; that so evil affections may die in me, and all things belonging to the Spirit may live and grow in me, and I be preserved in body and soul, and saved from the second death, and nourished unto eternal life, through him who loved me and gave himself for me, thy dear Son Jesus Christ. *Amen.*

MEDITATION AFTER COMMUNING.

NOW that I have commemorated my Master and Saviour according to his own gracious invitation, let me meditate on the meaning of these words of Jesus, when he said, Whoso eateth my flesh and drinketh my blood, hath eternal life, and I will raise him up at the last day. For my flesh is meat indeed, and my blood is drink indeed. He that eateth my flesh, and drinketh my blood, dwelleth in me, and I in him.

I trust that in this commemoration of my Lord, I have partaken of his own life, which is spiritual, sacred, and eternal. I trust that his doctrine and example are within me, and that neither things present nor things to come, will dissolve the divine fellowship between him the blessed Master and me his humble disciple.

PRAYER.

AND to thee, O God, my Father, do I give thanks for this holy communion. Grant that it may never turn to my judgment and condemnation, but that it may be, together with my other spiritual privileges, health and recovery under all weakness and infirmities; safety and defence against all the attacks of my spiritual enemies; vigor and strength to all my good purposes and resolutions; comfort and support under all the afflictions and calamities of life; assistance and direction under all difficulties and doubts; courage and constancy under all dangers and persecutions, in times of sickness, and in the hour of death. And be thou, O God, my Father, alway with me. Grant me pardon and peace in this life, mercy and favor at the day of judgment, and a never-fading crown of glory in thy heavenly kingdom. These things, for myself and for others, I devoutly ask in the name of Jesus Christ thy blessed Son our Lord. *Amen.*

AFTER THE SERVICE IS ENDED.

LORD, now lettest thou thy servant depart in peace; for mine eyes have seen thy salvation. Let me always hunger and thirst after righteousness; and nourish thou my soul to eternal life through Jesus Christ. *Amen.*

COMMUNION OF THE SICK.

If a sick person be desirous to receive the Communion at his house, he shall give notice to the Minister; and all things necessary being prepared, the Minister shall there celebrate the Communion, beginning with the Collect, Epistle, and Gospel here following.

THE COLLECT.

A LMIGHTY, everlasting God, maker of man-kind, who dost correct those whom thou dost love, and chastise every one whom thou dost receive ; we beseech thee to have mercy upon this thy servant visited with thine hand ; and to grant that *he* may take *his* sickness patiently ; and to restore *his* bodily health, if it be thy gracious will ; and that whensoever *his* soul shall depart from the body, it may be without spot presented unto thee, through Jesus Christ our Lord. *Amen.*

THE EPISTLE.
Heb. xii. 5.

M Y son, despise not thou the chastening of the Lord, nor faint when thou art rebuked of him. For whom the Lord loveth, he chasteneth, and scourgeth every son whom he receiveth.

THE GOSPEL.

St. John v. 24.

VERILY, verily, I say unto you, he who loveth my word, and believeth on him who sent me, hath everlasting life, and shall not come into condemnation ; but is passed from death unto life.

Ye who do truly, &c.

END OF THE COMMUNION.

THE BAPTISM OF INFANTS.

There should be for every Child two or three Sponsors: who may most properly be Parents or nearest Relations.

Minister.

HEAR the words of our Saviour Christ to his Apostles ·

Go ye, and make disciples of all nations, baptizing them in the name of the Father, and of the Son, and of the Holy Ghost.

Hear what is said of him in another place ·

They brought young children to him, that he should touch them; and his disciples rebuked those that brought them. But when Jesus saw it, he was much displeased, and said unto them, Suffer the little children to come unto me, and forbid them not; for of such is the kingdom of God. Verily I say unto you, Whosoever shall not receive the kingdom of God as a little child, he shall not enter therein. And he took them up in his arms, put his hands upon them, and blessed them.

Hear also what St. Peter saith

The baptism which saveth us, is not the putting

away the filth of the flesh, but the answer of a good conscience toward God.

Dearly beloved,

Ye have brought this child here to be baptized ; I demand therefore,

Will ye faithfully and earnestly exhort this child to renounce the hurtful vanities of this world, with all covetous desires of the same, and carnal desires of the flesh, so that *he* may not follow, nor be led by them?

Answ. I will.

Min. Will ye instruct *him* in the Gospel of our Lord Jesus Christ?

Answ. I will.

Min. Will ye exhort *him* to keep God's holy will and commandments, and to walk in the same all the days of *his* life?

Answ. I will.

Then shall the Minister take the child into his hands.

Name this child.

Then, naming it after them and either dipping it in the water, or sprinkling water upon it, he shall say,

I BAPTIZE thee in the name of the Father, and of the Son, and of the Holy Ghost.

Min. Let us pray.

ALMIGHTY and ever blessed God, by whose providence the different generations of mankind are raised up to know thee, and to enjoy thy favor for ever ; grant that this child, now dedicated to thee by our office and ministry, may be endued with heavenly virtues, and everlastingly saved through thy mercy, who dost live and govern all things, world without end. We beseech thee to enable thy servants who are intrusted with the care of this child, to perform their duty faithfully ; give them wisdom to be *his* defence against the temptations incident to childhood and youth ; and as *he* grows up in life, graciously assist them to enlarge *his* understanding and to open *his* heart to the impressions of religion and virtue. This our petition we humbly present in the name of Jesus Christ our Mediator and Redeemer. *Amen.*

WE give thee humble thanks, O Heavenly Father, that thou hast vouchsafed to call us to the knowledge of thy grace, and faith in thee ; increase this knowledge, and confirm this faith in us evermore, that we may be enabled to mortify all our evil and corrupt affections, and daily to proceed in all virtue and godliness of living, till we come to that eternal kingdom, which thou hast promised by Jesus Christ our Lord. *Amen.*

NOW unto him who is able to keep us from falling, and to present us faultless before the presence of his glory, with exceeding joy, to the only wise God our Saviour, be glory and majesty, dominion and power, through Jesus Christ, for ever and ever. *Amen.*

EXHORTATION TO PARENTS AFTER BAPTISM.

To be read or omitted at the discretion of the Minister.

THE design of receiving infants by baptism into the Church of Christ, is, to remind parents of their duty to them in their innocent and helpless age, to train them up as his disciples and the children of God; that as they have been the instruments of bringing them into this mortal life, they may have the comfort of contributing to their future happiness in a life which will never end.

Remember then that this child belongs to God who gave it to you, that it may be educated and fitted for himself; and if, through your criminal neglect or bad example, his reasonable creature be lost, he will require it at your hands.

Instil therefore into *his* tender mind the knowledge, reverence, and love of God, the Heavenly Father and Maker of all; and a deep sense of the duty which *he* owes to him. Acquaint *him* with his benevolent designs from the beginning, for the recovery of a degenerate and perishing world, to their duty and happiness; and lead *him* to learn the mind and will of God for *his* salvation, from that inestimable treasure of wisdom, the Holy Scriptures, especially the words of Christ and his apostles; and not from the doctrines and inventions of men.

Check the first risings of envy and pride in *his* breast, by teaching *him* humility and a just knowledge of *himself;* that all *he* possesses or hopes for is from God, whose free bounty alone maketh the difference between his creatures. But, at the same time, inform *him* of the dignity of *his* nature ; of the importance of reason, the light of God within *him*, by which *he* is to govern *himself*, to restrain *his* appetites and passions, moderate *his* affections, to know the God who made *him*, to learn his will, to become like unto him, holy, just, and good. Teach *him* above all things to abhor falsehood and lies ; and to love and cultivate truth and integrity, which will make *him* amiable in the eyes of all, and acceptable to God. Tell *him* that *he* is to love and to do good to all men, because all are equally the children of God with *himself*, and the objects of his fatherly kindness and care ; that *he* is not born only for *himself*, but for others ; to serve *his* country and mankind, by promoting truth and virtue, and the public good. Sow in *him* betimes these seeds of piety, charity, sincerity, and all goodness ; for otherwise the weeds of evil will spring up in *his* heart, which ye may never afterward be able to root out. And although no pains which ye can take, can ensure success, yet whatever happens, ye will have discharged your duty, and not have the guilt and mortifying reflection of having contributed to the ruin and misery of those you love. Remember the saying of the wise man, *Train up a child in the way he should go, and when he is old he will not depart from it.* If your labors should be successful, it will be a source of the highest and purest pleasure and satisfaction to you ; and ye will have the joy of leaving behind you those who may live and do good in the world, when ye shall be no more in it.

And may the supreme Father and Governor of all things direct and bless you in the faithful discharge of your duty, for his glory, the good of mankind, and the advancement of the Gospel of our Lord Jesus Christ. *Amen.*

Where there are other Sponsors who present the Child to be baptized, and not the Parents, the Minister may thus begin the Exhortation.

Y E who have now undertaken the care of this child, who naturally belongs to the parents, must take heed and remember that it is also a child of God, for whom it is to be educated and fitted ; and if, through your, &c.

END OF BAPTISM OF INFANTS.

THE BAPTISM

OF THOSE WHO ARE OF RIPER YEARS.

The Minister may begin the Service with the following Observations, relating to the Institution, Nature, and Use of Baptism.

OUR blessed Saviour, the Lord Jesus Christ, having himself published his religion for the salvation of the world, to the Jewish nation, commissioned his apostles to complete the work he had begun, by preaching his Gospel to all nations.

All power, said he, is given unto me in heaven and in earth. Go ye, therefore, and make disciples of all nations, baptizing them in the name of the Father, and of the Son, and of the Holy Ghost; teaching them to observe all things whatsoever I have commanded you; and lo, I am with you always, even to the end of the world.

By this direction of our Saviour, all persons are to be acknowledged as members of his Church, by baptism in the name of the Father, and of the Son, and of the Holy Ghost. They are then consecrated to the divine service, in that religion which came from God the Father, was published to the world by his Son, and confirmed by the operations of his Holy Spirit.

By this ordinance Christ hath wisely provided to keep up in his Church a sense of the purity of his doctrines, and the obligations to universal holiness of life, which are incumbent upon his disciples. Water is employed as an emblem of purity, or of that moral and religious improvement, in which all our Christian advantages should terminate.

Let us, therefore, as many as are here present, remember the purity of our Christian faith and pro-fessions ; and, by the present administration of bap-tism, take occasion to establish in our minds a lively sense of our obligations to serve God, according to the Gospel of his Son, in holiness and righteousness all our days.

Then shall the Minister say to the Person desiring to

OUR Lord Jesus commanded, that all persons baptized should be instructed in his holy Gos-pel. You, in the profession of the Christian faith, present yourself to be baptized according to his in-stitution. Do you now promise, that you will receive the instructions of the Christian religion, and govern your faith and practice by its doctrines and laws ?

Answ. This I now promise, and, by the help of God, will endeavor to perform.

The Minister shall then baptize the Person, saying.

I BAPTIZE thee in the name of the Father, and of the Son, and of the Holy Ghost.

Min. Let us pray.

ALMIGHTY God, the Father of our Lord Jesus Christ, regard in mercy the prayers of thy people; and bless thy servant, who hath now been acknowledged as a member of the Christian Church, by baptism. Incline *his* heart to receive with all readiness the doctrines and instructions of Christ, and to submit faithfully to the authority of his laws. Give *him* strength to triumph over the temptations of vice, and to be steadfast in the practice of that holiness which baptism is designed to represent; that, living as becometh a good and faithful member of the Christian Church here on earth, *he* may at length partake in heaven of that eternal kingdom which thou hast revealed to us by Jesus Christ our Lord. *Amen.*

WE give thee humble thanks, O Heavenly Father, that thou hast vouchsafed to call us to the knowledge of thy grace, and faith in thee; increase this knowledge, and confirm this faith in us evermore, that we may be enabled to mortify all our evil and corrupt affections, and daily to proceed in all virtue and godliness of living, till we come to that eternal kingdom, which thou hast promised by Jesus Christ our Lord. *Amen.*

NOW unto him who is able to keep us from falling, and to present us faultless before the presence of his glory, with exceeding joy, to the only wise God our Saviour, be glory and majesty, dominion and power, through Jesus Christ, for ever and ever. *Amen.*

THE EXHORTATION.

Christian Brother,

IN obedience to the command of our Lord Jesus Christ, that all persons baptized be instructed in his holy religion ; you have now engaged, by a solemn promise before God and this assembly, that you will receive the instructions of the Christian religion, and govern your faith and practice by its doctrines and laws. May you carefully keep in mind this promise, and endeavor to perform it faithfully. You are to endeavor to improve in every virtue which relates to God, your neighbor, or yourself ; and to this end, you are diligently and honestly to search the Scriptures. These contain everything necessary to eternal salvation ; and from these sacred records of our religion you may obtain all that information which is necessary to improve your understanding and confirm your faith. Above all, you are carefully to obey the precepts of the Gospel, and to cultivate that purity of heart and affections which all its laws, ordinances, and doctrines are designed to promote.

Having the fear of God before your eyes, be you now exhorted to discharge with fidelity and exactness the duty you have now acknowledged. To the due observance of it may God incline your heart ; and may he bless you with success, for your improvement in Christian knowledge, and holiness of life, for the honor of religion, and the glory of his holy name, through Jesus Christ our Lord. *Amen.*

END OF BAPTISM OF THOSE OF RIPER YEARS.

CONFIRMATION

D EARLY beloved, in your infancy, when you could not know the blessedness of the Christian religion, those who best loved you expressed in the most solemn manner, with prayer to Almighty God, their desire that you should be partakers of this inestimable blessedness; and pledged themselves to instruct you in the Gospel of our Lord Jesus Christ. You have now reached an age at which it might reasonably be hoped that you would, by your own voluntary act, take upon yourselves the responsibility of a public Christian profession: and forasmuch as you have signified your desire so to do, let me ask you in the presence of God and of this congregation, Do you now renounce the fellowship of evil, and resolve to learn and do the will of God as revealed by Jesus Christ?

Each of those who are to be confirmed shall answer:

I do.

Then shall the Minister say the following Prayer.

ALMIGHTY and ever-living God, the Father of our spirits, who delightest to do us good; strengthen, we beseech thee, these thy servants with the Holy Ghost the Comforter; and daily increase in them thy manifold gifts of grace, the spirit of wisdom and understanding, the spirit of counsel and inward strength, the spirit of knowledge and true godliness. Grant this, O blessed God, through thy love to us in Jesus Christ. *Amen.*

Then, all standing, the Minister may lay his hand upon the head of each one, saying,

Defend, O Lord, this thy child with thy heavenly grace, that *he* may continue thine forever, and may daily increase in thy Holy Spirit more and more, until *he* come unto thy everlasting kingdom. *Amen.*

The Lord be with you.
Answer. And with thy spirit.
Minister. Our help is in the name of the Lord;
Answer. Who hath made heaven and earth.
Minister. Blessed be the name of the Lord;
Answer. Henceforth, world without end.
Minister. Lord, hear our prayers;
Answer. And let our cry come unto thee.

Then...

OUR Father who art in heaven, Hallowed be thy name. Thy kingdom come; Thy will be done on earth, as it is in heaven. Give us this day our daily bread. And forgive us our trespasses, As we forgive those who trespass against us. And lead us not into temptation. But deliver us from evil. For thine is the kingdom, and the power, and the glory, For ever and ever. *Amen.*

Then shall the Minister say the following Collects.

ALMIGHTY and ever-living God, who makest us both to will and to do those things that be good and acceptable unto thy Divine Majesty ; we would offer our humble supplications unto thee for these thy servants who have made a public profession of their Christian faith, and expressed their earnest desire and prayer to be enabled to fulfil their duties as disciples of Jesus Christ. Let thy fatherly hand ever be over them; let thy Holy Spirit ever be with them; guide and help, strengthen and sanctify them, we beseech thee ; that, by the living bond of obedience and charity, they may be united to thee and thy beloved Son. *Amen.*

LORD of all power and might, who art the author and giver of all good things, graft in our hearts the love of thy name ; increase in us true religion ; nourish us with all goodness, and, of thy great mercy, keep us in the same, through Jesus Christ our Lord. *Amen.*

THE grace of our Lord Jesus Christ, and the love of God, and the fellowship of the Holy Spirit, be with us all evermore. *Amen.*

THE peace of God, which passeth all understanding, keep our hearts and minds through Jesus Christ. *Amen.*

MATRIMONY.

PUBLISH the Banns of marriage between *M.* of —— and *N.* of ——. If any of you know cause or just impediment why these two persons should not be joined together in matrimony, ye are to declare it. This is the first [*second or third*] time of asking.

DEARLY beloved, we are gathered together here in the sight of God, and in the face of this congregation, to join together this man and this woman in holy matrimony; which is an honorable estate, instituted of God in the time of man's innocency; which holy estate Christ adorned and beautified with his presence, and first miracle that he wrought in Cana of Galilee; and is commended of St. Paul to be honorable among all men; and therefore is not by any to be enterprised, or taken in hand, lightly or unadvisedly ; but reverently, discreetly, soberly, and in the fear of God.

And then, speaking to the Persons who are to be married, he shall say.

I REQUIRE and charge you both, as ye will answer at the dreadful day of judgment, when the secrets of all hearts shall be disclosed, that if either of you know any impediment why ye may not be lawfully united in matrimony, ye do now confess it.   For be ye well assured, that so many as are joined together otherwise than God's word doth allow, are not joined together by God, neither is their matrimony lawful.

If no impediment be alleged, then shall the Minister say unto the Man.

M. WILT thou have this woman to thy wedded wife, to live together after God's ordinance, in the estate of matrimony ?   Wilt thou love her, comfort her, honor and keep her, in sickness and in health, in sorrow and in joy; and, forsaking all other, keep thee only unto her, so long as ye both shall live?

I will.

Then shall the Minister say unto the Woman,

N. WILT thou have this man to thy wedded husband, to live together after God's ordinance, in the estate of matrimony ?   Wilt thou love him, comfort him, honor and keep him, in sickness and in health, in sorrow and in joy ; and, forsaking all other, keep thee only unto him, so long as ye both shall live?

The Woman shall answer.

I will.

Then shall the Minister say.

Who giveth this woman to be married to this man?

Then shall Minister, receiving the Woman at her Father's or a friend's hands, shall cause the Man with his right

I, *M.* take thee, *N.* to my wedded wife, to have and to hold, from this day forward, for better for worse, for richer for poorer, in sickness and in health, to love and to cherish, till death us do part, according to God's holy ordinance ; and thereto I plight thee my troth.

I, *N.* take thee, *M.* to my wedded husband, to have and to hold, from this day forward, for better for worse, for richer for poorer, in sickness and in health, to love and to cherish, till death us do part, according to God's holy ordinance ; and thereto I plight thee my troth.

T͡l shall they loo · t i͡r ha ds, a d the Ma͡r shall give unto the Woman a Ring, putting it upon the fourth finger of her left hand. And the Man hold-ing the Ring there, and taught by the Minister, shall say.

WITH this ring I thee wed ; with all my worldly goods I thee endow ; and to thee only do I promise to keep myself, so long as we both shall live. *Amen.*

The then Minister shall say.

Let us pray.

O ETERNAL God, creator and preserver of all mankind, giver of all spiritual grace, the author of everlasting life ; send thy blessing upon these thy servants, whom we bless in thy name. Enable them to perform the covenant which they have now made in thy presence. May they seriously attend to the duties of the new relation in which they stand to each other ; that it may not be to them a state of temptation and sorrow, but of holiness and com-fort ; may they live together in peace and love ; and wilt thou, the God of peace and love, be al-ways with them, and lead them in the paths of in-nocence and virtue to eternal life ; through Jesus Christ our Lord. *Amen.*

Then shall the Minister say to the People.

FORASMUCH as *M.* and *N.* have consented together in wedlock, and have witnessed the same before God and this company, and thereto have engaged and pledged themselves to each other, and have declared the same by giving and receiving a ring, and by joining hands; I pronounce that they be Man and Wife; and those whom God hath joined together, let no man put asunder.

Let us pray.

( ) MERCIFUL God and Heavenly Father who art the guide, the support, and the felicity of all who put their trust in thee; we beseech thee to bless these thy servants, and give them grace to fear and serve thee all the days of their life. May their hearts be united in the closest bonds of love and purity; may they be blessings and comforts to one another, sharers of each other's joys, consolers of each other's sorrows, and helpers to one another in all the changes of the world; and grant that they may so faithfully discharge the duties which belong to the condition into which they have entered, that they, and all who may be committed to their care, may meet together in that world of perfect felicity which thou hast revealed to us by Jesus Christ our Lord. *Amen.*

BLESSING.

THE Lord God Almighty bless, preserve, and keep you; the Lord mercifully with his favor look upon you, and fill you with all spiritual benediction and grace ; that ye may so live together in this life, that in the world to come ye may have life everlasting. *Amen.*

EXHORTATION TO THE PARTIES AFTER MARRIAGE.

To be read or omitted at the discretion of the Minister

IT will become you to consider seriously the sacred and important engagement into which ye have now entered. Marriage is the union of one man with one woman for their joint happiness, and for the pious education of children, where God gives them ; and, by the original appointment of God, confirmed by our Saviour, (*Gen.* ii. 24 ; *Matt.* xix. 4, 5, 6,) this union is to be perpetual, to be dissolved only by death. It was intended by the benevolent Parent of mankind to be a source of the purest satisfactions, to soften the unavoidable cares, and increase the innocent pleasures of life, by affording opportunities of sharing them with a most intimate friend and partner. By Christians in particular it is to be looked upon as a state of perfect indissoluble friendship, in which ye are to carry your regards for each other beyond the grave ; that ye may so live in virtue and holiness here, that ye may live hereafter in that state where there will be no marrying nor giving in marriage, but ye shall be as the angels in heaven. Study then to correct what is amiss in your respective tempers and dispositions, which may disturb your mutual love and peace. And· be severe censors of yourselves, but exact not too much one from another ; and bear with each other's infirmities, for there is nothing perfect here below. None are faultless, but all are to endeavor to become such. Cultivate in yourselves, and in each other, the knowledge and practice of virtue and true religion, as the only foundation of present comfort and future hopes. Study the Scriptures and the precepts and example of Christ, who alone hath the words of eternal life. And be not extravagant in your expectations from the world; for although it abound with many innocent joys and pleasures, yet it is not, nor is it intended to be, a place of unmixed prosperity and enjoyment, but a transitory scene of trial and improvement for a better and more enduring state.

The other great end of marriage is for the well ordering of families and right education of children. This is a matter of the highest moment. For families are the nurseries and schools, in which the successive generations of men are to be instructed and fitted for their different stations and employments in life, to bear their part and burden in it, to be helpful to others, good citizens, useful magistrates, faithful husbands, virtuous wives, patterns of all that is excellent and worthy in every relation. Of a number of families united, nations are composed; and of all of them together, the whole community of mankind. And as these little seminaries are well tutored and governed, or neglected, kingdoms, nations, and the world are happy or miserable.

Take heed therefore to set an example of piety and virtue yourselves; and then ye may with authority require those who belong to you to follow it. Let the God of heaven be publicly acknowledged and worshipped each day in your family. At least let not his name and worship be forgotten in it on the Lord's day. Keep a strict watch over all who depend upon you ; and suffer no vice to go unreproved, or to remain in your house persisted in and unamended. For this would be to encourage it, and put a snare before others. By this domestic care, and godly discipline, ye will ensure your own peace, and be a blessing to your family, your neighbors, and country ; but, which is above all to be valued and sought for, ye will be approved by Almighty God, and rank with prophets and apostles in that future world, where we are told, that they who are wise shall shine as the brightness of the firmament ; and they who turn many to righteousness as the stars for ever and ever.

END OF THE MARRIAGE SERVICE.

THE

VISITATION OF THE SICK.

TO BE USED WHEN THE SICK PERSON DESIRES IT.

The Minister now begin with saying.

PEACE be to this house, and to all who dwell in it.

And he may exhort the Sick Person after this form, or

DEARLY beloved, know this, that Almighty God is the Lord of life and death, and of all things to them pertaining, as youth, strength, health, age, weakness, and sickness. Wherefore, whatsoever your sickness is, know you certainly, that it is God's visitation. And for what cause soever this sickness is sent unto you; whether it be to try your patience for the example of others, and that your faith may be found in the day of the Lord, laudable, glorious, and honorable, to the increase of glory and endless felicity; or whether it be sent unto you to correct and amend in you whatsoever doth offend the eyes of your Heavenly Father; know

17 *   261

you certainly, that if you truly repent of your sins, and bear your sickness patiently, trusting in God's mercy, manifested by his dear Son Jesus Christ, and render unto him humble thanks for his fatherly visitation, submitting yourselves wholly unto his will, it shall turn to your profit, and help you forward in the right way that leadeth unto everlasting life.

If he think fit, the Minister may proceed in his Exhortation.

TAKE therefore in good part the chastisement of the Lord; for as St. Paul saith, Whom the Lord loveth, he chasteneth, and scourgeth every son whom he receiveth. If ye endure chastening, God dealeth with you as with sons; for what son is he whom the father chasteneth not? Furthermore, we have had fathers of our flesh, who corrected us, and we gave them reverence; shall we not much rather be in subjection unto the Father of spirits, and live? For they verily for a few days chastened us after their own pleasure; but he for our profit, that we might be partakers of his holiness. These words, good *brother*, are written in Holy Scripture for our comfort and instruction; that we should patiently, and with thanksgiving bear our Heavenly Father's correction, whensoever by any manner of adversity it shall please his gracious goodness to visit us. And there should be no greater comfort to Christian persons than to be made like unto Christ, by suffering patiently adversities, troubles, and sicknesses. For he himself went not up to joy, but first he suffered pain; he entered not into his glory before he was crucified. So truly our way to eternal joy is to suffer here with Christ; and our door to enter into eternal life is gladly to die with Christ; that we may rise again from death, and dwell with him in everlasting life.

HEAR further what the Scripture saith for the comfort of those who are in sickness and distress.

BEHOLD, happy is the man whom God correcteth; therefore despise not thou the chastening of the Almighty; for he maketh sore, and bindeth up; he woundeth, and his hands make whole. *Job* v. **17, 18.**

I remember thee upon my bed, and meditate on thee in the night watches. Because thou hast been my help, therefore under the shadow of thy wings will I rejoice. My soul followeth hard after thee; for thy right hand hath upholden me. *Psal.* lxiii. 6, 7, 8.

God restoreth my soul; he leadeth me in the path of righteousness, for his name's sake. Yea, though I walk through the valley of the shadow of death, I will fear no evil; for thou art with me; thy rod and thy staff they comfort me. *Psal.* xxiii. 3, 4.

The Lord is my portion, saith my soul; therefore will I hope in him. The Lord is good unto those who wait for him, to the soul that seeketh him. It is good that a man should both hope and quietly wait for the salvation of the Lord. *Lam.* iii. 24, 25, 26.

For the Lord will not cast off forever; but though he cause grief, yet will he have compassion according to the multitude of his mercies. For he doth not afflict willingly, nor grieve the children of men. *Lam.* iii. 31, 32, 33.

I am like a broken vessel. But I trusted in thee, O Lord; I said, thou art my God. My times are in thy hand; make thy face to shine upon thy servant; save me for thy mercy's sake. *Psal.* xxxi. 12, 14, 15, 16.

I said in my haste, I am cut off from before thine eyes; nevertheless, thou heardest the voice of my supplication when I cried unto thee. *Psal.* xxxi. 22.

Be of good courage, and he shall strengthen your heart, all ye who hope in the Lord. *Psal.* xxxi. 24.

Then shall be said over the following Prayer as

O LORD, look down from heaven, behold, visit, and relieve this thy servant. Look upon *him* with the eyes of thy mercy; give *him* comfort, and sure confidence in thee; support *him* under all the trials of *his* present sickness, relieve *his* pains, if it seem good unto thee, and keep *him* in perpetual peace and safety; through Jesus Christ our Lord. *Amen.*

ALMIGHTY and everlasting God, maker of mankind, who dost correct those whom thou dost love, and chastise every one whom thou dost receive; we beseech thee to have mercy upon this thy servant visited with thy hand, and grant that *he* may take thy visitation patiently; and fit *him*, O Lord, for whatever in thy righteous providence thou hast appointed for *him;* that *he* may have cause to glorify thy name for *his* present sufferings, and find that thou, O God, of very faithfulness, hast caused *him* to be troubled. Hear our prayers, O Lord, and grant our requests, for thy mercy's sake in Christ Jesus our Lord. *Amen.*

HEAR us, almighty and most merciful God and Father; extend thy accustomed goodness to this thy servant who is grieved with sickness. Sanctify, we beseech thee, this thy fatherly correction to *him*, that the sense of *his* weakness may add strength to *his* faith, and seriousness to *his* repentance; that if it shall be thy good pleasure to restore *him* to *his* former health, *he* may lead the residue of *his* life in thy fear and to thy glory; or else give *him* grace so to take thy visitation, that after this painful life is ended, *he* may dwell with thee in life everlasting, through Jesus Christ our Lord. *Amen.*

Instead of the three preceding prayers, may be said the

OUR Father in heaven, look down with mercy and pity upon thy servant, and lay not thy chastening hand upon *him* more heavily than *he* can bear. Let *him* acknowledge, with submission and humility, that even in judgment thou art merciful, and that of very faithfulness thou hast caused *him* to be troubled. Thou dost afflict *him* with a Parent's wisdom, — O sustain *him* with a Parent's love. Let thy grace be sufficient for *him* in all *his* need, and let the holy influences of thy Spirit hold *him* up in *his* weakness, and inspire *his* heart with strength, and hope, and confidence. Let not any pain or suffering, however acute, discompose the order of *his* thoughts, *his* submission, *his* gratitude, or *his* duty Together with *his* trials, wilt thou provide a way for *his* escape, even by the mercies of a longer and holier life, or by the mercies of a peaceful and blessed death, — even as it pleaseth thee, O Lord.

Thou knowest all the necessities and all the infirmities of thy servant ; fortify *his* soul, we beseech thee, with spiritual joys and perfect resignation, and fill *him* with desires of holiness and of thy heavenly kingdom. Make *his* repentance entire, and *his* faith strong, and *his* hope steadfast, so that if thou dost please to continue *him* yet longer in life, *he* may serve thee with a devoted heart, and whenever thou shalt call *his* spirit away from earth, it may enter into the rest of the sons of God, and be with thee, and the holy Jesus, and the spirits of the just made perfect, for ever and ever.

O Lord, hear ; O Lord, be merciful ; O Lord, heal, and pity, and save. Accept the prayer now offered in behalf of thine afflicted servant. Bless all *his* friends, and reward all the kindness which is shown *him.* Forgive *him his* trespasses, as *he* forgives those who trespass against *him.* Be with *him* every moment; be with *him* in the hour of death, and O in the day of judgment deliver *him,* through thine infinite mercy in Christ Jesus our Lord. *Amen.*

Then may be said this Psalm following.

De Profundis. Psalm CXXX.

OUT of the deep have I called unto thee, O Lord; Lord, hear my voice.

O let thine ears consider well the voice of my complaint.

If thou, Lord, wilt be extreme to mark what is done amiss, O Lord, who may abide it?

For there is mercy with thee, therefore shalt thou be feared.

I look for the Lord, my soul doth wait for him, in his word is my trust.

My soul waiteth for the Lord, more than they that watch for the morning; I say, more than they that watch for the morning.

O Israel, trust in the Lord; for with the Lord there is mercy, and with him is plenteous redemption.

And he shall redeem Israel from all his sins.

THE Almighty Lord, who is a most strong tower to all those who put their trust in him; to whom all things in heaven, in earth, and under the earth, do bow and obey, be now and evermore thy defence; and make thee know and feel, that there is none other name under heaven given to man, in whom, and through whom, thou mayest receive health and salvation, but only the name of our Lord Jesus Christ. *Amen.*

UNTO God's gracious mercy and protection we commit thee. The Lord bless thee and keep thee. The Lord make his face to shine upon thee, and be gracious unto thee. The Lord lift up his countenance upon thee, and give thee peace, both now and evermore. *Amen.*

Note. *The prayers of the above Service may be*

PRAYER FOR A SICK PERSON WHEN THERE IS SMALL HOPE OF RECOVERY.

O FATHER of mercies, God of all comfort, our only help in time of need; we fly unto thee for succor in behalf of this thy servant, here lying under thy hand in great weakness of body. Look graciously upon *him*, O Lord; and the more the outward man decayeth, strengthen *him*, we beseech thee, so much the more continually with thy grace and Holy Spirit in the inner man. Give *him* unfeigned repentance for the errors of *his* life past, and steadfast faith in thy Son Jesus, that *his* sins may be done away by thy mercy, and *his* pardon sealed in heaven, before *he* go hence and be no more seen. We know, O Lord, that there is no word impossible with thee; and that if thou wilt, thou canst even yet raise *him* up, and grant *him* a longer continuance amongst us. Yet forasmuch as in all appearance the time of *his* dissolution draweth near; so fit and prepare *him*, we beseech thee, against the hour of death, that after *his* departure hence in peace, and in thy favor, *he* may in thy appointed time be received into thine everlasting kingdom, which thou hast promised by Jesus Christ our Lord and Saviour. *Amen.*

COMMENDATORY PRAYERS FOR A SICK PERSON AT THE POINT OF DEPARTURE.

O ALMIGHTY God and Father of mankind, with whom the spirits of just men made perfect shall live forever; we humbly commend the soul of this thy servant, our dear *brother*, into thy hands, as into the hands of a faithful Creator, and most merciful Saviour; most humbly beseeching thee that it may be precious in thy sight. And teach us who survive, in this and other like daily spectacles of mortality, to see how frail and uncertain our own condition is, and so to number our days, that we may seriously apply our hearts to that holy and heavenly wisdom, while we live here, which may in the end bring us to life everlasting, through Jesus Christ thy Son our Lord. *Amen.*

O LORD God Almighty, most holy and gracious Father, we humbly commend the soul of thy servant into thy hands, thy most merciful hands. Impute not unto *him* the follies of *his* youth, nor any of the errors of *his* life ; but strengthen *him* in *his* agony, and carry *him* safely through *his* last distress. Let not *his* faith waver, nor *his* hope fail ; may *he* die in peace, and rest in hope, and rise in glory, for thine infinite mercy's sake in Jesus Christ our Lord. *Amen.*

PRAYER IN CASE OF SUDDEN EXTREMITY.

O MOST gracious Father, Judge of the living and the dead, behold thy servants running to thee for pity and mercy in behalf of this thy servant whom thou hast smitten with thy hasty rod and a swift angel. If it be thy will, O spare *him* a little, that *he* may recover *his* strength before *he* go hence, and be no more seen. But if thou hast otherwise appointed, let the miracles of thy compassion and thy wonderful mercy supply to *him* the want of the usual measures of time, and the periods of repentance, and the trimming of *his* lamp. O thou, who regardest the heart and the measures of the mind more than the delay and the measures of time, let it be thy pleasure to rescue the soul of thy servant from all the evils *he* hath deserved, and all the evils *he* fears. Stir up in *him* such effectual contrition for sin, and fervent love for thee, as may make *him* to be accepted with thee ; so that among the songs, which to eternal ages thy saints and holy angels shall sing to the honor of thy mercy, it may be ascribed to thy glory, that thou hast redeemed thy servant from the second death, and made him partaker of the gift of God, eternal life through Jesus Christ our Lord. *Amen.*

PRAYER FOR A SICK CHILD.

O ALMIGHTY God and merciful Father, to whom alone belong the issues of life and death; look down from heaven, we humbly beseech thee, with the eyes of mercy upon this child, now lying upon the bed of sickness; visit *him*, O Lord, with thy salvation; deliver *him* in thy good appointed time from *his* bodily pain, and sanctify this thy fatherly chastisement to *him;* that if it shall be thy pleasure to prolong *his* days here on earth, *he* may live to thee, and be an instrument of thy glory, by serving thee faithfully and doing good in *his* generation; or else receive *him* to thyself among those who have fallen asleep in the Lord Jesus, and who shall be raised by thee to endless life and happiness at the last day. Grant this, O Lord, for thy mercy's sake, in the name of thy Son our Lord Jesus Christ. *Amen.*

PRAYER FOR A LUNATIC.

O LORD, the only wise God, from whom we have received all the faculties of our souls; thou art good and righteous in all thy dispensations, though the reasons of them may be unknown to us thine imperfect creatures. We humbly beseech thee to dispel, if it be agreeable to thine infinite wisdom, the clouds in which the soul of thy servant is now involved; that *he* may regain *his* understanding, and the right use of *his* faculties. Heal *his* disordered mind, compose *his* passions, pacify *his* imagination; prosper the means used for *his* recovery; make *him* tractable in the use of remedies, and willing to comply with the advice of *his* friends. But if no means can effect *his* cure, let *him* possess *his* soul in peace, and in every interval of reason address *his* prayer unto thee; that when *his* earthly tabernacle shall be dissolved, *he* may rejoice in *his* former inability to pursue the pleasures of the world, and be presented unto thee pure and undefiled. Hear our prayer when we call upon thee; hear us for *him*, who is not able to pray for *himself*, for the sake of thine infinite mercv in Jesus Christ our Lord. *Amen.*

PRAYER FOR PERSONS TROUBLED IN MIND OR IN CONSCIENCE.

O BLESSED Lord, the Father of mercies, and the God of all comforts, we beseech thee to look down in pity and compassion upon this thine afflicted servant. Thou writest bitter things against *him*, and makest *him* to possess *his* former iniquities; thy wrath lieth hard upon *him*, and *his* soul is full of trouble. But, O merciful God, who hast written thy holy word for our learning, that we through patience and comfort of thy Holy Scriptures might have hope; give *him* a right understanding of *himself*, and of thy threats and promises, that *he* may neither cast away *his* confidence in thee, nor place it anywhere but in thee. Give *him* strength against all *his* temptations, and heal all *his* troubles. Break not the bruised reed, nor quench the smoking flax. Shut not up thy tender mercies in displeasure; but make *him* to hear of joy and gladness, that the bones which thou hast broken may rejoice. Deliver *him* from all disquieting fears, and lift up the light of thy countenance upon *him*, and give *him* peace, through the mediation of Jesus Christ our Lord. *Amen.*

PRAYER FOR ONE UNDER THE DREAD OF GOD'S WRATH.

O ALMIGHTY God, the aid of all who are in need, and the helper of all who flee to thee for succor; accept, we beseech thee, our humble supplications for this thy servant laboring under the dreadful apprehensions of thy wrath. O Lord, enter not into judgment with *him;* but make *him* sensible, that though the wages of sin are death, the gift of God is eternal life; that thou wouldest not the death of a sinner, and art not willing that any should perish; that thou dost always punish less than we deserve, and in the midst of judgment dost remember mercy. Revive *his* soul with a sense of thy love, and the hopes of obtaining thy pardon, and the joy of thy salvation; that *he* may be raised from this dejection, and show with gladness what thou hast done for *his* soul; and this we humbly ask in the name of Jesus Christ our Lord. *Amen.*

THANKSGIVING FOR THE BEGINNING OF A RECOVERY.

GREAT and mighty God, who bringest down to the grave and bringest up again ; we bless thy wonderful goodness, for having turned our heaviness into joy, and our mourning into gladness, by restoring this our *brother* to some degree of *his* former health. Blessed be thy name, that thou didst not forsake *him* in *his* sickness ; but didst visit *him* with comforts from above ; didst support *him* in patience and submission to thy will, and at last didst send *him* relief. Perfect, we beseech thee, this thy mercy towards *him*, and prosper the means which shall be made use of for *his* cure ; that being restored to health of body, vigor of mind, and cheerfulness of spirit, *he* may offer thee a spiritual oblation with great gladness, and bless thy holy name for all thy goodness towards *him*, through Jesus Christ our Saviour, through whom we ascribe unto thee all honor and glory, world without end. *Amen.*

END OF THE VISITATION OF THE SICK.

BURIAL OF THE DEAD.

*When the Processi ı is enter 'ng the Church, the ʿM n-
ster shall utte tl e e Senten es*

I AM the resurrection and the life, saith the Lord;
he who believeth in me, though he were dead,
yet shall he live; and whosoever liveth and believeth in me shall never die. *St. John* xi. 25, 26.

I KNOW that my Redeemer liveth, and that he
shall stand at the latter day upon the earth.
And though after my skin, worms destroy this body,
yet in my flesh shall I see God. *Job* xix. 25, 26.

WE brought nothing into this world, and it is
certain that we can carry nothing out. The
Lord gave, and the Lord hath taken away; blessed
be the name of the Lord. 1 *Tim.* vi. 7; *Job* i. 21.

*Then shall be said the following Passages from the
39th and 90th Psalms.*

PSALM XXXIX.

LORD, make me to know mine end, and the
measure of my days, that I may know how
frail I am.

Behold thou hast made my days as it were a span long, and mine age is even as nothing in respect of thee; and verily every man at his best state is altogether vanity.

For man walketh in a vain shadow, and disquieteth himself in vain; he heapeth up riches, and cannot tell who shall gather them.

And now, Lord, what is my hope? truly my hope is even in thee.

I became dumb, and opened not my mouth; for it was thy doing.

But take thy stroke away from me; for I am consumed by the blow of thy heavy hand.

When thou with rebukes dost chasten man for sin, thou makest his beauty to consume away, like as it were a moth fretting a garment; surely every man is vanity.

Hear my prayer, O Lord, and with thine ears consider my calling; hold not thy peace at my tears.

For I am a stranger with thee, and a sojourner, as all my fathers were.

O spare me a little, that I may recover my strength, before I go hence, and be no more seen.

Psalm XC.

LORD, thou hast been our dwelling-place in all generations.

Before the mountains were brought forth, or ever thou hadst formed the earth and the world, even from everlasting to everlasting, thou art God.

Thou turnest man to destruction; and sayest, Return, ye children of men.

For a thousand years in thy sight are but as yesterday when it is past, or a watch in the night.

Thou carriest them away as with a flood; they are even as a sleep; and fade away suddenly like the grass ·

In the morning it is green, and groweth up; but in the evening it is cut down, dried up, and withered.

The days of our age are threescore years and ten; and though men be so strong, that they come to fourscore years, yet is their strength then but labor and sorrow; so soon passeth it away, and we are gone.

So teach us to number our days, that we may apply our hearts unto wisdom.

Then may follow John xiv. or these Selections from
1 *Cor.* xv

NOW is Christ risen from the dead, and become the first fruits of those who slept. For since by man came death, by man came also the resurrection of the dead.

For as in Adam all die, even so in Christ shall all be made alive.

There is one glory of the sun, and another glory of the moon, and another glory of the stars; for one star differeth from another star in glory. So also is the resurrection of the dead. It is sown in corruption, it is raised in incorruption; it is sown in dishonor, it is raised in glory; it is sown in weakness, it is raised in power; it is sown a natural body, it is raised a spiritual body.

Now this I say, brethren, that flesh and blood cannot inherit the kingdom of God; neither doth corruption inherit incorruption. For this corruptible must put on incorruption, and this mortal must put on immortality. So when this corruptible shall have put on incorruption, and this mortal shall have put on immortality, then shall be brought to pass the saying that is written, Death is swallowed up in victory. O death, where is thy sting? O grave, where is thy victory? The sting of death is sin, and the strength of sin is the law; but thanks be to God, who giveth us the victory, through our Lord Jesus Christ.

Then the Minister, either at the Grave, or in the body of the Church, shall say.

MAN who is born of a woman, hath but a short time to live, and is full of misery. He cometh up, and is cut down like a flower; he fleeth as it were a shadow, and never continueth in one stay.

In the midst of life we are in death; of whom may we seek for succor, but of thee, O Lord, who for our sins art justly displeased?

Yet, O Lord God most holy, O Lord most mighty, O holy and most merciful Father, deliver us not into the bitter pains of eternal death.

Thou knowest, Lord, the secrets of our hearts; shut not thy merciful ears to our prayers; but spare us, Lord most holy, O God most mighty, O holy and merciful Father, thou most worthy Judge eternal, suffer us not, at our last hour, for any pains of death, to fall from thee.

Then, while the Earth shall be cast upon the Body by some standing by, the Minister shall say,

FORASMUCH as it hath pleased Almighty God to take unto himself the soul of our *brother* here departed, we therefore commit *his* body to the ground; earth to earth, ashes to ashes, dust to dust; in sure and certain hope of the resurrection to eternal life, through our Lord Jesus Christ, when the earth and the sea shall give up their dead, and the corruptible bodies of those who sleep in Jesus shall be changed and made like unto his glorious body, according to the mighty working whereby he is able to subdue all things to himself.

Then shall be said,

I HEARD a voice from heaven, saying unto me, Write, From henceforth, blessed are the dead who die in the Lord; even so saith the Spirit; for they rest from their labors, and their works do follow them.

At the Burial of a young Child, may be said, instead of the above,

I HEARD the voice of Jesus, saying, Suffer little children to come unto me, for of such is the kingdom of heaven.

Then shall the Minister say one of the following Prayers, at his discretion.

Let us pray.

ALMIGHTY God, with whom do live the spirits of those who depart hence in the Lord; and with whom the souls of the faithful, after they are delivered from the burthen of the flesh, are in joy and felicity; we give thee hearty thanks for the good examples of all those thy servants, who, having finished their course in faith, do now rest from their labors. And we beseech thee, that we, with all those who are departed in the true faith of thy holy name, may have our perfect consummation and bliss in thy heavenly and everlasting glory, through Jesus Christ our Lord. *Amen.*

O MERCIFUL God, the Father of our Lord Jesus Christ, who is the resurrection and the life; in whom whosoever believeth shall live, though he die; and whosoever liveth and believeth in him shall not die eternally; who also hath taught us by his holy apostle, St. Paul, not to be sorry, as men without hope, for those who sleep in him; we humbly beseech thee, O Father, to raise us from the death of sin unto the life of righteousness; that, when we shall depart this life, we may rest in him; and that, at the resurrection to eternal life, we may be found acceptable in thy sight, and receive that blessing which thy well-beloved Son shall then pronounce to all that love and fear thee, saying, Come, ye blessed children of my Father, receive the kingdom prepared for you from the beginning of the world. Grant this, we beseech thee, O merciful Father, through Jesus Christ our Mediator and Redeemer. *Amen.*

O ALMIGHTY and ever-living God, we fly to thee as to our eternal refuge; we rest ourselves upon thee, the Rock of Ages. We see thy hand in all the circumstances of our lives. We confess the wisdom which created us of the dust; and bow to the decree which has determined, that unto dust we shall return. Thou knowest our frame, thou rememberest that we are but dust; we therefore pray thee, help our infirmities, and pitifully behold the sorrows of our hearts. Sanctify to this family the affliction which thou hast called them to bear. Pour into their troubled minds the consolations of thy Spirit, and teach them to turn this sorrow to their eternal good. May they be still, and know that thou art God, and that thou dost not willingly afflict or grieve the children of men. May they resign, without murmuring, this object of their love, assured that though lost to them, *he* lives to thee. May they endure tribulation as becometh thy children, and disciples of thy Son Jesus Christ.

O Lord, regard all thy servants in mercy. Lead us through this valley of tears with safety and peace, with holiness and religion, with spiritual comfort and joy; that when we shall have served thee in our generations, we may be gathered unto our fathers, having the testimony of a good conscience, and in the hope that neither death nor life, nor things present, nor things to come, shall be able to separate us from the love of God, which is in Christ Jesus our Lord. *Amen.*

O LORD, our God, who sendest forth thy spirit, and we are created, who takest away our breath, and we die, and return to the dust; blessed be thy name for the assurance of eternal life which thou hast given us by thy beloved Son. Blessed be thy holy name for the faith which we cherish, that this corruptible shall put on incorruption, and this mortal, immortality; and that when the night of the grave is past, a glorious morning will come; when thou shalt wipe away all tears from our eyes, and there shall be no more death, neither sorrow, nor crying, nor pain.

Let this immortal hope, and the comforts of thy gracious Spirit, sustain, in this their bereavement, the family and friends of our departed *brother.* Be thou, O God, their refuge, and their consolation, and their sure trust. The more they are brought to perceive that things seen are temporal, so much the more may they find that the things which are unseen are eternal; that thou art faithful, and that Christ is worthy, and that heaven, and not earth, is their home. May they embrace thy promises and be thankful; may they know that thou art God, and be still.

And grant, we beseech thee, O holy Father and eternal Judge, that we may all live mindful of our mortality, and prepared for thy will; and that, when thou sayest unto us, Return, ye children of men, we may hear the command without dismay, and obey it without reluctance; knowing whom we have believed, and persuaded that he is able to keep that which we have committed to him, against that day. We offer our prayers through him who is the resurrection and the life, thy Son Jesus Christ. *Amen.*

THE grace of our Lord Jesus Christ, and the love of God, and the fellowship of the Holy Ghost, be with us all evermore. *Amen.*

At the Burial of the Dead at Sea, the preceding Service may be used: only instead of these words, We therefore commit *his* body to the ground, earth to earth, ashes to ashes, dust to dust ; looking for, &c., *shall b said.* We therefore commit *his* body to the deep, to be turned into corruption ; in sure and certain hope, etc.

END OF THE BURIAL SERVICE.

The Psalter.

A SELECTION FROM

THE PSALMS OF DAVID

The First Day .

MORNING PRAYER.

PSALM I.

The righteous man is blessed.

BLESSED is the man who walketh not in the counsel of the ungodly, nor standeth in the way of sinners, nor sitteth in the seat of the scornful.

But his delight is in the law of the Lord, and in his law doth he exercise himself day and night.

He shall be like a tree planted by the water side, that will bring forth his fruit in due season.

His leaf also shall not wither; and whatsoever he doeth, it shall prosper.

As for the ungodly, it is not so with them; but they are like the chaff which the wind scattereth away.

Therefore the ungodly shall not be able to stand in the judgment; neither the sinners, in the congregation of the righteous.

For the Lord knoweth the way of the righteous; but the way of the ungodly shall perish.

PSALM III.

Trust in God in a time of distress.

LORD, how are they increased who trouble me ! many are they who rise up against me.

Many there be who say of my soul, There is no help for him in his God.

But thou, O Lord, art my defender; thou art my glory, and the lifter up of my head.

I did call upon the Lord with my voice, and he heard me out of his holy hill.

I laid me down and slept, and rose up again; for the Lord sustained me.

Salvation belongeth unto the Lord, and thy blessing is upon thy people.

PSALM IV.

Thankfulness, Trust, and Contentment.

HEAR me when I call, O God of my righteousness; thou hast set me at liberty when I was in trouble; have mercy upon me, and hearken unto my prayer.

O ye sons of men, how long will ye turn my glory into shame, and have such pleasure in vanity, and seek after falsehood?

Know this, that the Lord hath chosen to himself the man who is godly; when **I** call upon the Lord he will hear me.

Stand in awe, and sin not; commune with your own heart, and in your chamber, and be still.

Offer the sacrifice of righteousness, and put your trust in the Lord.

There be many who say, Who will show us any good?

Lord, lift thou up the light of thy countenance upon us.

Thou hast put gladness in my heart, more than theirs, when their corn, and wine, and oil, increased.

I will lay me down in peace, and take my rest, for it is thou, O Lord, only, who makest me dwell in safety.

Now unto the King eternal, etc.

Be honor and glory, etc.

EVENING PRAYER.

PSALM V.

Prayer for aid against enemies.

GIVE ear unto my words, O Lord; consider my meditation.

O hearken thou unto the voice of my calling, my King and my God; for unto thee will I make my prayer.

My voice shalt thou hear betimes, O Lord; early in the morning will I direct my prayer unto thee, and will look up.

For thou art a God who hath no pleasure in wickedness; neither shall any evil dwell with thee.

Such as be foolish shall not stand in thy sight; for thou hatest all those who work iniquity.

Thou wilt destroy those who speak falsehood; the Lord will abhor both the bloodthirsty and deceitful man.

But as for me, I will come unto thy house, even upon the multitude of thy mercies; and in thy fear will I worship toward thy holy temple.

Lead me, O Lord, in thy righteousness, because of mine enemies; make thy way plain before my face.

Let all those who put their trust in thee rejoice; they shall ever be giving of thanks, because thou defendest them; they who love thy name shall be joyful in thee.

For thou, Lord, wilt give thy blessing unto the righteous; and with thy favorable kindness wilt thou defend him as with a shield.

Psalm VII.

Prayer against false accusers. See 1 Sam. Chap 24.

O LORD my God, in thee have I put my trust; save me from all those who persecute me, and deliver me;

Lest mine enemy devour my soul like a lion, and tear it in pieces, while there is none to help.

O Lord my God, if I have done this thing; or if there be any wickedness in my hands;

If I have rewarded evil unto him who dealt

friendly with me ; (yea, I have delivered him who without any cause is mine enemy ;)

Then let mine enemy persecute my soul, and take it ; yea, let him tread my life down upon the earth, and lay mine honor in the dust.

The Lord shall judge the people ; give sentence with me, O Lord, according to my righteousness, and according to the innocency that is in me.

O let the wickedness of the ungodly come to an end ; but guide thou the just.

For the righteous God trieth the very hearts and reins.

My help cometh of God, who preserveth those who are true of heart.

God is a righteous judge ; and God is provoked every day.

I will give thanks unto the Lord, according to his righteousness ; and I will praise the name of the Lord most high.

Now unto the King eternal, etc.

Be honor and glory, etc.

The Second Day.

MORNING PRAYER.

Psalm VIII.

David watching his flocks by night, meditates on the sky and the earth.

O LORD our Governor, how excellent is thy name in all the world ! thou who hast set thy glory above the heavens !

Out of the mouth of very babes and sucklings hast thou ordained praise, to put thine adversaries to shame and to still the enemy and the revengeful.

When I consider thy heavens, even the work of thy fingers ; the moon and the stars which thou hast ordained ;

What is man, that thou art mindful of him ? and the son of man, that thou visitest him ?

Thou madest him a little lower than the angels, and hast crowned him with glory and honor.

Thou makest him to have dominion over the works of thy hands ; and thou hast put all things under his feet ;

All sheep and oxen, yea, and the beasts of the field ;

The fowls of the air, and the fishes of the sea, and whatsoever passeth through the paths of the seas.

O Lord our Governor, how excellent is thy name in all the world !

Psalm IX.

Thanksgiving for Victory.

I WILL give thanks unto thee, O Lord, with my whole heart ; I will speak of all thy marvellous works.

I will be glad and rejoice in thee; I will sing praise to thy name, O thou Most High.

Thou hast rebuked the heathen, and destroyed the ungodly ; thou hast put out their name for ever and ever.

Desolations have consumed the enemy forever; and as to the cities which thou hast destroyed, their memory is perished with them.

But the Lord shall endure forever; he hath prepared his throne for judgment.

And he shall judge the world in righteousness, and minister true judgment unto the people.

The Lord also will be a defence for the oppressed, even a refuge in time of trouble.

And they, who know thy name, will put their trust in thee; for thou, Lord, hast never failed those who seek thee.

O praise the Lord who dwelleth in Sion: show the people of his doings.

For when he maketh inquisition for blood, he remembereth them, and forgetteth not the complaint of the poor.

The heathen are sunk down in the pit that they made; in the same net which they hid privily, is their own foot taken.

Thus the Lord is known by the judgment which he executeth; the ungodly is ensnared in the work of his own hands.

The wicked shall be turned into the pit, and all the people who forget God.

For the poor shall not always be forgotten; the patient abiding of the meek shall not perish forever.

Arise, O Lord, and let not man prevail; let the heathen be judged in thy sight.

Put them in fear, O Lord ; that the heathen may know themselves to be but men.

Now unto the King eternal, etc.

Be honor and glory, etc.

EVENING PRAYER.

PSALM XI.

Trust in God.

IN the Lord put I my trust; how say ye then to my soul, that she should flee as a bird unto the hill ?

" For lo, the ungodly bend their bow, and make ready their arrows upon the string, that they may privily shoot at those who are true of heart."

" If the foundations be cast down, what can the righteous do ? "

The Lord is in his holy temple ; the Lord's throne is in heaven. His eyes consider the poor ; and his eyelids try the children of men.

The Lord trieth the righteous ; but the ungodly and him who delighteth in wickedness, doth his soul abhor.

Upon the ungodly he shall rain snares, fire and brimstone, storm and tempest ; this shall be the portion of their cup.

For the righteous Lord loveth righteousness ; his countenance will behold the thing that is just.

PSALM XII.

A Prayer for protection from calumniators.

HELP, Lord, for the godly man ceaseth, for the faithful fail from among the children of men.

They speak vanity every one with his neighbor; they do but flatter with their lips, and dissemble in their double heart.

The Lord shall root out all deceitful lips, and the tongue that speaketh proud things;

Who have said, "With our tongue will we prevail; we are they who ought to speak; who is lord over us?"

Now for the oppression of the needy, and because of the deep sighing of the poor;

I will arise, saith the Lord, and will help every one from him who swelleth against him, and will set him at rest.

The words of the Lord are pure words; even as the silver which from the earth is tried, and purified seven times in the fire.

Thou wilt keep them, O Lord; thou wilt preserve them from this generation forever.

PSALM XV.

Picture of an upright man.

LORD, who shall dwell in thy tabernacle? or who shall rest upon thy holy hill?

Even he who leadeth an uncorrupt life, and doeth the thing which is right, and speaketh the truth from his heart:

He who hath used no deceit in his tongue, nor done evil to his neighbor, nor slandered his neighbor:

He who setteth not by himself, but honoreth those who fear the Lord ·

He who sweareth unto his neighbor, and disappointeth him not, though it were to his own hindrance :

He who hath not given his money upon usury, nor taken a bribe against the innocent.

Whoso doeth these things shall never fall.

PSALM XVI.

Trust in God, and gratitude for Divine protection.

PRESERVE me, O God; for in thee have I put my trust.

O my soul, thou hast said unto the Lord, Thou art my God ; I have nothing good without thee.

The saints who are on the earth, and the excellent, in them is all my delight.

They who run after other gods shall have great trouble.

Their drink offerings of blood will I not offer ; neither make mention of their names with my lips.

The Lord himself is the portion of mine inheritance, and of my cup ; thou shalt maintain my lot.

The lines are fallen unto me in pleasant places ; yea, I have a goodly heritage.

I will thank the Lord who careth for me ; my secret thoughts also instruct me in the night season.

I have set the Lord alway before me ; for he is on my right hand, therefore I shall not fall.

Wherefore my heart is glad, and my tongue rejoiceth ; my flesh also shall rest in hope.

For why ? thou wilt not leave my soul in the

grave ; neither wilt thou suffer thy holy one to see corruption.

Thou wilt show me the path of life ; in thy presence is fulness of joy ; and at thy right hand there are pleasures for evermore.

Now unto the King eternal, etc.

Be honor and glory, etc.

●

The Third Day

MORNING PRAYER.

PSALM XVIII.

God, the Almighty Deliverer. 2 Sam. Chap. 22.

I WILL love thee, O Lord, my strength ; the Lord is my rock, and my defence ; my Saviour, my God, and my might, in whom I will trust ; my buckler, the horn also of my salvation, and my refuge.

I will call upon the Lord, who is worthy to be praised ; so shall I be safe from mine enemies.

When the waves of death compassed me, and the floods of ungodliness made me afraid ;

When the sorrows of the grave surrounded me and the snares of death encompassed me ;

In my distress I called upon the Lord, and cried unto my God.

He heard my voice out of his holy temple ; and my complaint came before him, even into his ears.

Then the earth trembled and quaked ; the very foundations also of the hills shook, and were removed, because he was wroth.

There went up a smoke from his presence, and a consuming fire out of his mouth ; so that coals were kindled at it.

He bowed the heavens also, and came down ; and it was dark under his feet.

He rode upon the cherubim, and did fly ; he came flying upon the wings of the wind.

He made darkness his pavilion ; his tent round about him was dark waters and thick clouds of the skies.

At the brightness of his presence black clouds swept along, bolts of fire were kindled.

The Lord also thundered in the heaven, and the Highest gave his voice, amid hailstones, and coals of fire.

He sent out his arrows, and scattered them ; he cast forth lightnings, and destroyed them.

The springs of waters were seen, and the foundations of the round world were discovered at thy chiding, O Lord, at the blasting of the breath of thy displeasure.

He stretched forth his hand from above ; he took me, he drew me out of many waters.

He delivered me from my strong enemy, and from those who hated me ; for they were too mighty for me.

They assaulted me in the day of my trouble ; but the Lord was my upholder.

He brought me forth into a place of liberty ; he brought me forth, even because he had a favor unto me.

The Lord rewarded me according to my right-eous dealings; according to the cleanness of my hands did he recompense me.

For I have kept the ways of the Lord, and have not wickedly departed from my God.

For all his judgments were before me, and I did not put away his statutes from me.

I was also upright before him; and I kept myself from iniquity.

Therefore hath the Lord rewarded me according to my righteous dealing, according to the cleanness of my hands in his sight.

With the merciful thou wilt show thyself merciful; with an upright man thou wilt show thyself upright.

With the pure thou wilt show thyself pure, and with the froward thou wilt deal according to their frowardness.

For thou wilt save the people who are in adversity; and wilt bring down the high looks of the proud.

Thou also wilt light my candle; the Lord my God will make my darkness to be light.

The way of God is an undefiled way; the word of the Lord is tried; he is the defender of all who put their trust in him.

For who is God, but the Lord? or who hath any strength, except our God?

It is God who girdeth me with strength, and maketh my way plain.

Thou hast given me the shield of thy salvation;

thy right hand also hath holden me up, and thy loving-kindness hath made me great.

Thou hast enlarged my path under me, so that my feet shall not slide.

The Lord liveth, and blessed be my strong helper ; and praised be the God of my salvation.

It is he who delivereth me from mine enemies, and setteth me up above mine adversaries, and shall rid me from the violent man.

For this cause will I give thanks unto thee, O Lord, among the nations, and sing praises unto thy name.

Now unto the King eternal, etc.

Be honor and glory, etc.

EVENING PRAYER.

PSALM XIX.

The glory of God manifested in the heavenly bodies and in the Holy Scriptures.

THE heavens declare the glory of God ; and the firmament showeth his handy work.

Day unto day uttereth speech ; night unto night showeth knowledge.

There is no speech nor language where their voice is not heard.

Their sounds are gone out into all lands ; and their words unto the ends of the world.

Therein hath he set a tabernacle for the sun, who cometh forth as a bridegroom out of his chamber, and rejoiceth as a strong man to run his course.

He goeth forth from the uttermost part of the heaven, and his circuit is unto the end of it again ; and there is nothing hid from his heat.

The law of the Lord is perfect, converting the soul ; the testimony of the Lord is sure, and giveth wisdom unto the simple.

The statutes of the Lord are right, and rejoice the heart ; the commandment of the Lord is pure, and giveth light unto the eyes.

The fear of the Lord is clean, and endureth forever ; the judgments of the Lord are true, and righteous altogether.

More to be desired are they than gold, yea, than much fine gold ; sweeter also than honey, and the honeycomb.

Moreover, by them is thy servant taught ; and in keeping of them there is great reward.

Who can understand his errors? O cleanse thou me from my secret faults.

Keep thy servant also from presumptuous sins, lest they get the dominion over me ; so shall I be upright, and innocent from the great offence.

Let the words of my mouth, and the meditation of my heart, be always acceptable in thy sight,

O Lord, my strength, and my redeemer.

PSALM XX.

Prayer of the people for their king going to war.

THE Lord hear thee in the day of trouble ; the name of the God of Jacob defend thee ;

Send thee help from the sanctuary, and strengthen thee out of Sion ;

Grant thee thy heart's desire, and fulfil all thy mind.

We will rejoice in thy salvation, and triumph in the name of the Lord our God ; the Lord perform all thy petitions.

Now know I, that the Lord helpeth his anointed, and will hear him from his holy heaven, even with the wholesome strength of his right hand.

Some put their trust in chariots, and some in horses ; but we will remember the name of the Lord our God.

They are brought down, and fallen ; but we are risen and stand upright.

Save, Lord, and hear us, O King of heaven, when we call upon thee.

Now unto the King eternal, etc.

Be honor and glory, etc.

The Fourth Day,

MORNING PRAYER.

Psalm XXIII.

God our Shepherd.

THE Lord is my shepherd ; therefore can I lack nothing.

He maketh me to lie down in green pastures, he leadeth me beside the still waters.

He restoreth my soul, and bringeth me forth in the paths of righteousness for his name's sake.

Yea, though I walk through the valley of the shadow of death, I will fear no evil; for thou art with me, thy rod and thy staff comfort me.

Thou preparest a table before me in the presence of mine enemies; thou anointest my head with oil, and my cup runneth over.

Surely thy loving-kindness and mercy shall follow me all the days of my life; and I will dwell in the house of the Lord forever.

PSALM XXIV.

Bringing the ark into the temple. 2 Sam. Chap. 6, ver. 15.

THE earth is the Lord's, and all that therein is; the world, and they who dwell therein.

For he hath founded it upon the seas, and established it upon the floods.

Who shall ascend unto the hill of the Lord? or who shall rise up in his holy place?

Even he who hath clean hands and a pure heart, and who hath not lifted up his mind unto vanity, nor sworn deceitfully.

He shall receive a blessing from the Lord, and righteousness from the God of his salvation.

This is the generation of those who seek him, even of those who seek thy face, O God of Jacob.

Lift up your heads, O ye gates, and be ye lifted up, ye everlasting doors; and the King of glory shall come in.

"Who is the King of glory?" It is the Lord, strong and mighty, even the Lord mighty in battle.

Lift up your heads, O ye gates, and be ye lifted up, ye everlasting doors; and the King of glory shall come in.

"Who is the King of glory?" Even the Lord of hosts, he is the King of glory.

Now unto the King eternal, etc.

Be honor and glory, etc.

EVENING PRAYER.

Psalm XXV.

Prayer of the penitent.

UNTO thee, O Lord, will I lift up my soul; my God I have put my trust in thee; O let me not be confounded, neither let mine enemies triumph over me.

For all they who hope in thee shall not be ashamed; but such as wickedly forsake thee shall be put to confusion.

Show me thy ways, O Lord, and teach me thy paths.

Lead me forth in thy truth, and teach me; for thou art the God of my salvation; in thee hath been my hope all the day long.

Call to remembrance, O Lord, thy tender mercies, and thy loving-kindnesses, which have been ever of old.

O remember not the sins and offences of my youth; but according to thy mercy think thou upon me, for thy goodness' sake, O Lord.

Gracious and righteous is the Lord; therefore will he teach sinners in the way.

Those who are meek shall he guide in judgment; and such as are gentle, them shall he teach his way.

All the paths of the Lord are mercy and truth, unto such as keep his covenant and his testimonies.

For thy name's sake, O Lord, be merciful unto my sin, for it is great.

What man is he who feareth the Lord? Him shall he teach in the way that he shall choose.

His soul shall dwell at ease; and his seed shall inherit the land.

The secret of the Lord is among those who fear him; and he will show them his covenant.

Mine eyes are ever looking unto the Lord, for he shall pluck my feet out of the net.

Turn thee unto me, and have mercy upon me; for I am desolate and in misery.

The sorrows of my heart are enlarged; O bring thou me out of my troubles.

Look upon my adversity and misery, and forgive me all my sin.

O keep my soul, and deliver me; let me not be confounded; for I have put my trust in thee.

Let perfectness and righteous dealing preserve me; for my hope hath been in thee.

Deliver Israel, O God, out of all his troubles.

Now unto the King eternal, etc.

Be honor and glory, etc.

The Fifth Day.

MORNING PRAYER.

PSALM XXVI.

Confidence in innocence.

BE thou my judge, O Lord, for I have walked innocently; my trust hath been also in the Lord; therefore shall I not fall.

Examine me, O Lord, and prove me; try my reins and my heart.

For thy loving-kindness is ever before mine eyes, and I will walk in thy truth.

I have not dwelt with vain persons; neither will I have fellowship with the deceitful.

I have hated the congregation of the wicked; and will not sit among the ungodly.

I will wash my hands in innocency, O Lord, and so will I go to thine altar;

That I may show the voice of thanksgiving, and tell of all thy wondrous works.

Lord, I have loved the habitation of thy house, and the place where thine honor dwelleth.

O shut not up my soul with sinners, nor my life with the bloodthirsty;

In whose hands is wickedness, and their right hand is full of bribes.

But as for me, I will walk innocently; O deliver me, and be merciful unto me.

My foot standeth right; I will praise the Lord in the congregations.

PSALM XXVII.

Confidence in God's protection.

THE Lord is my light and my salvation; whom then shall I fear? The Lord is the strength of my life; of whom then shall I be afraid?

Though an host of men encamp against me, yet shall not my heart be afraid; and though there rise up war against me, yet will I put my trust in him.

One thing have I desired of the Lord, which I will seek after; even that I may dwell in the house of .the Lord all the days of my life, to behold the fair beauty of the Lord, and to inquire in his temple.

For in the time of trouble he will hide me in his tabernacle; yea, in the secret place of his dwelling will he hide me, and set me upon a rock of stone.

Therefore will I offer in his dwelling an oblation with great gladness; I will sing and speak praises unto the Lord.

Hearken unto my voice, O Lord, when I cry unto thee; have mercy upon me, and hear me.

When thou saidst, Seek ye my face; my heart said unto thee, Thy face, Lord, will I seek.

O hide thou not thy face from me, nor cast thy servant away in displeasure.

Thou hast been my succor; leave me not, neither forsake me, O God of my salvation.

Though my father and my mother forsake me, yet the Lord taketh me up.

Teach me thy way, O Lord, and lead me in the right way, because of mine enemies.

I should utterly have fainted, but that I believe verily to see the goodness of the Lord in the land of the living.

O tarry thou the Lord's leisure; be of good courage and he shall strengthen thine heart; and put thou thy trust in the Lord.

Now unto the King eternal, etc.

Be honor and glory, etc.

EVENING PRAYER.

PSALM XXVIII.

Prayer for aid, with confidence of being heard.

UNTO thee will I cry, O Lord my strength; be not silent to me; lest, if thou make as though thou hearest not, I become like those who go down into the pit.

Hear the voice of my humble petitions when I cry unto thee, when I hold up my hands toward the mercy-seat of thy holy temple.

O pluck me not away, neither destroy me with the ungodly and wicked doers, who speak friendly to their neighbors, but imagine mischief in their hearts.

Praised be the Lord, for he hath heard the voice of my humble petitions.

The Lord is my strength and my shield; my heart trusted in him, and I am helped; therefore my heart danceth for joy, and in my song will I praise him.

The Lord is my strength, and he is the wholesome defence of his anointed.

O save thy people, and give thy blessing unto thine inheritance ; feed them, and set them up for-ever.

PSALM XXIX.

The glory of God, manifested in a thunder-storm.

GIVE unto the Lord, O ye mighty, give unto the Lord glory and strength.

Give the Lord the honor due unto his name ; worship the Lord in the beauty of holiness.

The voice of the Lord is upon the waters, the voice of the glorious God ; the Lord thundereth over the great waters.

The voice of the Lord is mighty ; the voice of the Lord is a glorious voice.

The voice of the Lord breaketh the cedar-trees ; yea, the Lord breaketh the cedars of Lebanon.

The voice of the Lord scattereth flames of fire ; the voice of the Lord shaketh the wilderness ; yea, the Lord shaketh the wilderness of Kadesh.

The voice of the Lord causeth the oaks to quake, and layeth bare the forests ; in his temple doth every man speak of his honor.

The Lord sitteth above the water-flood ; yea, the Lord remaineth King forever.

The Lord will give strength unto his people ; the Lord will give his people the blessing of peace.

Now unto the King eternal, etc.

Be honor and glory, etc.

The Sixth Day.

MORNING PRAYER.

PSALM XXX.

On recovery from sickness.

I WILL magnify thee, O Lord; for thou hast set me up, and not made my foes to triumph over me.

O Lord my God, I cried unto thee, and thou hast healed me.

Thou, Lord, hast brought my soul from the grave; thou hast kept me alive that I should not go down to the pit.

Sing praises unto the Lord, O ye saints of his, and give thanks unto him at the remembrance of his holiness.

For his wrath endureth but the twinkling of an eye, and in his favor is life; heaviness may endure for a night, but joy cometh in the morning.

In my prosperity I said, "I shall never be moved; thou, Lord, of thy goodness, hast made my hill so strong."

Thou didst turn thy face from me, and I was troubled.

Then I cried unto thee, O Lord, and besought the Lord right humbly.

"What profit is there in my blood, when I go down to the pit?

"Shall the dust give thanks unto thee? or shall it declare thy truth?

"Hear, O Lord, and have mercy upon me; Lord, be thou my helper."

Thou hast turned my heaviness into joy; thou hast put off my sackcloth, and girded me with gladness.

Therefore will I sing thy praise without ceasing; O my God, I will give thanks unto thee forever.

Psalm XXXI.

A prayer for deliverance.

IN thee, O Lord, do I put my trust; let me never be put to confusion; deliver me in thy righteousness.

Bow down thine ear to me; make haste to deliver me.

And be thou my strong rock, and house of defence, that thou mayest save me.

For thou art my strong rock and my castle; be thou also my guide, and lead me for thy name's sake.

Into thy hands I commend my spirit; for thou hast redeemed me, O Lord, thou God of truth.

I have hated those who regard superstitious vanities, and my trust hath been in the Lord.

I will be glad and rejoice in thy mercy; for thou hast considered my trouble, and hast known my soul in adversities.

O how plentiful is thy goodness which thou hast laid up for those who fear thee, and that thou hast prepared for those who put their trust in thee, even before the sons of men!

Thou shalt hide them, in the place of thine own presence, from the insults of men; thou shalt keep them secretly, in thy tabernacle, from the strife of tongues.

Thanks be to the Lord; for he hath shown me his marvellous kindness, as in a strong city.

For I had said in my haste, I am cast out of the sight of thine eyes.

Nevertheless, thou heardest the voice of my prayer, when I cried unto thee.

O love the Lord, all ye his saints; for the Lord preserveth those who are faithful, and plenteously requiteth the proud doer.

Be strong, and he shall establish your heart, all ye who put your trust in the Lord.

Now unto the King eternal, etc.

Be honor and glory, etc.

EVENING PRAYER.

PSALM XXXII.

Penitential psalm.

BLESSED is he whose unrighteousness is forgiven, and whose sin is covered.

Blessed is the man unto whom the Lord imputeth no sin, and in whose spirit there is no guile.

While I held my tongue, my bones consumed away through my daily complaining.

For thy hand was heavy upon me day and night; and my moisture was turned into the drought of summer.

I acknowledged my sin unto thee, and mine unrighteousness have I not hid.

I said, I will confess my sins unto the Lord; and so thou forgavest the wickedness of my sin.

For this shall every one who is godly make his prayer unto thee, in a time when thou mayest be found; and in the great water-floods they shall not come nigh him.

Thou art a place to hide me in; thou shalt preserve me from trouble; thou shalt compass me about with songs of deliverance.

" I will inform thee, and teach thee the way wherein thou shouldst go, and I will guide thee with mine eye.

" Be ye not like to horse and mule, which have no understanding; whose mouths must be held with bit and bridle, lest they tread upon thee.

" Great plagues remain for the ungodly; but whoso putteth his trust in the Lord, mercy embraceth him on every side."

Be glad, O ye righteous, and rejoice in the Lord; and be joyful all ye who are true of heart.

PSALM XXXIII.

Praise to God as the Creator and Governor of the world.

REJOICE in the Lord, O ye righteous; for it becometh well the just to be thankful.

Sing unto the Lord a new song; sing praises unto him skilfully, with an exalted voice.

For the word of the Lord is true, and all his works are faithful.

He loveth righteousness and judgment; the earth is full of the goodness of the Lord.

By the word of the Lord were the heavens made, and all the hosts of them by the breath of his mouth.

He gathereth the waters of the sea together, as it were upon a heap ; and layeth up the deep, as in a treasure-house.

Let all the earth fear the Lord ; stand in awe of him, all ye who dwell in the world.

For he spake, and it was done ; he commanded, and it stood fast.

The Lord bringeth the counsel of the heathen to naught, and maketh the devices of the people to be of none effect, and casteth out the counsels of princes.

The counsel of the Lord shall endure forever · and the thoughts of his heart from generation to generation.

Blessed is the nation whose God is the Lord ; and blessed are the people that he hath chosen to him to be his inheritance.

The Lord looketh down from heaven, and beholdeth all the children of men ; from the habitation of his dwelling he considereth all those who dwell on the earth.

He fashioneth all the hearts of them, and understandeth all their works.

There is no king who can be saved by the multitude of an host ; neither is any mighty man delivered by much strength.

A horse is but a vain thing for safety ; neither shall he deliver any man by his great strength.

Behold, the eye of the Lord is upon those who fear him, and upon those who put their trust in his mercy ;

To deliver their soul from death, and to feed them in the time of famine.

Our soul hath patiently tarried for the Lord ; for he is our help and our shield.

For our hearts shall rejoice in him ; because we have trusted in his holy name.

Let thy merciful kindness, O Lord, be upon us, as we do put our trust in thee.

Now unto the King eternal, etc.

Be honor and glory, etc.

The Seventh Day.

MORNING PRAYER.

Psalm XXXIV.

The happiness of the righteous and misery of the wicked.

I WILL alway give thanks unto the Lord ; his praise shall ever be in my mouth.

My soul shall make her boast in the Lord ; the humble shall hear thereof, and be glad.

O praise the Lord with me, and let us magnify his name together.

I sought the Lord, and he heard me ; yea, he delivered me out of all my fear.

They looked unto him, and were enlightened ; and their faces were not ashamed.

Lo, the poor crieth, and the Lord heareth him ; yea, and saveth him out of all his troubles.

The angel of the Lord encampeth round about those who fear him, and delivereth them.

O taste, and see how gracious the Lord is ; blessed is the man who trusteth in him.

O fear the Lord, ye who are his saints ; for those who fear him lack nothing.

The lions do lack, and suffer hunger ; but they who seek the Lord shall want no manner of thing that is good.

Come, ye children, and hearken unto me ; I will teach you the fear of the Lord.

What man is he who desireth to live, and would fain see good days?

Keep thy tongue from evil, and thy lips, that they speak no guile.

Depart from evil, and do good ; seek peace, and pursue it.

The eyes of the Lord are over the righteous, and his ears are open unto their prayer.

The countenance of the Lord is against those who do evil, to root out the remembrance of them from the earth.

The righteous cry, and the Lord heareth them and delivereth them out of all their troubles.

The Lord is nigh unto those who are of a contrite heart, and will save such as are of an humble spirit.

Great are the troubles of the righteous ; but the Lord delivereth him out of them all.

He keepeth all his bones ; so that not one of them shall be broken.

But misfortune shall slay the ungodly; and they who hate the righteous shall be desolate.

The Lord delivereth the souls of his servants; and all they who put their trust in him shall not be destitute.

PSALM XXXVI.

The wickedness of men contrasted with the goodness of God.

MY heart showeth me the wickedness of the ungodly, that there is no fear of God before his eyes.

For he flattereth himself in his own sight, that his abominable sin will not be found out.

The words of his mouth are unrighteous and full of deceit; he hath left off to behave himself wisely, and to do good.

He imagineth mischief upon his bed, and hath set himself in no good way; neither doth he abhor anything that is evil.

Thy mercy, O Lord, reacheth unto the heavens, and thy faithfulness unto the clouds.

Thy righteousness standeth like the strong mountains; thy judgments are like the great deep.

Thou, Lord, preservest both man and beast. How excellent is thy mercy, O God! therefore the children of men shall put their trust under the shadow of thy wings.

They shall be satisfied with the plenteousness of thy house; and thou shalt give them to drink of thy pleasures as out of a river.

For with thee is the fountain of life, and in thy light shall we see light.

O continue thy loving-kindness unto those who know thee, and thy righteousness unto those who are true of heart.

Now unto the King eternal, etc.

Be honor and glory, etc.

EVENING PRAYER.

PSALM XXXVII.

The righteous and the wicked contrasted.

FRET not thyself because of the ungodly; neither be thou envious against the evil doers.

For they shall be soon cut down like the grass; and be withered even as the green herb.

Put thou thy trust in the Lord, and be doing good; so shalt thou dwell in the land, and verily thou shalt be fed.

Delight thou in the Lord, and he shall give thee thy heart's desire.

Commit thy way unto the Lord, and put thy trust in him, and he shall bring it to pass.

He shall make thy righteousness as clear as the light, and thy just dealing as the noonday.

Repose thyself in the Lord, and abide patiently upon him, but grieve not thyself at him whose way doth prosper, or against the man who doeth after evil counsels.

Cease from wrath, and let go displeasure; fret not thyself, else shalt thou be moved to do evil.

Wicked doers shall be rooted out; and they who patiently wait on the Lord shall inherit the land.

Yet a little while, and the ungodly shall be gone;

thou shalt look after his place, and he shall be away.

But the meek shall inherit the earth, and shall be refreshed in the abundance of peace.

The ungodly have drawn out the sword, and have bent their bow, to cast down the poor and needy, and to slay such as are of a right conversation.

Their sword shall go through their own heart, and their bow shall be broken.

A small thing that the righteous hath, is better than great riches of the ungodly.

For the arms of the ungodly shall be broken, but the Lord upholdeth the righteous.

The Lord knoweth the days of the godly; their inheritance shall endure forever.

They shall not be confounded in the perilous time, and in the days of dearth they shall have enough.

The Lord ordereth a good man's going, and maketh his way acceptable to himself.

Though he fall, he shall not be cast away; for the Lord upholdeth him with his hand.

I have been young, and now am old, and yet saw I never the righteous forsaken, nor his seed begging their bread.

The righteous is ever merciful, and lendeth, and his seed is blessed.

Flee from evil, and do the thing that is good, and dwell forevermore.

For the Lord loveth the thing that is right; he forsaketh not his who are godly, but they are preserved forever.

The unrighteous shall be punished; as for the seed of the ungodly, it shall be rooted out.

The righteous shall inherit the land and dwell therein forever.

The mouth of the righteous is exercised in wisdom, and his tongue will be talking of judgment.

The law of his God is in his heart, and his goings shall not slide.

The ungodly watcheth the righteous, and seeketh occasion to slay him.

The Lord will not leave him in his hand, nor condemn him when he is judged.

Hope thou in the Lord, and keep his way, and he shall promote thee, that thou shalt possess the land; when the ungodly shall perish, thou shalt see it.

I myself have seen the ungodly in great power, and flourishing like a green bay-tree.

I went by, and lo, he was gone; I sought him, but his place could nowhere be found.

Keep innocency, and take heed unto the thing that is right; for that shall bring a man peace at the last.

As for the transgressors, they shall perish together; and the end of the ungodly is, they shall be rooted out at the last.

But the salvation of the righteous cometh of the Lord, who is also their strength in the time of trouble.

And the Lord shall stand by them, and save them ; he shall deliver them from the ungodly, and shall save them, because they put their trust in him.

Now unto the King eternal, etc.

Be honor and glory, etc.

The Eighth Day.

MORNING PRAYER.

PSALM XXXIX.

The shortness and vanity of human life.

I SAID, I will take heed to my ways, that I offend not with my tongue.

I will keep my mouth as it were with a bridle, while the ungodly is in my sight.

I held my tongue and spake nothing ; I kept silence, yea, even from good words ; and it was pain and grief to me.

My heart was hot within me ; and while I was thus musing, the fire burned ; and at the last I spake with my tongue.

Lord, let me know my end, and the measure of my days ; that I may know how frail I am.

Behold, thou hast made my days as it were a span long ; and mine age is even as nothing in respect of thee ; and verily every man at his best state is altogether vanity.

For man walketh in a vain shadow, and disquieteth himself in vain ; he heapeth up riches, and cannot tell who shall gather them.

And now, Lord, what is my hope? truly my hope is even in thee.

Deliver me from all mine offences, and make me not the reproach of scoffers.

I became dumb and opened not my mouth; for it was thy doing.

Take thy stroke away from me; I am crushed by the blow of thy heavy hand.

When thou with rebukes dost chasten man for sin, thou makest his beauty to consume away, like as it were a moth fretting a garment; every man therefore is but vanity.

Hear my prayer, O Lord, and with thine ears consider my calling; hold not thy peace at my tears.

For I am a stranger with thee, and a sojourner, as all my fathers were.

O spare me a little, that I may recover my strength, before I go hence, and be no more seen.

PSALM XL.

Thanksgiving, with resolutions of obedience.

I WAITED patiently for the Lord, and he inclined unto me, and heard my calling.

He brought me out of the horrible pit, and out of the mire and clay, and set my feet upon the rock, and established my goings.

And he hath put a new song in my mouth, even a thanksgiving unto our God.

Many shall see it, and fear, and shall put their trust in the Lord.

Blessed is the man who hath set his hope in the

Lord, and turned not unto the proud, and such as go about with lies.

Many, O Lord my God, are the wondrous works which thou hast done, and thy thoughts which are to us-ward ; they cannot be numbered unto thee.

If I should declare them, and speak of them, they would be more than I am able to express.

Sacrifice and meat-offering thou wouldest not ; so hast thou taught me.

Burnt-offerings and sacrifice for sin hast thou not required ; then said I, " Lo, I come.

" In the volume of the book it is written of me, that I should fulfil thy will, O my God ; I am content to do it ; yea, thy law is within my heart."

I have declared thy righteousness in the great congregation ; lo, I have not refrained my lips, O Lord, and that thou knowest.

I have not hid thy righteousness within my heart ; my talk hath been of thy truth, and of thy salvation.

I have not kept back thy loving mercy and truth from the great congregation.

Withdraw not thou thy mercy from me, O Lord ; let thy loving-kindness and thy truth alway preserve me.

For innumerable troubles are come about me ; my sins have taken such hold upon me, that I am not able to look up ; yea, they are more in number than the hairs of my head, and my heart hath failed me.

O Lord, let it be thy pleasure to deliver me; make haste, O Lord, to help me.

Let all those who seek thee be joyful and glad in thee; and let such as love thy salvation say alway, The Lord be praised.

As for me, I am poor and needy; but the Lord careth for me.

Thou art my helper and redeemer; make no long tarrying, O my God.

Now unto the King eternal, etc.

Be honor and glory, etc.

EVENING PRAYER.

PSALM XLIII.

Longings of an exile for God's house.

GIVE sentence with me, O God, and defend my cause against the ungodly people; O deliver me from the deceitful and wicked man.

For thou art the God of my strength; why hast thou put me far from thee? and why go I so heavily while the enemy oppresseth me?

O send out thy light and thy truth, that they may lead me, and bring me unto thy holy hill, and to thy dwelling.

Then will I go unto the altar of God, even unto the God of my joy and gladness; and upon the harp will I give thanks unto thee, O God, my God.

Why art thou so heavy, O my soul? and why art thou so disquieted within me?

O put thy trust in God; for I will yet give him

thanks, who is the help of my countenance, and my God.

PSALM XLVI.

Deliverance from the Assyrians. 2 Chron. xxxii. 21.

GOD is our hope and strength, a very present help in trouble.

Therefore will we not fear, though the earth be moved, and though the hills be carried into the midst of the sea ;

Though the waters thereof rage and swell, and though the mountains shake at the tempest of the same.

There is a river, the streams whereof shall make glad the city of God, the holy place of the tabernacle of the Most High.

God is in the midst of her, therefore shall she not be moved ; God shall help her, and that right early.

The heathen raged, and the kingdoms were moved ; but God uttered his voice, and the earth melted away.

The Lord of hosts is with us ; the God of Jacob is our refuge.

O come hither, and behold the works of the Lord, what destruction he hath brought upon the earth.

He maketh wars to cease in all the world ; he breaketh the bow, and snappeth the spear in sunder, and burneth the chariots in the fire.

" Be still, and know that I am God ; I will be

exalted among the heathen, and I will be exalted in the earth."

The Lord of hosts is with us, the God of Jacob is our refuge.

PSALM XLVII.

Song of Victory.

O CLAP your hands together, all ye people ; O sing unto God with the voice of melody.

For the Lord is high, and to be feared ; he is the great King over all the earth.

He shall subdue the people under us, and the nations under our feet.

He shall choose out an heritage for us, even the excellency of Jacob whom he loved.

God is gone up with a shout, and the Lord with the sound of the trumpet.

O sing praises, sing praises unto our God ; O sing praises, sing praises unto our King.

For God is the King of all the earth ; sing ye praises with understanding.

God reigneth over the nations ; God sitteth upon his holy throne.

The princes of the heathen are joined unto the people of the God of Abraham ; for the mighty of the earth belong unto God. He is over all.

PSALM XLVIII.

Thanksgiving for national blessings.

GREAT is the Lord, and highly to be praised, in the city of our God, even upon his holy hill.

As we have heard, so have we seen in the city of the Lord of hosts, in the city of our God, God upholdeth the same forever.

We think of thy loving-kindness, Ȯ God, in the midst of thy temple.

O God, according to thy name, so is thy praise unto the world's end ; thy right hand is full of righteousness.

Let the mount Sion rejoice, and the daughters of Judah be glad, because of thy judgments.

For this God is our God for ever and ever ; he shall be our guide unto death.

Now unto the King eternal, etc.

Be honor and glory, etc.

The Ninth Day.

MORNING PRAYER.

PSALM L.

Formal worship of no avail without holiness of heart and life.

THE Lord, even the most mighty God, speaketh and calleth the world, from the rising up of the sun unto the going down thereof.

Out of Sion, the perfection of beauty, doth God shine forth.

Our God cometh, and shall not keep silence ; there goeth before him a consuming fire, and a mighty tempest is stirred up round about him.

He calleth to the heavens above, and to the earth, while he judgeth his people.

"Gather my servants together unto me, those who have made a covenant with me with sacrifice."

And the heavens shall declare his righteous sentence, for God himself is judge.

"Hear, O my people, and I will speak; I myself will testify against thee, O Israel; for I am God, even thy God.

"I will not reprove thee because of thy sacrifices, or for thy burnt-offerings, because they were not alway before me.

"I will take no bullock out of thine house, nor he-goat out of thy folds.

"For all the beasts of the forest are mine, and so are the cattle upon a thousand hills.

"I know all the fowls upon the mountains, and the wild beasts of the field are in my sight.

"If I were hungry, I would not tell thee; for the whole world is mine, and all that is therein.

"Offer unto God thanksgiving, and pay thy vows unto the Most High.

"And call upon me in the time of trouble; so will I hear thee, and thou shalt praise me."

But unto the ungodly saith God, "Why dost thou preach my laws, and take my covenant in thy mouth;

"Whereas thou hatest instruction, and hast cast my words behind thee?

"When thou sawest a thief thou consentedst unto him, and hast been partaker with the adulterers.

"Thou hast let thy mouth speak wickedness, and with thy tongue thou hast set forth deceit.

"Thou didst sit, and speak against thy brother; yea, and hast slandered thine own mother's son.

"These things hast thou done, and, because I was silent, thou thoughtest wickedly, that I was even such a one as thyself; but I will reprove thee, and set before thee the things that thou hast done.

" O consider this, ye who forget God; lest I pluck you away, and there be none to deliver you.

"Whoso offereth me thanks and praise, he honoreth me; and to him who ordereth his conversation right will I show the salvation of God."

Now unto the King eternal, etc.

Be honor and glory, etc.

EVENING PRAYER.

PSALM LI.

Penitential Psalm, called Miserere.

HAVE mercy upon me, O God, after thy great goodness; according to the multitude of thy mercies, do away mine offences.

Wash me thoroughly from my wickedness; and cleanse me from my sin.

For I acknowledge my transgressions, and my sin is ever before me.

Against thee especially have I sinned, and done this evil in thy sight; that thou mightest be justified in thy sentence, and be clear when thou judgest.

Thou requirest truth in the heart, and in the heart shalt make me to understand wisdom.

Purge me as with hyssop, and I shall be clean; wash me, and I shall be whiter than snow.

Make me to hear of joy and gladness, that the bones which thou hast broken may rejoice.

Turn thy face from my sins, and blot out my misdeeds.

Make me a clean heart, O God, and renew a right spirit within me.

Cast me not away from thy presence, and take not thy Holy Spirit from me.

O give me the comfort of thy help again, and establish me with thy free Spirit.

Then will I teach thy ways unto the wicked, and sinners shall be converted unto thee.

Open my lips, O Lord, and my mouth shall show forth thy praise.

For thou desirest no sacrifice, else would I give it thee ; but thou delightest not in burnt-offerings.

The sacrifice of God is a troubled spirit ; a broken and a contrite heart, O God, thou wilt not despise.

PSALM LVI.

A prayer for help by one surrounded by enemies.

BE merciful unto me, O God, for man goeth about to devour me ; he is daily fighting and troubling me.

Mine enemies would daily swallow me up ; for they be many who fight against me, O thou Most High.

Nevertheless, though I am some time afraid, yet put I my trust in thee.

I will praise God because of his word ; I have put my trust in God, and will not fear what flesh can do unto me.

They daily pervert my words ; all that they imagine is to do me evil.

They gather themselves together, they hide themselves, and mark my steps, when they lay wait for my life.

Shall they escape by their wickedness? Thou, O God, in thy displeasure shalt cast them down.

Thou tellest my offences ; put my tears before thee ; are not these things noted in thy book?

Whensoever I call upon thee, then shall mine enemies be put to flight ; this I know, for God is on my side.

In God's word will I rejoice ; in the Lord's word will I comfort me.

Yea, in God have I put my trust ; I will not be afraid of what man can do unto me.

Unto thee, O God, will I· pay my vows ; unto thee will I give thanks.

For thou hast delivered my soul from death, and my feet from falling, that I may walk before God in the light of the living.

Now unto the King eternal, etc.

Be honor and glory, etc.

The Tenth Day.

MORNING PRAYER.

Psalm LVII.

Prayer for help ; gratitude for deliverance.

BE merciful unto me, O God, be merciful unto me, for my soul trusteth in thee ; and under the shadow of thy wings shall be my refuge, until this calamity be overpast.

I will call unto the most high God, even unto the God who will perform all things for me.

He shall send from heaven, and save me from the reproach of him who would swallow me up.

Be thou exalted, O God, above the heavens, and let thy glory be above all the earth.

My heart is fixed, O God, my heart is fixed; I will sing, and give praise.

Awake up, my glory: awake, lute and harp; I myself will awake right early.

I will give thanks unto thee, O Lord, among the people, and I will sing unto thee among the nations.

For the greatness of thy mercy reacheth unto the heavens, and thy truth unto the clouds.

Be thou exalted, O God, above the heavens, and let thy glory be above all the earth.

Psalm LXI.

Prayer of an exile for himself and for his king.

HEAR my crying, O God; give ear unto my prayer.

From the ends of the earth will I call upon thee, when my heart is in heaviness.

O lead me to the rock that is higher than I; for thou art my hope, and a strong tower for me against the enemy.

I will dwell in thy tabernacle forever, and my trust shall be under the covering of thy wings.

For thou, O Lord, hast heard my desires, and hast given me the heritage of those who fear thy name.

O grant the king a long life, that his years may endure throughout many generations.

Let him dwell before God forever; O prepare thy loving mercy and faithfulness, that they may preserve him.

So will I alway sing praise unto thy name, and daily perform my vows.

PSALM LXII.

Trust in God.

MY soul truly waiteth still upon God; for of him cometh my salvation.

He verily is my strength and my salvation; he is my defence, so that I shall not greatly fall.

My soul, wait thou still upon God; for my hope is in him.

He truly is my strength and my salvation; he is my defence, so that I shall not fall.

In God is my health and my glory, the rock of my might; and in God is my trust.

O put your trust in him alway, ye people; pour out your hearts before him; for God is our hope.

As for the men of low degree, they are but vanity; the men of high degree are deceit; laid in the balance, they are altogether lighter than vanity itself.

O trust not in wrong and robbery; give not yourselves unto vanity; if riches increase, set not your heart upon them.

God spake once, and twice I have also heard the same, that power belongeth unto God;

And that thou, Lord, art merciful; for thou renderest to every man according to his work.

Now unto the King eternal, etc.

Be honor and glory, etc.

EVENING PRAYER.

' PSALM LXIII.

Trust in God; a morning prayer.

O GOD, thou art my God; early will I seek thee.

My soul thirsteth for thee, my flesh also longeth after thee, in a barren and dry land, where no water is;

To behold thy power and glory, as I have seen thee in the sanctuary.

Because thy loving-kindness is better than life itself, my lips shall praise thee.

Thus will I magnify thee as long as I live, and lift up my hands in thy name.

My soul shall be satisfied, even as it were with marrow and fatness, and my mouth shall praise thee with joyful lips.

Have I not remembered thee in my bed, and thought upon thee when I was waking?

Because thou hast been my helper, therefore under the shadow of thy wings will I rejoice.

My soul cleaveth to thee; thy right hand upholdeth me.

Psalm LXV.

The greatness and goodness of God.

THOU, O God, art praised in Sion, and unto thee shall the vow be performed.

O thou who hearest prayer, unto thee shall all flesh come.

My misdeeds prevail against me ; O be ' thou merciful unto our sins.

Blessed is the man whom thou choosest, and receivest unto thee ; he shall dwell in thy courts, and shall be satisfied with the pleasures of thy house, even of thy holy temple.

Thou dost show us wonderful things in thy righteousness, O God of our salvation ; thou, who art the hope of all the ends of the earth, and of those who are afar off upon the sea ;

Who in thy strength settest fast the mountains, and art girded about with power ;

Who stillest the raging of the sea, and the noise of its waves, and the madness of the people.

They who dwell in the uttermost parts of the earth are awed at thy tokens ; thou makest the outgoings of the morning and of the evening to praise thee.

Thou visitest the earth and blessest it ; thou makest it very plenteous.

The river of God is full of water ; thou providest their corn when thou hast so prepared the earth.

Thou waterest her furrows, thou sendest rain into the little valleys thereof, thou makest it soft with the drops of rain, and blessest the springing thereof.

Thou crownest the year with thy goodness, and thy clouds drop fatness.

They drop upon the pastures of the wilderness, and the little hills rejoice on every side.

The mountains are clothed with sheep; the valleys also stand so thick with corn, that they laugh and sing.

Now unto the King eternal, etc.

Be honor and glory, etc.

𝕿𝖍𝖊 𝕰𝖑𝖊𝖛𝖊𝖓𝖙𝖍 𝕯𝖆𝖞.

MORNING PRAYER.

PSALM LXVI.

Thanksgiving, after great deliverance.

O BE joyful in God, all ye lands; sing praises unto the honor of his name; make his praise to be glorious.

Say unto God, O how wonderful art thou in thy works! Through the greatness of thy power shall thine enemies submit themselves unto thee.

For all the world shall worship thee, sing of thee, and praise thy name.

O come, and behold the works of God; how wonderful he is in his doing toward the children of men!

He turned the sea into dry land, so that they went through the water on foot; there did we rejoice in him.

He ruleth with his power forever; his eyes behold the people; and such as are rebellious shall not be able to exalt themselves.

O praise our God, ye people, and make the voice of his praise to be heard;

Who holdeth our soul in life, and suffereth not our feet to slip.

For thou, O God, hast proved us; thou also hast tried us, like as silver is tried.

Thou broughtest us into the snare, and laidst trouble upon us.

Thou sufferedst men to ride over our heads; we went through fire and through water; but thou broughtest us out into a place of refreshment.

O come hither and hearken, all ye who fear God, and I will tell you what he hath done for my soul.

I called unto him with my mouth, and gave him praises with my tongue.

If I incline unto wickedness with my heart, the Lord will not hear me.

But God hath heard me, and considered the voice of my prayer.

Praised be God, who hath not cast out my prayer, nor turned his mercy from me.

Psalm LXVIII.

Hymn on the removal of the ark to Mount Zion. Numb. x. 35.

LET God arise, and let his enemies be scattered; let those also who hate him flee before him.

Like as the smoke vanisheth, so shalt thou drive them away; and like as wax melteth at the fire, so shall the ungodly perish at the presence of God.

But let the righteous be glad, and rejoice before God ; yea, let them exceedingly rejoice.

O sing unto God, and sing praises unto his name ; magnify him who rideth upon the heavens : praise him in his name JEHOVAH, and rejoice before him.

He is a Father of the fatherless, and defendeth the cause of the widows; even God in his holy habitation.

God restoreth the solitary to their families, and bringeth the prisoners out of captivity ; but letteth the rebellious continue in a dry land.

O God, when thou wentest forth before the people, when thou didst march through the wilderness;

The earth shook, and the heavens dropped at the presence of God ; even Sinai itself was moved at the presence of God, the God of Israel.

Thou, O God, sentest a gracious rain upon thine inheritance, and refreshedst it when it was weary.

Thy people dwelt in the midst of thy food ; for thou, O God, didst of thy goodness provide for their need.

The Lord gave the song of victory ; great was the company of those who published it.

Kings with their armies did flee and were discomfited, and she who staid at home divided the spoil.

The chariots of God's host are numberless, even thousands of thousands, and the Lord is among them, as in the holy place of Sinai.

Thou art gone up on high, thou hast led captivity captive, and received gifts from men, yea, even from thine enemies; and here wilt thou dwell, O Lord God.

Praised be the Lord daily; even the God who helpeth us, and poureth his benefits upon us.

He is our God, even the God of whom cometh salvation; God is the Lord, by whom we escape death.

The Lord hath said, I will bring my people again, as I did from Bashan; mine own will I bring again, as I did once from the deep of the sea.

Sing unto God, O ye kingdoms of the earth; O sing praises unto the Lord;

Who sitteth in the heavens over all, from the beginning; lo, he doth send out his voice, yea, and that a mighty voice.

Ascribe ye the power to God; his excellency is over Israel; his strength is in the clouds.

O God, wonderful art thou in thy holy places; the God of Israel will give strength and power unto his people; blessed be God.

Now unto the King eternal, etc.

Be honor and glory, etc.

EVENING PRAYER.

PSALM LXXI.

Prayer of the aged.

IN thee, O Lord, have I put my trust; let me never be put to confusion, but rescue me, and deliver me in thy righteousness ; incline thine ear unto me, and save me.

Be thou my stronghold, whereunto I may alway resort ; thou hast promised to help me, for thou art my house of defence and my castle.

Deliver me, O God, out of the hand of the ungodly, out of the hand of the unrighteous and cruel man.

For thou art my hope, O Lord God ; thou art my hope, even from my youth.

Through thee have I been holden up, ever since I was born ; my praise shall be always of thee.

I am become a wonder unto many ; but my sure trust is in thee.

O let my mouth be filled with thy praise, that I may sing of thy glory and honor all the day long.

Cast me not away in the time of age ; forsake me not when my strength faileth me.

For mine enemies speak against me, and they who lay wait for my life take their counsel together, saying, "God hath forsaken him ; persecute him, and take him ; for there is none to deliver him."

Go not far from me, O God ; my God, haste thee to help me.

As for me, I will patiently abide alway, and will praise thee more and more.

My mouth shall daily speak of thy righteousness and salvation ; for I know no end thereof.

I will go forth in the strength of the Lord God,

and will make mention of thy righteousness, even of thine only.

Thou, O God, hast taught me from my youth up until now; therefore will I tell of thy wondrous works.

Forsake me not, O God, in mine old age, when I am gray-headed, until I have shown thy strength unto this generation, and thy power to all those who are yet to come.

Thy righteousness, O God, is very high, and great things are those which thou hast done; O God, who is like unto thee?

O what great troubles and adversities hast thou shown me! And yet didst thou turn and refresh me, yea, and broughtest me from the depths of the earth again.

Thou hast brought me to great honor, and comforted me on every side.

Therefore will I praise thee and thy faithfulness, O God, playing upon an instrument of music; unto thee will I sing upon the harp, O thou Holy One of Israel.

My lips shall greatly rejoice when I sing unto thee; and so will my soul, which thou hast delivered.

My tongue also shall talk of thy righteousness all the day long; for they are confounded and brought unto shame, who seek to do me evil.

Now unto the King eternal, etc.

Be honor and glory, etc.

The Twelfth Day,

MORNING PRAYER.

PSALM LXXII.

David's prayer for Solomon.

GIVE the king thy justice, O God, and thy right-eousness unto the king's son.

Then shall he judge thy people according unto right, and defend the poor.

The mountains also shall bring forth peace, and the hills, righteousness unto the people.

He shall judge the poor of the people, defend the children of the needy, and punish the wrong-doer.

They shall fear thee as long as the sun and moon endure, from one generation to another.

He shall come down like rain upon the mown grass, even as the drops that water the earth.

In his time shall the righteous flourish, yea, and abundance of peace, so long as the moon endureth.

His dominion shall be also from the one sea to the other, and from the river unto the ends of the earth.

They who dwell in the wilderness shall kneel before him; his enemies shall lick the dust.

The kings of Tharsis and of the Isles shall give presents; the kings of Arabia and Saba shall bring gifts.

All kings shall fall down before him; all nations shall do him service.

For he shall deliver the poor when he crieth, the needy also, and him who hath no helper.

He shall be favorable to the simple and needy, and shall preserve the souls of the poor.

He shall deliver them from falsehood and wrong; and dear shall their blood be in his sight.

He shall flourish, and unto him shall be given of the gold of Arabia; prayer shall be made for him continually; and daily shall he be praised.

There shall be abundance of corn in the earth; its fruit shall wave like Lebanon; and they of the city shall flourish like the grass of the earth.

His name shall endure forever; his name shall be continued as long as the sun; and men shall be blessed in him: all nations shall call him blessed.

Praised be the Lord God, even the God of Israel, who only doth wondrous things;

And blessed be the name of his majesty forever; and all the earth shall be filled with his majesty. Amen, Amen.

Now unto the King eternal, etc.

Be honor and glory, etc.

EVENING PRAYER.

PSALM LXXIII.

A meditation on the ways of Providence.

TRULY God is good unto Israel, even unto such as are of a clean heart.

Nevertheless, my feet were almost gone; my steps had wellnigh slipped.

For I was envious at the wicked, when I saw the ungodly in such prosperity.

For they are in no distress; but are firm and strong.

They come in no misfortune like other men; neither are they afflicted like other men.

And this is the cause that they are so lifted up with pride, and filled with cruelty.

They are corrupt, and speak wicked blasphemy; their talking is against the Most High.

For they set their mouth against the heaven, and their tongue goeth through the world.

Therefore his people walk in their ways, and drink therein from full fountains.

For they say, "How should God perceive it? Is there knowledge in the Most High?"

Lo, these are the ungodly, these prosper in the world, and these have riches in possession; and I said, Then have I cleansed my heart in vain, and washed my hands in innocency.

For all the day long have I been smitten, and chastened every morning.

Yea, and I had almost said even as they; but lo, then I should have condemned the generation of thy children.

Then thought I to understand this; but it was too hard for me;

Until I went into the sanctuary of God; then understood I the end of these men.

Truly thou dost set them in slippery places, and dost cast them down, and destroy them.

O how suddenly do they consume, perish, and come to a fearful end !

Yea, even like as a dream when one awaketh, so shalt thou destroy their splendor in thy wrath.

Thus when my heart was embittered with envy, and my thoughts were troubled;

Then was I foolish, and ignorant, even as it were a brute before thee

Nevertheless, I am alway with thee; for thou hast holden me by my right hand.

Thou wilt guide me with thy counsel, and after that receive me to glory.

Whom have I in heaven but thee? and there is none upon earth that I desire in comparison of thee.

My flesh and my heart fail; but God is the strength of my heart, and my portion forever.

For lo, they who forsake thee shall perish; thou wilt destroy all those who follow after other gods.

But it is good for me to hold me fast by God, to put my trust in the Lord God, and to speak of all thy glorious works.

Now unto the King eternal, etc.

Be honor and glory, etc.

The Thirtenth Day.

MORNING PRAYER.

PSALM LXXV.

God the supreme ruler.

UNTO thee, O God, do we give thanks; yea, unto thee do we give thanks.

For that thy name is nigh, do thy wondrous works declare.

"When the promised time cometh, I shall judge according unto right.

· "The land is weak, and all the inhabitants thereof; I will bear up the pillars of it."

I said unto the fools, Deal not so madly; and to the ungodly, Boast not of your strength.

Boast not of your strength, and speak not with a stiff neck.

For promotion cometh neither from the east, nor from the west, nor yet from the south.

And why? God is the Judge; he putteth down one, and setteth up another.

For in the hand of the Lord there is a cup, and the wine is red; it is full mixed, and he poureth out of the same.

Even to the dregs thereof, all the ungodly of the earth shall wring them out and drink them.

But I will magnify the God of Jacob, and praise him forever.

Psalm LXXVI.

Song of victory. 2 Kings xix. 35.

IN Judah is God known; his name is great in Israel.

At Salem is his tabernacle, and his dwelling in Sion.

There broke he the arrows of the bow, the shield, the sword, and the battle.

Thou art of more honor and might, O Sion, than the hills of the robbers.

The proud are spoiled, they have sunk into sleep; and all their strength hath availed them nothing.

At thy rebuke, O God of Jacob, both the chariot and the horse are fallen.

Thou, even thou, art to be feared ; and who may stand in thy sight when thou art angry?

Thou didst cause thy sentence to be heard from heaven ; the earth trembled and was still,

When God arose to judgment, and to help all the meek upon earth.

The fierceness of man shall turn to thy praise ; and the remainder of wrath shalt thou restrain.

Promise unto the Lord your God, and keep it, all ye who are round about him ; bring presents unto him who ought to be feared.

For he breaketh down the spirit of princes ; he is terrible among the kings of the earth.

Now unto the King eternal, etc.

Be honor and glory, etc.

EVENING PRAYER.

Psalm LXXVII.

Hope derived from recollection of God's former mercies.

I WILL cry unto God with my voice, even unto God will I cry with my voice ; and O that he would hearken unto me.

In the time of my trouble I sought the Lord ; I stretched out my hands to him all the night long ; my soul refused comfort.

When I am in heaviness, I will think upon God; when my heart is vexed, I will complain.

I consider the days of old, and remember the years that are past.

I call to remembrance my song in the night; I commune with mine own heart, and search out my spirit.

Will the Lord absent himself forever? and will he be no more entreated?

Is his mercy clean gone forever? and is his promise come utterly to an end forevermore?

Hath God forgotten to be gracious? and will he shut up his loving-kindness in displeasure?

And I said, It is mine own infirmity; I will remember the years of the right hand of the Most High.

I will remember the works of the Lord, and call to mind thy wonders of old time.

I will think also of all thy works, and my talk shall be of thy doings.

Thy way, O God, is holy; who is so great a God as our God?

Thou art the God who doest wonders, and hast declared thy power among the nations.

Thou didst mightily deliver thy people, even the sons of Jacob and Joseph.

The waters saw thee, O God, the waters saw thee, and were afraid; the depths also were troubled.

The clouds poured out water, the air thundered, and thine arrows went abroad.

The voice of thy thunder was heard round about; the lightnings shone upon the ground; the earth was moved and shook withal.

Thy way was in the sea, and thy path in the great waters, and thy footsteps were not found.

Thou leddest thy people like a flock, by the hand of Moses and Aaron.

Psalm LXXXII.

Against unjust magistrates.

GOD has come up into the judgment-seat; he rebuketh the judges of the earth.

"How long will ye give wrong judgment, and accept the persons of the ungodly?

"Defend the poor and fatherless; do justice to the afflicted and needy.

"Deliver the outcast and poor; save them from the hand of the ungodly.

"They know not, neither understand, but walk on still in darkness; therefore all the foundations of the land are disturbed.

"I have said, Ye are gods; and ye are all the children of the Most High.

"But ye shall die like other men, and fall like tyrants."

Arise, O God, and judge thou the earth; for thou shalt take all nations to thine inheritance.

Now unto the King eternal, etc.

Be honor and glory, etc.

The Fourteenth Day.

MORNING PRAYER.

Psalm LXXXIV.

Song of worshippers going up to Jerusalem.

O HOW amiable are thy dwellings, thou Lord of hosts!

My soul longeth, yea, even fainteth for the courts

of the Lord ; my heart and my flesh cry out for the living God.

As the sparrow findeth an house, and the swallow a nest, where she may lay her young, so let me dwell at thine altars, O Lord of hosts, my king and my God.

Blessed are they who dwell in thy house ; they will be alway praising thee.

Blessed are the men whose strength is in thee, in whose heart are thy ways.

For them the desert valley of Baka hath fountains; and they are refreshed with abundant showers.

They go from strength to strength, till every one of them appeareth before God, in Sion.

O Lord God of hosts, hear my prayer ; hearken, O God of Jacob.

Behold, O God our defender, and look upon the face of thine anointed.

For one day in thy courts is better than a thousand elsewhere.

I had rather be a doorkeeper in the house of my God, than to dwell in the tents of ungodliness.

For the Lord God is a sun and shield ; the Lord will give grace and glory ; and no good thing will he withhold from those who walk uprightly.

O Lord God of hosts, blessed is the man who putteth his trust in thee.

PSALM LXXXV.

Prayer for the restoration of the Jewish state after the captivity.

LORD, thou art become gracious unto thy land ; thou hast turned away the captivity of Jacob.

Thou hast forgiven the offence of thy people, and covered all their sins.

Thou hast taken away all thy displeasure, and turned thyself from thy wrathful indignation.

Restore us then, O God our Saviour, and let thine anger cease from us.

Wilt thou be displeased at us forever? and wilt thou stretch out thy wrath from one generation to another?

Wilt thou not turn again and quicken us, that thy people may rejoice in thee?

Show us thy mercy, O Lord, and grant us thy salvation.

I will hear what God the Lord will speak ; for he will speak peace to his people and his saints ; only let them not return to their folly again.

For his salvation is nigh those who fear him, that glory may dwell in our land.

Mercy and truth are met together ; righteousness and peace have kissed each other.

Truth shall spring out of the earth ; and righteousness shall look down from heaven.

Yea, the Lord shall show his loving-kindness ; and our land shall yield her increase.

Righteousness shall go before him, and shall keep his path continually.

Now unto the King eternal, etc.
Be honor and glory, etc.

EVENING PRAYER.

Psalm LXXXVI.

A prayer of David under the persecutions of Saul.

BOW down thine ear, O Lord, and hear me, for I am poor and in misery.

Preserve thou my soul, for thou art my hope; my God, save thy servant who putteth his trust in thee.

Be merciful unto me, O Lord, for I will call daily upon thee.

Comfort the soul of thy servant; for unto thee, O Lord, do I lift up my soul.

For thou, Lord, art good and gracious, and of great mercy unto all those who call upon thee.

Give ear, Lord, unto my prayer, and ponder the voice of my humble desires.

In the time of my trouble I will call upon thee; for thou hearest me.

Among the gods there is none like unto thee, O Lord; there is not one who can do as thou doest.

All nations whom thou hast made, shall come and worship thee, O Lord, and shall glorify thy name.

For thou art great, and doest wondrous things; thou art God alone.

Teach me thy way, O Lord, and I will walk in thy truth; O knit my heart unto thee, that I may fear thy name.

I will thank thee, O Lord my God, with all my heart, and will praise thy name forevermore.

For great is thy mercy toward me ; and thou hast delivered my soul from the terrors of death.

O God, the proud are risen against me ; bands of violent men seek my life, and have not set thee before their eyes.

But thou, O Lord God, art full of compassion and mercy, long-suffering, plenteous in goodness and truth.

O turn thee then unto me, and have mercy upon me ; give thy strength unto thy servant, and help the son of thine handmaid.

Show some token upon me for good, that they who hate me may see it, and be ashamed ; because thou, Lord, hast holpen me, and comforted me.

PSALM LXXXIX.

God's mercy, power, and equity.

MY song shall be alway of the loving-kindness of the Lord ; with my mouth will I ever be showing thy truth from one generation to another.

For I have said, Mercy shall be set up forever ; thy truth shalt thou establish in the heavens.

O Lord, the very heavens shall praise thy wondrous works, and the congregation of the saints thy truth.

For who is he in the heavens, that shall be compared unto the Lord?

And who is he among the gods, that shall be likened unto the Lord?

God is very greatly to be feared in the assembly of the saints, and to be had in reverence of all those who are round about him.

O Lord God of hosts, who is like unto thee? thy truth, most mighty Lord, is on every side.

Thou rulest the raging of the sea; thou stillest the waves thereof, when they rise.

Thou hast subdued Egypt, and destroyed it; thou hast scattered thine enemies abroad with thy mighty arm.

The heavens are thine, the earth also is thine; thou hast laid the foundation of the round world, and all that therein is.

Thou hast made the north and the south; Tabor and Hermon rejoice in thy name.

Thou hast a mighty arm; strong is thy hand, and high is thy right hand.

Righteousness and equity are the foundation of thy throne; mercy and truth go before thy face.

Blessed is the people, O Lord, who know the joyful sound; they shall walk in the light of thy countenance.

Their delight shall be daily in thy name; and in thy righteousness shall they make their boast.

For thou art the glory of their strength; and in thy loving-kindness we shall greatly prosper.

For the Lord is our defence; the Holy One of Israel is our King.

Now unto the King eternal, etc.

Be honor and glory, etc.

MORNING PRAYER.

PSALM XC.

The eternity of God, the frailty of man.

LORD, thou hast been our refuge from one generation to another.

Before the mountains were brought forth, or ever thou hadst formed the earth and the world, even from everlasting to everlasting, thou art God.

Thou turnest man to destruction; and sayest, Return, ye children of men.

For a thousand years in thy sight are but as yesterday when it is past, or a watch in the night.

Thou carriest them away as with a flood; they are even as a sleep; and fade away suddenly like the grass:

In the morning it is green, and groweth up; but in the evening it is cut down, dried up, and withered.

For we consume away in thy displeasure, and are afraid at thy wrathful indignation.

Thou hast set our misdeeds before thee, and our secret sins in the light of thy countenance.

For when thou art angry, all our days are gone; we bring our years to an end, as it were a tale that is told.

The days of our age are threescore years and ten; and though men be so strong that they come to fourscore years, yet is their strength then but labor and sorrow; so soon passeth it away, and we are gone.

But who regardeth the power of thy wrath? or feareth thy displeasure as he ought?

So teach us to number our days, that we may apply our hearts unto wisdom.

Turn thee again, O Lord, at the last, and be gracious unto thy servants.

O satisfy us with thy mercy, and that soon ; so shall we rejoice and be glad all the days of our life.

Comfort us again, now according to the time that thou hast afflicted us, and for the years wherein we have suffered adversity.

Show thy servants thy work, and their children thy glory.

And the glorious majesty of the Lord our God be upon us ; prosper thou the work of our hands upon us ; O prosper thou our handy work.

PSALM XCI.

The happiness of him who trusts in God.

WHOSO dwelleth under the defence of the Most High, shall abide under the shadow of the Almighty.

I will say unto the Lord, Thou art my hope, and my stronghold ; my God, in whom I will trust.

For he shall deliver thee from the snare of the hunter, and from the noisome pestilence.

He shall defend thee under his wings, and thou shalt be safe under his feathers ; his faithfulness and truth shall be thy shield and buckler.

Thou shalt not be afraid for any terror by night; nor for the arrow that flieth by day;

For the pestilence that walketh in darkness; nor for the sickness that destroyeth in the noon-day.

A thousand shall fall beside thee, and ten thousand at thy right hand; but it shall not come nigh thee.

But with thine eyes shalt thou behold, and see the reward of the ungodly.

For the Lord is thy hope; thou hast made the Most High thy refuge.

There shall no evil happen unto thee, neither shall any plague come nigh thy dwelling.

For he shall give his angels charge over thee, to keep thee in all thy ways.

They shall bear thee in their hands, that thou hurt not thy foot against a stone.

Thou shalt tread upon the lion and adder; the young lion and the dragon shalt thou tread under thy feet.

" Because he hath set his love upon me, therefore will I deliver him; I will set him up, because he hath known my name.

" He shall call upon me, and I will hear him; yea, I am with him in trouble; I will deliver him, and bring him to honor.

"With long life will I satisfy him, and show him my salvation."

Now unto the King eternal, etc.

Be honor and glory, etc.

EVENING PRAYER.

Psalm XCII.

God the supreme ruler and judge.

IT is a good thing to give thanks unto the Lord, and to sing praises unto thy name, O Most High;

To tell of thy loving-kindness early in the morning, and of thy truth in the night season.

For thou, Lord, hast made me glad through thy works; and I will rejoice in giving praise for the operations of thy hands.

O Lord, how glorious are thy works! thy thoughts are very deep!

An unwise man doth not consider this; and a fool doth not understand it.

When the ungodly spring up as the grass, and when all the workers of wickedness do flourish, then shall they be destroyed forever; but thou, Lord, art the Most High forevermore.

For lo, thine enemies, O Lord, lo, thine enemies shall perish; and all the workers of wickedness shall be destroyed.

The righteous shall flourish like a palm-tree; and shall spread abroad like a cedar in Lebanon.

Those that be planted in the house of the Lord, shall flourish in the courts of the house of our God.

They shall bring forth fruit even in their age; and shall be full of sap and flourishing.

That they may show how true the Lord my strength is, and that there is no unrighteousness in him.

PSALM XCIII.

God the ruler of the Sea.

THE Lord reigneth ; he is clothed with majesty ; the Lord hath clothed himself with majesty and girded himself with strength.

Therefore the earth standeth firm and cannot be moved.

Thy throne is established of old ; thou art from everlasting.

The floods have lifted, O Lord, the floods have lifted up their voice ; the floods lift up their waves.

The Lord on high is mightier than the noise of many waters, yea, than the mighty waves of the sea.

Thy testimonies, O Lord, are very sure ; holiness becometh thine house forever.

Now unto the King eternal, etc.

Be honor and glory, etc.

The Sixteenth Day.

MORNING PRAYER.

PSALM XCIV.

For the nation, under oppression.

O LORD God, to whom vengeance belongeth ; thou God, to whom vengeance belongeth, arise !

Arise, thou Judge of the world, and reward the proud after their deserving.

Lord, how long shall the ungodly, how long shall the ungodly triumph ?

How long shall all wicked doers speak so disdainfully, and make such proud boasting?

They smite down thy people, O Lord, and trouble thine heritage.

They murder the widow and the stranger, and put the fatherless to death.

And yet they say, The Lord shall not see ; neither shall the God of Jacob regard it.

Take heed, ye most foolish of men ; O ye fools, when will ye understand ?

He who planted the ear, shall he not hear? or he who made the eye, shall he not see ?

He who chastiseth the nations, shall not he correct ? or he who teacheth man knowledge, shall not he know?

The Lord knoweth the thoughts of man, that they are but vain.

Blessed is the man whom thou chastenest, O Lord, and teachest him in thy law ;

To give him patience in time of adversity, until the pit be digged for the ungodly.

For the Lord will not fail his people, neither will he forsake his inheritance ;

Until righteousness turn again unto judgment ; and all such as are true in heart shall rejoice in it.

Who will rise up with me against the wicked? or who will take my part against the evil doers ?

If the Lord had not helped me, it had not failed but my soul had been put to silence.

But when I said, I am fallen, thy mercy, O Lord, held me up.

In the multitude of the sorrows that I had in my heart, thy comforts have refreshed my soul.

Wilt thou have any fellowship with the throne of those wicked ones, who make mischief their law?

They gather them together against the soul of the righteous, and condemn the innocent blood.

But the Lord is my refuge; and my God is the strength of my confidence.

Now unto the King eternal, etc.

Be honor and glory, etc.

EVENING PRAYER.

PSALM XCVI.

Exhortation to the praise and worship of God.

O SING unto the Lord a new song; sing unto the Lord, all the earth.

Sing unto the Lord, and praise his name; be telling of his salvation from day to day.

Declare his honor unto the heathen, and his wonders unto all the people.

For the Lord is great, and cannot worthily be praised; he is more to be feared than all gods.

As for all the gods of the heathen, they are but idols; but it is the Lord who made the heavens.

Glory and worship are before him; power and honor are in his sanctuary.

Ascribe unto the Lord, O ye families of the people, ascribe unto the Lord worship and power.

Ascribe unto the Lord the honor due unto his name; bring offerings, and come into his courts.

O worship the Lord in the beauty of holiness; let the whole earth stand in awe of him.

Tell it out among the heathen, that the Lord is King; that it is he who hath made the world so fast that it cannot be moved; and that he shall judge the people righteously.

Let the heavens rejoice, and let the earth be glad; let the sea make a noise, and all that therein is.

Let the field be joyful and all that is in it; let all the trees of the wood rejoice before the Lord.

For he cometh, for he cometh to judge the earth; and with righteousness to judge the world, and the people with his truth.

PSALM XCVII.

Praise to God as the supreme ruler.

THE Lord is King, let the earth be glad thereof; yea, let the multitude of the isles be glad thereof.

Clouds and darkness are round about him; righteousness and judgment are the foundation of his throne.

There shall go a 'fire before him, and burn up his enemies on every side.

His lightnings shone through the world; the earth saw, and was afraid.

The hills melted like wax at the presence of the

Lord, at the presence of the Lord of the whole earth.

The heavens have declared his righteousness; and all the people have seen his glory.

Confounded be all they who worship carved images, and who delight in vain gods; worship him, all ye gods.

Sion heard, and rejoiced; and the daughters of Judah were glad, because of thy judgments, O Lord.

For thou, Lord, art high above all the earth; thou art exalted far above all gods.

O´ ye who love the Lord, see that ye hate the thing which is evil; the Lord preserveth the souls of his saints; he shall deliver them from the hand of the ungodly.

There is sprung up a light for the righteous, and joyful gladness for such as are true of heart.

Rejoice in the Lord, ye righteous; and give thanks at the remembrance of his holiness.

Now unto the King eternal, etc.

Be honor and glory, etc.

The Seventeenth Day.

MORNING PRAYER.

PSALM XCIX.

Hymn of praise.

THE Lord is King, let the nations tremble; he sitteth between the cherubim, let the earth be moved.

The Lord is great in Sion, and high above all the people.

Let them praise thy great and wonderful name; for it is holy.

The king's power loveth justice; thou hast established equity; thou hast executed judgment and righteousness in Jacob.

O magnify the Lord our God, and fall down before his footstool; for he is holy.

Moses and Aaron, the chief among his ministers, and Samuel among such as call upon his name, these called upon the Lord, and he heard them.

He spake unto them out of the cloudy pillar; for they kept his testimonies, and the law that he gave them.

Thou heardest them, O Lord our God; thou forgavest them, O God, though thou punishedst their iniquities.

O magnify the Lord our God, and worship him upon his holy hill; for the Lord our God is holy.

PSALM CII.

Prayer of an aged exile for the restoration of Israel.

HEAR my prayer, O Lord, and let my crying come unto thee.

Hide not thy face from me in the time of my trouble; incline thine ears unto me when I call; O hear me, and that right soon.

For my days are consumed away like smoke; and my bones are burnt up as it were a firebrand.

I am become like a pelican in the wilderness, and like an owl that is in the desert.

I have watched, and am even as it were a bird of the night, that sitteth alone upon the house-top.

My days are gone like a shadow, and I am withered like grass.

But thou, O Lord, shalt endure forever, and thy remembrance throughout all generations.

Thou wilt arise, and have mercy upon Sion; for it is time that thou have mercy upon her; yea, the time is come.

For thy servants love the very stones thereof, and it pitieth them to see her in the dust.

Then the heathen shall fear thy name, O Lord, and all the kings of the earth thy majesty.

For the Lord will build up Sion, he will appear in his glory.

He will regard the prayer of the poor destitute, and will not despise their desire.

This shall be written for those who come after; and the people who shall be born shall praise the Lord.

For he looketh down from his sanctuary; out of the heaven doth the Lord behold the earth;

To hear the mournings of such as are in captivity, and deliver the people appointed unto death;

That they may declare the name of the Lord in Sion, and his worship at Jerusalem;

When the people are gathered together, and the kingdoms also to serve the Lord.

Thou, Lord, in the beginning hast laid the foundations of the earth ; and the heavens are the work of thy hands.

They shall perish, but thou shalt endure ; they all shall wax old as doth a garment ;

And as a vesture shalt thou change them, and they shall be changed ; but thou art the same, and thy years shall not fail.

The children of thy servants shall continue ; and their seed shall stand fast in thy sight.

Now unto the King eternal, etc.

Be honor and glory, etc.

EVENING PRAYER.

PSALM CIII.

God's mercies; man's frailty.

BLESS the Lord, O my soul; and all that is within me, bless his holy name.

Bless the Lord, O my soul, and forget not all his benefits ;

Who forgiveth all thy sin, and healeth all thine infirmities ;

Who saveth thy life from destruction, and crowneth thee with mercy and loving-kindness ;

Who filleth the evening of thy life with good things, and reneweth thy youth like the eagle's.

The Lord executeth righteousness and judgment for all those who are oppressed.

He showed his ways unto Moses, his works unto the children of Israel.

The Lord is full of compassion and mercy, long suffering, and of great goodness.

He will not alway be chiding; neither keepeth he his anger forever.

He hath not dealt with us after our sins; nor rewarded us according to our wickednesses.

For as the heaven is high above the earth, so great is his mercy toward those who fear him.

As far as the east is from the west, so far hath he removed our transgressions from us.

Yea, like as a father pitieth his own children; even so the Lord pitieth those who fear him.

For he knoweth our frame; he remembereth that we are but dust.

The days of man are but as grass; he flourisheth as a flower of the field.

For the wind passeth over it, and it is gone; and the place thereof shall know it no more.

But the merciful goodness of the Lord endureth for ever and ever upon those who fear him, and his righteousness upon children's children;

Even upon such as keep his covenant, and think upon his commandments to do them.

The Lord hath established his throne in heaven; and his kingdom ruleth over all.

O praise the Lord, ye angels of his, ye who excel in strength, ye who fulfil his commandment, and hearken unto the voice of his words.

O praise the Lord, all ye his hosts, ye servants of his who do his pleasure.

O praise the Lord, all ye works of his, in all

places of his dominion; praise thou the Lord, O my soul.

Now unto the King eternal, etc.

Be honor and glory, etc.

The Eighteenth Day.

MORNING PRAYER.

PSALM CIV.

God, the Creator and Preserver.

PRAISE the Lord, O my soul; O Lord my God, thou art exceeding glorious; thou art clothed with majesty and honor.

Thou deckest thyself with light as it were with a garment; and spreadest out the heavens like a curtain.

He layeth the beams of his chambers in the waters, and maketh the clouds his chariot, and walketh upon the wings of the wind.

He maketh the winds his messengers, his ministers the flaming fires.

He laid the foundations of the earth, that it should never be moved.

Thou coveredst it with the deep as with a garment; the waters stood above the hills.

At thy rebuke they fled; at the voice of thy thunder they hasted away.

They sunk from the hills, down to the valleys beneath, even unto the place which thou hadst appointed for them.

Thou hast set them their bounds, which they shall not pass, neither turn again to cover the earth.

Thou pourest out the springs into the rivers, which run among the hills.

All beasts of the field drink thereof, and the wild asses quench their thirst.

Beside them the fowls of the air have their habitation, and sing among the branches.

Thou waterest the hills from thy chambers; the earth is filled with the fruit of thy works.

He bringeth forth grass for the cattle, and green herb for the service of men;

That he may bring food out of the earth, and wine that maketh glad the heart of man, and oil to make him a cheerful countenance, and bread to strengthen man's heart.

The trees of the Lord are full of sap, even the cedars of Lebanon which he hath planted;

Wherein the birds make their nests; and the fir-trees are a dwelling for the stork.

The high hills are a refuge for the wild goats, and the stony rocks for the conies.

He appointeth the moon for seasons; and the sun knoweth his going down.

Thou makest darkness, and it is night, wherein all the beasts of the forest do move.

The lions, roaring after their prey, do seek their meat from God.

The sun ariseth, and they get them away together, and lay them down in their dens.

Then man goeth forth to his work, and to his labor until the evening.

O Lord, how manifold are thy works! in wisdom hast thou made them all; the earth is full of thy riches.

So is the great and wide sea also, wherein move creatures innumerable, both small and great.

There go the ships, and there the leviathan, which thou hast made to take his pastime therein.

These wait all upon thee, that thou mayest give them their meat in due season.

Thou givest it them, and they gather it; thou openest thy hand, they are filled with good.

Thou hidest thy face, they are troubled; thou takest away their breath, they die, and are turned again to their dust.

Thou sendest forth thy spirit, they are created; and thou renewest the face of the earth.

The glorious majesty of the Lord shall endure forever; the Lord shall rejoice in his works.

He looketh on the earth, and it trembleth; he toucheth the hills, and they smoke.

I will sing unto the Lord as long as I live; I will praise my God while I have my being.

And so shall my words please him; my joy shall be in the Lord.

As for sinners, they shall be consumed out of the earth, and the ungodly shall come to an end; praise thou the Lord, O my soul; praise the Lord.

Now unto the King eternal, etc.

Be honor and glory, etc.

EVENING PRAYER.

Psalm CVII.

The goodness of God to various classes of men.

O GIVE thanks unto the Lord, for he is gracious, and his mercy endureth forever.

Let them give thanks, whom the Lord hath redeemed, and delivered from the hand of the enemy ;

And gathered them out of the lands, from the east, and from the west, from the north, and from the south.

They wandered in the wilderness in a solitary way, and found no city to dwell in ;

Hungry and thirsty, their soul fainted in them.

So they cried unto the Lord in their trouble, and he delivered them from their distress.

He led them forth by the right way, that they might go to an inhabited city.

O that men would therefore praise the Lord for his goodness, and for the wonders that he doeth for the children of men !

For he satisfieth the empty soul, and filleth the hungry soul with good.

Such as sat in darkness, and in the shadow of death, being fast bound in misery and iron ;

Because they rebelled against the words of the Lord, and lightly regarded the counsel of the Most High ;

He brought down their heart through calamity ; they fell down, and there was none to help them.

Then they cried unto the Lord in their trouble, and he delivered them out of their distress.

For he brought them out of darkness, and out of the shadow of death, and brake their bonds in sunder.

O that men would therefore praise the Lord for his goodness, and for the wonders that he doeth for the children of men!

For he hath broken the gates of brass, and smitten the bars of iron in sunder.

Foolish men were afflicted for their offences, and because of their wickedness.

Their soul refused all manner of food, and they were even at death's door.

Then they cried unto the Lord in their trouble, and he delivered them out of their distress.

He sent his word, and healed them; and they were saved from their destruction.

O that men would therefore praise the Lord for his goodness, and for the wonders that he doeth for the children of men!

That they would offer unto him the sacrifice of thanksgiving, and tell out his works with gladness!

They who go down to the sea in ships, and pursue their business in the great waters,

These men see the works of the Lord, and his wonders in the deep.

For at his word the stormy wind ariseth, which lifteth up the waves thereof.

They are carried up to the heaven, and down

again to the depths; their soul melteth away because of the trouble.

So they cry unto the Lord in their trouble, and he delivereth them out of their distress.

For he maketh the storm to cease, and the waves to be still.

Then are they glad because they are at rest; and so he bringeth them unto the haven where they would be.

O that men would therefore praise the Lord for his goodness, and declare the wonders that he doeth for the children of men!

That they would exalt him also in the congregation of the people, and praise him in the assembly of the elders!

He turneth rivers into a wilderness, and water-springs into dry ground.

A fruitful land maketh he barren, for the wickedness of those who dwell therein.

Again he maketh the wilderness a standing water, and water-springs of a dry ground.

And there he setteth the hungry, that they may build them a city to dwell in;

That they may sow their land, and plant vineyards, to yield them fruits of increase.

He blesseth them, so that they multiply exceedingly, and suffereth not their cattle to decrease.

And again, when they are minished and brought low through oppression, through any plague or trouble;

Though he suffer them to be evil entreated

through tyrants, and let them wander out of the way in the wilderness;

Yet helpeth he the poor out of misery, and maketh him households like a flock.

The righteous will consider this and rejoice; and the mouth of all wickedness shall be stopped.

Whoso is wise will ponder these things, and understand the loving-kindness of the Lord.

Now unto the King eternal, etc.

Be honor and glory, etc.

The Nineteenth Day.

MORNING PRAYER.

PSALM CXI.

God's goodness in his works and word.

I WILL give thanks unto the Lord with my whole heart, secretly among the faithful, and in the congregation.

The works of the Lord are great, sought out by all those who have pleasure therein.

His works are worthy to be praised and had in honor; and his righteousness endureth forever.

He hath made his wonderful works to be remembered; the Lord is gracious and full of compassion.

He hath given food unto those who fear him; for he will ever be mindful of his covenant.

He hath shown his people the power of his works, when he gave them the heritage of the heathen.

The works of his hands are verity and judgment; all his commandments are true.

They stand fast for ever and ever, and are done in truth and equity.

He sent redemption unto his people; he hath confirmed his covenant forever; holy and reverend is his name.

The fear of the Lord is the beginning of wisdom; a good understanding have all they who obey him; his praise endureth forever.

PSALM CXII.

The blessedness of the righteous man.

BLESSED is the man who feareth the Lord, and who hath great delight in his commandments.

His posterity shall be mighty upon earth; the generation of the faithful shall be blessed.

Riches and plenteousness shall be in his house; and his righteousness endureth forever.

Unto the godly there ariseth up light in the darkness; he is merciful, loving, and righteous.

A good man is merciful, and lendeth; and will guide his affairs with discretion.

Surely he shall never be moved; and the righteons shall be had in everlasting remembrance.

He will not be afraid of any evil tidings; for his heart standeth fast, and believeth in the Lord.

He hath dispersed abroad, and given to the poor; his righteousness remaineth forever; his horn shall be exalted with honor.

Now unto the King eternal, etc.

Be honor and glory, etc.

EVENING PRAYER.

Psalm CXIII.

The condescending goodness of God.

PRAISE the Lord, ye servants of his ; ·O praise the name of the Lord.

Blessed be the name of the Lord, from this time forth forevermore.

Let the Lord's name be praised, from the rising up of the sun unto the going down of the same.

The Lord is high above all nations, and his glory above the heavens.

Who is like unto the Lord our God, who hath his dwelling so high, and yet humbleth himself to behold the things that are in heaven and earth ?

He taketh up the simple out of the dust, and lifteth the poor out of the mire ;

That he may set him with the princes, even with the princes of his people.

Psalm CXV.

The folly of idolatry.

NOT unto us, O Lord, not unto us, but unto thy name give the praise, for thy loving mercy, and for thy truth's sake.

Wherefore should the heathen say, "Where is now their God ?"

As for our God, he is in heaven ; he hath done whatsoever pleased him.

Their idols are silver and gold, even the work of men's hands.

They have mouths, but speak not; eyes have they, but see not.

They have ears, but hear not; noses have they, but smell not.

They have hands, but handle not; feet have they, and walk not; neither speak they through their throat.

They who make them are like unto them; and so are all they who put their trust in them.

But thou, house of Israel, trust thou in the Lord; he is our succor and defence.

Thou house of Aaron, trust thou in the Lord; he is our helper and defender.

Ye, who fear the Lord, put your trust in the Lord; he is our helper and defender.

The Lord hath been mindful of us, and he will bless us; he will bless the house of Israel, he will bless the house of Aaron.

He will bless those who fear the Lord, both small and great.

The Lord shall increase you more and more, you and your children.

Ye are the blessed of the Lord, who made heaven and earth.

All the whole heavens are the Lord's; the earth hath he given to the children of men.

The dead praise not the Lord, neither they who go down into silence.

But we will praise the Lord, from this time forth forevermore.   Praise the Lord.

Now unto the King eternal, etc.

Be honor and glory, etc.

𝕮𝖍𝖊 𝕿𝖜𝖊𝖓𝖙𝖎𝖊𝖙𝖍 𝕯𝖆𝖞.

MORNING PRAYER.

PSALM CXVI.

On recovery from sickness.

I LOVE the Lord, because he heard the voice of my prayer.

He hath inclined his ear unto me; therefore will I call upon him as long as I live.

The snares of death compassed me round about; and the pains of the grave took hold upon me.

I found trouble and heaviness; then I called upon the name of the Lord; "O Lord, I beseech thee, deliver my soul."

Gracious is the Lord, and righteous; yea, our God is merciful.

The Lord preserveth the simple; I was in misery, and he helped me.

Turn again then unto thy rest, O my soul; for the Lord hath dealt bountifully with thee.

For thou hast delivered my soul from death, mine eyes from tears, and my feet from falling.

I shall walk before the Lord in the land of the living.

I believed, although I said, "I am sore troubled." I said in my haste, "All men are false."

What shall I render unto the Lord for all the benefits that he hath done unto me?

I will pour out the cup of salvation, and call upon the name of the Lord.

I will pay my vows now in the presence of all

his people ; right dear in the sight of the Lord is the death of his saints.

Behold, O Lord, I am thy servant ; I am thy servant, and the son of thine handmaid ; thou hast broken my bonds in sunder.

I will offer to thee the sacrifice of thanksgiving, and will call upon the name of the Lord.

I will pay my vows unto the Lord, in the sight of all his people, in the courts of the Lord's house, even in the midst of thee, O Jerusalem. Praise the Lord.

PSALM CXVII.

A psalm of praise.

O PRAISE the Lord, all ye people ; praise him, all ye nations.

For his merciful kindness is great toward us ; and the truth of the Lord endureth forever. Praise the Lord.

Now unto the King eternal, etc.

Be honor and glory, etc.

EVENING PRAYER.

PSALM CXVIII.

Thanksgiving and triumph.

O GIVE thanks unto the Lord, for he is gracious, and his mercy endureth forever.

Let Israel now confess that his mercy endureth forever.

Let the house of Aaron now confess that his mercy endureth forever.

Yea, let those now who fear the Lord confess that his mercy endureth forever.

I called upon the Lord in trouble, and the Lord heard and delivered me.

The Lord is on my side; I will not fear; what can man do unto me?

It is better to trust in the Lord, than to put confidence in man.

It is better to trust in the Lord, than to put confidence in princes.

The Lord is my strength and my song, and is become my salvation.

The voice of joy and salvation is in the dwellings of the righteous; the right hand of the Lord bringeth mighty things to pass.

The right hand of the Lord is exalted; the right hand of the Lord bringeth mighty things to pass.

I shall not die, but live, and declare the works of the Lord.

The Lord hath chastened and, corrected me; but he hath not given me over unto death.

Open me the gates of holiness, that I may go in by them, and give thanks unto the Lord.

"This is the gate of the Lord, by which the righteous shall enter."

I will thank thee, for thou hast heard me, and art become my salvation.

The same stone which the builders refused is become the head stone in the corner.

This is the Lord's doing; and it is marvellous in our eyes.

This is the day which the Lord hath made ; we will rejoice and be glad in it.

Save now, O Lord ; O Lord, send us now prosperity.

" Blessed be he who cometh in the name of the Lord ! we bless you, ye who are of the house of the Lord."

Thou art my God, and I will thank thee ; thou art my God, and I will praise thee.

O give thanks unto the Lord, for he is gracious, and his mercy endureth forever.

Now unto the King eternal, etc.

Be honor and glory, etc.

The Ascension Day.

MORNING PRAYER.

PSALM CXIX.

The excellence of the divine laws, and the happiness of those who observe them.

ALEPH.

BLESSED are they who are undefiled in the way, and walk in the law of the Lord.

Blessed are they who keep his testimonies, and seek him with their whole heart ;

Who do no wickedness, but walk in his ways.

Thou hast charged that we shall diligently keep thy commandments.

O that my ways were so directed, that I might keep thy statutes !

So shall I not be confounded, while I have respect unto all thy commandments.

I will thank thee with uprightness of heart, when I shall have learned thy righteous judgments.

I will keep thy laws; O forsake me not utterly.

BETH.

WHEREWITHAL shall a young man cleanse his way? Even by ruling himself after thy word.

With my whole heart have I sought thee; O let me not go wrong out of thy commandments.

Thy words have I hid within my heart, that I should not sin against thee.

Blessed art thou, O Lord; O teach me thy statutes.

With my lips have I been telling of all the judgments of thy mouth.

I have had as great delight in the way of thy testimonies as in all manner of riches.

I will meditate on thy commandments, and have respect unto thy ways.

My delight shall be in thy statutes, and I will not forget thy word.

Now unto the King eternal, etc.

Be honor and glory, etc.

EVENING PRAYER.

PSALM CXIX.

GIMEL.

O DEAL kindly unto thy servant, that I may live and keep thy word.

Open thou mine eyes, that I may see the wondrous things of thy law.

I am a stranger upon earth; O hide not thy commandments from me.

My soul trembles for the very fervent desire that it hath alway unto thy judgments.

Thou hast rebuked the proud; and cursed are they who do err from thy commandments.

O turn from me reproach and contempt; for I have kept thy testimonies.

Though princes sit and speak against me, thy servant is occupied in thy statutes.

For thy testimonies are my delight and my counsellors.

DALETH.

MY soul cleaveth to the dust; O quicken thou me according to thy word.

I have acknowledged my ways, and thou heardest me; O teach me thy statutes.

Make me to understand the way of thy commandments; and so shall I talk of thy wondrous works.

My soul melteth away for very heaviness; comfort thou me according unto thy word.

Remove me from the deceitful way; and cause thou me to make much of thy law.

I have chosen the way of truth; and thy judgments have I laid before me.

I have kept close unto thy testimonies; O Lord, confound me not.

I will run the way of thy commandments, when thou hast set my heart at liberty.

Now unto the King eternal, etc.

Be honor and glory, etc.

𝕮𝖍𝖊 𝕿𝖜𝖊𝖓𝖙𝖞-𝖘𝖊𝖈𝖔𝖓𝖉 𝕭𝖆𝖞.

MORNING PRÀYER.

PSALM CXIX.

HE.

TEACH me, O Lord, the way of thy statutes; and I will keep it unto the end.

Give me understanding, and I will keep thy law; yea, I will keep it with my whole heart.

Make me to go in the path of thy commandments; for therein is my desire.

Incline my heart unto thy testimonies, and not to covetousness.

O turn away mine eyes, lest they behold vanity; and quicken thou me in thy way.

O establish thy word in thy servant, that I may fear thee.

Take away the reproach that I am afraid of; for thy judgments are good.

Behold, my delight is in thy commandments; O quicken me in thy righteousness.

VAU.

LET thy loving mercy come unto me, O Lord, even thy salvation, according unto thy word.

So shall I make answer unto those who reproach me; for my trust is in thy word.

O take not the word of thy truth utterly out of my mouth; for my hope is in thy judgments.

So shall I alway keep thy law; yea, for ever and ever.

And I will walk at liberty; for I seek thy commandments.

I will speak of thy testimonies also, even before kings, and will not be ashamed.

And my delight shall be in thy commandments, which I have loved.

My hands also will I lift up unto thy commandments, which I have loved ; and my study shall be in thy statutes.

Now unto the King eternal, etc.

Be honor and glory, etc.

EVENING PRAYER.

PSALM CXIX.

ZAIN.

O THINK upon thy word of promise to thy servant, wherein thou hast caused me to put my trust.

The same is my comfort in my trouble ; for thy word hath quickened me.

The proud have had me exceedingly in derision ; yet have I not shrunk from thy law.

For I remembered thy judgments of old, O Lord, and received comfort.

Horror hath taken hold upon me, because of the wicked who forsake thy law.

Thy statutes have been my songs in the house of my pilgrimage.

I have thought upon thy name, O Lord, in the night season ; and have kept thy law.

I esteemed myself rich in that I have kept thy commandments.

CHETH.

THOU art my portion, O Lord ; I have promised to keep thy law.

I entreated thy favor with my whole heart ; O be merciful unto me according to thy word.

I called my ways to remembrance, and turned my feet unto thy testimonies.

I made haste and delayed not to keep thy commandments.

The bands of the ungodly have robbed me ; but I have not forgotten thy law.

At midnight I will rise to give thanks unto thee, because of thy righteous judgments.

I am a companion of all those who fear thee and keep thy commandments.

The earth, O Lord, is full of thy mercy ; O teach me thy statutes.

Now unto the King eternal, etc.

Be honor and glory, etc.

The Twenty-third Day.

MORNING PRAYER.

PSALM CXIX.

TETH.

O LORD, thou hast dealt graciously with thy servant according unto thy word.

O teach me true understanding and knowledge ; for I have believed thy commandments.

Before I was afflicted, I went astray ; but now have I kept thy word.

Thou art good and doest good ; O teach me thy statutes.

The proud have forged a lie against me ; but I will keep thy commandments with my whole heart.

It is good for me that I have been in trouble, that I might learn thy statutes.

The law of thy mouth is dearer unto me than thousands of gold and silver.

JOD.

THY hands have made me, and fashioned me ; O give me understanding, that I may learn thy commandments.

They who fear thee will be glad when they see me, because I have put my trust in thy word.

I know, O Lord, that thy judgments are right, and that thou of very faithfulness hast caused me to be troubled.

O let thy merciful kindness be my comfort, according to thy word unto thy servant.

O let thy loving mercies come unto me, that I may live ; for thy law is my delight.

Let such as fear thee, and have known thy testimonies, be turned unto me.

O let my heart be sound in thy statutes, that I be not ashamed.

CAPH.

MY soul hath longed for thy salvation ; and I have a good hope because of thy word.

Mine eyes languish for thy word, saying, O when wilt thou comfort me ?

O quicken me according to thy loving-kindness ; and so shall I keep the testimonies of thy mouth.

Now unto the King eternal, etc.

Be honor and glory, etc.

EVENING PRAYER.

PSALM CXIX.

LAMED.

O LORD, thy word endureth forever in the heavens.

Thy truth also remaineth from one generation to another ; thou hast laid the foundation of the earth, and it abideth.

They continue this day according to thine ordinance ; for all things serve thee.

If my delight had not been in thy law, I should have perished in my misery.

I will never forget thy commandments ; for with them thou hast quickened me.

I am thine ; O save me ; for I have sought thy commandments.

The ungodly laid wait for me, to destroy me ; but I will consider thy testimonies.

I see that all things come to an end ; but thy commandment is eternal.

MEM.

O HOW I love thy law ! all the day long is my study in it !

Thou, through thy commandments, hast made me wiser than mine enemies ; for they are ever with me.

I have more understanding than my teachers; for thy testimonies are my study.

I am wiser than the aged; because I keep thy commandments.

I have refrained my feet from every evil way, because I keep thy word.

I have not shrunk from thy judgments; for thou teachest me.

How sweet are thy words unto my taste, yea, sweeter than honey unto my mouth.

Through thy commandments I get understanding; therefore I hate all evil ways.

Now unto the King eternal, etc.

Be honor and glory, etc.

The Twenty-fourth Day.

MORNING PRAYER.

PSALM CXIX.

NUN.

THY word is a lamp unto my feet, and a light unto my paths.

I have sworn and am steadfastly purposed to keep thy righteous judgments.

I am troubled above measure; revive me, O Lord, according to thy word.

Let the free-will offerings of my mouth please thee, O Lord; and teach thou me thy judgments.

My life is in constant peril; yet do I not forget thy law.

The ungodly have laid a snare for me ; but yet I swerve not from thy commandments.

Thy testimonies have I claimed as mine heritage forever ; and why? they are the very joy of my heart.

I have applied my heart to fulfil thy statutes, which are an everlasting reward.

SAMECH.

I HATE wicked imaginations ; but thy law do I love.

Thou art my defence and shield ; and my trust is in thy word.

Depart from me, ye wicked ; I will keep the commandments of my God.

O stablish me according to thy word, that I may live ; and let me not be disappointed of my hope.

Hold thou me up, and I shall be safe ; yea, my delight shall be ever in thy statutes.

Thou hast trodden down all those who depart from thy statutes ; for they imagine but deceit.

Thou puttest away all the ungodly of the earth like dross ; therefore I love thy testimonies.

My flesh trembleth for fear of thee, and I am afraid of thy judgments.

AIN.

I HAVE done judgment and justice ; O give me not over unto mine oppressors.

O lead thy servant in safety, that the proud do me no wrong.

Mine eyes are wasted away with looking for thy help, and for thy gracious promise.

O deal with thy servant according unto thy loving mercy, and teach me thy statutes.

I am thy servant; O grant me understanding, that I may know thy testimonies.

It is time for thee, Lord, to execute judgment; for they have set at naught thy law.

For I love thy commandments above gold and precious stones.

Therefore I direct my way according to all thy commandments; and all false ways I utterly abhor.

Now unto the King eternal, etc.

Be honor and glory, etc.

EVENING PRAYER.

PSALM CXIX.

PE.

THY testimonies are wonderful; therefore doth my soul keep them.

When thy word goeth forth, it giveth light and understanding unto the simple.

I open my mouth, and pant for thy commandments; for they are my exceeding delight.

O look thou upon me, and be merciful unto me, as thou usest to do unto those who love thy name.

Order my steps in thy word; and let no wickedness have dominion over me.

O deliver me from the wrongful dealings of men; so shall I keep thy commandments.

Show the light of thy countenance upon thy servant; and teach me thy statutes.

Mine eyes gush out with rivers of water, because men keep not thy law.

TZADDI.

R IGHTEOUS art thou, O Lord, and true is thy judgment.

The testimonies that thou hast commanded are exceeding righteous and true.

My indignation hath consumed me, because mine enemies have forgotten thy words.

Thy word is approved to the utmost; and thy servant loveth it.

I am small, and of no reputation; yet do I not forget thy commandments.

Thy righteousness is an everlasting righteousness; and thy law is the truth.

When trouble and heaviness take hold upon me, my delight is in thy commandments.

The righteousness of thy testimonies is everlasting; O grant me understanding, and I shall live.

KOPH.

I CALL with my whole heart; hear me, O Lord; I will keep thy statutes.

Yea, even unto thee do I call; help me, and I shall keep thy testimonies.

·Early in the morning do I cry unto thee; for in thy word is my trust.

Mine eyes anticipate the night watches, that I may be occupied in thy words.

Hear my voice, O Lord, according unto thy loving-kindness; quicken me according as thou art wont.

389

They draw nigh who of malice persecute me, and are far from thy law.

But thou also art nigh, O Lord; all thy commandments are true.

Concerning thy testimonies, I have known long since, that thou hast established them forever.

Now unto the King eternal, etc.

Be honor and glory, etc.

The Twenty-fifth Day.

MORNING PRAYER.

PSALM CXIX.

RESH.

O CONSIDER mine adversity, and deliver me; for I do not forget thy law.

Plead thou my cause, and deliver me; preserve me according to thy word.

Salvation is far from the ungodly; for they regard not thy statutes.

Great is thy mercy, O Lord; quicken me according to thy judgments.

Many there are who trouble me, and persecute me; yet do I not swerve from thy testimonies.

It grieveth me, when I see the transgressors, because they keep not thy law.

Consider, O Lord, how I love thy commandments; O revive me according to thy loving-kindness.

Thy word is true from everlasting; all the judgments of thy righteousness endure forevermore.

SCHIN.

PRINCES have persecuted me without a cause; but my heart standeth in awe of thy word.

I am as glad of thy word as one who findeth great spoils.

As for lies, I hate and abhor them; but thy law do I love.

Seven times a day do I praise thee, because of thy righteous judgments.

Great is the peace that they have who love thy law; and nothing shall offend them.

Lord, I have looked for thy saving health, and done after thy commandments.

My soul hath kept thy testimonies, and loved them exceedingly.

I have kept thy commandments and testimonies; for all my ways are before thee.

TAU.

LET my prayer come before thee, O Lord; give me understanding according to thy word.

Let my supplication come before thee; deliver me according to thy word.

My lips shall speak of thy praise, when thou hast taught me thy statutes.

Yea, my tongue shall speak of thy word; for all thy commandments are righteous.

Let thine hand help me; for I have chosen thy commandments.

I have longed for thy saving health, O Lord; and in thy law is my delight.

O let my soul live, and it shall praise thee; and thy judgments shall help me.

I have gone astray like a sheep that is lost; O seek thy servant, for I do not forget thy commandments.

Now unto the King eternal, etc.

Be honor and glory, etc.

EVENING PRAYER.

PSALM CXXI.

Trust in God's protection.

I WILL lift up mine eyes unto the hills, from whence cometh my help.

My help cometh even from the Lord, who hath made heaven and earth.

He will not suffer thy foot to be moved; and he who keepeth thee will not sleep.

Behold, he who keepeth Israel shall neither slumber nor sleep.

The Lord himself is thy keeper; the Lord is thy shade upon thy right hand;

So that the sun shall not smite thee by day, neither the moon by night.

· The Lord shall preserve thee from all evil; yea, it is even he who shall keep thy soul.

The Lord shall preserve thy going out and thy coming in, from this time forth forevermore.

PSALM CXXII.

Hymn of worshippers going up to Jerusalem.

I WAS glad when they said unto me, Let us go up to the house of the Lord.

Our feet shall stand within thy gates, O Jerusalem.

Jerusalem is rebuilt as a city, and is at unity in itself.

Thither the tribes go up, even the tribes of the Lord, according to the law of Israel, to give thanks unto the name of the Lord.

For there is the seat of judgment, even the throne of the house of David.

O pray for the peace of Jerusalem; they shall prosper who love thee.

Peace be within thy walls, and prosperity within thy palaces.

For my brethren and companions' sakes, I will say, Peace be within thee.

Yea, because of the house of the Lord our God, I will seek to do thee good.

Now unto the King eternal, etc.

Be honor and glory, etc.

The Twenty-sixth Day.

MORNING PRAYER.

Psalm CXXIII.

Prayer of the exiles.

UNTO thee lift I up mine eyes, O thou who dwellest in the heavens.

Behold, even as the eyes of servants look unto the hand of their masters, and as the eyes of a maiden unto the hand of her mistress;

Even so our eyes wait upon the Lord our God, until he have mercy upon us.

Have mercy upon. us, O Lord, have mercy upon us ; for we are utterly despised.

Our soul is filled with the insolence of the prosperons, and with the despitefulness of the proud.

PSALM CXXIV.

Exiles giving thanks.

IF the Lord himself had not been on our side, now may Israel say, if the Lord himself had not been on our side, when men rose up against us ;

They had swallowed us up alive, when they were so wrathfully displeased at us ;

Yea, the waters had drowned us ; and the stream had gone over our soul ;

The proud waters had gone over our soul.

But praised be the Lord, who hath not given us over for a prey unto their teeth.

Our soul is escaped, even as a bird out of the snare of the fowler ; the snare is broken, and we are delivered.

Our help is in the name of the Lord, who hath made heaven and earth.

PSALM CXXV.

Exiles trusting in God.

THEY who put their trust in the Lord, shall be even as the mount Sion, which may not be removed, but standeth fast forever.

As the hills stand about Jerusalem, even so

standeth the Lord round about his people, from this time forth forevermore.

For the sceptre of the ungodly shall not rule over the righteous ; unless the righteous put their hand unto wickedness.

Do well, O Lord, unto those who are good and true of heart.

As for such as turn aside unto their crooked ways, the Lord shall lead them forth with the evil doers ; but peace shall be upon Israel.

Now unto the King eternal, etc.

Be honor and glory, etc.

EVENING PRAYER.

PSALM CXXVI.

Exiles rejoicing in their restoration.

WHEN the Lord turned again the captivity of Sion, then were we like unto those who dream.

Then was our mouth filled with laughter, and our tongue with joy.

Then said they among the heathen, "The Lord hath done great things for them."

Yea, the Lord hath done great things for us, whereof we rejoice.

Thou hast restored our captives, O Lord, as the rivers in the south.

They who sow in tears shall reap in joy.

He who goeth on his way weeping, and beareth forth good seed, shall doubtless come again with joy, and bring his sheaves with him.

PSALM CXXVII.

Family blessings the gift of God.

EXCEPT the Lord build the house, their labor is but lost who build it.

Except the Lord keep the city, the watchman waketh but in vain.

It is but lost labor that ye haste to rise up early, and so late take rest, and eat the bread of carefulness ; for surely he giveth his beloved sleep.

Lo, children are an heritage and gift that cometh of the Lord.

Like as the arrows in the hand of the mighty man, even so are the young children.

Happy is the man who hath his quiver full of them ; they shall not be ashamed when they speak with their enemies in the gate.

PSALM CXXVIII.

The blessings of home are of God.

BLESSED is he who feareth the Lord, and walketh in his ways.

For thou shalt eat the labor of thine hands ; O blessed art thou, and happy shalt thou be.

Thy wife shall be as the fruitful vine upon the walls of thine house.

Thy children like olive branches round about thy table.

Lo, thus shall the man be blessed, who feareth the Lord.

The Lord from out of Sion shall so bless thee, that thou shalt see Jerusalem in prosperity all thy life long ;

Yea, that thou shalt see thy children's children, and peace upon Israel.

Now unto the King eternal, etc.

Be honor and glory, etc.

𝔗𝔥𝔢 𝔗𝔴𝔢𝔫𝔱𝔶 𝔰𝔢𝔳𝔢𝔫𝔱𝔥 𝔇𝔞𝔶.

MORNING PRAYER.

PSALM CXXX.

Penitential Psalm, De Profundis.

OUT of the deep have I called unto thee, O Lord; Lord, hear my voice.

O let thine ears consider well the voice of my complaint.

If thou, Lord, wilt be extreme to mark what is done amiss, O Lord, who may abide it?

But there is mercy with thee; therefore shalt thou be feared.

I look for the Lord; my soul doth wait for him; in his word is my trust.

My soul waiteth for the Lord, more than they that watch for the morning, I say, more than they that watch for the morning.

O Israel, trust in the Lord; for with the Lord there is mercy, and with him is plenteous redemption.

And he shall redeem Israel from all his sin.

PSALM CXXXI.

Humility and contentment.

LORD, my heart is not haughty, nor mine eyes lofty.

I will not exercise myself in great matters, which are too high for me;

But will refrain my soul and keep it low, like as a child that is weaned from his mother; yea, my soul shall be even as a weaned child.

O Israel, trust in the Lord, from this time forth forevermore.

Psalm CXXXII.

Dedication of the temple. 1 Chron. Chap. 22, verse 14.

LORD, remember David, and all his troubles;
How he sware unto the Lord, and vowed a vow unto the Almighty God of Jacob;

"I will not come within the tabernacle of mine house, nor climb up into my bed;

"I will not suffer mine eyes to sleep, nor mine eyelids to slumber;

"Until I find out a place for the temple of the Lord, a habitation for the mighty God of Jacob."

We will go into his tabernacle, we will worship before his footstool.

Arise, O Lord, into thy resting-place, thou, and the ark of thy strength.

Let thy priests be clothed with righteousness; and let thy saints sing with joyfulness.

For thy servant David's sake, turn not away thy face from thine anointed.

The Lord hath made a faithful oath unto David, and he will not shrink from it;

"Of the fruit of thy body will I set upon thy throne.

"If thy children will keep my covenant, and my

testimonies that I shall teach them, their children also shall sit upon thy throne forevermore."

For the Lord hath chosen Sion; he hath desired it for his habitation.

"This shall be my rest forever; here will I dwell, for I have a delight therein.

"I will bless her provision with increase; and will satisfy her poor with bread.

"I will clothe her priests with salvation; and her saints shall rejoice and sing."

Now unto the King eternal, etc.

Be honor and glory, etc.

EVENING PRAYER.

PSALM CXXXIII.

Blessedness of unity among brethren.

BEHOLD, how good and joyful a thing it is for brethren to dwell together in unity.

It is like the precious ointment upon the head, that ran down upon the beard, even unto Aaron's beard, and went down to the skirts of his clothing.

Like as the dew of Hermon, and the dew which falleth upon the hill of Sion.

For there the Lord promiseth his blessing, and life forevermore.

PSALM CXXXIV.

The servants of the temple exhorted to praise God.

O PRAISE the Lord, all ye servants of the Lord.

Ye who by night stand in the house of the Lord, even in the courts of the house of our God;

Lift up your hands in the sanctuary and praise the Lord.

The Lord, who made heaven and earth, give thee his blessing out of Sion.

PSALM CXXXV.

A psalm of praise.

O PRAISE the Lord; praise ye the name of the Lord; praise it, O ye servants of the Lord.

Ye who stand in the house of the Lord, in the courts of the house of our God;

O praise the Lord, for the Lord is gracious; O sing praises unto his name, for it is lovely.

The Lord hath chosen Jacob unto himself, and Israel for his own possession.

I know that the Lord is great, and that our Lord is above all gods.

Whatsoever the Lord pleaseth, that doeth he in heaven and in earth, in the sea, and in all depths.

He bringeth forth the clouds from the ends of the world, and sendeth forth lightnings with the rain, bringing the winds out of his treasuries.

Thy name, O Lord, endureth forever; and thy memorial, O Lord, from one generation to another.

For the Lord will defend his people, and be gracious unto his servants.

As for the idols of the heathen, they are but silver and gold, the work of men's hands.

They have mouths, and speak not; eyes have they, but they see not;

They have ears, and yet they hear not; neither is there any breath in their mouths.

They who make them are like unto them; and so are all they who put their trust in them.

Praise the Lord, ye house of Israel; praise the Lord, ye house of Aaron.

Praise the Lord, ye house of Levi; ye who fear the Lord, praise the Lord.

Now unto the King eternal, etc.

Be honor and glory, etc.

The Twenty-eighth Day.

MORNING PRAYER.

PSALM CXXXVI.

A psalm of thanksgiving.

O GIVE thanks unto the Lord; for he is gracious, and his mercy endureth forever.

O give thanks unto the God of all gods; for his mercy endureth forever.

O thank the Lord of all lords; for his mercy endureth forever.

Who only doeth great wonders; for his mercy endureth forever.

Who by his excellent wisdom made the heavens; for his mercy endureth forever.

Who laid out the earth above the waters; for his mercy endureth forever.

Who hath made great lights; for his mercy endureth forever.

The sun to rule by day; for his mercy endureth forever.

The moon and the stars to govern the night; for his mercy endureth forever.

Who remembered us when we were in trouble; for his mercy endureth forever.

And delivered us from our enemies; for his mercy endureth forever.

Who giveth food to all flesh; for his mercy endureth forever.

O give thanks unto the God of heaven; for his mercy endureth forever.

PSALM CXXXVIII.

Thanksgiving for deliverance.

I WILL give thanks unto thee, O Lord, with my whole heart; even before princes will I sing praise unto thee.

I will worship toward thy holy temple, and praise thy name, because of thy loving-kindness and truth; for thou hast magnified thy name and thy word above all things.

When I called upon thee, thou heardest me, and enduedst my soul with much strength.

All the kings of the earth shall praise thee, O Lord, when they shall have heard the words of thy mouth.

Yea, they shall sing of thy ways, that great is the glory of the Lord.

For though the Lord be high, yet hath he respect unto the lowly; as for the proud, he beholdeth them afar off.

Though I walk in the midst of trouble, yet shalt thou refresh me ; thou shalt stretch forth thine hand against the furiousness of mine enemies, and thy right hand shall save me.

The Lord shall make good his loving-kindness toward me ; yea, thy mercy, O Lord, endureth forever ; forsake not then the works of thine own hands.

Now unto the King eternal, etc.

Be honor and glory, etc.

EVENING PRAYER.

PSALM CXXXIX.

The universal presence and knowledge of God.

O LORD, thou hast searched me out, and known me ; thou knowest my downsitting, and mine uprising ; thou understandest my thoughts afar off.

Thou art about my path, and about my bed, and beholdest all my ways.

For lo, there is not a word in my tongue, but thou, O Lord, knowest it altogether.

Thou dost encompass me behind and before, and layest thine hand upon me.

Such knowledge is too wonderful and excellent for me ; I cannot attain unto it.

Whither shall I go then from thy spirit ? or whither shall I flee from thy presence ?

If I climb up into heaven, thou art there ; if I go down to the grave, thou art there also.

If I take the wings of the morning, and dwell in the uttermost parts of the sea ;

Even there also shall thy hand lead me, and thy right hand shall hold me.

If I say, Peradventure the darkness shall cover me ; even the night shall be light about me.

Yea, the darkness is no darkness with thee ; but the night is as clear as the day ; the darkness and light to thee are both alike.

I will give thanks unto thee, for I am fearfully and wonderfully made ; marvellous are thy works, and that my soul knoweth right well.

My substance was not hid from thee, when I was made secretly, and fashioned beneath in the earth.

Thine eyes did see my substance, yet being imperfect ; and in thy book were all my members written ;

Which day by day were fashioned, when as yet there was none of them.

How dear are thy thoughts unto me, O God ! O how great is the sum of them !

If I should count them, they are more in number than the sand ; when I awake I am still with thee.

Try me, O God, and seek the ground of my heart ; prove me, and examine my thoughts.

Look well if there be any way of wickedness in me, and lead me in the way everlasting.

Now unto the King eternal, etc.

Be honor and glory, etc.

The Twenty-ninth Day.

MORNING PRAYER.

Psalm CXLI.

Prayer for watchfulness and submission.

LORD, I call upon thee; haste thee unto me, and consider my voice, when I cry unto thee.

Let my prayer be set forth in thy sight as incense; and let the lifting up of my hands be an evening sacrifice.

Set a watch, O Lord, before my mouth, and keep the door of my lips.

O let not mine heart be inclined to any evil thing; let me not be occupied in ungodly works, with wicked men, nor eat of such things as please them.

Let the righteous smite me, it shall be a kindness; let him reprove me, it shall be an oil to my head which I will not refuse; for yet my prayer shall be for them in their calamities.

Our bones lie scattered at the grave's mouth, like as when one breaketh and heweth wood upon the earth.

But mine eyes look unto thee, O Lord God; in thee is my trust; O cast not out my soul.

Psalm CXLII.

A prayer of David when he was in the cave. 1 Sam. Chap. 24.

I CRIED unto the Lord with my voice; yea, even unto the Lord did I make my supplication.

I poured out my complaints before him; and showed him of my trouble.

When my spirit was in heaviness, thou knewest my path; in the way wherein I walked, have they privily laid a snare for me.

I looked also upon my right hand, and saw there was no man who would know me.

I had no place to flee unto; and no man cared for my soul.

I cried unto thee, O Lord, and said, Thou art my hope, and my portion in the land of the living.

Consider my complaint; for I am brought very low.

O deliver me from my persecutors; for they are stronger than I.

Bring my soul out of prison, that I may give thanks unto thy name; the righteous shall compass me about, when thou hast dealt so bountifully with me.

PSALM CXLIII.

Penitential psalm.

HEAR my prayer, O Lord, and consider my desire; hearken unto me for thy truth and righteousness' sake.

And enter not into judgment with thy servant; for in thy sight shall no man living be justified.

I remember the days of old; I muse upon all thy works; yea, I meditate on the works of thy hands.

I stretch forth my hands unto thee; my soul gaspeth unto thee as a thirsty land.

Hear me, O Lord, and that soon, for my spirit waxeth faint; hide not thy face from me, lest I be like unto those who go down into the pit.

O let me hear thy loving-kindness betimes in the morning, for in thee is my trust; show thou me the way that I should walk in, for I lift up my soul unto thee.

Deliver me, O Lord, from mine enemies; for I flee unto thee to hide me.

Teach me to do the thing that pleaseth thee; for thou art my God; let thy loving Spirit lead me forth into the land of righteousness.

Quicken me, O Lord, for thy name's sake; and for thy righteousness' sake bring my soul out of trouble.

Now unto the King eternal, etc.

Be honor and glory, etc.

EVENING PRAYER.

Psalm CXLIV.

Thanksgiving and supplication for blessings.

BLESSED be the Lord, my strength; my hope and my fortress; my castle and deliverer; my defender, in whom I trust.

Lord, what is man, that thou hast such respect unto him? or the son of man, that thou so regardest him?

Man is like a thing of naught; his life passeth away like a shadow.

Bow thy heavens, O Lord, and come down; touch the mountains, and they shall smoke.

Stretch forth thine hand from above; deliver

me, and take me out of the great waters, from the hand of strange nations;

Whose mouth talketh vanity, and their right hand is a right hand of wickedness.

I will sing a new song unto thee, O God; and sing praises unto thee upon a ten-stringed lute.

Save me, and deliver me from the hand of strange nations, whose mouth talketh vanity, and their right hand is a right hand of iniquity;

That our sons may grow up as the young plants; and that our daughters may be as the polished columns of the temple;

That our garners may be full and plenteous with all manner of store; that our sheep may bring forth thousands, and ten thousands in our streets;

That our oxen may be strong to labor; that there be no decay, no leading into captivity, and no complaining in our streets.

Happy are the people that are in such a case; yea, blessed are the people whose God is the Lord.

Psalm CXLVI.

The justice and mercy of God.

PRAISE the Lord, O my soul; while I live will I praise the Lord; yea, as long as I have any being, I will sing praises unto my God.

O put not your trust in princes, nor in any child of man; for there is no help in them.

Their breath goeth forth: they return to the dust; and then all their thoughts perish.

Blessed is he who hath the God of Jacob for his help, and whose hope is in the Lord his God;

Who made heaven and earth, the sea, and all that therein is; who keepeth his promise forever.

Who helpeth those to right who suffer wrong; who feedeth the hungry.

The Lord looseth men out of prison; the Lord openeth the eyes of the blind.

The Lord helpeth those who are fallen; the Lord careth for the righteous.

The Lord careth for the strangers; he defendeth the fatherless and widow; but the way of the ungodly he doth utterly overturn.

The Lord shall reign forever; even thy God, O Sion, unto all generations. Praise ye the Lord.

Now unto the King eternal, etc.

Be honor and glory, etc.

The Thirtieth Day.

MORNING PRAYER.

Psalm CXLVII.

The power of God, and his goodness to Israel.

O PRAISE the Lord; for it is a good thing to sing praises unto our God; yea, a joyful and pleasant thing it is to be thankful.

The Lord doth build up Jerusalem, and gather together the outcasts of Israel.

He healeth those who are broken in heart, and bindeth up their wounds.

He numbereth the stars; and calleth them all by their names.

Great is our Lord, and great is his power; yea, and his wisdom is infinite.

The Lord lifteth up the meek; and bringeth the ungodly down to the ground.

O sing unto the Lord with thanksgiving; sing praises upon the harp unto our God;

Who covereth the heaven with clouds, and prepareth rain for the earth, and maketh the grass to grow upon the mountains;

Who giveth to the beast his food, and feedeth the young ravens that cry.

He hath no pleasure in the strength of the horse; neither delighteth he in the force of man;

But the Lord's delight is in those who fear him, and put their trust in his mercy.

Praise the Lord, O Jerusalem; praise thy God, O Sion.

For he hath made fast the bars of thy gates; and hath blessed thy children within thee.

He maketh peace in thy borders; and filleth thee with the finest of the wheat.

He sendeth forth his commandment upon earth; and his word is instantly obeyed.

He giveth snow like wool; he scattereth the hoar-frost like ashes.

He casteth forth his ice like morsels; who can stand before his cold?

He sendeth out his word and melteth them; he bloweth with his wind, and the waters flow.

He showeth his word unto Jacob, his statutes and ordinances unto Israel.

He hath not dealt so with any other nation; neither hath the heathen knowledge of his laws. Praise ye the Lord.

Now unto the King eternal, etc.

Be honor and glory, etc.

EVENING PRAYER.

Psalm CXLVIII.

The heavens and the earth called to praise the Lord.

PRAISE ye the Lord. Praise ye the Lord from the heavens; praise him in the height.

Praise him, all ye angels of his; praise him all his hosts.

Praise him, sun and moon; praise him, all ye stars and light.

Praise him, ye heavens of heavens, and ye waters of the skies.

Let them praise the name of the Lord, for he commanded and they were created.

He hath made them fast for ever and ever; he hath given them a law which shall not be broken.

Praise the Lord, upon earth, ye whales, and all deeps;

Fire and hail, snow and vapors, wind and storm, fulfilling his word;

Mountains and all hills, fruitful trees and all cedars;

Beasts and all cattle, creeping things and feathered fowls;

Kings of the earth and all people, princes and all judges of the world;

Young men and maidens, old men and children; praise the name of the Lord; for his name alone is excellent, and his praise is above heaven and earth.

He shall increase the glory of his people; all his saints shall praise him, even the children of Israel, even the people that serveth him. Praise ye the Lord.

Psalm CXLIX.

Exhortation to praise God.

PRAISE ye the Lord. Sing unto the Lord a new song; let the congregation of saints praise him.

Let Israel rejoice in him who made him; and let the children of Sion be joyful in their king.

For the Lord hath pleasure in his people; he will beautify the meek with salvation.

Let the saints be joyful with glory; let them rejoice in their congregations.

Psalm CL.

Exulting praise.

PRAISE ye the Lord. Praise God in his sanctuary. Praise him in the firmament of his power.

Praise him for his noble acts; praise him according to his excellent greatness.

Praise him with the sound of the trumpet; praise him upon the lute and harp.

Praise him upon the well-tuned cymbals ; praise him upon the loud cymbals.

Let everything that hath breath praise the Lord. Praise ye the Lord.

Now unto the King eternal, etc.

Be honor and glory, etc.

END OF THE PSALMS.

ANTHEMS AND PSALMS.

FOR CHRISTMAS DAY.

Antſ em.

To be used at Morning Prayer, instead of the Psalm,
O come, let us sing, &c.

GLORY be to God in the highest, on earth peace, good will toward men.

Blessed are the people who know the joyful sound; they shall walk, O Lord, in the light of thy countenance;

Through the tender mercies of our God, whereby the dayspring from on high hath visited us;

To give light to those who sit in darkness and in the shadow of death, and to guide our feet in the way of peace.

How beautiful on the mountains are the feet of him who bringeth good tidings; who publisheth peace; who bringeth good tidings of good; who publisheth salvation; who saith unto Sion, Thy God reigneth.

There is sprung up a light for the righteous, and joyful gladness for such as are true of heart.

Rejoice in the Lord, ye righteous, and give thanks at the remembrance of his holiness.

Sing unto the Lord, and praise his name; be telling of his salvation from day to day.

Let all those who seek him be joyful and glad in him, and let all such as love his salvation say always, The Lord be praised.

Proper Psalms

MORNING PRAYER.

PSALM XLV.

M Y heart is inditing joyful words; I speak of the things concerning the King; my tongue is as the pen of a ready writer.

Thou art the fairest of the children of men; full of grace are thy lips; for God hath blessed thee forever.

Gird thy sword upon thy thigh, O thou Mighty One, with thy glory and thy majesty.

And in thy majesty ride prosperously, for the cause of truth and meekness and righteousness; and thy right hand shall teach thee terrible things.

Thy throne, O God, endureth forever; the seeptre of thy kingdom is a right sceptre.

Thou hast loved righteousness, and hated iniquity; wherefore God, even thy God, hath anointed thee with the oil of gladness above thy fellows.

I will make thy name to be remembered to all generations; so that the people shall praise thee for ever and ever.

Psalm LXXXV.

LORD, thou art become gracious unto thy land; thou hast turned away the captivity of Jacob.

Thou hast forgiven the offence of thy people, and covered all their sins.

Thou hast taken away all thy displeasure, and turned thyself from thy wrathful indignation.

Turn us then, O God, our Saviour, and let thine anger cease from us.

Wilt thou be displeased at us forever? and wilt thou stretch out thy wrath from one generation to another?

Wilt thou not turn again and quicken us, that thy people may rejoice in thee?

Show us thy mercy, O Lord, and grant us thy salvation.

I will hear what God the Lord will speak; for he will speak peace to his people and his saints; only let them not return to their folly again.

For his salvation is nigh those who fear him, that glory may dwell in our land.

Mercy and truth shall meet together; righteousness and peace shall kiss each other.

Truth shall flourish out of the earth; and righteousness shall look down from heaven.

Yea, the Lord shall show his loving-kindness; and our land shall yield her increase.

Righteousness shall go before him; and shall keep his path continually.

Now unto the King eternal, etc.

Be honor and glory, etc.

EVENING PRAYER.

Psalm CX.

THE Lord said unto my.lord, Sit thou on my right hand, until I make thine enemies thy footstool.

The Lord shall extend the sceptre of thy power out of Sion; rule thou in the midst of thine enemies.

In the day of thy power shall the people offer thee free-will offerings with a holy worship; thy youth shall come forth like dew from the womb of the morning.

The Lord sware, and will not repent, Thou art a priest forever after the order of Melchisedeck.

The Lord at thy right hand shall destroy even kings in the day of his wrath.

He shall judge among the nations; he shall fill the places with dead bodies, and shall wound the heads of his enemies over many countries.

Thou shalt drink of the brook in the way, and lift up thy head on high.

Psalm CXXXII.

LORD, remember David, and all his troubles; How he sware unto the Lord, and vowed a vow unto the Almighty God of Jacob;

" I will not come within the tabernacle of mine house, nor climb up into my bed;

" I will not suffer mine eyes to sleep, nor mine eyelids to slumber;

"Until I find out a place for the temple of the Lord, a habitation for the mighty God of Jacob."

We will go into his tabernacle, we will worship before his footstool.

Arise, O Lord, into thy resting-place; thou, and the ark of thy strength.

Let thy priests be clothed with righteousness; and let thy saints sing with joyfulness.

For thy servant David's sake, turn not away thy face from thine anointed.

The Lord hath made a faithful oath unto David, and he shall not shrink from it;

"Of the fruit of thy body will I set upon thy throne.

"If thy children will keep my covenant, and my testimonies that I shall teach them, their children also shall sit upon thy throne forevermore."

For the Lord hath chosen Sion; he hath desired it for his habitation.

"This shall be my rest forever; here will I dwell, for I have a delight therein.

"I will bless her provision with increase; and will satisfy her poor with bread.

"I will clothe her priests with salvation; and her saints shall rejoice and sing."

Now unto the King eternal, etc.

Be honor and glory, etc.

FOR GOOD FRIDAY.

Anthem.

THE people stood up, and the rulers took counsel together against the Lord, and against his anointed.

They cast their heads together with one consent, and were confederate against him.

They spake against him with false tongues, and encompassed him about with words of hatred, and fought against him without a cause.

False witnesses also did rise up against him; they laid to his charge things that he knew not.

For the sins of the people, and the iniquity of the priests, they shed the blood of the just, in the midst of Jerusalem.

He was oppressed and he was afflicted, yet he opened not his mouth; he was led as a lamb to the slaughter, and as a sheep before her shearers is dumb, so he opened not his mouth.

But thou, Lord, hast highly exalted him, and given him a name that is above every name;

That in the name of Jesus every knee should bow, and every tongue confess that Christ Jesus is Lord, to the glory of God the Father.

Proper Psalms.

MORNING PRAYER.

PSALM XXII.

MY God, my God, look upon me; why hast thou forsaken me, and art so far from my help, and from the words of my complaint?

O my God, I cry in the day time, but thou hearest not; and in the night season also I take no rest.

But thou continuest holy, O thou worship of Israel.

Our fathers trusted in thee; they trusted in thee, and thou didst deliver them.

They called upon thee, and were delivered; they put their trust in thee, and were not confounded.

But as for me, I am a worm and no man; a very scorn of men, and the outcast of the people.

All they who see me, laugh me to scorn; they shoot out their lips, and shake their heads, saying,

"He trusted in God, that he would deliver him; let him deliver him, if he will have him."

But thou art he who brought me into being; thou wast my hope when I hanged yet upon my mother's breasts.

I have been left unto thee ever since I was born; thou art my God even from my birth.

O go not from me, for trouble is hard at hand, and there is none to help me.

My strength is dried up like a potsherd, and my tongue cleaveth to my jaws; and thou hast brought me into the dust of death.

For the hunters are come about me; and the counsel of the wicked layeth siege against me.

They have pierced my hands and my feet; I may tell all my bones; they look and stare upon me.

They part my garments among them, and cast lots upon my vesture.

But be not thou far from me, O Lord; thou art my succor; haste thee to help me.

Deliver my life from the sword; my soul from the power of the hunter.

I will declare thy name unto my brethren; in the midst of the congregation will I praise thee.

O praise the Lord, ye who fear him; magnify him, all ye of the seed of Jacob, and fear him, all ye seed of Israel.

For he hath not despised nor abhorred the low estate of the afflicted; he hath not hid his face from him, but when he cried unto him, he heard him.

My praise shall be of thee in the great congregation; my vows will I perform in the sight of those who fear thee.

The poor shall eat, and be satisfied; they who seek after the Lord, shall praise him; your hearts shall be glad forever.

All the ends of the world shall remember themselves, and be turned unto the Lord; and all the kindreds of the nations shall worship before him.

For the kingdom is the Lord's; and he is the governor among the nations.

All the wealthy on earth shall worship him;

All those who are miserable shall kneel before him ; and he who cannot keep alive his own soul.

Future generations shall serve him ; the race which is to come shall hear of the Lord.

They shall come, and shall declare his righteousness unto the people who shall be born ; for he hath done this.

PSALM LIV.

SAVE me, O God, for thy name's sake, and defend me in thy strength.

Hear my prayer, O God, and hearken unto the words of my mouth.

For the proud are risen up against me ; and tyrants, who have not God before their eyes, seek my life.

But God is my helper ; the Lord is with those who uphold me.

The offerings of a free heart will I give thee ; and will praise thy name, O Lord, for it is good.

Now unto the King eternal, etc.

Be honor and glory, etc.

EVENING PRAYER.

PSALM LXIV.

HEAR my voice, O God, in my prayer ; preserve my life from fear of the enemy.

Hide me from the gathering together of the froward, and from the insurrection of wicked doers ;

Who have whet their tongue like a sword, and have fitted their arrows, even bitter words ;

That they may privily shoot at him who is upright; suddenly do they shoot at him, and fear not.

They encourage themselves in mischief, and commune among themselves how they may lay snares; and say, Who shall see them?

But God shall strike them with a swift arrow, and they shall be suddenly wounded.

Yea, their own tongues shall make them fall; and whoso seeth them shall fly from them.

And all men who see it shall say, This hath God done! for they shall perceive that it is his work.

The righteous shall rejoice in the Lord, and put his trust in him; and all they who are true of heart shall be glad.

Psalm LXIX.

SAVE me, O God, for the waters are come in, even unto my soul.

I sink in the deep mire, where no ground is; I am come into deep waters, where the floods rush over me.

I am weary of crying; my throat is dried; my sight faileth me, for waiting so long upon my God.

They who hate me without a cause, are more than the hairs of my head; they who are mine enemies, and would destroy me guiltless, are mighty.

Let not those who trust in thee, O Lord God of hosts, be ashamed for my cause; let not those who seek thee be confounded through me, O God of Israel.

Because for thy sake have I suffered reproach; shame hath covered my face.

I am become a stranger unto my brethren, even an alien unto my mother's children.

For the zeal of thine house hath eaten me up; and the rebukes of those who rebuked thee, are fallen upon me.

I wept and chastened myself with fasting, and that was turned to my reproof.

I put on sackcloth also; and they jested upon me.

But, Lord, I make my prayer unto thee in an acceptable time.

Hear me, O God, in the multitude of thy mercy, even in the truth of thy salvation.

Take me out of the mire, that I sink not; O let me be delivered from those who hate me, and out of the deep waters.

Let not the water-flood drown me, neither let the deep swallow me up, and let not the pit shut her mouth upon me.

Hear me, O Lord, for thy loving-kindness is good; turn thee unto me, according to the multitude of thy mercies.

And hide not thy face from thy servant, for I am in trouble; O haste thee, and hear me.

Draw nigh unto my soul, and save it; O deliver me, because of mine enemies.

Thou hast known my reproach, my shame, and my dishonor; mine adversaries are all in thy sight.

Reproach hath broken my heart; I am full of heaviness; I looked for some to have pity on me, but there was no man, neither found I any to comfort me.

They gave me gall to eat; and when I was thirsty, they gave me vinegar to drink.

As for me, I am poor and in heaviness, but thy help, O God, shall lift me up.

I will praise the name of God with a song, and magnify it with thanksgiving.

The humble shall consider this and be glad; the hearts of those that fear God shall be revived.

For the Lord heareth the poor, and despiseth not his people in their bonds.

Let heaven and earth praise him, the sea, and all that moveth therein.

For God will save Sion, and build the cities of Judah, that men may dwell there, and have it in possession.

The posterity also of his servants shall inherit it; and they who love his name shall dwell therein.

Now unto the King eternal, etc.

Be honor and glory, etc.

FOR EASTER DAY.

Anthem.

CHRIST our passover is sacrificed for us; therefore let us keep the feast; not with the old leaven, neither with the leaven of malice and wickedness; but with the unleavened bread of sincerity and truth.

Christ, being raised from the dead, dieth no more; death hath no more dominion over him.

For in that he died, he died unto sin once ; but in that he liveth, he liveth unto God. Likewise reckon ye also yourselves to be dead indeed unto sin, but alive unto God, through Jesus Christ our Lord.

Christ is risen from the dead, and become the first fruits of those who slept.

For since by man came death, by man came also the resurrection of the dead. For as in Adam all die, even so in Christ shall all be made alive.

Blessing, and honor, and glory, and power, be unto him, who sitteth upon the throne, and unto the Lamb, for ever and ever. *Amen.*

Proper Psalms.

MORNING PRAYER.

PSALM II.

WHY do the heathen rage? and why do the nations imagine a vain thing?

The kings of the earth stand up, and the rulers take counsel together against the Lord, and against his anointed ;

" Let us break," say they, " their bonds asunder, and cast away their cords from us."

He who dwelleth in heaven shall laugh them to scorn ; the Lord shall have them in derision.

He shall speak unto them in his wrath, and rebuke them in his sore displeasure.

" I myself have set my king upon my holy hill of Sion."

I will declare the decree·; the Lord hath said unto me, "Thou art my Son, this day have I begotten thee.

"Ask of me, and I will give thee the heathen for thine inheritance, and the utmost parts of the earth for thy possession.

"Thou shalt break them with a rod of iron, and dash them in pieces like a potter's vessel."

Be wise now therefore, O ye kings; be admonished, ye who are judges of the earth.

Serve the Lord in fear; and rejoice before him with reverence.

Submit to the Son, lest he be angry, and so ye perish from the right way, if his wrath be kindled, yea, but a little. Blessed are all they who put their trust in him.

Psalm LVII.

BE merciful unto me, O God, be merciful unto me, for my soul trusteth in thee; and under the shadow of thy wings shall be my refuge, until this calamity be overpast.

I will call unto the most high God, even unto the God who will perform all things for me.

He shall send from heaven, and save me from the reproach of him who would swallow me up.

Be thou exalted, O God, above the heavens, and let thy glory be above all the earth.

My heart is fixed, O God, my heart is fixed; I will sing and give praise.

Awake up, my glory; awake, lute and harp; I myself will awake right early.

I will give thanks unto thee, O Lord, among the people, and I will sing unto thee among the nations.

For the greatness of thy mercy reacheth unto the heavens, and thy truth unto the clouds.

Be thou exalted, O God, above the heavens, and let thy glory be above all the earth.

Now unto the King eternal, etc.

Be honor and glory, etc.

EVENING PRAYER.

Psalm CXIII.

PRAISE the Lord, ye servants of his ; O praise the name of the Lord.

Blessed be the name of the Lord, from this time forth forevermore.

Let the Lord's name be praised, from the rising up of the sun unto the going down of the same.

The Lord is high above all nations, and his glory above the heavens.

Who is like unto the Lord our God, who hath his dwelling so high, and yet humbleth himself to behold the things that are in heaven and earth ?

He taketh up the simple out of the dust, and lifteth the poor out of the mire ;

That he may set him with the princes, even with the princes of his people.

Psalm CXVIII.

O GIVE thanks unto the Lord, for he is gracious, and his mercy endureth forever.

Let Israel now confess that his mercy endureth forever.

Let the house of Aaron now confess that his mercy endureth forever.

Yea, let those now who fear the Lord confess that his mercy endureth forever.

I called upon the Lord in trouble, and the Lord heard and delivered me.

The Lord is on my side; I will not fear; what can man do unto me?

It is better to trust in the Lord, than to put confidence in man.

It is better to trust in the Lord, than to put confidence in princes.

The Lord is my strength and my song, and is become my salvation.

The voice of joy and salvation is in the dwellings of the righteous; the right hand of the Lord bringeth mighty things to pass.

The right hand of the Lord is exalted; the right hand of the Lord bringeth mighty things to pass.

I shall not die, but live, and declare the works of the Lord.

The Lord hath chastened and corrected me; but he hath not given me over unto death.

Open me the gates of holiness, that I may go in by them, and give thanks unto the Lord.

" This is the gate of the Lord, through which the righteous shall enter."

I will thank thee, for thou hast heard me, and art become my salvation.

The same stone which the builders refused is become the head-stone in the corner.

This is the Lord's doing ; and it is marvellous in our eyes.

This is the day which the Lord hath made ; we will rejoice and be glad in it.

Save now, O Lord ; O Lord, send us now prosperity.

" Blessed is he who cometh in the name of the Lord ; we bless you, ye who are of the house of the Lord."

Thou art my God, and I will thank thee ; thou art my God, and I will praise thee.

O give thanks unto the Lord, for he is gracious, and his mercy endureth forever.

Now unto the King eternal, etc.

Be honor and glory, etc.

FOR WHITSUNDAY.

O GIVE thanks unto the Lord, and call upon his name ; tell the people what things he hath done.

O let your songs be of him, and praise him ; and let your talking be of all his wondrous works.

Seek the Lord and his strength, seek his face forevermore.

The Lord gave the word, and great was the company of those who published it.

His salvation is nigh unto those who fear him, that glory may dwell in the land.

Mercy and truth are met together, righteousness and peace have kissed each other.

Truth shall flourish on the earth, and righteousness shall look down from heaven.

The Lord will give strength unto his people; the Lord will give unto his people the blessing of peace.

Blessed are the people whose strength is from thee, and in whose heart are thy ways.

Teach us to do thy will, for thou art our God; O let thy good spirit lead us into the paths of righteousness.

Gloria in Excelsis.

GLORY be to God on high, and on earth peace, good will towards men. We praise thee, we bless thee, we worship thee, we glorify thee, we give thanks to thee, for thy great glory; O Lord God, heavenly King, God the Father Almighty.

O Lord, through thy only-begotten Son Jesus Christ, Lamb of God, Son of the Father, who taketh away the sins of the world, have mercy upon us! Through him that taketh away the sins of the world, have mercy upon us. Through him that taketh away the sins of the world, receive our prayer. Through him that sitteth at thy right hand, O God, our Father, have mercy upon us. For thou only art holy, thou only art the Lord. And to thee, O God, through Christ, by the Holy Ghost, be honor and glory for ever. *Amen.*

𝔓roper 𝔓salms.

MORNING PRAYER.

Psalm LXVIII.

L ET God arise, and let his enemies be scattered; let those also who hate him flee before him.

Like as the smoke vanisheth, so shalt thou drive them away; and like as wax melteth at the fire, so shall the ungodly perish at the presence of God.

But let the righteous be glad, and rejoice before God; yea, let them exceedingly rejoice.

O sing unto God, and sing praises unto his name; magnify him who rideth upon the heavens; praise him in his name JEHOVAH, and rejoice before him.

He is a Father of the fatherless, and defendeth the cause of the widows; even God in his holy habitation.

God restoreth the solitary to their families, and bringeth the prisoners out of captivity; but letteth the rebellious continue in a dry land.

O God, when thou wentest forth before the people, when thou didst march through the wilderness;

The earth shook, and the heavens dropped at the presence of God; even Sinai itself was moved at the presence of God, the God of Israel.

Thou, O God, sentest a gracious rain upon thine inheritance, and refreshedst it when it was weary.

Thy people dwelt in the midst of thy food; for thou, O God, didst of thy goodness provide for their need.

The Lord gave the song of victory ; great was the company of those who published it.

Kings with their armies did flee and were discomfited, and she who staid at home divided the spoil.

The chariots of God's host are numberless, even thousands of thousands, and the Lord is among them, as in the holy place of Sinai.

Thou art gone up on high, thou hast led captivity captive, and received gifts from men ; yea, even from thine enemies ; and here wilt thou dwell, O Lord God.

Praised be the Lord daily ; even the God who helpeth us, and poureth his benefits upon us.

He is our God, even the God of whom cometh salvation ; God is the Lord, by whom we escape death.

The Lord hath said, I will bring my people again as I did from Bashan ; mine own will I bring again as I did once from the deep of the sea.

Sing unto God, O ye kingdoms of the earth ; O sing praises unto the Lord ;

Who sitteth in the heavens over all, from the beginning ; lo, he doth utter his voice, yea, and that a mighty voice.

Ascribe ye the power to God ; his excellency is over Israel ; his strength is in the clouds.

O God, wonderful art thou in thy holy places ; the God of Israel will give strength and power unto his people ; blessed be God.

PSALM LXXVIII.

HEAR my law, O my people ; incline your ears unto the words of my mouth.

I will open my mouth in a parable ; I will utter sayings of old time ;

Which we have heard and known, and such as our fathers have told us ;

That we should not hide them from the children of the generations to come, but show the honor of the Lord, his mighty and wonderful works that he hath done.

He made a covenant with Jacob, and gave Israel a law, which he commanded our forefathers to teach their children ;

That their posterity might know it, and the children who were yet unborn ;

To the intent that when they came up, they might show their children the same ;

That they might put their trust in God, and not forget the works of God, but keep his commandments.

Now unto the King eternal, etc.

Be honor and glory, etc.

EVENING PRAYER.

PSALM XLIV

WE have heard with our ears, O God, our fathers have told us, what thou hast done in their time of old.

How thou didst drive out the heathen with thy

hand, and planted them in ; how thou didst destroy the nations, and cast them out.

For they gat not the land in possession through their own sword, neither was it their own arm that helped them ;

But thy right hand, and thine arm, and the light of thy countenance, because thou hadst favor unto them.

Thou art my King, O God ; send help unto Jacob.

For I will not trust in my bow ; it is not my sword that shall help me.

But it is thou who savest us from our enemies, and puttest them to confusion who hate us.

We make our boast of God all day long, and will praise thy name forever.

Psalm CV.

O GIVE thanks unto the Lord, and call upon his name ; tell the people what things he hath done.

O let your songs be of him, and praise him ; and let your talking be of all his wondrous works.

Rejoice in his holy name ; let the heart of those rejoice who seek the Lord.

Seek the Lord and his strength ; seek his face evermore.

Remember the marvellous works that he hath done ; his wonders, and the judgments of his mouth ;

O ye seed of Abraham his servant, ye children of Jacob his chosen.

He is the Lord our God ; his judgments are in all the world.

He hath been alway mindful of his covenant and promise that he made to a thousand generations ;

Even the covenant that he made with Abraham, and the oath that he sware unto Isaac ;

And appointed the same unto Jacob for a law, and to Israel for an everlasting testament ;

Saying, " Unto thee will I give the land of Canaan, the lot of your inheritance."

When there were yet but a few of them, and they strangers in the land ;

What time as they went from one nation to another, from one kingdom to another people ;

He suffered no man to do them wrong, but reproved even kings for their sakes.

" Touch not mine anointed, and do my prophets no harm."

And he brought forth his people with joy, and his chosen with gladness ;

And gave them the lands of the heathen ; and they took the labors of the people in possession ;

That they might keep his statutes, and observe his laws.

Now unto the King eternal, etc.

Be honor and glory, etc.

A SERVICE

FOR DAYS OF THANKSGIVING.

The Minister may use the common Service for Morning or Evening Prayer, till he comes to the Psalms for the Day of the Month; instead of which, the following Psalms are to be said.

PSALM XLVII.

O CLAP your hands together all ye people; O sing unto God with the voice of melody.

For the Lord is high, and to be feared; he is the great King over all the earth.

He shall subdue the people under us, and the nations under our feet.

He shall choose out an heritage for us, even the excellency of Jacob whom he loved.

God is gone up with a shout, and the Lord with the sound of the trumpet.

O sing praises, sing praises unto our God; O sing praises, sing praises unto our King.

For God is the King of all the earth; sing ye praises with understanding.

God reigneth over the nations ; God sitteth upon his holy throne.

The princes of the heathen are joined unto the people of the God of Abraham ; for God, who is high exalted, doth defend the earth as it were with a shield.

PSALM CXLVII.

PRAISE ye the Lord : for it is a good thing to sing praises unto our God ; yea, a joyful and pleasant thing it is to be thankful.

The Lord doth build up Jerusalem and gather together the outcasts of Israel.

He healeth those who are broken in heart, and bindeth up their wounds.

He telleth the number of the stars ; and calleth them all by their names.

Great is our Lord, and great is his power ; yea, and his wisdom is infinite.

The Lord lifteth up the meek ; and bringeth the ungodly down to the ground.

O sing unto the Lord with thanksgiving ; sing praises upon the harp unto our God ;

Who covereth the heaven with clouds, and prepareth rain for the earth, and maketh the grass to grow upon the mountains ;

Who giveth to the beast his food, and feedeth the young ravens that cry.

He hath no pleasure in the strength of the horse ; neither delighteth he in the force of man.

But the Lord's delight is in those who fear him and put their trust in his mercy.

Praise the Lord, O Jerusalem ; praise thy God, O Sion.

For he hath strengthened the bars of thy gates ; and hath blessed thy children within thee.

He maketh peace in thy borders ; and filleth thee with the finest of the wheat.

He sendeth forth his commandment upon earth ; and his word is instantly obeyed.

He giveth snow like wool ; he scattereth the hoar-frost like ashes.

He casteth forth his ice like morsels ; who can stand before his cold ?

He sendeth out his word and melteth them ; he bloweth with his wind, and the waters flow.

He showeth his word unto Jacob, his statutes and ordinances unto Israel.

He hath not dealt so with any other nation ; neither have the heathen knowledge of his laws. Praise ye the Lord.

PSALM CL.

PRAISE ye the Lord. Praise God in his sanctuary. Praise him in the firmament of his power.

Praise him for his noble acts ; praise him according to his excellent greatness.

Praise him with the sound of the trumpet ; praise him upon the lute and harp.

Praise him upon the well-tuned cymbals ; praise him upon the loud cymbals.

Let everything that hath breath praise the Lord.

Now unto the King eternal, immortal, invisible, the only wise God ;

Be honor and glory, through Jesus Christ for ever and ever. *Amen.*

Then may follow an Anthem or a Voluntary on the Organ; and then the Minister shall read the FIRST LESSON, *which may be either of the following por- tions from the Old Testament :* Deut. viii. or xxvi. or xxviii. to v. 15. Isaiah xii. or xxv. to v. 10. *And at the end of the Lesson shall say* Here endeth the First Lesson. *Then shall be sung or said the follow- ing Anthem.*

PSALM C.

O BE joyful in the Lord all ye lands ; serve the Lord with gladness, and come before his pres- ence with a song.

Be ye sure that the Lord he is God ; it is he who hath made us, and not we ourselves ; we are his people and the sheep of his pasture.

O go your way into his gates with thanksgiving, and into his courts with praise ; be thankful unto him, and speak good of his name.

For the Lord is gracious, his mercy is everlasting, and his truth endureth from generation to generation.

Then shall the Minister read the SECOND LESSON, *which may be either of the following portions from th N Testament :* St. Luke xii. 13 to 32. Philipp. iv. 4 to 14. *And at the end of the Lesson he shall say,* Here endeth the Second Lesson. *Then shall be sung or said the following Psalm.*

PSALM CXXXVI.

O GIVE thanks unto the Lord ; for he is gracious, and his mercy endureth forever.

O give thanks unto the God of all gods; for his mercy endureth forever.

O thank the Lord of all lords; for his mercy endureth forever.

Who by his excellent wisdom made the heavens; for his mercy endureth forever.

Who laid out the earth above the waters; for his mercy endureth forever.

Who hath made great lights; for his mercy endureth forever.

The sun to rule by day; for his mercy endureth forever.

The moon and the stars to govern the night; for his mercy endureth forever.

Who remembereth us when we are in trouble; for his mercy endureth forever.

And hath delivered us from our enemies; for his mercy endureth forever.

Who giveth food to all flesh; for his mercy endureth forever.

O give thanks unto the God of heaven; for his mercy endureth forever.

Min. The Lord be with you.

Answ. And with thy spirit.

Min. Glory be to God in the highest;

Answ. And on earth peace, good will toward men.

Min. Let us pray.

O Lord, show thy mercy upon us;

Answ. And grant us thy salvation.

Min. O God, make clean our hearts within us;

Answ. And take not thy Holy Spirit from us.

A THANKSGIVING.

O THOU who art good unto all, who exercisest loving-kindness in all the earth, and who hast come nigh to us by Jesus Christ thy Son ; it is thou who givest our daily bread, health in our habitations, and peace in our borders, and who crownest the year with thy goodness. We desire this day gratefully to recount thy mercies, and to ascribe blessing and honor, and glory and praise, to thee our rock and fortress, our strength and redeemer.

How precious have been thy thoughts unto us, O God, how great has been the sum of them! We bless thee for preserving our houses from the ravages of fire, for all the health and pleasure which we have enjoyed in them, for the bread which has given strength to our bodies, for the medicine which has arrested the progress of disease, for the sympathy which has comforted us under trouble, for divine preservation in our journeys by land, for favorable winds on the ocean, for refreshing showers upon the fields. We thank thee for every cheerful sensation when alone, for the pleasures of friendly intercourse, for the benefits of good neighborhood, for the privileges of public worship, for the maintenance of civil order, the continuance of peace, the administration of justice, for every encouragement to well doing, every manifestation of useful truth, and for all the advantages of our condition.

Graciously direct us, O God, to a right improvement of all thy mercies. Preserve us from the wicked indulgence of all fleshly lusts, and from wasting our substance in riotous living. May we enjoy our temporal possessions with temperance, cheerfulness, and contentment. Protect us from the snares of prosperity. May we honor thee with our substance, be rich in good works, and duly esteem and praise thee the rock of our salvation.

Continue to us the enjoyment of our civil rights; rule in the hearts of our rulers, and direct them in all their designs and measures by thy wisdom and grace; make our land a quiet habitation; grant peace, order, and plenty in our families, our villages and towns, and throughout our country; bless all fountains of useful science; heal and cleanse their waters; dispel the mists of ignorance; arrest the progress of profaneness and vice; make the people of our land humble before thee, peaceable in their civil and social relations, and zealous for the establishment of liberty, order, and truth. May we never by our ingratitude incur that censure, I have nourished and brought up children, but they have rebelled against me. Grant this, O Father, for thine infinite mercy's sake in Jesus Christ our Lord. *Amen.*

CONCLUDING PRAYER.

ALMIGHTY God, who hast given us grace at this time with one accord to make our common supplications unto thee, and hast promised by thy beloved Son, that where two or three are gathered together in his name, thou wilt grant their requests ; fulfil now, O Lord, the desires and petitions of thy servants, as may be most expedient for them, granting us in this world knowledge of thy truth, and in the world to come life everlasting. *Amen.*

THE Lord bless us, and keep us ; may he be gracious unto us, and give us peace, now and forevermore. *Amen.*

Or this.

NOW unto him who is able to keep us from falling, and to present us faultless before the presence of his glory with exceeding joy, to the only wise God our Saviour, be glory and majesty, dominion and power, through Jesus Christ, for ever and ever. *Amen.*

END OF SERVICE FOR DAYS OF THANKSGIVING.

A SERVICE

FOR DAYS OF FASTING AND HUMILIATION.

The Minister may use the common Service for Morning Service, O come let us sing, &c., instead of which shall be said or sung the following Anthem, from the fifty-fifth Psalm.

PSALM LV.

Reliance upon God in the time of trouble.

HEAR my prayer, O God, and hide not thyself from my petition.

Take heed unto me, and hear me ; how I mourn in my prayer, and am troubled.

My heart is disquieted within me, and the terrors of death are fallen upon me.

Fearfulness and trembling are come upon me, and an horrible dread hath overwhelmed me.

And I say, O that I had wings like a dove ; for then would I flee away, and be at rest.

Lo, then would I get me away far off, and remain in the wilderness.

I would make haste to escape from the stormy wind and tempest.

But yet I will call upon God, and the Lord shall save me.

In the evening, and morning, and at noonday will I pray, and that instantly ; and he shall hear my voice.

O cast thy burden upon the Lord, and he will sustain thee, and will not suffer the righteous to fall utterly.

And then, instead of the Psalms for the Day of the Month, shall be said the following Psalms.

PSALM VI.

Penitential Psalm.

O LORD, rebuke me not in thine indignation ; neither chasten me in thy heavy displeasure.

Have mercy upon me, O Lord, for I am weak ; O Lord, heal me, for my bones tremble.

My soul also is sore troubled ; but thou, O Lord, how long ?

Turn thee, O Lord, and deliver my soul ; O save me for thy mercies' sake.

Depart from me, all ye who work vanity ; for the Lord hath heard the voice of my weeping.

The Lord hath heard my petition ; the Lord will receive my prayer.

PSALM XLII.

Longings of an exile for God's house.

A S the hart panteth after the water-brooks, so longeth my soul after thee, O God.

My soul is athirst for God, yea, even for the living God ; when shall I come and appear before God ?

My tears have been my food day and night; while they continually say unto me, "Where is now thy God?"

When I remember these things, I pour out my soul in grief; how I once walked with the multitude to the house of God, with the voice of joy and praise, with the multitude that kept holy day.

Why art thou so full of heaviness, O my soul; and why art thou so disquieted within me;

Put thy trust in God; for I will yet give him thanks for the help of his countenance.

Once the Lord granted his loving-kindness in the daytime; and in the night season did I sing unto him, and made my prayer unto the God of my life.

Now I say unto the God of my strength, Why hast thou forgotten me? Why go I thus heavily, while the enemy oppresseth me?

As with a sword in my bones, mine enemies reproach me; while they say daily unto me, " Where is now thy God?"

Why art thou so cast down, O my soul; and why art thou so disquieted within me?

O put thy trust in God; for I will yet thank him, who is the help of my countenance, and my God.

PSALM LXXX.

Prayer for deliverance in a time of calamity.

HEAR, O thou Shepherd of Israel, thou that leadest Joseph like a flock; shine forth, thou that sittest between the cherubim.

Turn us again, O God, show the light of thy countenance, and we shall be whole.

O Lord, God of hosts, how long wilt thou be angry against the prayer of thy people?

Thou feedest them with the bread of tears, and givest them plenteousness of tears to drink.

Turn us again, thou God of hosts, show the light of thy countenance, and we shall be whole.

Thou didst bring a vine out of Egypt; thou didst cast out the heathen, and plantedst it.

Thou madest room for it; and when it had taken root, it filled the land.

The hills were covered with the shadow of it, and the boughs thereof were like the goodly cedar-trees.

She stretched out her branches unto the sea, and her boughs unto the river.

Why hast thou then broken down her hedges, that all those who go by pluck off her grapes?

The wild boar out of the wood doth root it up, and the wild beasts of the field devour it.

Turn thee again, thou God of hosts, look down from heaven; behold, and visit this vine;

And the vineyard that thy right hand planted, and the branch that thou madest so strong for thyself.

It is burnt with fire and cut down; they perish at the rebuke of thy countenance.

Let thy hand uphold the man of thy right hand, and the son of man, whom thou madest so strong for thyself.

So will not we go back from thee ; O let us live, and we will call upon thy name.

Turn us again, O Lord, God of hosts, show the light of thy countenance, and we shall be whole.

Now unto the King eternal, immortal, invisible, the only wise God ;

Be honor and glory, through Jesus Christ for ever and ever. *Amen.*

Here may follow an Anthem or a Voluntary on the Organ ; and then the Minister shall read the FIRST LESSON, *which may be one of the following :* Isaiah lviii. Hosea xiv. Joel ii.

And at the end of the Lesson he shall say, Here endeth the First Lesson.

Then shall be said or sung, the following instead of

PSALM CIII.

THE Lord is full of compassion and mercy, long suffering, and of great goodness.

He will not always chide ; neither keepeth he his anger forever.

He hath not dealt with us after our sins ; nor rewarded us according to our wickedness.

For as the heaven is high above the earth, so great is his mercy toward those who fear him.

As far as the east is from the west, so far hath he removed our transgressions from us.

Yea, like as a father pitieth his children ; even so the Lord pitieth those who fear him.

· For he knoweth our frame ; he remembereth that we are but dust.

The days of man are but as grass ; he flourisheth as a flower of the field.

For the wind passeth over it, and it is gone ; and the place thereof shall know it no more.

But the merciful goodness of the Lord endureth for ever and ever upon those who fear him, and his righteousness upon children's children ;

Even upon such as keep his covenants, and think upon his commandments to do them.

Then shall the ministers read the Second Lesson, *which may be either of the following portions from the New Testament*. St. Matt. vi. 1 to 19. St. Mark ii. 15 to 21.

And at the end of the Lesson he shall say, Here endeth the Second Lesson.

Then shall be said or sung the following Psalm.

PSALM LXVII.

GOD be merciful unto us, and bless us ; and show us the light of his countenance, and be merciful unto us.

That thy way may be known upon earth, thy saving health among all nations.

Let the people praise thee, O God; yea, let all the people praise thee.

O let the nations rejoice and be glad; for thou shalt judge the folk righteously, and govern the nations upon earth.

Let the people praise thee, O God ; yea, let all the people praise thee.

Then shall the earth bring forth her increase ;

and God, even our own God, shall give us his blessing.

God shall bless us, and all the ends of the world shall fear him.

Min. The Lord be with you.
Answ. And with thy spirit.
Min. Let us pray.
O Lord, show thy mercy upon us ;
Answ. And grant us thy salvation.
Min. O God, make clean our hearts within us ;
Answ. And take not thy Holy Spirit from us.

Min. O God, merciful Father, who despisest not the sighing of a contrite heart, nor the desire of such as be sorrowful ; mercifully assist our prayers which we make before thee, in all our troubles and adversities, whensoever they oppress us ; and graciously hear us, that all evils which are devised against us may, by the providence of thy goodness, be brought to naught ; that we, thy servants, being hurt by no persecutions, may evermore give thanks unto thee in thy holy Church, through Jesus Christ our Lord.

O Lord, arise, help us, and deliver us for thy name's sake.

O God, we have heard with our ears, and our fathers have declared unto us, the noble works that thou didst in their days, and in the old time before them.

O Lord, arise, help us, and deliver us for thine honor.

From our enemies defend us, O God.

Graciously look upon our afflictions.

Pitifully behold the sorrows of our hearts.

Mercifully forgive the sins of thy people.

Favorably with mercy hear our prayers.

O gracious Father, have mercy upon us.

Both now and ever vouchsafe to hear us, O Lord.

Graciously hear us, O Lord; graciously hear us, O Lord God.

O Lord, let thy mercy be shown upon us ;

As we do put our trust in thee.

PRAYER FOR FAST DAY.

A LMIGHTY and most merciful God, who lovest righteousness and hatest iniquity, and art a compassionate Father to those who repent and turn unto thee ; we would come before thee this day, humbly confessing our sins, and beseeching thee to impress upon our minds every motive to sincere repentance and a holy life.

O thou Supreme Director of the affairs of human society ; we thank thee for the advantages of our condition ; that we enjoy liberty, safety, and plenty ; that the lines are fallen to us in pleasant places, and that we have a goodly heritage. Yet we have made unworthy returns for thy loving-kindness ; we have shown ourselves undeserving of thy mercy. We lament that plenty has been abused by luxury, and liberty by licentiousness ; our peace and safety by strife, envyings, and divisions ; that so little of the power of godliness is manifested ; that so many restrain prayer before thee, and, notwithstanding

the expressions of thy will, do yet despise or neglect thy laws. Surely it is of thy mercy that we
are not consumed, and because thy compassions
fail not.

We beseech thee to grant thy mercy unto us who
have corrupted our manners, who have been indif-
ferent to thy worship; indulged too much a spirit
of pride and uncharitableness, and have become
too strongly attached to the world and the things
of the world. Awaken us to a sense of our unworthiness; pardon the sins of our nation; forgive
all those who humble themselves this day before
thee, and spare thy people; animate us to unite
with one heart in promoting the honor of thy name,
the interests of religion, and the prosperity and happiness of our country. May we keep the fast which
thou hast chosen; and, loosing every band of wickedness, become a peculiar people zealous of good
works, that thy displeasure may be turned away
from us, and that thou mayest delight to build us
up and not destroy us.

O thou, who art the Lord of lords, and the Fountain of all power, we commend to thy care and
blessing the President of the United States, the
Governor of this State, and all others in authority.
May they have wisdom to discern, and firmness to
pursue the true interests of this people; may they
employ all their influence to promote peace and
virtue; and under their government may justice
and judgment run down as waters, and righteousness as a mighty stream. Endue with grace and
clothe with godliness the ministers of religion. May

they do honor to thy truth in their public services and their private conduct; and wilt thou so direct and bless them, both in their preaching and living, that they may save themselves, and those who hear them. We beseech thee to bless all seminaries of learning, all governors and instructors of youth, all patrons and promoters of sound literature and knowledge; and grant that all the means and opportunities of mental, moral, and religious advancement which are enjoyed among us, may be thankfully acknowledged and diligently improved.

Universal Parent and Governor; be merciful to the whole race of man; enlighten all who sit in darkness; send forth a spirit of peace and good will; restrain the violence of unreasonable men; may no weapon formed against the rights of mankind prosper; multiply the patterns of Christian virtue and the instruments of beneficence; direct all flesh to the knowledge of thy Son; and may thy kingdom come and thy will be done on earth as it is in heaven; which we ask as disciples of Jesus Christ. *Amen.*

CONCLUDING PRAYER.

ETERNAL and all-seeing God, we thy creatures sink into nothing before thy supreme majesty; we feel our weakness; we acknowledge our folly; we repeatedly bewail our sins; thee only would we adore with awful veneration; thee would we thank with fervent zeal; to thy power we humbly submit; of thy goodness we devoutly implore protection; on thy wisdom we firmly and cheerfully rely. Whenever we address thee, O Father, if our prayers are unwise, wilt thou pity us ; if they are presumptuous, wilt thou pardon us ; if acceptable to thee, grant them, all powerful God ; and as we now express our submission to thy decrees, adore thy providence, and bless thy dispensations, so, in that future state, to which we reverently hope thy goodness will raise us, may we continue praising, venerating, worshipping thee, more and more, through worlds without number, and ages without end. *Amen.*

THE Lord bless us and keep us ; the Lord make his face shine upon us, and be gracious unto us ; the Lord lift up his countenance upon us, and give us peace, now and evermore. *Amen.*

END OF SERVICE FOR FAST DAYS.

FORMS OF PRAYER

TO BE USED AT SEA.

*Its Service may commence with the following Psalm ;
after which the Person officiating may use such parts
of the common Morning or Evening Prayer as he
shall judge proper.*

PSALM XCIII.

THE Lord is King, and hath put on glorious
apparel ; the Lord hath clothed himself with
majesty, and girded himself with strength.

Therefore the earth standeth firm and cannot be
moved.

Ever since the world began, hath thy throne been
established ; thou art from everlasting.

The floods have lifted up, O Lord, the floods
have lifted up their voice ; the floods lift up their
waves.

The Lord on high is mightier than the noise
of many waters, yea, than the mighty waves of
the sea.

Thy testimonies, O Lord, are very sure ; holiness
becometh thine house forever.

Prayer

O ETERNAL Lord God, who alone spreadest out the heavens, and rulest the raging of the sea; who hast compassed the waters with bounds, until day and night come to an end; be pleased to receive into thine almighty and most gracious protection the persons of us thy servants, who now call upon thy name from the bosom of the mighty deep. Borne on the surface of a changing element, and exposed to the vicissitudes of the inconstant skies, may we always feel ourselves in the presence and merciful care of that infinite and holy God, who hath measured the waters in the hollow of his hand, and meted out heaven with a span. Preserve us, we pray thee, from the dangers of the sea; from shipwreck; from fire; from the wrath of the tempest; from the violence of enemies; and grant that we may arrive at our desired haven in safety, health, and peace, and with a thankful remembrance of thy rich and manifold mercies. But we do more especially pray, O Lord our God, that if thou shouldst see fit to bring us into peril and misfortune, we may bear thy whole will with perfect submission, and surrender ourselves in every event to thine absolute and all-wise disposal. Whether we are in danger or at rest, in sickness or health, in life or death, let us be thine, O Lord, and wholly thine.

Hear us in behalf of our country, and grant that it may constantly prosper under thy care, and be defended with thy favorable kindness as with a shield.   Bless our absent friends, wherever they may be ; preserve them from evil ; and, in thy great mercy, permit us to see them again, and rejoice in their society and welfare.

We thank thee, that thou hast thus far preserved us ; we thank thee for this opportunity of calling upon thy name ; we commend ourselves and our interests to thy holy keeping ; and ascribe unto thee all honor and glory, dominion and praise, through Jesus Christ our Lord.   *Amen.*

Or this

O LORD, our God, who madest heaven, and earth, and sea, and all that therein is, and who keepest thy promise forever ; mercifully hear the prayers of thy servants ; deliver us from the dangers of the seas ; protect and prosper us in the way we go, and bring us to our haven and to our friends in peace ; but above all things grant that we may always submit to thy will and pleasure, and obey thy most holy law, and so pass the waves of this changing and troublesome world, that we may finally come to the land of everlasting life ; through Jesus Christ our Lord.   *Amen.*

Then may be used either Prayers of the Morning or Evening Service, or else the Benediction may be made with the following.

PRAYER IN STORMS AT SEA.

O MOST glorious and gracious Lord God, who dwellest in heaven, but beholdest all things below; look down, we beseech thee, and hear us, calling out of the depth of misery; and out of the jaws of this death, which is now ready to swallow us up. Save, Lord, or else we perish. The living, the living shall praise thee. O send thy word of command to rebuke the raging winds and the roaring sea; that we, being delivered from this distress, may live to serve thee, and to glorify thy name all the days of our life. Hear, Lord, and save us, in the name of our blessed Saviour, thy Son, our Lord Jesus Christ. *Amen.*

THOU, O Lord, who stillest the raging of the sea, hear, hear us, and save us that we perish not.

O God, whose Son Jesus Christ did save his disciples ready to perish in a storm; hear us, and save us, we beseech thee.

Lord be merciful to us sinners, and save us for thy mercies' sake.

THANKSGIVING AFTER A STORM.

Psalm cvii.

O THAT men would praise the Lord for his goodness; and declare the wonders that he doeth for the children of men!

That they would offer unto him the sacrifice of thanksgiving; and tell out his works with gladness!

They that go down to the sea in ships; and occupy their business in great waters;

These men see the works of the Lord, and his wonders in the deep.

For at his word the stormy wind ariseth ; which lifteth up the waves thereof.

They are carried up to the heaven, and down again to the deep ; their soul melteth away because of the trouble.

Then they cry unto the Lord in their trouble, and he delivereth them out of their distress.

For he maketh the storm to cease, so that the waves are still.

Then are they glad, because they are at rest ; and so he bringeth them unto the haven where they would be.

O that men would therefore praise the Lord for his goodness ; and declare the wonders that he doeth for the children of men !

That they would exalt him also in the congregation of the people ; and praise him in the assembly of the elders !

COLLECT OF THANKSGIVING.

O MOST mighty and graciously good God, thy mercy is over all thy works, but in special manner hath been extended towards us, whom thou hast so powerfully and wonderfully defended. Thou hast showed us terrible things, and wonders in the deep, that we might see how powerful and gracious a God thou art ; how able and ready to help those who trust in thee. Thou hast showed us how both winds and seas obey thy command ; that we may learn even from them hereafter to obey thy voice, and to do thy will. We therefore bless and glorify thy name, for this thy mercy, in saving us when we were ready to perish. And we beseech thee, make us as truly sensible now of thy mercy, as we were then of our danger; and give us hearts always ready to express our thankfulness, not only by words, but also by our lives, in being more obedient to thy holy commandments. Continue, we beseech thee, this thy goodness to us ; that we, whom thou hast saved, may serve thee, in holiness and righteousness, all the days of our life, through Jesus Christ our Lord and Saviour. *Amen.*

END OF PRAYERS TO BE USED AT SEA.

TWO ADDITIONAL SERVICES

FOR MORNING OR EVENING.

FIRST SERVICE.

This Service is to be introduced by the following Address from the Minister to the People.

O BE joyful in the Lord, all ye people; serve the Lord with gladness, and come before his presence with a song.

Be ye sure that the Lord he is God; it is he who hath made us, and we are his; we are his people and the sheep of his pasture.

Enter into his gates with thanksgiving, and into his courts with praise; be thankful unto him, and speak good of his name.

For the Lord is gracious, his mercy is everlasting, and his truth endureth from generation to generation.

People.

Unto the Lord our God will we lift up our souls, and magnify his name together.

THE INTRODUCTORY PRAYER.

O LORD God Almighty, before whom all creatures bow, the fountain of life and the father of all mercies, we thine unworthy servants come before thee in humble acknowledgment of thine eternal power and majesty. Thou art the living and true God; thy kingdom ruleth over all, and thy goodness is without bounds. Assist us to worship thee in spirit and in truth; may we celebrate thy perfections, and speak of thy wonderful works, with reverence; give thanks unto thee, and sing thy praises with joy; humble ourselves before thee with sincere and contrite hearts; and pray unto thee in the faith that thou hearest and answerest prayer. Graciously accept these our devotions, which we offer in the name and as disciples of Jesus Christ our Lord.

People.

May the words of our mouths, and the meditations of our hearts, be acceptable in thy sight, O Lord, our strength and our redeemer.

Then shall be recited the following Anthem, or instead of it the Psalter appointed for the day.

Minister.

WE praise thee, O God; we worship thee, the most glorious and the best of beings; the creator and governor of all things, visible and invisible.

Peo. O Lord God, thou art greatly to be praised; and to be had in reverence by all who draw nigh unto thee.

Min. We acknowledge thee, the one, living, and

true God, God in heaven above, and in earth beneath, and throughout all worlds ; there is none beside thee.

Peo. Unto us there is but one God ; to whom be glory forever.

Min. Thou alone art from everlasting, without beginning of days, or end of years ; thou livest and reignest for ever and ever.

Peo. We magnify thee, the high and lofty One, who inhabitest eternity.

Min. Thou art a spiritual and incorruptible being ; who dwellest in light inaccessible and full of glory ; whom no mortal eye hath seen, or can see.

Peo. We would worship thee, who art a spirit, in spirit and in truth.

Min. Thou art perfect in wisdom, wonderful in counsel, and excellent in all thy works.

Peo. To the only wise God be honor and glory forever.

Min. Holy art thou, O God ; thou art of purer eyes than to behold iniquity ; thy countenance regardeth the upright.

Peo. We reverence thy name ; for thou art holy.

Min. Thy righteousness is like the great mountains ; thy truth reacheth to the heavens ; justice and judgment are the everlasting foundations of thy throne.

Peo. Just and true are all thy ways, O thou King of saints.

Min. Thou art good, and thou doest good continually ; all thy works bear testimony to thy rich

and overflowing bounty; every good and every per-
feet gift is from above, and cometh down from thee,
the Father of all.

Peo. O Lord, thy goodness is above all praise;
universal as thy works, and endless as eternity.

Min. All glory and honor, blessing and praise
be unto God forever. *Amen.*

*Then may follow a Voluntary on the Organ; after
which the* FIRST LESSON *is to be read out of the
Old Testament; then may follow an Anthem; after
which the Service is to proceed with the following
Thanksgiving.*

Minister.

Let us now offer up unto God our sincere and
humble thanksgivings, for his great goodness to us,
and to all mankind.

People.

Bless the Lord, O our souls, and forget not all
his benefits.

Minister.

We thank thee, O Father, Lord of heaven and
earth, for the innumerable mercies which thou hast
bestowed upon us. We thank thee for the wise
and useful frame of our bodies; and for the nobler
powers of our minds; by which we are enabled to
contemplate the beauty of thy works, and the wonderful order of thy providence; and to attain the
knowledge and love of thee, the creator of the
world, and the author of all good.

We thank thee, O ever bountiful and most gra-
cions God, for the continual preservation of our

lives ; our food and raiment are the daily gifts of thy bounty ; thou givest us health and fruitful seasons, and fillest our hearts with joy and gladness.

People.

Blessed be the Lord for his goodness and for his wonderful works to the children of men.

Minister.

Above all, we praise and magnify thee for thy goodness in the manifestation of thy Son Jesus Christ, whom thou hast raised up to bless mankind, to turn them from darkness to light, and from the power of sin, to the worship and obedience of thee, the true God.

We thank thee for the promises of thy mercy and forgiveness, upon repentance and newness of life ; for the aid of thy gracious influence to help our infirmities ; and for the blessed hope of eternal life, confirmed to us in the Gospel.

People.

Blessed be the God and Father of our Lord Jesus Christ, for his goodness, and for his wonderful works to the children of men.

Here the Second Lesson may be read ... with Ner.

Minister.

IF we say that we have no sin, we deceive ourselves, and the truth is not in us.

If we confess and forsake our sins, God is faithful and just to forgive us our sins, and to cleanse us from all unrighteousness.

Let us therefore, with humble and contrite hearts, confess our sins at the throne of the heavenly grace.

The GENERAL CONFESSION ; *to be read by the Minister alone.*

ALMIGHTY God, Father of our Lord Jesus Christ, maker of all things, and judge of all men ; we acknowledge and lament before thee the manifold errors and follies of our lives. Our only hope is in thy mercy, which endureth forever. We bow ourselves before the throne of thy grace, imploring thy pardon. O God, have mercy upon the works of thy hands ; forgive and accept thy people, according to thy promises in Jesus Christ our Lord. Enable us, O God, by the assistance of thy Holy Spirit, to forsake every evil way, to correct whatever is wrong in our tempers and conduct, and to delight in the practice of everything good and virtuous ; that we may obtain from thee, the God of all mercy, the forgiveness of our sins, and an inheritance among those who are sanctified, through the redemption which is in Jesus Christ.

People.

Create in us, O God, a clean heart, and renew a right spirit within us.

Then shall be read the COLLECT FOR THE DAY, *a d one or more of the following Prayers.*

FOR RESIGNATION.

O LORD God, whose never failing providence ordereth all things both in heaven and in earth, we submit ourselves to the disposal of that wisdom which cannot err, and to the care of that goodness which is unchangeable and everlasting. Lead us whither thou pleasest ; place us in what circumstances thou shalt judge proper ; we would do thy whole will with fidelity and pleasure ; we would bear thy whole will with submission and patience. Defend us, O gracious Father, from every real evil ; confer upon us every needful good ; may all events conspire to the improvement and establishment of our virtue ; and may we be conducted by thine unerring hand through all the changes of this mortal life, and finally be admitted to the everlasting habitations of the just, which thou hast promised to thy faithful servants by Jesus Christ our Lord. *Amen.*

FOR ALL MANKIND.

A LMIGHTY and everlasting God, who hast taught us to offer prayers, supplications, and intercessions for all men, we beseech thee to extend thy mercy to all mankind ; may all the families and kingdoms of the earth be brought to the knowledge and pure worship of thee, the only true God ; enlarge the kingdom of thy Son, that kingdom of truth and righteousness, which shall never be destroyed ; may the spirit of persecution forever cease ; and may truth and righteousness, peace and charity, everywhere abound, through Jesus Christ our Lord. *Amen.*

FOR OUR COUNTRY.

O LORD God, high and mighty, who dost from thy throne behold all the dwellers upon the earth ; look down with favor and mercy upon these United States. May public virtue prevail, and on that lasting foundation may the public happiness be established ; may our liberties be preserved inviolate, and handed down to the latest posterity. Bless us with health and fruitful seasons ; crown the year with thy goodness ; dispose us all to a grateful and temperate enjoyment of the bounties of thy providence, and a faithful obedience of thy laws, through Jesus Christ our Lord. *Amen.*

FOR RULERS.

A LMIGHTY God, the King of kings, and fountain of all power, we humbly beseech thee to behold with thy favor the President of the United States, and all others in authority. May they discharge the duties of their stations with understanding and wisdom, with integrity and honor ; and under their government may we and all thy people lead quiet and peaceable lives in all godliness and honesty ; keeping the unity of the spirit in the bond of peace, and in righteousness of life. *Amen.*

FOR THE MINISTERS OF RELIGION.

O GOD, the Father of lights, and fountain of all good, endue the ministers of thy true religion, of every denomination, and in every part of the world, with the spirit and temper of Jesus Christ; and in all the duties of their office may they conduct themselves as examples to their flocks; and by the excellence of their doctrines, and the holiness of their lives, may they save themselves and those who hear them, through the only Mediator, Jesus Christ our Lord. *Amen.*

FOR THOSE IN AFFLICTION.

MOST merciful and gracious God, the God of all consolation and hope; we humbly recommend to thy fatherly goodness all those who are any ways afflicted or distressed, in mind, body, or estate; be thou, in thy great mercy, a father to the fatherless, and the defender of the widow; provide for the poor, give health to the sick, and ease to those who are in oppression; give to all fortitude in the day of trial, and in due time a happy deliverance out of their afflictions. And from the various calamities we meet with in life, may we learn to pity the distressed, to sympathize with the afflicted, to be patient under all the appointments of thy providence, and be excited to the pursuit of that happiness which ariseth from the practice of virtue and piety, and from the glorious hope of immortality, which thou hast promised to the faithful followers of Jesus Christ our Lord. *Amen.*

CONCLUDING PRAYER.

O LORD, our Heavenly Father, almighty and everlasting God, who hast permitted us to make our united supplications unto thee ; accept the praises and hear the prayers which we have offered to thy divine Majesty ; and fulfil, O Lord, the desires and petitions of thy servants, as may be most expedient for them ; granting us in this world knowledge of thy truth, and in the world to come life everlasting, through our Lord and Saviour Jesus Christ, in whose words we conclude our prayers ;

OUR Father, who art in Heaven, Hallowed be thy name. Thy kingdom come ; Thy will be done on earth as it is in Heaven. Give us this day our daily bread. And forgive us our trespasses, As we forgive those who trespass against us. And lead us not into temptation, But deliver us from evil. For thine is the kingdom, and the power, and the glory, For ever and ever. *Amen.*

NOW unto him who is able to keep us from falling, and to present us faultless before the presence of his glory with exceeding joy, to the only wise God our Saviour, be glory and majesty, dominion and power, through Jesus Christ, for ever and ever. *Amen.*

END OF FIRST SERVICE.

SECOND SERVICE.

The Service is to be introduced by the following Address from the Minister to the People.

HEAR, all ye people; give ear, all ye inhabitants of the world; for the Lord God omnipotent reigneth.

Let the heaven and the earth praise him; the sea, and everything that moveth therein.

Trust in him at all times, ye people; pour out your hearts before him; for God is our refuge.

People.

The Lord reigneth; let the earth rejoice.

INTRODUCTORY PRAYER.

O EVER blessed and most glorious God, the object of supreme veneration, on whom all the families of the earth continually depend; we would present ourselves before thee with reverence and humility; we would offer unto thee our sacrifice of praise and thanksgiving with joy and gratitude. By celebrating thy perfections, may we be excited to an ardent love and imitation of thee, our Father in heaven. May we confess our sins with unfeigned sorrow, and steady purposes of amendment; may we pray unto thee, as the bountiful dispenser of every good thing; may our intercessions be accompanied with charity to all men; may no vain thoughts distract our minds, no unworthy object withdraw our affections; but may our whole hearts be engaged in thy worship, and may the influence of these our religious services be manifested in our future lives; which we humbly ask in the name and as disciples of Jesus Christ our Lord.

People.

Graciously hear us, O God, graciously hear us, O Lord God.

Then shall be read the following Anthem, or the first of the Psalms appointed for the Day.

Minister.

WE praise thee, O God, we worship thee, the one true and living God, who art infinite and unchangeable in all thy perfections.

Peo. Blessed art thou, O Lord God, and worthy to be praised forever.

Min. Before the mountains were brought forth, or ever thou hadst formed the earth and the world, from everlasting to everlasting thou art God.

Peo. Thou livest, and reignest forever.

Min. Thou art the Lord, and changest not; of old hast thou laid the foundations of the earth, and the heavens are the work of thy hands; they shall perish, but thou shalt endure; thy counsel standeth fast, and thy thoughts unto all generations.

Peo. Thou art the same, yesterday, to-day, and forever.

Min. Whither can we flee from thy presence? heaven is thy throne, the earth is thy footstool, and the universe thy habitation.

Peo. All things are full of thee.

Min. Thou hast founded the earth by thy wisdom, and stretched out the heavens by thine understanding; by thy knowledge the depths are broken up, and the clouds drop down the dew; thou art mighty in wisdom, wonderful in counsel, and excellent in all thy works.

Peo. O Lord, how manifold are thy works; in wisdom hast thou made them all.

Min. Thou art the righteous Lord, who exercisest judgment in the earth; thy righteousness is like the great mountains, thy faithfulness reacheth above the clouds; eternal truth is thy law.

Peo. Upright art thou, O Lord; all thy works are just and true.

Min. O Lord God, holy and reverend is thy name; thou art of purer eyes than to behold iniquity; sinners cannot stand before thee; but the upright in heart are always in the light of thy countenance.

Peo. We reverence thee, O Lord, for thou art holy.

Min. Above all we praise thee, we worship thee, as the Lord God gracious and merciful, the God of love, and of all consolation; thou exercisest loving-kindness and benignity; thou delightest to make all thy creatures happy; thou doest good continually ; and thy tender mercies are over all thy works.

Peo. O that men would praise the Lord for his goodness, and for his wonderful works to the children of men.

Min. But who, O Lord, can show forth all thy praise ? We behold the monuments of thy power ; we trace the footsteps of thy wisdom ; and, every moment of our lives, partake of the riches of thy goodness ; but none can say how great, and wise, and good thou art.

Peo. Who can find out thee, the Almighty, unto perfection ?

Min. With one consent, and with our whole hearts, we would celebrate thy glorious perfections here below, until our souls become prepared for thy kingdom and service above, there to worship thee in a more perfect manner, through the ages of eternity. *Amen.*

Then may follow a Voluntary on the Organ, after which the FIRST LESSON *is to be read out of the Old Testament. Then shall be sung an Anthem ; and then the Service is to proceed with the following Thanksgiving.*

Minister.

REJOICE in the Lord, all ye people ; come into his presence with thanksgiving, and be devout and joyful in his service.

Sing praises unto him, and bless him ; for he is good, and his mercy endureth forever.

People.

We will give thanks unto the Lord, for he is good, and his mercy endureth forever.

Minister.

Almighty God, Father of all mercies ; we would offer unto thee our unfeigned thanksgivings for thy goodness and loving-kindness to us and to all men.

We thank thee for the breath of life, the light of reason and conscience, the benevolent and friendly affections, and all the useful and noble powers of our minds. We thank thee for our continual preservation, for the food we eat, the raiment with which we are clothed, and the habitations wherein we dwell ; for health and peace and safety ; for every personal and family and public blessing ; for every friendly and social enjoyment, and for all the happiness of our lives.

People.

Bless the Lord, O our souls, and forget not all his benefits.

Minister.

But above all we bless thee, O ever gracious Father, for thine inestimable love in the redemption of the world by our Lord Jesus Christ, for the means of grace, and the hope of glory. We thank thee for those pure and heavenly doctrines which he hath taught, to lead mankind in the way of truth and salvation ; for those holy and excellent rules of virtue and true religion which he hath laid down in his Gospel; and for the perfect example which he hath left us, that we might follow his steps. We thank thee, that in obedience to thine authority, and to fulfil all righteousness, he submitted unto death, that, being made perfect by suffering, he might become the author of eternal salvation to all who obey him.

And finally we bless thee, the God and Father of our Lord Jesus Christ, that by raising him from the dead, thou hast confirmed to us the glorious and joyful hope of an inheritance incorruptible, undefiled, and which fadeth not away, reserved in the heavens for us.

People.

Glory be to God in the highest; on earth peace, good will to men.

Minister.

O Lord our God, who can number all thy mercies? Thy bounty prevents our requests, seasonably supplies every returning want, and gives us all things richly to enjoy. Write a law of thankfulness on our hearts, we beseech thee, and grant that we may walk before thee, in holiness and righteousness, all the days of our lives. *Amen.*

Here the SECOND LESSON *is to be read out of the New Testament; after which may be sung an Anthem; and then the Service may proceed as follows.*

Minister

SURELY it is meet to be said unto God, we have done iniquity.

To the Lord our God belong mercies and for-
givenesses, though we have sinned against him.

Let us therefore confess and lament our manifold transgressions before the throne of grace.

GENERAL CONFESSION.

ALMIGHTY and most merciful Father, we confess that in many things we have all offended ;
we have not duly improved the talents with which
thou hast intrusted us; we have too often neglected
our duty to ourselves and to our fellow-creatures,
and our consciences witness against us. With humble and penitent hearts we lament before thee, O
our Father, every instance of disobedience ; whatever we have done amiss in thought, word, or deed ;
every offence against thee, our neighbor, or ourselves. Forgive our sins, we beseech thee, and
cleanse us from all unrighteousness ; and may we
bring forth the fruits which are meet for repentance, by walking in newness of life, in humble
expectation of thy mercy declared unto mankind
through Jesus Christ our Lord.

People.

O God, make clean our hearts within us, and
take not thy Holy Spirit from us.

Then shall be read the COLLECT FOR THE DAY, *and*
one or more of the following Prayers.

FOR TEMPORAL MERCIES.

ALMIGHTY God, the giver of every good and
perfect gift, we commend ourselves and all

our concerns to the disposal of thy gracious providence. Thou knowest what is truly good for us,
and it is our highest happiness that we are under
thy fatherly care. In humble submission to thy
wise and gracious will, we beseech thee to bless us
with health of body, and peace of mind ; and to
bestow upon us such a share of the good things
of this life as thou knowest to be best for us.
Conduct us by thy gracious hand through all the
changes of this world ; and may we at last be per-
feet and happy, in that heavenly inheritance, which
is incorruptible, and fadeth not away. *Amen.*

FOR ALL MANKIND.

O GOD, the Father of all mankind, we offer up
unto thee our prayers and intercessions for
our fellow-creatures. Mercifully regard the work
of thy hands. Let thy name be known, and thy
pure worship prevail throughout the world. May
all people, nations, and languages acknowledge
thee, the true God. May wisdom and goodness,
liberty and peace, charity and happiness everywhere
abound ; and thy kingdom of truth and righteousness spread and flourish, until it cover the face of
the whole earth. *Amen.*

FOR RULERS.

O LORD God, high and mighty, King of kings,
Lord of lords, we humbly beseech thee with
thy favor to behold the President of the United
States, and all others in authority. May they be
the faithful guardians of our public liberties, and

the instruments of transmitting them to posterity. May we have reason to rejoice in them as the ministers of thy providence to us for good ; and may they finally be found worthy of everlasting life. *Amen.*

FOR CHRISTIAN MINISTERS.

O GOD, the Father of our Lord Jesus Christ, the fountain of light, from whom cometh every good and perfect gift, we humbly beseech thee to send down thy blessing upon Christian Ministers of every denomination ; may they be so replenished with the truth of thy doctrines, and so exemplary in unaffected piety and goodness of life, that they may become the means of turning many to righteousness, and of promoting the knowledge and practice of the pure and holy Gospel of Jesus Christ our Lord. *Amen.*

FOR THE AFFLICTED.

O GOD of mercy, we humbly implore thy favorable regard for all our brethren in affliction ; may thy wisdom be their direction, thy power their support, and thy goodness their confidence ; and by a patient behavior under their afflictions, and a thankful acknowledgment of all thy mercies, may they be prepared for unmixed happiness in a future and better world. *Amen.*

CONCLUDING PRAYER.

O LORD God, our Heavenly Father, who hast permitted us with one accord to make our common supplications unto thee, fulfil, we beseech thee, the desires and petitions of thy servants, as thou in thy wisdom knowest to be good for us. We commit ourselves to the care of thy providence; mercifully defend us from all the dangers to which we may be exposed; graciously accept these our services, and grant that in all our works begun, continued, and ended, we may glorify thy holy name, and finally obtain everlasting life and felicity; which we humbly ask in the name and as the disciples of Jesus Christ our Lord; in whose words we conclude our prayers.

OUR Father, who art in heaven, Hallowed be thy name. Thy kingdom come; Thy will be done on earth, as it is in heaven. Give us this day our daily bread, And forgive us our trespasses, As we forgive those who trespass against us. And lead us not into temptation, But deliver us from evil. For thine is the kingdom, and the power, and the glory, For ever and ever. *Amen.*

NOW unto the King eternal, immortal, invisible, the only wise God, be honor and glory, through Jesus Christ, for ever and ever. *Amen.*

END OF SECOND SERVICE.

Prayers

FAMILIES AND SUNDAY SCHOOLS.

FAMILY PRAYERS.

ALMIGHTY and ever blessed God, source of all being, and fountain of all good; we, thy children, come before thee this morning, to express our sense of thy goodness to us, to acknowledge our dependence upon thee, to adore thy greatness, and commend ourselves to thy care.

Glory be to thy name that thou hast made us capable of holding communion with thee, the Father of our spirits, and of receiving the revelations of thy word and will. Glory be to thy name for the heavenly doctrines, precepts, and promises of the Gospel of thy Son. We make it our earnest prayer to thee, that our hearts may be touched by its holy influences, that our characters may be formed by its spirit, that our lives may be governed by its laws. O guide us, we beseech thee, in the ways of its truth to the everlasting home which it promises to the righteous.

Let our attendance this day on thy public worship, and the services and instructions of thy house, conduce to our spiritual improvement and our eternal good. Let us enter thy gates with thanksgiving, and thy courts with praise, and take with us our best affections and resolutions to the temple of the Lord. Let not our thoughts, which ought to be engaged in the holiest offices, be still returning to the cares, pleasures, and follies of a transitory world; neither let us take thy name upon our lips when our hearts are far from thee. But let our prayers and meditations exalt and purify us, and assist us to discharge our duties in this life, and contribute to prepare us for that eternal world to which we are rapidly hastening.

Bless all who call upon thy name this day. May they approach thee in sincerity, humility, and love. May all denominations of Christians, however divided in opinion, be joined together in the bond of peace, and an earnest regard for the interests of true religion and virtue. And O let the name and the Gospel of thy Son be known and glorified more and more, till the whole world shall come to the perfect light, and embrace the truth as it is in Jesus. In his worthy name, and as his disciples, we offer these our petitions; ascribing to thee, the King eternal, immortal, invisible, the only wise God, all glory and honor, might, majesty, and dominion, now and forevermore. *Amen.*

SUNDAY EVENING.

OUR Father, who art in heaven; accept, we beseech thee, our grateful acknowledgments for all thy goodness to us this day; and especially for the privileges of holy rest, worship, and instruction. We fervently pray that whatever good impressions may have been made upon us may be durable; that whatever good resolutions we may have formed may be steadfastly kept; that every devout aspiration we may have breathed in the sanctuary may be remembered in the world, to guard us against temptation, and preserve us holy and undefiled. Help us to set our affections on things above. May we constantly live as in thy world, in thy sight, as thy children. Let it be our study at home and abroad, by day and by night, to love and fear thee as we ought, and to do those things which are well pleasing in thy sight.

We acknowledge, O thou Father and judge of men, that we have sinned against thee; that notwithstanding we have been continued in the world from day to day, and thy mercies have been borne to us on the wings of every hour, we have been undutiful and unthankful; we have often forgotten, and often disobeyed thee. O Father, pardon and reclaim us, and give us that repentance which needeth not to be repented of. Cleanse us from our secret faults, and let sin have no dominion over us. Enable us to become true followers of thy Son Jesus Christ in all things; to clothe ourselves with his humility, purity, and benevolence. Let thy will, as it was his, be ours also. Like him, may we go about doing good. May the contemplation of his character, and imitation of his example, bring us constantly nearer to his own perfection, and to those mansions of everlasting happiness which he has promised to his disciples, and gone before to prepare for them.

Take us, Almighty God, under thy sovereign protection. Make us in soul and body wholly thine. Sanctify our domestic relations ; bless our friends, and strengthen and purify the bonds of love which join thy servants together. May the blessings, which we receive from thee, excite our gratitude, and animate our obedience. May those sorrows, and privations, and pains, with which, in thy wisdom, thou mayest afflict us, be endured with fortitude and resignation, and improved to our eternal peace. Watch over us during the darkness of this night, and the defenceless hours of sleep ; preserve us from all dangers ; and bring us to the light of another morning more inclined to love thee, and resolved to serve thee, than we ever have been. Accept our evening sacrifice of prayer and praise, which we offer in the name of Jesus Christ, our most blessed Lord and Saviour. *Amen.*

MONDAY MORNING.

GREAT and glorious Lord our God ; we, thy servants, whom thou hast brought to see the light of another morning, humbly acknowledge thee as the God of our lives and the giver of all good. It is thou who sustainest us in the defenceless hours of sleep, and when we awake we are still with thee. Encompassed by the same care which guarded us by night, we begin the occupations of the day. O God, our trust is in thee. Give us grace to perform our duty faithfully ; to use this world as not abusing it ; to hold fast our integrity as long as we live ; to remember that thou seest us always, and that we must render a final account of all that we do, to thee, the witness and judge of men.

We thank thee, O most merciful Father, for our domestic ties and family blessings. May we, the members of this household, mutually endeavor to discharge our several duties to each other with tenderness and fidelity. Let the gentle and pure spirit of the blessed Jesus possess our hearts, and influence our conduct. Let tranquillity, harmony, and love abide in our dwelling, and the voice of health and cheerfulness be continually heard in it. Extend thy loving-kindness to all our friends. Delight in their happiness here, and make them heirs of the inheritance of the saints in the future and eternal world.

O thou, whose blessing is on the habitation of the just, let us be the joyful objects of that blessing, now and forevermore. Let thy mercy encompass our abode, and follow us in all our ways. Throughout our earthly pilgrimage, be thou our guide and comforter; let thy rod and thy staff be our support in the valley of the shadow of death; and lift up the light of thy countenance upon us in the regions of eternal day. O God, hear us in thy great mercy; pity our infirmities; pardon our sins; and from our united hearts accept this tribute of devotion, through Jesus Christ our Lord. *Amen.*

MONDAY EVENING.

O THOU who dwellest in the heavens, but whom the heaven of heavens cannot contain, unto thee do we lift up our souls. Thou art never far from any one of us, and we cannot flee from thy presence. If we say, The darkness shall hide us, even the night shall be light about us; for the darkness and the light are both alike to thee. Thou seest us at this moment, and discernest every thought and intention of our hearts. Thou art acquainted with all our ways, and there is not a word in our tongues, but lo, O Lord, thou knowest it altogether. Let this momentous truth be deeply impressed upon our minds. However occupied, and in whatever place or circumstances we may be, may we remember that thou art with us; that no fault which we commit will be overlooked, no virtue we exercise be unnoticed, and no prayers which we utter be unheard by thee, our God. Encircled in thy protecting arms, may we fear no evil. Encompassed by thine awful presence, may we dread all sin. When discouraged by difficulties, let us look up to thee from whom our help cometh; and when distressed by calamity, may we take refuge in thy mercy, and find peace by staying our minds on the eternal One. Through life may we act always as seeing him who is invisible. In death, may we find our consolation in the presence of him, who, when flesh and heart fail, will be the strength of our heart and our portion forever.

Accept our thanks, most merciful Father, for thy great goodness in bringing us to the close of another day, in the enjoyment of so many blessings. While we gratefully receive the gifts of thy bounty, let us not incur the guilt of loving the creature more than the Creator, or of laying up treasure on earth to the neglect of our treasure in heaven ; but help us so to pass through things temporal, that we finally lose not things eternal.

Graciously regard whatever of duty we have this day performed. Forgive whatever has been sinful in us. Bless and protect our friends. Let no evil come near us in the night ; and bring us to the morning rejoicing still in thy great goodness, and praising thee, the Father of all mercies, through Jesus Christ our Lord. *Amen.*

TUESDAY MORNING.

ALMIGHTY God, maker of all things, whose we are, and on whom we entirely depend ; we bless thee that thou hast kept us during the past night ; that thou hast refreshed us with grateful slumbers ; that thou hast preserved us from the dangers which walk in darkness, and hast opened our eyes on the light of another day. We acknowledge, O God, that these are but a small part of thy mercies. Thou hast been always with us ; thou art continually doing us good. All the blessings which we enjoy, or have ever enjoyed, come down from thee, the Father and the Friend of all.

We would call upon our souls, and all that is within us, to bless and praise thy holy name, and not to forget all the benefits of him, who forgiveth our iniquities, who healeth our diseases, who redeemeth our lives from destruction, and crowneth us with loving-kindness and tender mercy. O teach us how to thank thee as we ought ; to show forth thy praise not only with our lips, but in our lives ; by giving up ourselves to thy service, and by walking before thee in holiness and righteousness all our days. Let us cherish that faith which is imbibed from a pure doctrine, and is manifested by a holy life. Let us cultivate that piety which deeply reverences and supremely loves a Being of infinite perfections, and which produces, as its natural fruit, a sincere love for all mankind. May every day of our lives be marked by some valuable improvement, some act of virtue, some victory over temptation and passion. May we be continually advancing nearer to perfection, to the moral likeness of our Saviour, and to thy rest and happiness above.

O God, we look to thee for thy protection through this day. Keep us from danger, from sickness, and from falling into sin. Enable us to be useful to society, and to obtain the approbation of those whom we love. Let us especially so conduct ourselves this day, and through all our days, as to secure thy favor which is life, and thy loving-kindness which is better than life. We ask all things in the name, and as disciples of thy blessed Son, our Saviour, Jesus Christ. *Amen.*

TUESDAY EVENING.

EVER gracious and indulgent God, who hast brought us to the close of this day in safety and peace ; we render thee our devout thanksgivings for the mercies which we have experienced, and commend ourselves to thy continued protection. Unworthy as we are, we yet would seek thy face and implore thy favor, for thou hast bid us look to thee as our merciful Father, who will never forget nor forsake his children, and is always ready to forgive those who truly turn to him.

We therefore pray thee, O Father, that above all things thou wouldst assist us in loving and serving thee. What our lot shall be, we leave to thy wise providence; but O teach us, under all circumstances, to be grateful to thee in prosperity, and resigned to thy will in affliction and distress. Inspire our hearts with a purer love to thee; enlighten our minds with heavenly wisdom; and make our desires conform themselves to thy purposes. Let gratitude be the pervading disposition of our souls. May we always feel that we are thy children; that we have received from thee infinitely more than we deserve; and that the least return which we can make to thee, is, to be contented and cheerful under thy paternal government.

May our reverence for thy will and commandments be displayed in our conduct toward our brethren of the human family; so that we may constantly regard them with feelings of pure benevolence, and do unto them as we should wish them to do unto us. Let us go to rest this night at peace with all mankind, and with bosoms free from all envy, hatred, malice, and uncharitableness; and grant that we may rise up in the morning with a firm resolution to imitate thee, according to the measure of our humble capacity, by doing good.

Hear, answer, forgive, and accept us, O Father

in heaven, for thine infinite mercy's sake in Jesus Christ our Lord. *Amen.*

WEDNESDAY MORNING.

O THOU infinite and eternal Spirit, by whose power the world in which we live, and the countless worlds by which we are surrounded, were created from nothing ; by whose wisdom they and all that they contain are constantly directed ; by whose goodness they are preserved in order and filled with happiness and beauty ; and without whose support they would all return to the nothing from which they came ; we, thy dependent offspring, come to thee this morning with the grateful acknowledgment of our dependence on thy bounty and protection. By thee our daily returning wants are supplied ; by thee our dwellings are defended ; our blessings are preserved ; our feet are kept from falling, our eyes from tears, and our souls from death.

Weak and ignorant as we are, we rejoice to know and to feel that we are subjected to thine all-wise control, and that we are surrounded by the presence of the omniscient and eternal God. And especially do we thank and bless thee, O Father, for thy love in the Gospel of thy Son Jesus Christ ; for the heavenly radiance which it sheds on the path of our duty, through the gloom of affliction, and on the bed of death. We thank thee that it enables us to look beyond the bounds of mortality and time, and defy the power of change and death ; and that it promises to the faithful servants of

God, and true disciples of Christ, those glorious rewards of a future life, which eye hath never seen, nor ear heard, nor the heart of man conceived.

All is from thee; all joy, all support, all improvement, all hope. O may we become worthy of thy mercies, by receiving them as from thee, and using them according to thy will; by renouncing and avoiding all that is evil, and following after and cleaving to all that is good; by living and dying in thy fear and love.

Hear us, O Father, in heaven where thou dwellest, and accept us in the name of Jesus Christ, our redeemer; as whose disciples we address thee, and through whom we ascribe unto thee everlasting honors. *Amen.*

WEDNESDAY EVENING.

O GOD, the unchangeable and everlasting fountain of life, perfection, and happiness; we lift up our hearts unto thee, the greatest, wisest, and best of beings. Grant that we may increase in the knowledge of thee, day by day; that we may constantly attain more pure and worthy conceptions of thy nature and providence; that we may manifest a more becoming reverence for thy perfections, and a truer concern for thy honor and service.

We also pray thee, O God, to teach us the knowledge and the government of ourselves; may we keep our hearts with all diligence, amidst all the trials and changes of the world; in prosperity may we be humble, temperate, and charitable; in adversity may we be patient, and wholly resigned to thy will. Save us, O gracious God, from anger and malice, from revenge and uncharitableness, from pride and presumption, from the snares of the wicked and the fatal influence of every evil example; give us prudence to direct our affairs, resolution to preserve our innocence, and wisdom and constancy to retain our integrity as long as we live. In whatever station thou art pleased to appoint our lot, and wherever we are, in public or in private, may it be our uniform and steady purpose to discharge our duty with fidelity; and in that solemn day, when thou, supreme over all, shalt judge the world by Jesus Christ, may we appear with humble confidence and joy, and be admitted into thy glorious and everlásting kingdom.

O God, we implore thy blessing on all that is dear and valuable to us. We pray thee to bless our country, our rulers, our friends, the churches of Christ, the ministers of religion, the instructors of youth, the rising generation, and all the means of establishing, preserving, and diffusing the principles of liberty, holiness, and virtue. Keep us this night by thine almighty power; be always our defender, guide, and friend; and to thee, the infinite and eternal God, we will ascribe continually all glory, honor, and praise, through Jesus Christ our Lord. *Amen.*

THURSDAY MORNING.

O THOU great Creator, governor, and supporter of men; thou dwellest in light, and art the father of lights, with whom is no variableness nor shadow of turning. Grateful for the care which thou hast exercised over us during the night past, we would cheerfully submit ourselves to thy guidance through the day upon which we have entered. Keep us in thy faith and fear, and secure us from every evil of soul and body. Impress on our hearts a solemn sense of thy universal presence. Preserve us from any snares and dangers to which we may be exposed, and especially from the sins which do most easily beset us. Prepare us for new occurrences, whether prosperous or adverse, and quicken us in the discharge of those duties which lie before us.

Thou prolongest our lives, that we may attain more and more to the true end of life. May this day witness some improvement in knowledge, piety, and virtue. May it witness our diligence in that occupation to which thou hast called us. We desire and purpose to keep consciences void of offence, and to abstain from every action offensive to the eye of divine purity; but the experience which we have had of our frailty makes us diffident of our strength. Our confidence is in thy power to strengthen our faith, invigorate our obedience, and cause us to run in the way of thy commandments. We implore thine aid, that we may walk before thee this day, and all the days of our lives. Help our endeavors after improvement and usefulness; enable us to make every day some progress in a holy life; teach us to feel the uncertainty and value of our days on earth; and when they shall be numbered and finished, receive us into the light and bliss of thy glorious presence, through Jesus Christ our Lord. *Amen.*

THURSDAY EVENING.

O GOD, the Father of mercies, the God of love and of all consolation ; we thy servants unite to present unto thee our unfeigned thanks, for all thy goodness and loving-kindness to us and all the children of men.

We thank thee, that thou hast created us in thine own image ; endued us with social affections ; implanted in our hearts a sense of good and evil ; and called us to the fear and love of thee, the greatest and best of beings. We praise thee for our continual support, and for all the comforts of our lives. Thou givest us health and fruitful seasons, and fillest our hearts with food and gladness. Blessed be the Lord, even the God of our salvation, who daily loadeth us with benefits.

Above all, we thank thee for thy great mercy, in sending thy well-beloved Son Jesus Christ into the world, to instruct us by his excellent doctrine ; to guide us by his perfect example ; and to fill us with the joyful hope of eternal life. Thou hast been mindful of us and blessed us ; thou hast dealt bountifully with us, and done great things for us. We will bless thee at all times ; thy praise shall be continually in our mouths.

We acknowledge before thee, O God, who rulest the children of men with wisdom and goodness, that we have not duly improved thy manifold mercies. Though thou hast nourished and brought us up as children, we have sinned against thee. We desire to forsake all our evil ways, and to return unto thee with our whole hearts; and we humbly beseech thee, who art slow to anger and ready to forgive, that thou wouldst pardon all our transgressions. O Lord, show thy mercy upon us, and grant us thy salvation.

Lead us by thy gracious hand in the path of our duty; and, in the time of temptation, let thy good Spirit be with us, to keep us from falling. May our minds be purified from all sinful affections; may falsehood and deceit have no place in our words; and, in all our ways, may we obey thy commandments; that, being holy in thy sight, we may obtain thy favor, and may finally be received into thine everlasting kingdom.

We pray unto thee, O gracious God, in behalf of all our friends. Supply their wants out of the stores of thy bounty; let thy watchful providence evermore defend them from evil; and let thy goodness and mercy follow them all the days of their lives.

We address our united devotions unto thee, the giver of all good things, in the name and as the disciples of Jesus Christ; and now unto the blessed and only potentate, the King of kings, and Lord of lords, dwelling in light to which no man can approach, whom no man hath seen or can see, be honor and power everlasting. *Amen.*

FRIDAY MORNING.

ALMIGHTY and everlasting God, in whom we live and move and have our being; we, thy needy creatures, render thee our humble praises, for thy preservation of us from the beginning of our lives to this day. We thank thee for refreshing us with the slumbers, and guarding us from the dangers, of the past night. For all thy mercies we bless and magnify thy glorious name, humbly beseeching thee to accept this our morning sacrifice of praise and thanksgiving.

And since it is by thy mercy, O gracious Father, that another day is added to our lives, we here dedicate both our souls and our bodies to thee and thy service, in a sober, righteous, and godly life ; in which resolution do thou, O merciful God, confirm and strengthen us ; that, as we grow in age, we may grow in grace, and in the knowledge of our Lord and Saviour Jesus Christ.

But, O God, who knowest the weakness of our nature, and the manifold temptations which we daily meet with, we humbly beseech thee to have compassion on our infirmities, and to give us the constant assistance of thy Holy Spirit, that we may be effectually restrained from sin and excited to our duty. Imprint upon our hearts such a dread of thy judgments, and such a grateful sense of thy goodness to us, as may make us both afraid and ashamed to offend thee ; and keep in our minds a lively remembrance of that great day, in which we must give an account of our thoughts, words, and actions, and, according to the works done in the body, be rewarded or punished by him, whom thou hast appointed the judge of the quick and dead, thy Son Jesus Christ.

In particular, we implore thy grace and protection for the ensuing day. Keep us temperate in our meats and drinks, and diligent in our several callings. Grant us patience under any afflictions thou shalt see fit to lay on us, and minds always contented with our present condition. Give us grace to be just and upright in all our dealings; quiet and peaceable; full of compassion; and ready to do good unto all men, according to our abilities and opportunities. Direct us in all our ways, and prosper the works of our hands in the business of our several stations. Defend us from all dangers and adversities; and be graciously pleased to take us and all things belonging to us under thy fatherly care and protection. These things, and whatever else thou shalt see necessary and convenient to us, we humbly beg in the name and as the disciples of Jesus Christ, our blessed Lord and Redeemer. *Amen.*

FRIDAY EVENING.

MOST merciful God, who art of purer eyes than to behold iniquity, and hast promised forgiveness to all those who confess and forsake their sins; we come before thee this evening, in an humble sense of our unworthiness, acknowledging our transgressions of thy righteous laws. But, O gracious Father, who desirest not the death of a sinner, look upon us, we beseech thee, in mercy, and forgive us the sins which we have committed against thee. Make us deeply sensible of the evil of all unrighteousness; and work in us a hearty contrition for our faults and offences, that we may obtain forgiveness at thy hands, who art ever ready to receive the humble and penitent.

And lest, through our own frailty, or the temptations which encompass us, we be drawn into further sin, grant us the direction and assistance of thy Holy Spirit. Reform whatever is amiss in the temper and disposition of our souls; that no unclean thoughts, unlawful designs, or inordinate desires may rest there. Purge our hearts from envy, hatred, and malice; that we may never suffer the sun to go down upon our wrath; but may always retire to our rest in peace, charity, and good will, with a conscience void of offence towards thee and towards man.

And accept, O Lord, our intercessions for all mankind. Let the light of thy Gospel shine upon all nations; and may as many as have received it, live as becomes it. Be gracious unto thy Church; and grant that every member of the same, in his vocation and ministry, may serve thee faithfully. Bless all in authority over us; and so rule their hearts and strengthen their hands, that they may punish wickedness and vice, and maintain thy true religion and virtue. Send down thy blessings, temporal and spiritual, upon all our relations, friends, and neighbors. Reward all who have done us good, and pardon all those who have done or wish us evil, and give them repentance and better minds. Be merciful to all who are in any trouble; and of thine abundant goodness minister unto them according to their several necessities.

To our prayers, O Lord, we join our unfeigned thanks for all thy mercies; for our being, our reason, and all other endowments and faculties of soul and body; for our health, friends, food, and raiment, and all the other comforts and conveniences of life. Above all we adore thy mercy in sending thy Son into the world to redeem us from sin and death, and to show us the Father. We bless thee for thy patience with us; for the assistances of thy Holy Spirit; for thy continual care and watchful providence over us, through the whole course of our lives. We pray thee to continue thy blessings to us; and to give us grace to show our thankfulness in a sincere obedience to thy laws.

We beseech thee to protect us this night. Defend us from all dangers, and give us such refreshing sleep as may fit us for the duties of the following day. Make us ever mindful of the time when we shall lie down in the dust; and grant us grace always to live in such a state, that we may never be afraid to die; so that living and dying we may be thine, and thine forevermore. We ask all in the name of thy Son Jesus Christ. *Amen.*

SATURDAY MORNING.

O GOD, our Creator and Heavenly Father, the giver of all good, upon whom we depend now and forever; we, thy children, thank thee for the watchful care of thy providence, by which we have been preserved, during the defenceless hours of the night, and brought in safety to the light of another day.

Thy mercies, O God, are renewed to us every morning. Let our gratitude and dutiful obedience to thee bear some proportion to thy favors, that we may be a family fearing thee, and glorifying thy name among men. We desire to set thee our God before us in all our ways, that thy blessing may constantly go along with us, and that we may never undertake anything which we dare not beg of thee to prosper.

Assist us, gracious God, in the discharge of all social and relative duties. May it be our prevailing aim to bear a nearer resemblance unto thee, the original of all perfection, and to proceed, after the example of Jesus Christ, thy Son, in the practice of all goodness. By the expectation of a happy immortality, may our virtue be supported, and our peace secured ; that we may live in a state of continual improvement, and of preparation for that heavenly kingdom, into which nothing unholy or impure shall ever enter.

O God, to the direction of thy wise and unerring providence we do entirely commit ourselves. Safe under thy protection, and happy in thy favor, we would cheerfully follow where thou pleasest to conduct us. Be with us this day, and all our days. Be also with our friends, to keep and preserve them both in body and in soul. In health and in sickness, in life and in death, may we lift up our hearts to thee, and make thy goodness alone our confidence and joy ; and may we so pass through the changing scenes of the present world, that we may be prepared for the pure and unmixed happiness of thy glorious presence forevermore. Mercifully hear and accept us, O God, through thy Son Jesus Christ our Lord. *Amen.*

SATURDAY EVENING.

O THOU, who alone art from everlasting, without beginning of days, or end of years ; we rejoice that, amid the continual changes of this our uncertain life, we can look to thee, O God, who endurest forever. Heaven and earth shall pass away, but thou remainest, and wilt never fail those who trust in thee, nor hide thy face from those who love thee.

Preserver of men, at the close of another day and week, we would render unto thee our sincere and humble thanks for all the mercies of thy providence, by which our lives have been supported and blest. We acknowledge with joy that it is thou alone who preservest us, and makest us to dwell in safety ; for in thy hands alone our life and breath are, and thine are all our ways.

Forgive, we beseech thee, the transgressions of the past day, the past week, and ·of all past time. Whatever has been amiss in our conduct, or irregular in our dispositions, whatever we have done which we ought not to have done, or omitted which we ought to have performed, do thou, in thy great mercy, forgive. Knowing our frailty and danger from the past, may we in future take more careful heed to our steps, and walk more uprightly before thee. Quicken our consciences, and sanctify our hearts. Make us more pure, humble, and devout, more benevolent and useful ; and so teach us to number our days, that we may apply our hearts unto wisdom.

Hitherto thou hast helped and sustained us. Truly our hope is in thee, and under the shadow of thy wings will we put our trust. Grant us refreshment this night by sleep ; and may we arise in thy favor in the morning, and be fitted for the sacred duties of the day. O thou who givest power to the faint, and, to those who have no might, increasest strength, give unto us strength to do and bear thy whole will and pleasure. In thine everlasting arms support us ; by thy mighty power defend us ; let thy grace be sufficient for us, and thy goodness and mercy follow us all our days. We dedicate ourselves to thee as our God and guide through life, our support and comfort in death, and, after death, our everlasting portion and felicity. When the present succession of days and nights shall cease, graciously receive us to that state where we shall serve thee without intermission and without weariness, through the day of eternity.

We commend to thee our relatives and friends. We ask thy compassion for the distressed, thy mercy for the erring and guilty, thy blessing upon all men. Promote the cause of knowledge and religion in the earth ; let the pure doctrines and practice of Christianity everywhere prevail, and the whole earth be filled with thy glory and praise.

Holy Watchman of thy people, who dost never slumber nor sleep ; the ever blessed God, who art able to do for us more exceedingly than we can ask or think; the Father almighty; the King eternal, immortal, and invisible; unto thee be all honor and glory, through Jesus Christ our Lord. *Amen.*

A PRAYER FOR MORNING OR EVENING.

O GOD, the Creator, Preserver, and Benefactor of men, we approach thee in an humble sense of our dependence upon thee, who, both by day and by night, dost constantly sustain and defend us, and delight to do us good. May we regard thee as the chief good, and the knowledge and love of thee as the greatest of blessings. May we earnestly desire, and diligently seek, and happily find thee. Thou art our Ruler and Governor. Reign, we beseech thee, in our hearts. Subdue and expel all rebellious passions; turn away from us vanity and self-deceit; preserve us from envy, covetousness, wrath, hardness of heart, and contempt of thy word; and make us humble, and gentle, and kind, and ready at all times to do thy will and submit to thy righteous pleasure. Thou art our merciful and indulgent Father. O grant to thy children those best of gifts, a firm and right faith, a steadfast and well-grounded hope, and a never failing charity. Thou art the God and Father of our Lord Jesus Christ. Give us grace to receive him as our Saviour, and learn of him as our teacher, and follow him as our guide and example, and love him as the friend who died for us; that so we may be numbered among his true disciples, and become fellow-heirs with him in thy heavenly kingdom. Help us to remember, and to imitate the benevolence which filled his soul. May we consider mankind as our brethren, and be heartily disposed to relieve their wants; to comfort their sorrows; to redress their wrongs; to pardon those who have offended us; to love those who hate us; to do good unto all.

May we walk within our houses with perfect hearts. May we study to advance each other's happiness, and to quicken each other's piety. May every good and holy disposition be daily improving in our breasts, until we become fit for that happy kingdom where love and peace and joy forever reign. Hear us in thy Son's name, for whom we bless thee, and through whom we ascribe unto thee all honor and glory forever. *Amen.*

A SECOND.

O GOD, our Heavenly Father, we beseech thee to incline thine ear unto thy children, and favorably hear our prayer. We pray that thou wouldst guide and lead us by thy providence, and comfort us by thy mercy, and protect us by thine almighty power. We submit to thee all our thoughts, words, actions, and sufferings; and we desire to have thee always in our minds, to do all our works in thy name, and in thy strength to bear all calamity with patience. Give us grace that we may be attentive to our spiritual concerns, temperate in our enjoyments, vigilant in our conduct, and steadfast and immovable in all good purposes. Dispose our hearts to admire and praise thy holiness; to hate all evil works; to love our neighbor, and to renounce the vanities of the world.

Enable us to conduct ourselves with prudence in all transactions, and show courage in danger, fortitude in trial, submissiveness in adversity, and in prosperity an humble mind. Let thy grace illuminate our understandings, direct our wills, sanctify our bodies, and bless and save our souls. Make us diligent in curbing all irregular affections ; zealous in imploring thy grace ; careful in keeping thy commandments, and constant in working out our salvation.

Finally, O God, make us sensible how little is the world, how great thy heavens, how short time, and how long a blessed eternity. O that we may well prepare ourselves for death ; that we may flee from the wrath to come, and obtain of thee everlasting life, through Jesus Christ our Lord. *Amen.*

A THIRD.

O LORD, our Heavenly Father, who hast preserved us to the present hour, and hast blessed us with unnumbered benefits, give us grace, we beseech thee, to be truly grateful, and sincerely to renew the dedication of ourselves and of our lives to thee.

We confess before thee our sins, which are more than we can number or express ; and we adore the riches of thy mercy which forgiveth our sins, and healeth our iniquities. Grant that, through the daily contemplation of the doctrines of thy Gospel, our hearts may be daily made better. May the faith of Christ be made effectual to bring down our pride, to subdue our selfishness, to improve our temper, to direct and restrain our tongues, to animate us with the purest zeal, and to fill us with charity to our neighbor. May it also sanctify our daily work, exciting our diligence in it, and teaching us to look to thee, O Lord, for our great and final recompense. O God, we pray thee to bless us to the end of our lives. Defend us in all future dangers; succor us in all sorrows, trials, and adversities; and, when the toils of this mortal life are over, conduct us in safety to thine everlasting peace and rest.

To thee, who hast been the support of our infancy, the help of our youth, and the guide of our advancing years, do we commit ourselves forever. To thee do we humbly resign all our affairs, and commend our bodies and our souls, our temporal and eternal interests. And to thee do we ascribe all glory and praise, through Jesus Christ our Lord and Saviour. *Amen.*

FOR SUNDAY MORNING OR EVENING.

ALMIGHTY God, Father of all thy creatures, we adore thee for thy great goodness, in providing not only for our temporal necessities, but also for the spiritual wants of our souls. We thank thee for thy holy Word, by which we are instructed in thy will and are made wise unto salvation. We thank thee for thy holy Sabbaths, on which our thoughts are especially called away from earthly things, to the consideration of those things which are heavenly and eternal.

We praise thee for the gift of thy Son Jesus

Christ; that he hath set us an example by his holy life; that he hath redeemed us by his painful and precious death; and that, by his resurrection from the dead on the third day, he hath given us assurance of immortality.

We pray thee, O Lord, to impress deeply on our minds these solemn truths, that we may not forget them amidst the cares and occupations of the world, but may daily be reminded of our Christian privileges and Christian duties. Save us from indifference and levity, as well as from wickedness and sin. Pardon our sins in times past; pardon our forgetfulness of thee our God, and grant us thy peace.

We pray thee to send the blessed Gospel of thy Son over the world. Bless the labors of thy ministers in every place; fill them with zeal for thine honor, and with love to thy name. May Christ be preached from the rising to the setting sun; and may each of us endeavor to recommend our faith by our conduct.

We intercede for our relations, connections, and friends; especially for those who may be in sorrow, sickness, or trouble. Grant unto them those consolations which thou only canst bestow, and put into their hearts a holy trust in thee. And may those who feel that their infirmities come upon them, and that their outward frame decays, be enabled to believe that, when earthly things fail, they shall have a building of God, a house not made with hands, eternal in the heavens.

Take us now, O God, under thy gracious care.

Let thy blessing attend us, and thy good Spirit rest upon us. May the truths which we hear with our outward ears sink into our hearts; and may we, through the ensuing week, rise up and lie down at peace with thee, and with all mankind. When our Sabbaths and all our days on earth are numbered and finished, receive us, O God, we beseech thee, to thine eternal rest; through Jesus Christ, our blessed Lord and Saviour. *Amen.*

PRAYER FOR A BEREAVED FAMILY.

O THOU eternal Lord our God, the Lord of life and death, who givest and who takest away, enable us all to say, with sincere and humble resignation, Thy name be blessed, and thy will be done. In all our troubles and adversities, whensoever they oppress us, we would come to thee, O Father, and put our whole trust and confidence in thee, and lay down the burthen of our sorrows before thee, and look to thee alone for consolation and help; for we know that thou art a God of mercy and compassion, and that, though clouds and darkness are round about thee, righteousness and judgment are the foundations of thy throne.

We desire to submit with all humility and patience to the recent afflictive dispensation of thy righteous providence. Be pleased to sanctify it to thy servants, the members of this family. Teach us to turn this sorrow to our eternal good; and let the sense of our loss make us cleave more steadfastly to thee. Let no repining thoughts rise in our hearts, but help us to place our affections more strongly on those immovable things which are above, and to resign unto thee all our thoughts and desires. By this chastisement may we be purified from sin, quickened in duty, mortified to the world, and raised above it. Send thy Holy Spirit to abide with and comfort our hearts, and enable us to endure tribulation as becometh disciples of thy Son Jesus Christ.

Bind more closely together the surviving members of this family. Increase in us a tender and faithful affection. May we learn how to promote each other's happiness, and mitigate the sorrows which have befallen, or yet await us. Teach us to feel the vanity of earthly things, to delight in thy word, to study thy will, to observe thy law, and to work out our own salvation ; that when we go the way of all the earth, we may be comforted by thy presence, and admitted to that heavenly state where all tears shall be wiped from our eyes, and there shall be no more decay, nor sickness, nor death ; which we ask in the name of thy Son Jesus Christ, the resurrection and the life, through whom to thee be rendered everlasting praises. *Amen.*

PRAYER FOR THE CHILDREN OF A FAMILY.

ALMIGHTY God, by whose gracious providence the successive generations of mankind are called into being, we implore thy fatherly blessing on the children of this family. To thy protection and guidance, to thy direction and disposal, we humbly and earnestly recommend them. May they remember their Creator in the days of their youth. Impress on their tender minds that reverence of thee which is the beginning of wisdom; and give them that understanding which shall incline them to keep thy commandments. Lead them by thy right hand in the path of duty, and preserve them amidst the temptations to which the young are particularly exposed, and amidst all the temptations of this present evil world. As they grow in years, may they grow in grace, and by a careful improvement of the talents committed to their trust, may they lay a foundation for their present comfort and eternal felicity.

Help us, O Lord, to train them up in thy fear. May we give them seasonable instructions, and set them good examples. Direct us in every part of their education; in the choice of their studies, employments, and stations of life, whereby they may be most happy in themselves, and most useful to society. Let a kind providence accompany them through life; may we have the comfort of seeing them behave wisely and well, and the hope that they will at last be received to the endless felicity of thy heavenly kingdom, through Jesus Christ our Lord. *Amen.*

A PRAYER FOR THE AGED.

GREAT God, and Heavenly Father, look down with peculiar favor and kindness upon thine aged servants. Have compassion upon their infirmities, and help them in all their weaknesses, difficulties, and distresses. Cast them not away, O Lord, in their old age. Forsake them not when their strength faileth. Remember not against them former iniquities, but, according to thy mercy, remember them, for thy goodness' sake, O Lord. Give them heavenly wisdom. Pour abundance of thy grace upon them, that their hoary heads may be found in the way of righteousness, and their souls be precious in thy sight. O let goodness and mercy follow them the remainder of their days. Let their last days be their best days, and their last comforts their strongest and sweetest comforts. And, when heart and flesh and all their powers shall fail them, be thou, O God, the strength of their hearts, their support, and their portion forever. *Amen.*

END OF FAMILY PRAYERS.

FIRST MORNING SERVICE

FOR A FAMILY.

The following Anthem is to be said by the Head of the Family, or Reader, in alternate verses with the other members of the Family.

BLESSED art thou, O Lord, our God, and the God of our fathers, who turnest the shadows of death into the morning, and renewest the face of the earth ;

Who scatterest the darkness by this return of light, and hast commanded night to give place to day ;

Who hast delivered us from the terror by night, and from the pestilence that walketh in darkness ;

Who makest the outgoings of the morning and of the evening to praise thee ;

For that we laid down and slept, and rose up again, because thou, O Lord, didst make us to dwell in safety ;

For that we awaked, and beheld, and our sleep was sweet unto us.

Blot out, we pray thee, as a cloud, our transgressions, and as the thickness of the morning cloud, our sins.

Grant us to walk as children of the light and of the day.

O let us hear thy loving-kindness betimes in the morning, for in thee is our trust.

Show thou us the way that we should walk in, for we lift up our souls unto thee.

Now unto the King eternal, immortal, invisible, the only wise God ;

Be honor and glory, through Jesus Christ, for ever and ever. *Amen.*

Then shall the Person who conducts the Service say,

The Lord be with you.
Answer. And with thy spirit.
Reader. Let us pray.

Then shall be read either of the following Prayers.

O GOD, whose light again shines upon us, we desire to unite with thy whole family in heaven and earth, to offer up to thee, the eternal Fountain of light, our morning adoration, and pay our tribute of gratitude and praise to thee our Preserver. O shine into our hearts with the light of truth, and disperse the shades of error and prejudice and sin. Inspire us with the hopes and comforts of true religion, and implant within us thy likeness, the image of our Creator, in righteousness and true holiness. Give us clear and consoling views of thy Providence, which so mercifully regards us, and our minutest concerns. Warm our hearts with love to thee ; with the love of goodness, of purity, and of all thy moral perfections ; that by these our faith and trust in thee may be increased and strengthened, and that we may rejoice that all the different dispensations of our lives are in thy hand, the hand of our Heavenly Father.

Encourage us in the faithful discharge of our duties. Guide us by thy counsel ; support us in our journey by thy strength ; hold us up by thy promises. Animate us with the patience and perseverance of our blessed Lord and Master, who, for the joy that was set before him, endured the cross, despised the shame, and is set down at the right hand of the throne of God. In his name we offer our prayers, and in his words conclude them. Our Father, &c.

SECOND.

O LORD our God, who hast brought us out from the shades of night to see another day, assist and accept our morning devotions which we offer up to thee, who both by night and by day art our Guardian and Deliverer. We thank thee that thou hast preserved us from the dangers of the past night, and we pray thee to continue thy goodness to us through the present day, and preserve us from all perils both of body and soul. We thank thee for all the time thou hast given us, and acknowledge that we have greatly wasted and misused it. May we do so no more. Make us each day to remember that every day is thy gift, to be used in thy service, and in doing the work of our salvation.

Let the Sun of Righteousness arise upon our souls with healing in his wings. Make us children of the light and of the day, and show us the way wherein we should walk. Quicken our dulness in thy service. Release our hearts from the bondage of sin and the fetters of temptation, and so assist us in all our doings with thy most gracious favor, that, when the few days of this our mortal life are ended, we may inherit that endless life which thou hast prepared for all who love and fear thee.

The blessings, which we ask for ourselves, we ask for others, for our friends, and also for our enemies, if we have them, and for the whole world of mankind, through Jesus Christ our Lord. *Amen.*

THIRD.

ALMIGHTY God, it is owing to thee that we have been preserved through the past night. It is through thy goodness that we have been refreshed with sleep, and that our eyes are now opened to the light of another day. Accept, we beseech thee, our grateful praise; and grant that this day we may be upheld by thy power, and led by thy hand, and kept from danger, from pain, and from sin. With the return of each morning may our thoughts and affections rise to thee; and as one day succeeds another, so may our love to thee be perpetually renewed in our hearts, and our service to thee be constant.

Help us, O God and Father, to love one another. Let thy love be shed abroad upon this family, and may each member of the same walk in the light of thy favor. May children know thee to be their God, and their father's God, and may they seek thy blessing as their greatest happiness, and make it their first duty, and find it their highest pleasure to keep thy commandments.

O God, we commit our ways to thee. To thee we commend all whom we love. Be with them and with us, by day and by night, in sorrow and in joy, in time and in eternity. Forgive us all our sins, and accept us freely through Jesus Christ our Lord and Saviour. *Amen.*

Then shall the whole Family together say the Lord's Prayer.

OUR Father, who art in heaven, Hallowed be thy name. Thy kingdom come ; Thy will be done on earth as it is in heaven. Give us this day our daily bread. And forgive us our trespasses, As we forgive those who trespass against us. And lead us not into temptation, But deliver us from evil. For thine is the kingdom, and the power, and the glory, For ever and ever. *Amen.*

———◆———

SECOND MORNING SERVICE.

The following Sentences are to be said alternately, as in the First Service, by the Reader and the Family.

THE Lord hath brought us safe to the beginning of this day ; let us give him thanks for this his goodness, and for all his mercies and loving-kind-nesses to us and to all men.

Every day will we give thanks unto thee, O Lord, and praise thy name for ever and ever.

Let all those who put their trust in thee rejoice ; they shall ever be giving of thanks, because thou defendest them ; they who love thy name shall be joyful in thee.

For thou, Lord, wilt give thy blessing unto thy people ; and with thy favorable kindness wilt thou defend them as with a shield.

Now unto the King eternal, immortal, invisible, the only wise God ;

Be honor and glory, through Jesus Christ, for ever and ever. *Amen.*

Then shall the Person who con d cts tl e Serv ce say,

LET us pray to God, that we may live in his fear, and in love and charity with our neighbors ; that his Holy Spirit may direct and rule our hearts, teaching us what to do and what to avoid ; and that we may continue his faithful servants this day, and all the days of our life.

Answer. Let our prayers and meditations be always acceptable in thy sight, O Lord, our strength and our Redeemer.

Reader. Let us pray.

Then s al he read eitl ɩ of tl e f llo ɩng Prayers.

O MOST gracious and merciful God, by whom the world is governed and preserved, we give thee humble thanks for thy fatherly care over us, in bringing us to the light of another day. We gratefully acknowledge our dependence upon thee for all the necessaries, conveniences, and comforts of our life ; for all the means of our well-being here, and of our everlasting happiness hereafter. We give thee thanks for the light of thy Gospel, and the help of thy grace, and the support of thy promises, and all the blessings which thou hast vouchsafed unto us in thy Son Jesus Christ.

May we ever walk as in thy sight ; and, fearing to offend thee, may we keep ourselves from all sin. Enable us to resist and overcome temptation ; to follow the motions of thy good Spirit ; to be true and just in our dealings ; watchful over our thoughts, words, and actions ; diligent in our business, and temperate in all things.

May thy blessing be upon our persons, our labors, our substance ; upon all that belongs to us, and all who are dear to us.

Give us, gracious God, what is needful for us, and give us grace not to abuse thy favors. Give us, we beseech thee, contentment for ourselves, and benevolence for others. Give us, in this world, the knowledge of thy truth, and in the world to come, life everlasting. *Amen.*

SECOND.

A LMIGHTY and eternal God, we, the work of thy hands, and the subjects of thy government, sensible of thy goodness to us hitherto, implore thy mercy and protection for the time to come. We ask thy pardon for our sins, and thy grace and powerful assistance, that we may not hazard thy favor by our transgressions.

May the same good providence that has watched over us for our good the past night, guard us this day from all evil and mischief, from all assaults of our spiritual enemies, from hardness of heart, and contempt of thy word and commandment. And seeing all men's labors are in vain without thy blessing, we beseech thee to bless every one of us in our several places and callings. Prosper thou the works of our hands upon us, and give us grace thankfully to accept, and soberly to use, whatever we shall this day receive from thee ; that we, owning thee for our benefactor, and using thy benefits according to thy pleasure, may continue to be the partakers of thy blessings.

Bless us at home and abroad. Bless the country in which we live, and its rulers and governors. Bless the Church universal of thy Son, and all the ministers of the holy Gospel. Bless all schools and seminaries of learning, and all instructors of youth. Preserve all who travel by sea and by land. Give health and strength to the sick and weak, and joy and comfort to the sorrowful and afflicted.

We commend ourselves, and all belonging to us, to thee, our merciful Creator. Hear us also in behalf of our friends, our relations, our benefactors, and all who desire our prayers. We humbly ask for them the mercies which suit their several conditions and needs. We implore for them thy favor, thy peace, and life eternal.

And now to thee, O God, Father Almighty, we ascribe all honor and glory through Jesus Christ, for ever and ever. *Amen.*

THIRD.

ALMIGHTY and eternal God, our Creator, Preserver, and Benefactor, we desire to begin this day with the acknowledgment of thy power and goodness, and of our obligation to love and serve thee ; and we beseech thee to grant us grace to pass the whole of it in thy fear, and in the fulfilment of thy commandments.

O Lord, enable us diligently to perform our respective duties. Let us not waste our time, nor be unfaithful to any trust. Let us have the testimony of our consciences, that in simplicity and sincerity we have our conversation in the world. Let truth be ever on our lips. May we perform a kind and Christian part to all who come within our influence.

We also beseech thee to give us patience to bear the several trials and vicissitudes of life, with an equal and contented mind. Let us not be perplexed with the cares of this world, nor overwhelmed with unnecessary fears ; but let us ever trust thy gracious Providence, and hope in thy goodness and mercy.

Bless unto us the afflictive circumstances through which we may pass. May we see thy hand in all thy various dispensations, and know that, if we truly love and serve thee, all things shall work together for our good.

We commend to thy kind and fatherly care all our friends and relations. We pray for the rising generation ; that thou wouldst be their hope, their refuge, and their strength. Hear the cry of the sick, and the aged, and the afflicted; and grant help and peace to all thy needy and dependent creatures; and pardon to sinful and sinning men, through Jesus Christ our Saviour. *Amen.*

Then shall the whole Family together say the Lord's Prayer

OUR Father, who art in heaven, Hallowed be thy name. Thy kingdom come; Thy will be done on earth, as it is in heaven. Give us this day our daily bread, And forgive us our trespasses, As we forgive those who trespass against us. And lead us not into temptation, But deliver us from evil. For thine is the kingdom, and the power, and the glory, For ever and ever. *Amen.*

———◆———

FIRST EVENING SERVICE

FOR A FAMILY.

The following Anthem is to be said by the Reader and Family alternately, as in the preceding Services

THE Lord hath commanded his loving-kindness in the day-time; and in the night season also our song shall be of him, and our prayer unto the God of our life.

As long as we live will we magnify thee in this manner, and lift up our hands in thy name.

Let our prayer be set forth in thy sight as the incense; and let the lifting up of our hands be an evening sacrifice.

For thou art the portion of our inheritance and of our cup, and thou shalt maintain our lot.

Behold, he who keepeth his people will neither slumber nor sleep. He is about our path, and about our bed, and beholdeth all our ways.

We will lay us down in peace, and take our rest, for it is thou, O Lord, only, who makest us to dwell in safety.

Now unto the King eternal, immortal, invisible, the only God;

Be honor and glory, through Jesus Christ, for ever and ever. *Amen.*

Then shall the Person who conducts the Service say.

The Lord be with you;
Answer. And with thy spirit.
Reader. Let us pray.

Then shall be used either of the following Prayers.

O ALMIGHTY and everlasting God; for all the blessings which we every day receive from thy bounty; for all the known, and all the unobserved favors, deliverances, visitations, and graces of thy Holy Spirit, we bless thy good providence; beseeching thee still to continue thy fatherly care over us, for we are weak and ignorant, and need thy constant protection and guidance.

Wilt thou, O God, be merciful unto us, who have broken thy laws, abused thy patience, wasted precious time, sinned against thy light, and resisted thy good Spirit. Lighten our darkness, we beseech thee, that we may be able to see the evil and danger of sin, and shun the snares of temptation, and walk with safety in the paths of pleasantness and peace. Forgive whatever we have done or thought amiss during the past day; and give us grace that we may render ourselves more worthy of thy favor for the time to come. Let us be excited to serve thee, our Heavenly Master, with fidelity, and finish our work with diligence, before that night overtakes us, wherein no man can work.

O thou who never slumberest nor sleepest, but, both by night and by day, dost watch over thy people, keep and defend us, we pray thee, this night. Let the shades which encompass us be as the shadow of thy wings. May our sleep be quiet and refreshing; and may we rise in the morning prepared and invigorated to serve thee in the duties of the day. May all our nights on earth be hallowed by thy blessing, and all our days devoted to thy service; so that when we have slept the sleep of the grave, we may awake to the resurrection of the just.

Hear us, we beseech thee, in thy Son's name, as whose disciples we approach thee, our Father, and ascribe unto thee all honor and glory forever. *Amen.*

SECOND.

OUR Father in heaven, thy children kneel before the throne of thy mercy, and humbly thank thee for all the blessings of this day, and for the privilege which we now enjoy of holding communion with thee.

O God, if this day we have fallen into any sin;

if we have weakly yielded to any temptation ; if we have been angry without cause, or beyond bounds ; if we have been uncharitable, unjust, undutiful, or in any way unmindful of thee and thy laws, we beseech thee to forgive us in thy great mercy, and grant us true repentance, that we may lie down this night in peace with the world, with ourselves, and with thee. And we pray thee, O Father, to watch over us this night, and protect us from all evil, and give to our eyes refreshing slumbers, so that we may rise in the morning with renewed power to serve thee. If we are to rise no more in this world, grant that we may wake, in the next, to life immortal, and the light of thy countenance forevermore.

We pray thee, also, to protect the whole sleeping world through the hours of darkness. And be graciously with those, who, by land or by sea, must wake and watch. Soothe the pains of the sick ; speak pardon and peace to sleepless consciences ; guide the traveller on his way ; preserve the mariner from the fury of the tempest, and direct him through the paths of the deep. Be a Father to the fatherless ; a Deliverer to the oppressed ; a Friend to all who are under neglect or contempt, or in want ; and especially to those who are persecuted for conscience' and righteousness' sake. Be kind to all our friends and to all our enemies ; to all who have prayed for us, and to all who have desired that we should pray for them. Mercifully, O God, Father Almighty, hear their prayers, and ours, which we offer in the name of our Lord Jesus Christ. *Amen.*

THIRD.

O LORD God, Father of all mercies, we desire to offer up to thee, before we seek repose, our evening sacrifice of prayer and praise. We bless thee for thy goodness to us during the past day, and we beseech thee to continue to us thy gracious protection during this night. Thou sustainest us, though we see thee not. Thou art our support in trouble; our guide in difficulty; our best consolation in time of sickness; our only refuge in the hour of death.

Thou knowest our ways, and our hearts. Pardon, we beseech thee, whatever evil we have said, or thought, or done, this day. Teach us continually to examine our hearts by the light of thy holy word; and grant unto us true repentance, and faith in our Lord and Saviour. May we manifest those tempers, and abound in those works, which his Gospel requires. May we be full of meekness and patience, of kindness and forbearance, of benevolence and charity; and, being established in the love of God, may we also love our neighbor, with a pure heart, fervently.

We beseech thee to bless unto us the events of thy providence; and so to order all things, during the remainder of our lives, that they may issue in our eternal good. We know not what a day may bring forth; but thou knowest all things. O sanctify unto us our prosperity and our adversity, our sickness and our health; and, in all conditions, grant unto us grateful and contented minds.

We commend to thee the young and the old, the strong and the feeble, the happy and the afflicted. Grant unto all the needful spirit of thy grace, the remission of sins, and life everlasting; through Jesus Christ our Lord. *Amen.*

Then shall the whole Family say the following Bene-diction, and the Service may be closed with a Hymn.

`T`HE Lord bless us and keep us; The Lord lift up the light of his countenance upon us, And give us peace, Now and evermore. *Amen.*

———◆———

SECOND EVENING SERVICE.

The following Psalm is to be said, alternately, as in the preceding Services.

`W`E will lift up our eyes unto the hills from whence cometh our help.

Our help cometh even from the Lord, who hath made heaven and earth.

He will not suffer thy foot to be moved; and he who keepeth thee will not sleep.

Behold he who keepeth Israel shall neither slumber nor sleep.

The Lord himself is thy keeper; the Lord is thy shade upon thy right hand.

So that the sun shall not smite thee by day, neither the moon by night.

The Lord shall preserve thee from all evil; yea, it is even he who shall keep thy soul.

The Lord shall preserve thy going out and thy coming in, from this time forth forevermore.

Now unto the King eternal, immortal, invisible, the only wise God;

Be honor and glory, through Jesus Christ, for ever and ever. *Amen.*

Then shall the Person who conducts the Service say,

BY the favor of God, we are come to the evening of this day. Let us pray to our Father to enable us, as we draw nearer to the grave, to draw nearer to himself, and to his heavenly kingdom.

Answer. O thou who hearest prayer, unto thee will we lift up our souls.

Reader. Let us pray.

Then shall be read either of the following Prayers.

O GOD, the light of every heart that sees thee, the life of every soul that loves thee, we, thy children, pray that thou wouldst lighten our darkness, sustain our faintings, save us from the death of sin, and grant us life eternal. Enter, we beseech thee, into our hearts, speak peace unto this house, and abide with us always.

Keep us continually, O God, in thy faith and fear. May we be followers of that which is good, and followers of thy Son Jesus Christ, obeying his precepts, and imitating his example. Let our bodies be in constant subjection to our souls, our senses to our reason, and our reason to thy divine and gracious instruction; that so, both outwardly and inwardly, we may be fully disposed to do thy will.

May we, thy children, know from our experience how good and how pleasant a thing it is to dwell together in unity.   May we be kind and faithful to each other, and to all with whom we are in any way connected.   And may we be always sensible of our relationship to thee, our Heavenly Father; and feel that, whether sleeping or waking, we are still with thee.   Keep and defend us this night. Grant unto us quiet and restoring slumbers.   Bring us to the light of another morning in safety; and, when our days and nights on earth are numbered and finished, grant that we may behold each other in the light of eternal day.   And this we ask in the name of Jesus Christ, our blessed Lord and Redeemer.   *Amen.*

SECOND.

WE humbly thank thee, merciful Father, for thy goodness in conducting us to the close of this day, and for all thy mercies from day to day bestowed upon us.   Add this to all thy favors, we beseech thee, that we may never forget to be thankful, but may constantly acknowledge thee as the source of all our blessings, and praise thee not only with our lips, but in our lives.   Write thy law upon our hearts, that all our desires, words, and actions may be conformable to thy holy will.   Remembering thy mercies hitherto vouchsafed to us, we do entirely trust thee for the time to come.   For this only we are anxious, and do earnestly pray, that we may all our days serve and please thee in such a constant practice of piety, righteousness, and mercy, of temperance, meekness, patience, truth, and fidelity, as may adorn the religion and name of our Lord and Master.

Accept, O God, as the testimony of our love and charity, our hearty intercessions for all mankind. Let the glorious light of thy Gospel shine upon all nations; and grant that all who have already received it, may live as becomes it.

O Lord, continue thy gracious protection to us this night. Into thy hands we commend ourselves, our souls and bodies, and all things belonging to us. And make us mindful, we pray thee, of that time when we shall lie down in the dust; and grant us grace always to live in such a state, that we may never be afraid or unfit to die. And now to thee, our God and Father, we ascribe all honor and glory, through Jesus Christ. *Amen.*

THIRD.

ALMIGHTY God, we draw nigh to thee, in faith and humility, to offer our evening worship. How great is the privilege of those, who can look up to thee, and call thee their Father! How blessed are they who have him for their friend who made heaven and earth, and orders all things therein! We pray that we may abide in thy favor; may be kept in thy family; may always find thee near. Having sought first the kingdom of God and his righteousness, may all other things be added unto us. May thy bounty supply our wants. May thine arm be stretched out to protect us. May thy Holy Spirit sustain and strengthen us.

And when it seems good unto thy wisdom to visit us with trials and afflictions, may thy grace sanctify all our sorrows, and make them instrumental to our eternal benefit.

To thy grace and care we commend our friends and relations. We beseech thee to guard them from evil, and grant them all things convenient to them ; and, when they shall have finished their appointed course on earth, to bring them to thine everlasting kingdom.

Bless the old and the young. May children be blessed in their parents, and parents in their children. Bless those who are coming on, and those who are in the midst of their work, and those who are passing away. Be thou the God and the Guide of all.

Let us go to rest, this night, secure in thy gracious protection. Let us rise, in the morning, prepared for the duties of the day. When we are called to sleep the sleep of death, may we fear no evil, but rejoice in the sure hope of a brighter morning, through Jesus Christ our Saviour. *Amen.*

Then shall the whole Family say the Benediction, as in the preceding Service.

END OF FAMILY SERVICES.

PETITIONS AND THANKSGIVINGS

FOR SUNDAY MORNING.

BE graciously present with all who this day meet to serve thee ; bless the labors of all those who watch for souls ; and give us all grace to hear with attention, to receive the word with meekness, and to serve the Lord with gladness. Teach us all things necessary to salvation ; enable us to understand and remember the sacred truths delivered to us, with full purpose of living accordingly, that our conversation may be holy, and our end everlasting life.

ANOTHER.

WE thank thee for the morning light of this day of rest, and for all the spiritual privileges which it brings with it. May we have rest and refreshment to our souls. May we read, and hear, and meditate, with profit, and lift up our hearts to thee in prayer and praise, with sincere devotion. And grant, most merciful God, that we may so improve all our sacred opportunities, that we fail not of a part in thine eternal rest, and in the hymns of angels and blessed spirits in the world to come.

FOR SUNDAY EVENING.

GLORY be to thy name for the especial blessings which this sacred day has brought to us. Pardon us, if in any manner we have abused its privileges. Cause the truths which we have heard to sink deep into our hearts, and bring forth in us the fruits of a holy and religious life, a peaceful and blessed death, and a glorious resurrection.

ANOTHER.

BLESSED be God, the God and Father of our Lord Jesus Christ, who hath vouchsafed to us the rest and the instruction of this Christian Sabbath. Blessed be God for the means of happiness and improvement which have been offered this day to us and our fellow Christians. Make us mindful, we pray thee, of our duty; that, as we often hear how we ought to walk and to please God, we may continue to do so unto our lives' end.

INTERCESSION FOR CHILDREN.

OUR Heavenly Father, we beseech thee to be a Father to our children. Take them into the arms of thy love. Strengthen them in the path of duty, and when they fall, raise them up again. Wherever they are, or may go, there be thou with them. Guide them; teach them; defend, pardon, and save them.

ANOTHER.

WE humbly and earnestly look to thee, O God, for a blessing, a plenteous blessing, on our dear children. Grant them thy best gifts. Grant them health, and strength, and understanding. Grant them, above all, virtue, holiness, good dispositions, the knowledge and love of thee, and of thy Son Jesus Christ. Help us to do all our duty to them, and help them to do their duty to us. Lead them and guard them through life; be with them in death; and grant that we may all meet together at last in the House of our Heavenly Father.

INTERCESSION FOR FRIENDS.

ALMIGHTY God, fountain of all goodness and all excellency; extend thine abundant favor and loving-kindness to our friends. Reward them for all the good which from thy merciful providence they have conveyed unto us. Let the light of thy countenance shine upon them, and never let them come into any affliction or sadness, but such as may be an instrument of thy glory, and their eternal comfort. Forgive them all their sins. Preserve them from spiritual dangers. Give supply to all their needs; guarding their persons; sanctifying their hearts; and leading them in the way of righteousness, by the waters of comfort, to the land of eternal rest and glory.

ANOTHER.

O LORD, graciously accept our prayers for all our kindred and friends. To those who are afflicted, give comfort and deliverance; to those who prosper, humility and temperance. Bless the sick with health; and keep the healthy from sickness. To all grant thy grace, O God, and show thy mercy. Let love bind us one to another, and religion knit us all to thee; that, however we suffer or scatter on earth, we may live and be in joy together, in the felicity of Heaven.

ON A JOURNEY.

O THOU who art everywhere present, and everywhere and always the same merciful and protecting God, protect us, we beseech thee, in the house and by the way. Save us from danger, from violence, and from sickness. May our way be pleasant to our feet, and improving to our minds and souls. Grant to us a safe arrival at home. Bless and protect those whom we have left behind us. After the journey of life is over, grant that we may all arrive safely in that blessed country, where there is no weariness, nor peril, nor parting.

ON A VOYAGE.

O THOU who art the confidence of those who are abroad upon the sea, protect us, we beseech thee, in this our voyage, and preserve us from all its dangers. But especially grant unto us a sure and steadfast trust in thee. Whatever changes may come over the deep, and whatever foes or perils we may encounter, let us know and feel that thou art near us, and that no real evil can befall us while we are with thee. Bring us to our desired haven, if it be thy will, and to our friends, in safety and peace. When the sea of life is past, and its storms are spent, then, O merciful God, land us on the calm and happy shore of thy heavenly kingdom.

AFTER RETURNING FROM A JOURNEY OR VOYAGE.

WE thank thee, O God, merciful Father, that, through thy great goodness, we are permitted to meet again around our own domestic altar. For thy protecting care of us, while we were away, and for this our safe return, we praise and bless thee. For all the comforts, pleasures, and duties of this our earthly home, we devoutly thank thee. But we know that we are strangers with thee, and sojourn-ers, as all our fathers were ; that our days on the earth are as a shadow, and here there is no abiding. O be thou with us, to lead and uphold us through the remainder of our pilgrimage, and at last receive us to our home in thine eternal heavens.

FOR CHRISTMAS DAY.

O GOD, our Father, through whose mercy the dayspring from on high hath visited us, to give light to those who sat in darkness, and in the shadow of death, to guide our feet into the way of peace ; we bless thee that unto us was born this day in the city of David, a Saviour, who is Christ the Lord ; and we pray that he may be also born in us spirit-ually, in faith, love, and obedience, and live and dwell in us continually, that we may in all things do thy will as he did, and at last become heirs with him in thy heavenly and everlasting glory.

FOR A NEW YEAR.

BLESSED be God, who has brought us safe to the beginning of another year. Make us sensible, O thou eternal and holy One, how short and uncertain is our mortal life. Pardon our misspent time, and make us henceforth careful to redeem it. Grant that we may begin this new year with new resolutions of serving thee more faithfully. Make us wise unto salvation ; that we may consider, in this our day, the things that belong to our peace ; and that we may pass the time of our sojourning here in thy fear and love ; and be ready to depart hence, whenever thou shalt say unto us, Return, ye children of men.

FOR A SICK CHILD.

HEAVENLY Father, we beseech thee to pity the troubles of the child whom thou hast visited with illness, and pity our sorrows, who are afflicted for it. Ease it of its pains, and strengthen it in its weakness. Raise it up again, if it shall please thee, to grow in years and stature, in wisdom and virtue ; and thereby to comfort us, and glorify thee. We believe that thou knowest best what is fit both for it, and for us, and wilt do what is fit for both ; and, therefore, we leave it to thy wise disposal. But let it be thine, O Lord, in life or death ; and either preserve it to be thy true and faithful servant on earth, or take it to the blessedness of thy children in the kingdom of heaven.

FOR A SICK PERSON.

LOOK graciously, O God, on thy servant, whom thou hast brought low with illness. Grant unto *him* a strong sense of *his* entire dependence upon thee; that, whether the means used for *his* relief succeed, *he* may ascribe the glory to thee alone, or whether thou thinkest fit to deny them their intended effects, *he* may humble himself under thy mighty hand, and bear the rod, knowing who hath appointed it. We pray thee to preserve thy servant to us, for *he* is dear to us. Nevertheless, not our will, but thine be done. If it be thy will that *he* should live, may *his* whole life praise thee. If *his* sickness be unto death, may *his* soul be prepared to meet thee, and our souls lie resigned at thy feet.

IN BEREAVEMENT.

SANCTIFY to thy servants, O God, the loss of one of our number by death. Look with pity upon our sorrows; and grant that the affliction which it has pleased thee to bring upon us, may awaken our consciences, and soften our hearts, and impress upon us such convictions of thy holiness and power, that we may place in thee our only felicity, and strive to please thee in all our ways. And give us grace constantly to look forward to that life which is beyond death, and over which death has no power, revealed to us by thy dear Son Jesus Christ.

IN ANY AFFLICTION.

MERCIFULLY regard us, O Lord, in our present trouble, and make us glad according to the days wherein thou hast afflicted us. Strengthen us to bear the cross which is laid upon us. Give us grace to look to the example of our blessed Master, who, for the joy which was set before him, endured a heavier cross than ours. By the sadness of our countenances may our hearts be made better ; and may we so improve thine afflictive dispensations, that they may all tend to our final happiness and glory.

END OF PETITIONS AND THANKSGIVINGS.

BURIAL OF CHILDREN.

The Service shall begin with the following Sentences; the Minister standing, if so were sent, at the Head of the Coffin.

I AM the resurrection and the life, saith the Lord; he who believeth in me, though he were dead, yet shall he live; and whosoever liveth and believeth in me, shall never die. *St. John* xi. 25, 26.

WE brought nothing into this world, and it is certain we can carry nothing out. The Lord gave, and the Lord hath taken away; blessed be the name of the Lord. 1 *Tim.* vi. 7. *Job* i. 21.

WHILE the child was yet alive, I fasted and wept; for I said, Who can tell whether God will be gracious to me, that the child may live? But now he is dead, wherefore should I fast? can I bring him back again? I shall go to him, but he shall not return to me. 2 *Sam.* xii. 22, 23.

Then shall be said the Psalm

PSALM XC.

LORD, thou hast been our dwelling-place in all generations.

Before the mountains were brought forth, or ever thou hadst formed the earth and the world, even from everlasting to everlasting, thou art God.

Thou turnest man to destruction; and sayest, Return, ye children of men.

Thou carriest them away as with a flood; they are even as a dream, and fade away suddenly as the grass.

In the morning it is green, and groweth up; but in the evening it is cut down, dried up, and withered.

Turn thee again, O Lord, at the last, and be gracious unto thy servants.

Comfort us again now, according to the time that thou hast afflicted us, and for the years wherein we have suffered adversity.

Show thy servants thy work, and their children thy glory.

Then shall the Minister say,

MY brethren, what is our life? It is even a vapor, that appeareth for a little while, and then vanisheth away. It is as the early dew of morning, that glittereth for a short time, and then is exhaled to heaven. The gray head is laid low; and the blossom of youth perisheth. All are in the hands of God.

The voice said, cry! And he said, What shall I cry? All flesh is grass, and all the goodliness thereof is as the flower of the field. The grass withereth, the flower fadeth, because the wind of the Lord bloweth upon it. The grass withereth, the flower fadeth, but the word of our God shall stand forever. And the word of God is his promise to you and to your children, through Christ Jesus. And this is the promise that he hath promised us, even eternal life. This corruptible shall put on incorruption, and this mortal shall put on immortality.

Forasmuch then, as it hath pleased Almighty God to take unto himself the soul of this deceased child, we therefore commit *his* body to the ground; earth to earth, ashes to ashes, dust to dust; looking for the resurrection to eternal life, when the earth and the sea shall give up their dead, and the corruptible bodies of those who sleep in Jesus shall be changed, and made like unto his glorious body, according to the mighty working whereby he is able to subdue all things to himself.

F OR we know that if our earthly house of this tabernacle be dissolved, we have a building of God, a house not made with hands, eternal in the heavens.

In my Father's house are many mansions; if it were not so, I would have told you. I go to prepare a place for you. And if I go and prepare a place for you, I will come again and receive you unto myself; that where I am, there ye may be also.

Peace I leave with you, my peace I give unto you : not as the world giveth give I unto you. Let not your heart be troubled, neither let it be afraid.

Come unto me all ye that labor and are heavy laden, and I will give you rest.

They brought young children to Christ, that he should touch them ; and his disciples rebuked those that brought them. But when Jesus saw it, he said, Suffer the little children to come unto me, and forbid them not ; for of such is the kingdom of God. Verily I say unto you, Whosoever shall not receive the kingdom of God as a little child, he shall not enter therein.

And he took them up in his arms, put his hands upon them, and blessed them.

Let us pray.

O GOD, our Heavenly Father, in whose hands are the souls of thy children, and with whom the spirits of the innocent, departed this life, are in everlasting peace and felicity, enable us, we pray thee, to understand and feel the wisdom of thine appointments, to bow with submission to thy decrees, and to acknowledge that the Judge of all the earth will do right ; that so our darkness may be dispelled, our tears wiped away, and our sorrow turned into joy.

It has pleased thee, O God, to send thine angel of death, to cut off a beloved child from the land of the living, in the morning of *his* days. We believe in thy loving mercy and truth, and in the Gospel of thy Son. We believe that it is well with the child. Give grace, we beseech thee, to the bereaved mourners, to say, It is well. Have compassion upon them in their grief. Sustain them by faith in thy sure promises ; comfort them by thy

Holy Spirit; and strengthen them with the consolations of Christ. Impress on their minds the assurance that thou didst call the child, because thou hadst need of *him*, and that *he* is now resting, peacefully and safely, in the arms of the holy Saviour, who, when he was on earth, took little children into his arms, and blessed them. And grant, O most merciful God, that this bereavement may so touch their hearts, that they may have a new sense of their relation to thee, and dependence upon thee, and a new desire to do thy will, and to devote themselves to thy service in holiness and righteousness, all their days.

May we all live as those who must die, and who, after death, must render an account to their Judge. May we enjoy thy mercies and good gifts with gratitude, and resign them with trust and submission. May the sorrows which thou shalt see fit to send us be so improved and sanctified, that we may be able to say, It is good for us that we have been afflicted, that we might learn thy statutes. And when thou shalt call us hence, may we be received, through thine infinite mercy, to that world where sorrow is unknown, and joy is eternal, revealed to us by Jesus Christ, our blessed Lord and Saviour. *Amen.*

THE grace of our Lord Jesus Christ, and the love of God, and the fellowship of the Holy Ghost, be with us all forevermore. *Amen.*

END OF BURIAL OF CHILDREN.

A CATECHISM

FOR THE INSTRUCTION OF CHILDREN.

PART I.

Question. Can you tell me who made you?

Answer. God made me and all things.

Q. For what did God make you?

A. To be good and happy.

Q. What is it to be good?

A. To love and obey my parents, to speak the truth always, and to be just and kind to all persons.

Q. Can God know whether you are good or not?

A. Yes; for though we cannot see God, yet he sees us, wherever we are, by night as well as by day.

Q. What will God do for you, if you be good?

A. He will love me, and make me happy.

Q. Can you do anything for God, who is so good to you?

A. I can only love him, obey him, and be thankful to him; I can do nothing for him.

Q. Can you speak to God?

A. Yes; he has bid us to pray to him for everything which is fit for us, and he is always ready to hear us.

Q. In what manner should you pray to God?

A. Our Saviour, Jesus Christ, has given us a form of prayer, called the Lord's Prayer.

Q. Repeat the Lord's Prayer.

A. Our Father, who art in heaven, Hallowed be thy name. Thy kingdom come; Thy will be done on earth as it is in heaven. Give us this day our daily bread. And forgive us our trespasses, As we forgive those who trespass against us. And lead us not into temptation, But deliver us from evil. For thine is the kingdom, and the power, and the glory, For ever and ever. *Amen.*

Q. What will God do to those who are not good?

A. He will punish them.

Q. Is God able to punish those who are not good?

A. Yes; he who made all things can do all things; he can take away all our friends, and everything which he has given us; and he can make us die, whenever he pleases.

Q. After you die, shall you live again?

A. Yes; God will raise us from the dead, and, if we be good, we shall die no more.

Q. Where shall you live again, if you have been good?

A. If I have been good, I shall go to heaven, where I shall be very happy forever.

Q. What will become of the wicked, when they die?

A. They will meet with their just punishment.

Q. When you do anything which is wrong, should you not be afraid that God, who sees you, will punish you?

A. Yes; but he has promised to forgive us, if we be sorry for our sins, and endeavor to sin no more.

Q. Who has told us that God will forgive us, if we repent of our sins, and endeavor to sin no more?

A. Many persons by whom God spake, and particularly Jesus Christ.

Q. Who was Jesus Christ?

A. The well-beloved Son of God, whom the Father sent to teach men their duty, and to persuade and encourage them to practise it.

Q. Where do we learn what we know concerning Christ, and what he did, taught, and suffered, for the good of men?

A. In the Bible, which we should diligently read and study, for our improvement in knowledge and goodness, in order to fit us for heaven.

Q. Is there any form of words in which Christians express the principal articles of their belief?

A. Yes; the Apostles' Creed, which was composed in the first ages of Christianity, is such a form.

Q. Repeat the Apostles' Creed.

A. I believe in God, the Father Almighty, maker of heaven and earth;

And in Jesus Christ, his only Son, our Lord; who was conceived by the Holy Ghost; born of the Virgin Mary; suffered under Pontius Pilate; was crucified, dead, and buried; the third day he arose again from the dead; he ascended into heaven; and sitteth at the right hand of God, the Father Almighty; from thence he shall come to judge the living and the dead.

I believe in the Holy Ghost; the communion of saints; the forgiveness of sins; the resurrection of the body; and the life everlasting. *Amen.*

PART II.

Q. Does the Bible inform us what God himself is?

A. Yes; it teaches us that he is a being who had no beginning, and that he will have no end; that he is almighty, perfectly wise, and infinitely good; that he is everywhere present; that he never changes in his nature or disposition.

Q. What does God require of us, in order to live and die in his favor?

A. All that God requires of us is comprehended in these two precepts; Thou shalt love the Lord thy God with all thy heart; and thy neighbor as thyself.

Q. In what manner must we express our love to God?

A. By a grateful sense of his goodness to us; by a constant care to do his will; and by an entire and cheerful submission to all the dispensations of his providence.

Q. How must we express our love to our fellow-men?

A. By doing to others as we should think it right in them to do to us in the same circumstances.

Q. By what methods must we cherish our love to God, and increase our confidence in him?

A. We must frequently consider the benefits he confers upon us. We must also address ourselves to him in prayer, thanking him for the mercies he bestows upon us, confessing our sins before him, and asking of him whatever he knows to be needful and good for us.

Q. How shall we bring ourselves into the best disposition for performing our duty to God and man?

A. By a proper government of our passions, according to the dictates of reason and conscience; by living in temperance and chastity; and never indulging a proud, malicious, or selfish temper.

Q. What should we do, when people affront and injure us?

A. We should not return evil for evil; and, if they repent, we must forgive them, as we hope that God will forgive us our offences against him.

Q. In what manner should we treat the inferior animals?

A. We should treat them with tenderness and humanity; and never torment them or destroy their lives to make ourselves sport; because they are the creatures of God, and because God has commanded us to be merciful unto them.

Q. Has God anywhere delivered distinct directions, concerning the several branches of our duty to him and to our neighbor?

A. Yes, in the Ten Commandments, which he delivered to the children of Israel from Mount Sinai.

Q. Which is the first commandment?

A. Thou shalt have no other gods but me.

Q. Which is the second commandment?

A. Thou shalt not make to thyself any graven image, nor the likeness of anything that is in heaven above, or in the earth beneath, or in the water under the earth; thou shalt not bow down to them, nor worship them; for I, the Lord thy God, am a jealous God, and visit the sins of the fathers upon the children, unto the third and fourth generation, of those who hate me; and show mercy unto thousands of those who love me, and keep my commandments.

Q. Which is the third commandment?

A. Thou shalt not take the name of the Lord thy God in vain; for the Lord will not hold him guiltless who taketh his name in vain.

Q. Which is the fourth commandment.

A. Remember, that thou keep holy the Sabbath day. Six days shalt thou labor, and do all that thou hast to do; but the seventh day is the Sabbath of the Lord thy God. In it thou shalt do no manner of work, thou, and thy son, and thy daughter; thy man-servant, and thy maid-servant; thy cattle, and the stranger who is within thy gates. For in six days the Lord made heaven and earth, the sea, and all that in them is, and rested the seventh day; wherefore the Lord blessed the seventh day, and hallowed it.

Q. Which is the fifth commandment?

A. Honor thy father and thy mother; that thy days may be long in the land, which the Lord thy God giveth thee.

Q. Which is the sixth commandment?

A. Thou shalt do no murder.

Q. Which is the seventh commandment?

A. Thou shalt not commit adultery.

Q. Which is the eighth commandment?

A. Thou shalt not steal.

Q. Which is the ninth commandment?

A. Thou shalt not bear false witness against thy neighbor.

Q. Which is the tenth commandment?

A. Thou shalt not covet thy neighbor's house; thou shalt not covet thy neighbor's wife; nor his servant, nor his maid, nor his ox, nor his ass, nor anything that is his.

Q. What are those principles which most effectually lead to the observance of these, and all other of God's commandments?

A. A high reverence of God, and a sincere good will to our fellow-creatures, joined with a just regard to our own real interest.

Q. What is the best method we can take to guard ourselves from all vice and wickedness?

A. By being careful not to indulge sinful thoughts; and by correcting everything which is amiss in the beginning, before we have become accustomed to it, and have formed a habit which cannot easily be broken; particularly by avoiding the company of wicked persons, who would soon make us like themselves; and by being, in a more especial manner, upon our guard against those vices, to which our situation and circumstances make us peculiarly prone.

Q. Is any man able to fulfil all the commands of God, so as to live entirely without sin?

A. No. Our merciful God and Father knows that we are not able to do this, and therefore doth not expect it from us. He only requires that we repent of the sins we commit, and endeavor to live better lives for the future.

Q. What should a sense of our frailty and proneness to sin teach us?

A. Humility and watchfulness, and earnestness in our prayers to God, to enable us to resist temptation, and to strengthen and confirm our good dispositions.

Q. Did Christ appoint any outward ordinances as means of promoting his religion?

A. He commanded his disciples to go and teach all nations, baptizing them in the name of the Father, and of the Son, and of the Holy Ghost; and he also commanded them to eat bread and drink wine in remembrance of him. This rite is called the Lord's Supper.

Q. What is the meaning of baptism?

A. The washing of water in baptism probably represents the purity of heart and life, required from all who become the disciples of Christ.

Q. What is the nature and use of the Lord's Supper?

A. By eating bread and drinking wine in remembrance of Christ, we keep alive the memory of his death and resurrection; we acknowledge ourselves to be Christians; we cherish a grateful sense of the blessings of the Gospel of Christ; and strengthen our resolutions to live as becomes his disciples.

Q. What has Jesus Christ become to us on account of what he did and suffered for the good of men?

A. Because he humbled himself to death, God has highly exalted him, and made him head over all things to his Church; and, at the end of the world, he will come to judge the living and the dead. For this hope which was set before him, he endured the cross, and despised the shame of that ignominious death.

Q. What does Christ, in the Scriptures, say concerning the day of judgment?

A. That, when the Son of man shall come in his glory, and all the holy angels with him, then shall he sit upon the throne of his glory; and before him shall be gathered all nations; and he shall separate them one from another, as a shepherd divideth his sheep from the goats;—that he will send the wicked into punishment; and take the righteous to a state of happiness, which is life eternal with himself.

END OF THE CATECHISM.

SERVICES FOR SUNDAY SCHOOLS.

FIRST SERVICE.

Instructor shall hearken to the Lord with Action in the words of Scripture

COME, ye children, hearken unto me; I will teach you the fear of the Lord.

The fear of the Lord is the beginning of wisdom; but the wicked despise wisdom and instruction. My children, if sinners entice you, consent ye not. If they say, Come with us, cast in your lot among us, — my children, walk not in the way with them; refrain your feet from their path; for their feet run to evil. When wisdom entereth into your hearts, and knowledge is pleasant unto your souls, discretion shall preserve you, understanding shall keep you; to deliver you from the way of those who leave the paths of uprightness, to walk in the ways of darkness.

My children, forget not the law of God; but let your hearts keep his commandments. For length of days, and years of life, and peace, shall they add to you. Let not mercy and truth forsake you. Bind them about your necks; write them upon the tables of your hearts.   So shall you find favor in the sight of God and man.

Th•n shall tl e Children say,

WE call with our whole hearts; hear us, O Lord; we will keep thy statutes.
Instructor.   Let us pray.

Then the Chil1•en sJall say, afte• the Ii st ne t •, tl•
•u•••u•••• P••••••.

O LORD, our Heavenly Father, give us wisdom, give us understanding.   May we fear to do evil, and learn to do well.   May we love the truth, And love goodness, And love thee, our God, And Jesus Christ, our Saviour.   We thank thee, O Lord, for the gift of thy Son ; Who came to teach us what is true and good, And died that we might live.   We thank thee, that, when he was on earth, He suffered little children to come to him, And took them in his arms and blessed them.   May we be worthy of his blessing ; May our souls rest in his arms.   May we be gentle and kind ; May we be patient and meek ; May we love each other with pure hearts ; So that our Heavenly Father may love us, And take us to heaven when we die.

We pray thee, O God, to bless our parents and our kindred, Our teachers and our friends.   O guard them from danger, And comfort them in trouble, And heal them in sickness, And deliver them from evil.   Bless all mankind.   Pardon our offences ; Help our infirmities ; And accept our prayers ; Through Jesus Christ, our Lord.   *Amen.*

Instructor. The Lord bless you and keep you; the Lord be gracious unto you, and give you peace, now and evermore. *Amen.*

———◆———

SECOND SERVICE.

The Instructor shall begin with the following Address.

MY dear children, — God our Father has preserved us since we last met together; he has been mindful of us, and has blessed us. We can say, How dear are thy thoughts unto us, O God! how great is the sum of them! If we should count them, they are more in number than the sand. He feeds us; he clothes us; he gives us friends. He gives us every good and perfect gift. We cannot repay him for all his loving-kindness; but he has graciously assured us that he will accept our praises and thanksgivings, if we offer them purely and sincerely. Let us join in offering praise to God with devout affections, and with holy words.

Then shall the Instructor and Pupils repeat the following verses alternately; the Instructor beginning.

BLESS the Lord, O my soul, and all that is within me, bless his holy name.

Bless the Lord, O my soul, and forget not all his benefits!

Who forgiveth all thy sins, and healeth all thine infirmities;

Who saveth thy life from destruction, and crown-eth thee with mercy and loving-kindness;

Who filleth the morning of thy life with good things, and reneweth thy youth like the eagle's.

He will bless those who fear the Lord, both small and great.

Ye are the blessed of the Lord, who made heaven and earth.

And we will praise the Lord from this time forth forevermore.

Here shall the Instructor say

NOW let us unite in prayer to the same Almighty Being. And let us remember that he is a God who heareth prayer, and knoweth all our thoughts, and all the secrets of our hearts. Let us pray to him humbly, and reverently, and sincerely.

PRAYER.

HOLY and blessed Lord, our God; We pray thee to hear us; We pray thee to bless us. Give unto us a pure heart and a right spirit. May we strive to do what is pleasing in thy sight. May we be careful not to offend thee. May we love and obey our parents and guardians; May we speak the truth always; And be just and kind to all persons. As we grow in stature, may we grow in wisdom, and in favor with God and man. When we sin, do thou forgive us. When we wander, do thou restore us. When we are in sorrow, do thou comfort us. While we live, may we love and serve thee. In the hour of death, may we rest upon thee; And after death may we rise to praise thee. Which we humbly ask in the name of Jesus Christ our Lord. *Amen.*

Instructor. Children, the grace of Christ be with you, and the peace of God rest upon you, now and forevermore. *Amen.*

———◆———

THIRD SERVICE.

The following Sentences are to be said alternately by the Instructor and Pupils.

Ins. WHEREWITHAL shall the young cleanse their way?

P. By taking heed thereto, according to God's word.

Ins. Teach them, O Lord, the way of thy statutes;

P. And we will keep it unto the end.

Ins. Give them understanding, and they shall keep thy law.

P. Yea, we will keep it with our whole heart.

Ins. O turn away their eyes, lest they behold vanity;

P. And quicken thou us in thy way.

Ins. The earth, O Lord, is full of thy mercy;

P. All thy commandments are truth.

Ins. Thou art good, and doest good.

P. O teach us thy statutes.

Ins. Thy testimonies have we claimed as our heritage forever; and why?

P. They are the very joy of our hearts.

Ins. Our hands also will we lift up unto thy commandments, which we have loved ;

P. And our study shall be in thy statutes.

Ins. Let us pray.

Then shall the Instructor say the following Prayer.

O GOD, who art the source of light, and fountain of all wisdom, help thy young servants, we pray thee, in acquiring a right knowledge of thee and of thy holy will and word. Dispose their hearts to the love of truth, and their minds to the attainment of all good learning. Assist them to search the Scriptures, and to find in them eternal life. Lead them to their Saviour, and incline them to reverence, imitate, and obey him. May they learn of him, who was meek and lowly in heart; and so learn of him, that they may finally live and reign with him, in glory and joy everlasting. This we humbly ask in the name of Jesus Christ our Lord. *Amen.*

Then shall he say.

O LORD, thy word endureth forever in heaven ; thy truth also remaineth from one generation to another.

P. Lord, have mercy upon us, and incline our hearts to keep thy law.

Ins. The righteousness of thy testimonies is everlasting ; O grant us understanding, and we shall live.

P. Lord, have mercy upon us, and write all thy laws in our hearts, we beseech thee.

Ins. May the Lord bless us and keep us ; may the Lord lift up the light of his countenance upon us, and give us peace, now and forevermore, through Jesus Christ our Saviour. *Amen.*

CLOSING PRAYER FOR A SUNDAY SCHOOL.

OUR Father, who art in heaven, We thank thee for the instruction which we have now received, And we pray that it may do us good. We thank thee for the blessings of the Gospel, And we pray that we may value and improve them. We thank thee for all thy good gifts, And we pray thee to make us worthy of them. May we depart from this place with thy blessing ; May we go home with thy peace in our hearts. Forgive us our errors and faults. Make us wiser and better every day. May we live on earth as thy dear children ; And live forever with thee in heaven ; Through Jesus Christ our Lord. *Amen.*

A Benediction, which may be added to the Closing Prayer.

THE Lord bless us and keep us ; the Lord lift up the light of his countenance upon us ; and give us peace, now and evermore. *Amen.*

THE END.

Made in the USA
Middletown, DE
13 September 2024

60891956R00328